SIX PLAYS BY
Lillian Hellman

SIX PLAYS BY
Lillian Hellman

The Children's Hour
Days to Come
The Little Foxes
Watch on the Rhine
Another Part of the Forest
The Autumn Garden

VINTAGE BOOKS
A Division of Random House
New York

Library of Congress Cataloging in Publication Data
Hillman, Lillian, 1905-
   Six plays.
   Reprint of the 1960 ed. published by Modern Library, New York.
   CONTENTS: The children's hour.—Days to come.—The little foxes.
   [etc.]
[PS3515.E343A6 1979] 812′.5′2 79-2160
ISBN 0-394-74112-9

Contents

The Children's Hour

FOR
D. HAMMETT
WITH THANKS

The Children's Hour was first produced at Maxine Elliot's Theatre, New York City, on November 20, 1934, with the following cast:

(In the order of their appearance)

PEGGY ROGERS	EUGENIA RAWLS
MRS. LILY MORTAR	ALINE MCDERMOTT
EVELYN MUNN	ELIZABETH SECKEL
HELEN BURTON	LYNNE FISHER
LOIS FISHER	JACQUELINE RUSLING
CATHERINE	BARBARA LEEDS
ROSALIE WELLS	BARBARA BEALS
MARY TILFORD	FLORENCE MCGEE
KAREN WRIGHT	KATHERINE EMERY
MARTHA DOBIE	ANNE REVERE
DOCTOR JOSEPH CARDIN	ROBERT KEITH
AGATHA	EDMONIA NOLLEY
MRS. AMELIA TILFORD	KATHERINE EMMET
A GROCERY BOY	JACK TYLER

Produced and directed by HERMAN SHUMLIN

Settings designed by ALINE BERNSTEIN

Scene

ACT ONE

Living room of the Wright-Dobie School.
Late afternon in April.

ACT TWO

Scene I. Living room at Mrs. Tilford's.
A few hours later.
Scene II. The same. Later that evening.

ACT THREE

The same as Act One. November.

Act One

SCENE: *A room in the Wright-Dobie School for girls, a converted farm-house eighteen miles from the town of Lancet. It is a comfortable, unpretentious room used as an afternoon study-room and at all other times as the living room.*

A large door Left Center faces the audience. There is a single door Right. Against both back walls are bookcases. A large desk is at Right; a table, two sofas, and eight or ten chairs.

It is early in an afternoon in April.

AT RISE: MRS. LILY MORTAR *is sitting in a large chair Right Center, with her head back and her eyes closed. She is a plump, florid woman of forty-five with obviously touched-up hair. Her clothes are too fancy for a classroom.*

Seven girls, from twelve to fourteen years old, are informally grouped on chairs and sofa. Six of them are sewing with no great amount of industry on pieces of white material. One of the others, EVELYN MUNN, *is using her scissors to trim the hair of* ROSALIE, *who sits, nervously, in front of her. She has* ROSALIE's *head bent back at an awkward angle and is enjoying herself.*

The eighth girl, PEGGY ROGERS, *is sitting in a higher chair than the others. She is reading aloud from a book. She is bored and she reads in a singsong, tired voice.*

PEGGY (*reading*) "It is twice blest; it blesseth him that gives and him that takes: 'tis mightiest in the mightiest;

5

it becomes the throned monarch better than his crown; his sceptre shows the force of temporal power, the attribute to awe and majesty, wherein . . ." (MRS. MORTAR *suddenly opens her eyes and stares at the haircutting. The children make efforts to warn* EVELYN. PEGGY *raises her voice until she is shouting*) "doth sit the dread and fear of kings; but mercy is above . . ."

MRS. MORTAR   Evelyn! What are you doing?

EVELYN   (*inanely. She lisps*)   Uh—nothing, Mrs. Mortar.

MRS. MORTAR   You are certainly doing something. You are ruining the scissors for one thing.

PEGGY   (*loudly*)   "But mercy is above. It . . ."

MRS. MORTAR   Just a moment, Peggy. It is very unfortunate that you girls cannot sit quietly with your sewing and drink in the immortal words of the immortal bard. (*She sighs*) Evelyn, go back to your sewing.

EVELYN   I can't get the hem thtraight. Honeth, I've been trying for three weekth, but I jutht can't do it.

MRS. MORTAR   Helen, please help Evelyn with the hem.

HELEN   (*rises, holding up the garment* EVELYN *has been working on. It is soiled and shapeless, and so much has been cut off that it is now hardly large enough for a child of five. Giggling*)   She can't ever wear *that*, Mrs. Mortar.

MRS. MORTAR   (*vaguely*)   Well, try to do something with it. Make some handkerchiefs or something. Be clever about it. Women must learn these tricks. (*To* PEGGY) Continue. "Mightiest in the mightiest."

PEGGY   " 'Tis mightiest in the mightiest; it becomes the throned monarch better than his crown; his sceptre— his sceptre shows the force of temporal power, the attribute to awe and majesty, wherein—"

LOIS   (*from the back of the room chants softly and monotonously through the previous speech*)   Ferebam, ferebas, ferebat, ferebamus, ferebatis, fere, fere—

CATHERINE   (*two seats away, the book propped in front of her*)   Fere*bant*.

LOIS   Ferebamus, ferebatis, fere*bant*.

MRS. MORTAR   Who's doing that?

PEGGY   (*the noise ceases. She hurries on*)   "Wherein doth sit the dread and fear of kings; but mercy is above this sceptred sway, it is enthroned in the hearts of kings, it is an attribute to God himself—"

MRS. MORTAR (*sadly, reproachfully*) Peggy, can't you imagine yourself as Portia? Can't you read the lines with some feeling, some pity? (*Dreamily*) Pity. Ah! As Sir Henry said to me many's the time, pity makes the actress. Now, why can't *you* feel pity?

PEGGY I guess I feel pity.

LOIS Ferebamus, ferebatis, fere—fere—fere—

CATHERINE Fere*bant*, stupid.

MRS. MORTAR How many people in this room are talking? Peggy, read the line again. I'll give you the cue.

PEGGY What's a cue?

MRS. MORTAR A cue is a line or word given the actor or actress to remind them of their next speech.

HELEN (*softly*) To remind *him* or *her*.

ROSALIE (*a fattish girl with glasses*) Weren't you ever in the movies, Mrs. Mortar?

MRS. MORTAR I had many offers, my dear. But the cinema is a shallow art. It has no—no— (*Vaguely*) no fourth dimension. Now, Peggy, if you would only try to submerge yourself in this problem. You are pleading for the life of a man. (*She rises and there are faint sighs from the girls, who stare at her with blank, bored faces. She recites hammily, with gestures*) "But mercy is above this sceptred sway; it is enthroned in the hearts of kings, it is an attribute to God himself; and earthly power doth then show likest God's when mercy seasons justice."

LOIS (*almost singing it*) Utor, fruor, fungor, potior, and vescor take the dative.

CATHERINE Take the *ablative*.

LOIS Oh, dear. Utor, fruor, fung—

MRS. MORTAR (*to* LOIS, *with sarcasm*) You have something to tell the class?

LOIS (*apologetically*) We've got a Latin exam this afternoon.

MRS. MORTAR And you intend to occupy the sewing and

elocution hour learning what should have been learnt yesterday?

CATHERINE (*wearily*) It takes her more than yesterday to learn it.

MRS. MORTAR Well, I cannot allow you to interrupt us like this.

CATHERINE But we're finished sewing.

LOIS (*admiringly*) I bet you were good at Latin, Mrs. Mortar.

MRS. MORTAR (*conciliated*) Long ago, my dear, long ago. Now, take your book over by the window and don't disturb our enjoyment of Shakespeare. (CATHERINE *and* LOIS *rise, go to window, stand mumbling and gesturing*) Let us go back again. "It is an attribute of—" (*At this point the door opens far enough to let* MARY TILFORD, *clutching a slightly faded bunch of wild flowers, squeeze cautiously in. She is fourteen, neither pretty nor ugly. She is an undistinguished-looking girl, except for the sullenly dissatisfied expression on her face*) "And earthly power doth then show likest God's when mercy seasons justice. We do pray for mercy, and that same prayer doth teach—"

PEGGY (*happily*) You've skipped three lines.

MRS. MORTAR In my entire career I've never missed a line.

PEGGY But you did skip three lines. (*Goes to* MRS. MORTAR *with book*) See?

MRS. MORTAR (*seeing* MARY *sidling along wall toward other end of the room, turns to her to avoid* PFGGY *and the book*) Mary!

HELEN (*in whisper to* MARY) You're going to catch it now.

MRS. MORTAR Mary!

MARY Yes, Mrs. Mortar?

MRS. MORTAR This is a pretty time to be coming to your sewing class, I must say. Even if you have no interest in your work you might at least remember that you owe me a little courtesy. Courtesy is breeding. Breeding is an excellent thing. (*Turns to class*) Always remember that.

ROSALIE Please, Mrs. Mortar, can I write that down?

MRS. MORTAR Certainly. Suppose you all write it down.

PEGGY But we wrote it down last week.

(MARY *giggles.*)

MRS. MORTAR Mary, I am still awaiting your explanation. Where have you been?

MARY I took a walk.

MRS. MORTAR So you took a walk. And may I ask, young lady, are we in the habit of taking walks when we should be at our classes?

MARY I am sorry, Mrs. Mortar, I went to get you these flowers. I thought you would like them and I didn't know it would take so long to pick them.

MRS. MORTAR (*flattered*) Well, well.

MARY (*almost in tears*) You were telling us last week how much you liked flowers, and I thought that I would bring you some and—

MRS. MORTAR That was very sweet of you, Mary; I always like thoughtfulness. But you must not allow anything to interfere with your classes. Now run along, dear, and get a vase and some water to put my flowers in. (MARY *turns, sticks out her tongue at* HELEN, *says:* "A-a-a," *and exits Left*) You may put that book away, Peggy. I am sure your family need never worry about your going on the stage.

PEGGY I don't want to go on the stage. I want to be a lighthouse-keeper's wife.

MRS. MORTAR Well, I certainly hope you won't read to him.

(*The laughter of the class pleases her.* PEGGY *sits down among the other girls, who are making a great show of doing nothing.* MRS. MORTAR *returns to her chair, puts her head back, closes her eyes.*)

CATHERINE How much longer, O Cataline, are you going to abuse our patience? (*To* LOIS) Now translate it, and for goodness' sakes try to get it right this time.

MRS. MORTAR (*for no reason*) "One master passion in the breast, like Aaron's serpent, swallows all the rest."

(*She and* LOIS *are murmuring during* KAREN WRIGHT's *entrance.* KAREN *is an attractive woman of twenty-eight, casually pleasant in manner, without sacrifice of warmth*

*or dignity. She smiles at the girls, goes to the desk.
With her entrance there is an immediate change in the
manner of the girls: they are fond of her and they respect her. She gives* MORTAR, *whose quotation has
reached her, an annoyed look.*)

LOIS   "Quo usque tandem a*butere*. . . ."

KAREN   (*automatically*) "Abu*tere*." (*Opens drawer in
desk*) What's happened to your hair, Rosalie?

ROSALIE   It got cut, Miss Wright.

KAREN   (*smiling*) I can see that. A new style? Looks as
though it has holes in it.

EVELYN   (*giggling*) I didn't mean to do it that bad, Mith
Wright, but Rothalie'th got funny hair. I thaw a picture in the paper, and I wath trying to do it that way.

ROSALIE   (*feels her hair, looks pathetically at* KAREN) Oh,
what shall I do, Miss Wright? (*Gesturing*) It's long
here, and it's short here and—

KAREN   Never mind. Come up to my room later and I'll
see if I can fix it for you.

MRS. MORTAR   And hereafter we'll have no more haircutting.

KAREN   Helen, have you found your bracelet?

HELEN   No, I haven't, and I've looked everywhere.

KAREN   Have another look. It must be in your room somewhere.

(MARY *comes in Right, with her flowers in a vase. When
she sees* KAREN, *she loses some of her assurance.* KAREN
looks at the flowers in surprise.)

MARY   Good afternoon, Miss Wright. (*Sits down, looks at*
KAREN, *who is staring hard at the flowers.*)

KAREN   Hello, Mary.

MRS. MORTAR   (*fluttering around*) Peggy has been reading Portia for us.

(PEGGY *sighs.*)

KAREN   (*smiling*) Peggy doesn't like Portia?

MRS. MORTAR   I don't think she quite appreciates it, but—

KAREN   (*patting* PEGGY *on the head*) Well, I didn't either.
I don't think I do yet. Where'd you get those flowers,
Mary?

MRS. MORTAR   She picked them for me. (*Hurriedly*)

It made her a little late to class, but she heard me say I loved flowers, and she went to get them for me. (*With a sigh*) The first wild flowers of the season.

KAREN But not the very first, are they, Mary?

MARY I don't know.

KAREN Where did you get them?

MARY Near Conway's cornfield, I think.

KAREN It wasn't necessary to go so far. There was a bunch exactly like this in the garbage can this morning.

MRS. MORTAR (*after a second*) Oh, I can't believe it! What a nasty thing to do! (*To* MARY) And I suppose you have just as fine an excuse for being an hour late to breakfast this morning, and last week— (*To* KAREN) I haven't wanted to tell you these things before, but—

KAREN (*hurriedly, as a bell rings off stage*) There's the bell.

LOIS (*walking toward door*) Ad, ab, ante, in, de, inter, con, post, præ— (*Looks up at* KAREN) I *can't* seem to remember the rest.

KAREN Præ, pro, sub, super. Don't worry, Lois. You'll come out all right. (LOIS *smiles, exits.* MARY *attempts to make a quick exit*) Wait a minute, Mary. (*Reluctantly* MARY *turns back as the girls file out.* KAREN *moves the small chairs, clearing the room as she talks*) Mary, I've had the feeling—and I don't think I'm wrong— that the girls here were happy; that they liked Miss Dobie and me, that they liked the school. Do you think that's true?

MARY Miss Wright, I have to get my Latin book.

KAREN I thought it was true until you came here a year ago. I don't think you're very happy here, and I'd like to find out why. (*Looks at* MARY, *waits for an answer, gets none, shakes her head*) Why, for example, do you find it necessary to lie to us so often?

MARY (*without looking up*) I'm not lying. I went out walking and I saw the flowers and they looked pretty and I didn't know it was so late.

KAREN (*impatiently*) Stop it, Mary! I'm not interested in hearing that foolish story again. I *know* you got the flowers out of the garbage can. What I do want to know is why you feel you have to lie out of it.

MARY (*beginning to whimper*) I *did* pick the flowers near Conway's. You never believe me. You believe everybody but me. It's always like that. Everything I say you fuss at me about. Everything I do is wrong.

KAREN You know that isn't true. (*Goes to* MARY, *puts her arm around her, waits until the sobbing has stopped*) Look, Mary, look at me. (*Raises* MARY's *face with her hand*) Let's try to understand each other. If you feel that you *have* to take a walk, or that you just *can't* come to class, or that you'd like to go into the village by yourself, come and tell me—I'll try and understand. (*Smiles*) I don't say that I'll always agree that you should do exactly what you want to do, but I've had feelings like that, too—everybody has—and I won't be unreasonable about yours. But this way, this kind of lying you do, makes everything wrong.

MARY (*looking steadily at* KAREN) I got the flowers near Conway's cornfield.

KAREN (*looks at* MARY, *sighs, moves back toward desk and stands there for a moment*) Well, there doesn't seem to be any other way with you; you'll have to be punished. Take your recreation periods alone for the next two weeks. No horseback-riding and no hockey. Don't leave the school grounds for any reason whatsoever. Is that clear?

MARY (*carefully*) Saturday, too?

KAREN Yes.

MARY But you said I could go to the boat-races.

KAREN I'm sorry, but you can't go.

MARY I'll tell my grandmother. I'll tell her how everybody treats me here and the way I get punished for every little thing I do. I'll tell her, I'll—

MRS. MORTAR Why, I'd slap her hands!

KAREN (*turning back from door, ignoring* MRS. MORTAR's *speech. To* MARY) Go upstairs, Mary.

MARY I don't feel well.

KAREN (*wearily*) Go upstairs now.

MARY I've got a pain. I've had it all morning. It hurts

right here. (*Pointing vaguely in the direction of her heart*) Really it does.

KAREN Ask Miss Dobie to give you some hot water and bicarbonate of soda.

MARY It's a bad pain. I've never had it before.

KAREN I don't think it can be very serious.

MARY My heart! It's my heart! It's stopping or something. I can't breathe. (*She takes a long breath and falls awkwardly to the floor.*)

KAREN (*sighs, shakes her head, kneels beside* MARY. *To* MRS. MORTAR) Ask Martha to phone Joe.

MRS. MORTAR (*going out*) Do you think—? Heart trouble is very serious in a child.

(KAREN *picks* MARY *up from the floor and carries her off Right. After a moment* MARTHA DOBIE *enters Center. She is about the same age as* KAREN. *She is a nervous, high-strung woman.*)

KAREN (*enters Right*) Did you get Joe?

MARTHA (*nodding*) What happened to her? She was perfectly well a few hours ago.

KAREN She probably still is. I told her she couldn't go to the boat-races and she had a heart attack.

MARTHA Where is she?

KAREN In there. Mortar's with her.

MARTHA Anything really wrong with her?

KAREN I doubt it. (*Sits down at desk and begins to mark papers*) She's a problem, that kid. Her latest trick was kidding your aunt out of a sewing lesson with those faded flowers we threw out. Then she threatened to go to her grandmother with some tale about being mistreated.

MARTHA And, please God, Grandma would believe her and take her away.

KAREN Which would give the school a swell black eye. But we ought to do something.

MARTHA How about having a talk with Mrs. Tilford?

KAREN (*smiling*) You want to do it? (MARTHA *shakes her head*) I hate to do it. She's been so nice to us. (*Shrugging her shoulders*) Anyway, it wouldn't do any good.

She's too crazy about Mary to see her faults very clearly —and the kid knows it.

MARTHA   How about asking Joe to say something to her? She'd listen to him.

KAREN   That would be admitting that we can't do the job ourselves.

MARTHA   Well, we can't, and we might as well admit it. We've tried everything we can think of. She's had more attention than any other three kids put together. And we still haven't the faintest idea what goes on inside her head.

KAREN   She's a strange girl.

MARTHA   That's putting it mildly.

KAREN   (*laughs*) It's funny. We always talk about the child as if she were a grown woman.

MARTHA   It's not so funny. There's something the matter with the kid. That's been true ever since the first day she came. She causes trouble here; she's bad for the other girls. I don't know what it is—it's a feeling I've got that it's wrong somewhere—

KAREN   All right, all right, we'll talk it over with Joe. Now what about our other pet nuisance?

MARTHA   (*laughs*) My aunt the actress? What's she been up to now?

KAREN   Nothing unusual. Last night at dinner she was telling the girls about the time she lost her trunks in Butte, Montana, and how she gave her best performance of Rosalind during a hurricane. Today in the kitchen you could hear her on what Sir Henry said to her.

MARTHA   Wait until she does Hedda Gabler standing on a chair. Sir Henry taught her to do it that way. He said it was a test of great acting.

KAREN   You must have had a gay childhood.

MARTHA   (*bitterly*) Oh, I did. I did, indeed. God, how I used to hate all that—

KAREN   Couldn't we get rid of her soon, Martha? I hate to make it hard on you, but she really ought not to be here.

MARTHA   (*after a moment*) I know.

KAREN We can scrape up enough money to send her away. Let's do it.

MARTHA (*goes to her, affectionately pats her head*) You've been very patient about it. I'm sorry and I'll talk to her today. It'll probably be a week or two before she can be ready to leave. Is that all right?

KAREN Of course. (*Looks at her watch*) Did you get Joe himself on the phone?

MARTHA He was already on his way. Isn't he always on his way over here?

KAREN (*laughs*) Well, I'm going to marry him some day, you know.

MARTHA (*looking at her*) You haven't talked of marriage for a long time.

KAREN I've talked of it with Joe.

MARTHA Then you *are* thinking about it—soon?

KAREN Perhaps when the term is over. By that time we ought to be out of debt, and the school should be paying for itself.

MARTHA (*nervously playing with a book on the table*) Then we won't be taking our vacation together?

KAREN Of course we will. The three of us.

MARTHA I had been looking forward to some place by the lake—just you and me—the way we used to at college.

KAREN (*cheerfully*) Well, now there will be three of us. That'll be fun, too.

MARTHA (*after a pause*) Why haven't you told me this before?

KAREN I'm not telling you anything we haven't talked about often.

MARTHA But you're talking about it as *soon* now.

KAREN I'm glad to be able to. I've been in love with Joe a long time. (MARTHA *crosses to window and stands looking out, her back to* KAREN. KAREN *finishes marking papers and rises*) It's a big day for the school. Rosalie's finally put an "l" in could.

MARTHA (*in a dull, bitter tone, not turning from window*) You really *are* going to leave, aren't you?

KAREN I'm not going to leave, and you know it. Why do you say things like that? We agreed a long time ago that my marriage wasn't going to make any difference to the school.

MARTHA   But it will. You know it will. It can't help it.

KAREN   That's nonsense. Joe doesn't want me to give up here.

MARTHA   (*turning from window*) I don't understand you. It's been so damned hard building this thing up, slaving and going without things to make ends meet—think of having a winter coat without holes in the lining again! —and now when we're getting on our feet, you're all ready to let it go to hell.

KAREN   This is a silly argument, Martha. Let's quit it. You haven't listened to a word I've said. I'm not getting married tomorrow, and when I do, it's not going to interfere with my work here. You're making something out of nothing.

MARTHA   It's going to be hard going on alone afterward.

KAREN   For God's sake, do you expect me to give up my marriage?

MARTHA   I don't mean that, but it's so—

(*Door Center opens and* DOCTOR JOSEPH CARDIN *comes in. He is a large, pleasant-looking, carelessly dressed man of about thirty-five.*)

CARDIN   Hello, darling. Hi, Martha. What's the best news?

MARTHA   Hello, Joe.

KAREN   We tried to get you on the phone. Come in and look at your little cousin.

CARDIN   Sure. What's the matter with her now? I stopped at Vernie's on the way over to look at that little black bull he bought. He's a baby! There's going to be plenty of good breeding done in these hills.

KAREN   You'd better come and see her. She says she has a pain in her heart. (*Goes out Right.*)

CARDIN   (*stopping to light a cigarette*) Our little Mary pops up in every day's dispatches.

MARTHA   (*impatiently*) Go and see her. Heart attacks are nothing to play with.

CARDIN   (*looks at her*) Never played with one in my life. (*Exits Right.*)

(MARTHA *walks around room and finally goes to stare out window.*)

(MRS. MORTAR *enters Right.*)

MRS. MORTAR I was asked to leave the room. (MARTHA *pays no attention*) It seems that I'm not wanted in the room during the examination.

MARTHA (*over her shoulder*) What difference does it make?

MRS. MORTAR What difference does it make? Why, it was a deliberate snub.

MARTHA There's very little pleasure in watching a man use a stethoscope.

MRS. MORTAR Isn't it natural that the child should have me with her? Isn't it natural that an older woman should be present? (*No answer*) Very well, if you are so thick-skinned that you don't resent these things—

MARTHA What are you talking about? Why, in the name of heaven, should *you* be with her?

MRS. MORTAR It—it's customary for an older woman to be present during an examination.

MARTHA (*laughs*) Tell that to Joe. Maybe he'll give you a job as duenna for his office.

MRS. MORTAR (*reminiscently*) It was I who saved Delia Lampert's life the time she had that heart attack in Buffalo. We almost lost her that time. Poor Delia! We went over to London together. She married Robert Laffonne. Not seven months later he left her and ran away with Eve Cloun, who was playing the Infant Phenomenon in Birmingham—

MARTHA Console yourself. If you've seen one heart attack, you've seen them all.

MRS. MORTAR So you don't resent your aunt being snubbed and humiliated?

MARTHA Oh, Aunt Lily!

MRS. MORTAR Karen is consistently rude to me, and you know it.

MARTHA I know that she is very polite to you, and— what's more important—very patient.

MRS. MORTAR Patient with me? *I*, who have worked my fingers to the bone!

MARTHA Don't tell yourself that too often, Aunt Lilly; you'll come to believe it.

MRS. MORTAR I *know* it's true. Where could you have gotten a woman of my reputation to give these children voice lessons, elocution lessons? Patient with me! Here I've donated my services—

MARTHA I was under the impression you were being paid.

MRS. MORTAR That small thing! I used to earn twice that for one performance.

MARTHA The gilded days. It was very extravagant of them to pay you so much. (*Suddenly tired of the whole thing*) You're not very happy here, are you, Aunt Lily?

MRS. MORTAR Satisfied enough, I guess, for a poor relation.

MARTHA (*makes a motion of distaste*) But you don't like the school or the farm or—

MRS. MORTAR I told you at the beginning you shouldn't have bought a place like this. Burying yourself on a farm! You'll regret it.

MARTHA We like it here. (*After a moment*) Aunt Lily, you've talked about London for a long time. Would you like to go over?

MRS. MORTAR (*with a sigh*) It's been twenty years, and I shall never live to see it again.

MARTHA Well, you can go any time you like. We can spare the money now, and it will do you a lot of good. You pick out the boat you want and I'll get the passage. (*She has been talking rapidly, anxious to end the whole thing*) Now that's all fixed. You'll have a grand time seeing all your old friends, and if you live sensibly I ought to be able to let you have enough to get along on. (*She begins to gather books, notebooks, and pencils.*)

MRS. MORTAR (*slowly*) So you want me to leave?

MARTHA That's not the way to put it. You've wanted to go ever since I can remember.

MRS. MORTAR You're trying to get rid of me.

MARTHA That's it. We don't want you around when we dig up the buried treasure.

MRS. MORTAR So? You're turning me out? At my age! Nice, grateful girl you are.

MARTHA Oh, my God, how can anybody deal with you?

You're going where you want to go, and we'll be better off alone. That suits everybody. You complain about the farm, you complain about the school, you complain about Karen, and now you have what you want and you're still looking for something to complain about.

MRS. MORTAR (*with dignity*)   Please do not raise your voice.

MARTHA You ought to be glad I don't do worse.

MRS. MORTAR I absolutely refuse to be shipped off three thousand miles away. I'm not going to England. I shall go back to the stage. I'll write to my agents tomorrow, and as soon as they have something good for me—

MARTHA The truth is I'd like you to leave soon. The three of us can't live together, and it doesn't make any difference whose fault it is.

MRS. MORTAR You wish me to go tonight?

MARTHA Don't act, Aunt Lily. Go as soon as you've found a place you like. I'll put the money in the bank for you tomorrow.

MRS. MORTAR You think I'd take your money? I'd rather scrub floors first.

MARTHA I imagine you'll change your mind.

MRS. MORTAR I should have known by this time that the wise thing is to stay out of your way when *he's* in the house.

MARTHA What are you talking about now?

MRS. MORTAR Never mind. I should have known better. You always take your spite out on me.

MARTHA Spite? (*Impatiently*) Oh, don't let's have any more of this today. I'm tired. I've been working since six o'clock this morning.

MRS. MORTAR Any day that he's in the house is a bad day.

MARTHA When *who* is in the house?

MRS. MORTAR Don't think you're fooling me, young lady. I wasn't born yesterday.

MARTHA Aunt Lily, the amount of disconnected unpleasantness that goes on in your head could keep a psychologist busy for years. Now go take your nap.

MRS. MORTAR I know what I know. Every time that man comes into this house, you have a fit. It seems like you just can't stand the idea of them being together. God knows what you'll do when they get married. You're jealous of him, that's what it is.

MARTHA   (*her voice is tense and the previous attitude of good-natured irritation is gone*)   I'm very fond of Joe, and you know it.

MRS. MORTAR   You're fonder of Karen, and I know that. And it's unnatural, just as unnatural as it can be. You don't like their being together. You were always like that even as a child. If you had a little girl friend, you always got mad when she liked anybody else. Well, you'd better get a beau of your own now—a woman of your age.

MARTHA   The sooner you get out of here, the better. Your vulgarities are making me sick and I won't stand for them any longer. I want you to leave—

(*At this point there is a sound outside the large doors Center.* MARTHA *breaks off, angry and ashamed. After a moment she crosses to the door and opens it.* EVELYN *and* PEGGY *are to be seen on the staircase. For a second she stands still as they stop and look at her. Then, afraid that her anger with her aunt will color anything she might say to the children, she crosses the room again and stands with her back to them.*)

MARTHA   What were you doing outside the door?

EVELYN   (*hurriedly*)   We were going upthtairth, Mith Dobie.

PEGGY   We came down to see how Mary was.

MARTHA   And you stopped long enough to see how we were. Did you deliberately listen?

PEGGY   We didn't mean to. We heard voices and we couldn't help—

MRS. MORTAR   (*fake social tone*)   Eavesdropping is something nice young ladies just don't do.

MARTHA   (*turning to face the children*)   Go upstairs now. We'll talk about this later. (*Slowly shuts door as they begin to climb the stairs.*)

MRS. MORTAR   You mean to say you're not going to do anything about that? (*No answer. She laughs nastily*)

That's the trouble with these new-fangled notions of discipline and—

MARTHA (*thoughtfully*) You know, it's really bad having you around children.

MRS. MORTAR What exactly does that mean?

MARTHA It means that I don't like them hearing the things you say. Oh, I'll "do something about it," but the truth is that this is their home, and things shouldn't be said in it that they can't hear. When you're at your best, you're not for tender ears.

MRS. MORTAR So now it's my fault, is it? Just as I said, whenever he's in the house you think you can take it out on me. You've got to have some way to let out steam and—

(*Door opens Right and* CARDIN *comes in.*)

MARTHA How is Mary?

(MRS. MORTAR, *head in air, gives* MARTHA *a malicious half-smile and makes what she thinks is majestic exit Center.*)

MRS. MORTAR Good day, Joseph.

CARDIN What's the matter with the Duchess? (*Nods at door Center.*)

MARTHA Just keeping her hand in, in case Sir Henry's watching her from above. What about Mary?

CARDIN Nothing. Absolutely nothing.

MARTHA (*sighs*) I thought so.

CARDIN I could have managed a better faint than that when I was six years old.

MARTHA Nothing the matter with her at all, then?

CARDIN (*laughs*) No, ma'am, not a thing. Just a little something she thought up.

MARTHA But it's such a silly thing to do. She knew we'd have you in. (*Sighs*) Maybe she's not so bright. Any idiots in your family, Joe? Any inbreeding?

CARDIN Don't blame her on me. It's another side of the family. (*Laughs*) You can look at Aunt Amelia and tell: old New England stock; never married out of Boston; still thinks honor is honor and dinner's at eight thirty. Yes, ma'am, we're a proud old breed.

MARTHA The Jukes were an old family, too. Look, Joe,

have you any idea what is the matter with Mary? I mean, has she always been like this?

CARDIN   She's always been a honey. Aunt Amelia's spoiling hasn't helped any, either.

MARTHA   We're reaching the end of our rope with her. This kind of thing—

CARDIN   (*looking at her*)   Aren't you taking this too seriously?

MARTHA   (*after a second*)   I guess I am. But you stay around kids long enough and you won't know what to take seriously, either. But I do think somebody ought to talk to Mrs. Tilford about her.

CARDIN   You wouldn't be meaning me now, would you, Miss Dobie?

MARTHA   Well, Karen and I were talking about it this afternoon and—

CARDIN   Listen, friend, I'm marrying Karen, but I'm not writing Mary Tilford in the contract. (*Martha moves slightly.* CARDIN *takes her by the shoulders and turns her around to face him again. His face is grave, his voice gentle*) Forget Mary for a minute. You and I have got something to fight about. Every time anything's said about marrying—about Karen marrying me—you— (*She winces*) There it is. I'm fond of you. I always thought you liked me. What is it? I know how fond you are of Karen, but our marriage oughtn't to make a great deal of difference—

MARTHA   (*pushing his hands from her shoulders*) God damn you. I wish— (*She puts her face in her hands.* CARDIN *waches her in silence, mechanically lighting a cigarette. When she takes her hands from her face, she holds them out to him. Contritely*) Joe, please, I'm sorry. I'm a fool, a nasty, bitter—

CARDIN   (*takes her hands in one of his, patting them with his other hand*) Aw, shut up. (*He puts an arm around her, and she leans her head against his lapel. They are standing like that when* KAREN *comes in Right.*)

MARTHA   (*to* KAREN, *as she wipes her eyes*) Your friend's got a nice shoulder to weep on.

KAREN   He's an admirable man in every way. Well, the angel child is now putting her clothes back on.

MARTHA   The angel child's influence is abroad even while she's unconscious. Her room-mates were busy listening at the door while Aunt Lily and I were yelling at each other.

KAREN   We'll have to move those girls away from one another.

(*A bell rings from the rear of the house.*)

MARTHA   That's my class. I'll send Peggy and Evelyn down. You talk to them.

KAREN   All right. (*As* MARTHA *exits Center,* KAREN *goes toward door Right. As she passes* CARDIN ' *she kisses him*) Mary!

(MARY *opens door, comes in, stands buttoning the neck of her dress.*)

CARDIN   (*to* MARY) How's it feel to be back from the grave?

MARY   My heart hurts.

CARDIN   (*laughing. To* KAREN) Science has failed. Try a hairbrush.

MARY   It's *my* heart, and it hurts.

KAREN   Sit down.

MARY   I want to see my grandmother. I want to—

(EVELYN *and* PEGGY *timidly enter Center.*)

KAREN   Sit down, girls, I want to talk to you.

PEGGY   We're awfully sorry, really. We just didn't think and—

KAREN   I'm sorry too, Peggy. (*Thoughtfully*) You and Evelyn never used to do things like this. We'll have to separate you three.

EVELYN   Ah, Mith Wright, we've been together almotht a year.

KAREN   It was evidently too long. Now, don't let's talk about it. Peggy, you will move into Lois's room, and Lois will move in with Evelyn. Mary will go in with Rosalie.

MARY   Rosalie hates me.

KAREN   That's a very stupid thing to say. I can't imagine Rosalie hating anyone.

MARY (*starting to cry*) And it's all because I had a pain. If anybody else was sick they'd be put to bed and petted. You're always mean to me. I get blamed and punished for everything. (*To* CARDIN) I do, Cousin Joe. All the time for everything.

(MARY *by now is crying violently and as* KAREN *half moves toward her,* CARDIN, *who has been frowning, picks* MARY *up and puts her down on the couch.*)

CARDIN You've been unpleasant enough to Miss Wright. Lie here until you've stopped working yourself into a fit. (*Picks up his hat and bag, smiles at* KAREN) I've got to go now. She's not going to hurt herself crying. The next time she faints, I'd wait until she got tired lying on the floor. (*Passing* MARY, *he pats her head. She jerks away from him.*)

KAREN Wait a minute. I'll walk to the car with you. (*To girls*) Go up now and move your things. Tell Lois to get her stuff ready.

(*She and* CARDIN *exit Center. A second after the door is closed,* MARY *springs up and throws a cushion at the door.*)

EVELYN Don't do that. She'll hear you.

MARY Who cares if she does? (*Kicks table*) And she can hear that, too.

(*Small ornament falls off table and breaks on floor.* EVELYN *and* PEGGY *gasp, and* MARY's *bravado disappears for a moment.*)

EVELYN (*frightened*) Now what are you going to do?

PEGGY (*stooping down in a vain effort to pick up the pieces*) You'll get the devil now. Dr. Cardin gave it to Miss Wright. I guess it was kind of a lover's gift. People get awfully angry about a lover's gift.

MARY Oh, leave it alone. She'll never know we did it.

PEGGY *We* didn't do it. You did it yourself.

MARY And what will you do if I say *we* did do it? (*Laughs*) Never mind, I'll think of something else. The wind could've knocked it over.

EVELYN Yeh. She'th going to believe that one.

MARY Oh, stop worrying about it. I'll get out of it.

EVELYN Did you really have a pain?

MARY I fainted, didn't I?

PEGGY I wish I could faint sometimes. I've never even worn glasses, like Rosalie.

MARY A lot it'll get you to faint.

EVELYN What did Mith Wright do to you when the clath left?

MARY Told me I couldn't go to the boat-races.

EVELYN Whew!

PEGGY But we'll remember everything that happens and we'll give you all the souvenirs and things.

MARY I won't let you go if I can't go. But I'll find some way to go. What were *you* doing?

PEGGY I guess we shouldn't have done it, really. We came down to see what was happening to you, but the doors were closed and we could hear Miss Dobie and Mortar having an awful row. Then Miss Dobie opens the door and there we were.

MARY And a lot of crawling and crying you both did too, I bet.

EVELYN We were thort of thorry about lithening. I gueth it wathn't—

MARY Ah, you're always sorry about everything. What were they saying?

PEGGY What was who saying?

MARY Dobie and Mortar, silly.

PEGGY (*evasively*) Just talking, I guess.

EVELYN Fighting, you mean.

MARY About what?

EVELYN Well, they were talking about Mortar going away to England and—

PEGGY You know, it really wasn't very nice to've listened, and I think it's worse to tell.

MARY You do, do you? You just don't tell me and see what happens.

(PEGGY *sighs.*)

EVELYN Mortar got awful thore at that and thaid they juth wanted to get rid of her, and then they thtarted talking about Dr. Cardin.

MARY What about him?

PEGGY   We'd better get started moving; Miss Wright will be back first thing we know.

MARY   (*fiercely*) Shut up! Go on, Evelyn.

EVELYN   They're going to be married.

MARY   Everybody knows that.

PEGGY   But everybody doesn't know that Miss Dobie doesn't want them to get married. How do you like that?

(*The door opens and* ROSALIE WELLS *sticks her head in.*)

ROSALIE   I have a class soon. If you're going to move your things—

MARY   Close that door, you idiot. (ROSALIE *closes door, stands near it*) What do you want?

ROSALIE   I'm trying to tell you. If you're going to move your things—not that I want you in with me—you'd better start right now. Miss Wright's coming in a minute.

MARY   Who cares if she is?

ROSALIE   (*starts for door*) I'm just telling you for your own good.

PEGGY   (*getting up*) We're coming.

MARY   No. Let Rosalie move our things.

ROSALIE   You crazy?

PEGGY   (*nervously*) It's all right. Evelyn and I'll get your things. Come on, Evelyn.

MARY   Trying to get out of telling me, huh? Well, you won't get out of it that way. Sit down and stop being such a sissy. Rosalie, you go on up and move my things and don't say a word about our being down here.

ROSALIE   And who was your French maid yesterday, Mary Tilford?

MARY   (*laughing*) You'll do for today. Now go on, Rosalie, and fix our things.

ROSALIE   You crazy?

MARY   And the next time we go into town, I'll let you wear my gold locket and buckle. You'll like that, won't you, Rosalie?

ROSALIE   (*draws back, moves her hands nervously*) I don't know what you're talking about.

MARY   Oh, I'm not talking about anything in particular.

You just run along now and remind me the next time to get my buckle and locket for you.

ROSALIE (*stares at her a moment*) All right, I'll do it this time, but just 'cause I got a good disposition. But don't think you're going to boss me around, Mary Tilford.

MARY (*smiling*) No, indeed. (ROSALIE *starts for door*) And get the things done neatly, Rosalie. Don't muss my white linen bloomers—

(*The door slams as* MARY *laughs.*)

EVELYN Now what do you think of that? What made her tho agreeable?

MARY Oh, a little secret we got. Go on, now, what else did they say?

PEGGY Well, Mortar said that Dobie was jealous of them, and that she was like that when she was a little girl, and that she'd better get herself a beau of her own because it was unnatural, and that she never wanted anybody to like Miss Wright, and that was unnatural. Boy! Did Miss Dobie get sore at that!

EVELYN Then we didn't hear any more. Peggy dropped a book.

MARY What'd she mean Dobie was jealous?

PEGGY What's unnatural?

EVELYN Un for not. Not natural.

PEGGY It's funny, because everybody gets married.

MARY A lot of people don't—they're too ugly.

PEGGY (*jumps up, claps her hand to her mouth*) Oh, my God! Rosalie'll find that copy of *Mademoiselle de Maupin*. She'll blab like the dickens.

MARY Ah, she won't say a word.

EVELYN Who getth the book when we move?

MARY You can have it. That's what I was doing this morning—finishing it. There's one part in it—

PEGGY What part?

(MARY *laughs.*)

EVELYN Well, what wath it?

MARY Wait until you read it.

EVELYN Don't forget to give it to me.

PEGGY It's a shame about being moved. I've got to go in

with Helen, and she blows her nose all night. Lois told me.

MARY   It was a dirty trick making us move. She just wants to see how much fun she can take away from me. She hates me.

PEGGY   No, she doesn't, Mary. She treats you just like the rest of us—almost better.

MARY   That's right, stick up for your crush. Take her side against mine.

PEGGY   I didn't mean it that way.

EVELYN   (*looks at her watch*)   We'd better get upthtairth.

MARY   I'm not going.

PEGGY   Rosalie isn't so bad.

EVELYN   What you going to do about the vathe?

MARY   I don't care about Rosalie and I don't care about the vase. I'm not going to be here.

EVELYN *and* PEGGY   (*together*)   Not going to be here! What do you mean?

MARY   (*calmly*)   I'm going home.

PEGGY   Oh, Mary—

EVELYN   You can't do that.

MARY   Can't I? You just watch. (*Begins to walk around the room*) I'm not staying here. I'm going home and tell Grandma I'm not staying any more. (*Smiles to herself*) I'll tell her I'm not happy. They're scared of Grandma—she helped 'em when they first started, you know—and when she tells 'em something, believe me, they'll sit up and listen. They can't get away with treating me like this, and they don't have to think they can.

PEGGY   (*appalled*)   You just going to walk out like that?

EVELYN   What you going to tell your grandmother?

MARY   Oh, who cares? I'll think of something to tell her. I can always do it better on the spur of the moment.

PEGGY   She'll send you right back.

MARY   You let me worry about that. Grandma's very fond of me, on account my father was her favorite son. I can manage *her* all right.

PEGGY   I don't think you ought to go, really, Mary. It's just going to make an awful lot of trouble.

EVELYN   What'th going to happen about the vathe?

MARY   Say I did it—it doesn't make a bit of difference any more to me. Now listen, you two got to help. They won't miss me before dinner if you make Rosalie shut the door and keep it shut. Now, I'll go through the field to French's, and then I can get the bus to Homestead.

EVELYN   How you going to get to the thtreet-car?

MARY   Taxi, idiot.

PEGGY   How are you going to get out of here in the first place?

MARY   I'm going to walk out. You know where the front door is, or are you too dumb even for that? Well, I'm going right out that front door.

EVELYN   Gee, I wouldn't have the nerve.

MARY   Of course you wouldn't. You'd let 'em do anything to you they want. Well, they can't do it to me. Who's got any money?

EVELYN   Not me. Not a thent.

MARY   I've got to have at least a dollar for the taxi and a dime for the bus.

EVELYN   And where you going to find it?

PEGGY   See? Why don't you just wait until your allowance comes Monday, and then you can go any place you want. Maybe by that time—

MARY   I'm going today. *Now.*

EVELYN   You can't *walk* to Lanthet.

MARY   (*goes to* PEGGY)   You've got money. You've got two dollars and twenty-five cents.

PEGGY   I—I—

MARY   Go get it for me.

PEGGY   No! No! I won't get it for you.

EVELYN   You can't have *that* money, Mary—

MARY   Get it for me.

PEGGY   (*cringes, her voice is scared*)   I won't. I won't. Mamma doesn't send me much allowance—not half as much as the rest of you get—I saved this so long—you took it from me last time—

EVELYN   Ah, she wantth that bithycle tho bad.

PEGGY   I haven't gone to the movies, I haven't had any candy, I haven't had anything the rest of you get all the time. It took me so long to save that and I—

MARY   Go upstairs and get me the money.

PEGGY   (*hysterically, backing away from her*) I won't. I won't. I won't.

(MARY *makes a sudden move for her, grabs her left arm, and jerks it back, hard and expertly.* PEGGY *screams softly.* EVELYN *tries to take* MARY'S *arm away. Without releasing her hold on* PEGGY, MARY *slaps* EVELYN'S *face.* EVELYN *begins to cry.*)

MARY   Just say when you've had enough.

PEGGY   (*softly, stifling*) All—all right—I'll get it.

(MARY *smiles, nods her head as the Curtain falls.*)

Act Two

SCENE: *Living room at* MRS. TILFORD'S. *It is a formal room, without being cold or elegant. The furniture is old, but excellent. The exit to the hall is Left; glass doors Right lead to a dining room that cannot be seen.*

AT RISE: *Stage is empty. Voices are heard in the hall.*

AGATHA (*off-stage*) What are you doing here? Well, come on in—don't stand there gaping at me. Have they given you a holiday or did you just decide you'd get a better dinner here? (AGATHA *enters Left, followed by* MARY. AGATHA *is a sharp-faced maid, not young, with a querulous voice*) Can't you even say hello?

MARY Hello, Agatha. You didn't give me a chance. Where's Grandma?

AGATHA Why aren't you in school? Look at your face and clothes. Where have you been?

MARY I got a little dirty coming home. I walked part of the way through the woods.

AGATHA Why didn't you put on your middy blouse and your old brown coat?

MARY Oh, stop asking me questions. Where's Grandma?

AGATHA Where ought any clean person be at this time of day? She's taking a bath.

MARY Is anybody coming for dinner?

AGATHA She didn't say anything about you coming.

MARY How could she, stupid? She didn't know.

31

AGATHA Then what are you doing here?

MARY Leave me alone. I don't feel well.

AGATHA Why don't you feel well? Who ever heard of a person going for a walk in the woods when they didn't feel well?

MARY Oh, leave me alone. I came home because I was sick.

AGATHA You look all right.

MARY But I don't feel all right. (*Whining*) I can't even come home without everybody nagging at me.

AGATHA Don't think you're fooling me, young lady. You might pull the wool over some people's eyes, but—I bet you've been up to something again. (*Stares suspiciously at* MARY, *who says nothing*) Well, you wait right here till I tell your grandmother. And if you feel so sick, you certainly won't want any dinner. A good dose of rhubarb and soda will fix you up. (*Exits Left.*)

(MARY *makes a face in the direction* AGATHA *has gone and stops sniffling. She looks nervously around the room, then goes to a low mirror and tries several experiments with her face in an attempt to make it look sick and haggard.*)

(MRS. TILFORD, *followed by* AGATHA, *enters Left.* MRS. TILFORD *is a large, dignified woman in her sixties, with a pleasant, strong face.*)

AGATHA (*to* MRS. TILFORD, *as she follows her into the room*) Why didn't you put some cold water on your chest? Do you want to catch your death of cold at your age? Did you have to hurry so?

MRS. TILFORD Mary, what are you doing home?

(MARY *rushes to her and buries her head in* MRS. TILFORD'S *dress, crying.* MRS. TILFORD *lets her cry for a moment while she pats her head, then puts an arm around the child and leads her to a sofa.*)

MRS. TILFORD Never mind, dear; now stop crying and tell me what is the matter.

MARY (*gradually stops crying, fondling* MRS. TILFORD'S *hand*) It's so good to see you, Grandma. You didn't come to visit me all last week.

MRS. TILFORD I couldn't, dear. But I was coming tomorrow.

MARY I missed you so. (*Smiling up at* MRS. TILFORD) I was awful homesick.

MRS. TILFORD I'm glad that's all it was. I was frightened when Agatha said you were not well.

AGATHA Did I say that? I said she needed a good dose of rhubarb and soda. Most likely she only came home for Wednesday night fudge cake.

MRS. TILFORD We all get homesick. But how did you get here? Did Miss Karen drive you over?

MARY I—I walked most of the way, and then a lady gave me a ride and— (*Looks timidly at* MRS. TILFORD.)

AGATHA Did she have to walk through the woods in her very best coat?

MRS. TILFORD Mary! Do you mean you left without permission?

MARY (*nervously*) I ran away, Grandma. They didn't know—

MRS. TILFORD That was a very bad thing to do, and they'll be worried. Agatha, phone Miss Wright and tell her Mary is here. John will drive her back before dinner.

MARY (*as* AGATHA *starts toward telephone*) No, Grandma, don't do that. Please don't do that. Please let me stay.

MRS. TILFORD But, darling, you can't leave school any time you please.

MARY Oh, please, Grandma, don't send me back right away. You don't know how they'll punish me.

MRS. TILFORD I don't think they'll be that angry. Come, you're acting like a foolish little girl.

MARY (*hysterically, as she sees* AGATHA *about to pick up the telephone*) Grandma! Please! I can't go back! I can't! They'll kill me! They will, Grandma! They'll kill me!

(MRS. TILFORD *and* AGATHA *stare at* MARY *in amazement. She puts her head in* MRS. TILFORD'S *lap and sobs.*)

MRS. TILFORD (*motioning with a hand for* AGATHA *to leave the room*) Never mind phoning now, Agatha.

AGATHA If you're going to let her—

(MRS. TILFORD *repeats the gesture.* AGATHA *exits Right, with offended dignity.*)

MRS. TILFORD   Stop crying, Mary.

MARY   (*raising her head from* MRS. TILFORD's *lap*)   It's so nice here, Grandma.

MRS. TILFORD   I'm glad you like being home with me, but at your age you can hardly— (*More seriously*) What made you say such a terrible thing about Miss Wright and Miss Dobie? You know they wouldn't hurt you.

MARY   Oh, but they would. They—I— (*Breaks off, looks around as if hunting for a clue to her next word; then dramatically*) I fainted today!

MRS. TILFORD   (*alarmed*)   Fainted?

MARY   Yes, I did. My heart—I had a pain in my heart. I couldn't help having a pain in my heart, and when I fainted right in class, they called Cousin Joe and he said I didn't. He said it was maybe only that I ate my breakfast too fast and Miss Wright blamed me for it.

MRS. TILFORD   (*relieved*)   I'm sure if Joseph said it wasn't serious, it wasn't.

MARY   But I did have a pain in my heart—honest.

MRS. TILFORD   Have you still got it?

MARY   I guess I haven't got it much any more, but I feel a little weak, and I was so scared of Miss Wright being so mean to me just because I was sick.

MRS. TILFORD   Scared of Karen? Nonsense. It's perfectly possible that you had a pain, but if you had really been sick your Cousin Joseph would certainly have known it. It's not nice to frighten people by pretending to be sick when you aren't.

MARY   I didn't *want* to be sick, but I'm always getting punished for everything.

MRS. TILFORD   (*gently*)   You mustn't imagine things like that, child, or you'll grow up to be a very unhappy woman. I'm not going to scold you any more for coming home this time, though I suppose I should. Run along upstairs and wash your face and change your dress, and after dinner John will drive you back. Run along.

MARY   (*happily*)   I can stay for dinner?

MRS. TILFORD   Yes.

MARY Maybe I could stay till the first of the week. Saturday's your birthday and I could be here with you.

MRS. TILFORD We don't celebrate my birthday, dear. You'll have to go back to school after dinner.

MARY But— (*She hesitates, then goes up to* MRS. TILFORD *and puts her arms around the older woman's neck. Softly*) How much do you love me?

MRS. TILFORD (*smiling*) As much as all the words in all the books in all the world.

MARY Remember when I was little and you used to tell me that right before I went to sleep? And it was a rule nobody could say another single word after you finished? You used to say: "Wor-rr-ld," and then I had to shut my eyes tight.

MRS. TILFORD And sometimes you were naughty and didn't shut them.

MARY I miss you an awful lot, Grandma.

MRS. TILFORD And I miss you, but I'm afraid my Latin is too rusty—you'll learn it better in school.

MARY But couldn't I stay out the rest of this term? After the summer maybe I won't mind it so much. I'll study hard, honest, and—

MRS. TILFORD You're an earnest little coaxer, but it's out of the question. Back you go tonight. (*Gives* MARY *a playful slap*) Let's not have any more talk about it now, and let's have no more running away from school ever.

MARY (*slowly*) Then I really have to go back there tonight?

MRS. TILFORD Of course.

MARY You don't love me. You don't care whether they kill me or not.

MRS. TILFORD Mary.

MARY You don't! You don't! You don't care what happens to me.

MRS. TILFORD (*sternly*) But I *do* care that you're talking this way.

MARY (*meekly*) I'm sorry I said that, Grandma. I didn't mean to hurt your feelings. (*Puts her arms around* MRS. TILFORD's *neck*) Forgive me?

MRS. TILFORD   What made you talk like that?

MARY   (*in a whisper*) I'm scared, Grandma, I'm scared. They'll do dreadful things to me.

MRS. TILFORD   Dreadful? Nonsense. They'll punish you for running away. You deserve to be punished.

MARY   It's not that. It's not anything I do. It never is. They —they just punish me anyhow, just like they got something against me. I'm afraid of them, Grandma.

MRS. TILFORD   That's ridiculous. What have they ever done to you that is so terrible?

MARY   A lot of things—all the time. Miss Wright says I can't go to the boat-races and— (*Realizing the inadequacy of this reply, she breaks off, hesitates, hunting for a more telling reply, and finally stammers*) It's—it's after what happened today.

MRS. TILFORD   You mean something else besides your naughtiness in pretending to faint and then running away?

MARY   I *did* faint. I didn't pretend. They just said that to make me feel bad. Anyway, it wasn't anything that I did.

MRS. TILFORD   What was it, then?

MARY   I can't tell you.

MRS. TILFORD   Why?

MARY   (*sulkily*) Because you're just going to take their part.

MRS. TILFORD   (*a little annoyed*) Very well. Now run upstairs and get ready for dinner.

MARY   It was—it was all about Miss Dobie and Mrs. Mortar. They were talking awful things and Peggy and Evelyn heard them and Miss Dobie found out, and then they made us move our rooms.

MRS. TILFORD   What has that to do with you? I don't understand a word you're saying.

MARY   They made us move our rooms. They said we couldn't be together any more. They're afraid to have us near them, that's what it is, and they're taking it out on me. They're scared of you.

MRS. TILFORD   For a little girl you're imagining a lot of

big things. Why should they be scared of me? Am I such
an unpleasant old lady?

MARY   They're afraid you'll find out.

MRS. TILFORD   Find out what?

MARY   (*vaguely*) Things.

MRS. TILFORD   Run along, Mary. I hope you'll get more
coherent as you get older.

MARY   (*slowly starting for door*) All right. But there're
a lot of things. They have secrets or something, and
they're afraid I'll find out and tell you.

MRS. TILFORD   There's not necessarily anything wrong with
people having secrets.

MARY   (*coming back in the room again*) But they've got
funny ones. Peggy and Evelyn heard Mrs. Mortar telling Miss Dobie that she was jealous of Miss Wright
marrying Cousin Joe.

MRS. TILFORD   You shouldn't repeat things like that.

MARY   But that's what she said, Grandma. She said it
was unnatural for a girl to feel that way.

MRS. TILFORD   What?

MARY   I'm just telling you what she said. She said there
was something funny about it, and that Miss Dobie had
always been like that, even when she was a little girl,
and that it was unnatural—

MRS. TILFORD   Stop using that silly word, Mary.

MARY   (*vaguely realizing that she is on the right track,
hurries on*) But that was the word *she* kept using,
Grandma, and then they got mad and told Mrs. Mortar
she'd have to get out.

MRS. TILFORD   That was probably not the reason at all.

MARY   (*nodding vigorously*) I bet it was, because honestly, Miss Dobie does get cranky and mean every time
Cousin Joe comes, and today I heard her say to him:
"God damn you," and then she said she was just a jealous
fool and—

MRS. TILFORD   You have picked up some very fine words,
haven't you, Mary?

MARY   That's just what she said, Grandma, and one time
Miss Dobie was crying in Miss Wright's room, and
Miss Wright was trying to stop her, and she said that

all right, maybe she wouldn't get married right away
if—

MRS. TILFORD   How do you know all this?

MARY   We couldn't help hearing because they—I mean
Miss Dobie—was talking awful loud, and their room
is right next to ours.

MRS. TILFORD   Whose room?

MARY   Miss Wright's room, I mean, and you can just ask
Peggy and Evelyn whether we didn't hear. Almost always Miss Dobie comes in after we go to bed and stays
a long time. I guess that's why they want to get rid of
us—of me—because we hear things. That's why they're
making us move our room, and they punish me all the
time for—

MRS. TILFORD   For eavesdropping, I should think. (*She
has said this mechanically. With nothing definite in her
mind, she is making an effort to conceal the fact that
*MARY's *description of the life at school has shocked her*)
Well, now I think we've had enough gossip, don't you?
Dinner's almost ready, and I can't eat with a girl who
has such a dirty face.

MARY   (*softly*)   I've heard other things, too.

MRS. TILFORD   (*abstractedly*)   What? What did you say?

MARY   I've heard other things. Plenty of other things,
Grandma.

MRS. TILFORD   What things?

MARY   Bad things.

MRS. TILFORD   Well, what were they?

MARY   I can't tell you.

MRS. TILFORD   Mary, you're annoying me very much. If
you have anything to say, then say it and stop acting
silly.

MARY   I mean I can't say it out loud.

MRS. TILFORD   There couldn't possibly be anything so terrible that you couldn't say it out loud. Now either tell
the truth or be still.

MARY   Well, a lot of things I don't understand. But it's
awful, and sometimes they fight and then they make up,
and Miss Dobie cries and Miss Wright gets mad, and

then they make up again, and there are funny noises and we get scared.

MRS. TILFORD   Noises? I suppose you girls have a happy time imagining a murder.

MARY   And we've seen things, too. Funny things. (*Sees the impatience of her grandmother*) I'd tell you, but I got to whisper it.

MRS. TILFORD   Why must you whisper it?

MARY   I don't know. I just got to. (*Climbs on the sofa next to* MRS. TILFORD *and begins whispering. At first the whisper is slow and hesitant, but it gradually works itself up to fast, excited talking. In the middle of it* MRS. TILFORD *stops her.*)

MRS. TILFORD   (*trembling*) Do you know what you're saying? (*Without answering,* MARY *goes back to the whispering until the older woman takes her by the shoulders and turns her around to stare in her face*) Mary? Are you telling me the truth?

MARY   Honest, honest. You just ask Peggy and Evelyn and— (*After a moment* MRS. TILFORD *gets up and begins to pace about the room. She is no longer listening to* MARY, *who keeps up a running fire of conversation*) They know too. And maybe there're other kids who know, but we've always been frightened and so we didn't ask, and one night I was going to go and find out, but I got scared and we went to bed early so we wouldn't hear, but sometimes I couldn't help it, but we never talked about it much, because we thought they'd find out and— Oh, Grandma, don't make me go back to that awful place.

MRS. TILFORD   (*abstractedly*) What? (*Starts to move about again.*)

MARY   Don't make me go back to that place. I just couldn't stand it any more. Really, Grandma, I'm so unhappy there, and if only I could stay out the rest of the term, why, then—

MRS. TILFORD   (*makes irritated gesture*) Be still a minute. (*After a moment*) No, you won't have to go back.

MARY   (*surprised*) Honest?

MRS. TILFORD   Honest.

MARY   (*hugging* MRS. TILFORD)   You're the nicest, loveliest grandma in all the world. You—you're not mad at me?

MRS. TILFORD   I'm not mad at you. Now go upstairs and get ready for dinner. (MARY *kisses her and runs happily out Left.* MRS TILFORD *stands staring after her for a long moment; then, very slowly, she puts on her eyeglasses and crosses to the phone. She dials a number*) Is Miss Wright—is Miss Wright in? (*Waits a second, hurriedly puts down the receiver*) Never mind, never mind. (*Dials another number*) Dr. Cardin, please. Mrs. Tilford. (*She remains absolutely motionless while she waits. When she does speak, her voice is low and tense*) Joseph? Joseph? Can you come to see me right away? Yes, I'm perfectly well. No, but it's important, Joseph, very important. I must see you right away. I—I can't tell you over the phone. Can't you come sooner? It's not about Mary's fainting— I said it's not about Mary, Joseph; in one way it's about Mary— (*Suddenly quiet*) But will the hospital take so long? Very well, Joseph, make it as soon as you can. (*Hangs up the receiver, sits for a moment undecided. Then, taking a breath, she dials another number*) Mrs. Munn, please. This is Mrs. Tilford. Miriam? This is Amelia Tilford. I have something to tell you—something very shocking, I'm afraid —something about the school and Evelyn and Mary—

Curtain

SCENE II

SCENE: *The same as Scene I. The curtain has been lowered to mark the passing of a few hours.*

AT RISE: MARY *is lying on the floor playing with a puzzle.* AGATHA *appears lugging blankets and pillows across the room. Almost at the door, she stops and gives* MARY *an annoyed look.*

AGATHA   And see to it that she doesn't get my good quilt all dirty, and let her wear your green pajamas.

MARY   Who?

AGATHA   Who? Don't you ever keep your ears open? Rosalie Wells is coming over to spend the night with you.

MARY   You mean she's going to sleep *here?*

AGATHA   You heard me.

MARY   What for?

AGATHA   Do I know all the crazy things that are happening around here? Your grandmother phones Mrs. Wells all the way to New York, three dollars and eighty-five cents and families starving, and Mrs. Wells wanted to know if Rosalie could stay here until tomorrow.

MARY   (*relieved*) Oh. Couldn't Evelyn Munn come instead?

AGATHA   Sure. We'll have the whole town over to entertain you.

MARY   I won't let Rosalie Wells wear my new pajamas.

AGATHA   (*exits as the front door-bell rings*) Don't tell me what you won't do. You'll act like a lady for once in your life. (*Off-stage*) Come on in, Rosalie. Just go on in there and make yourself at home. Have you had your dinner?

ROSALIE   (*off-stage*)   Good evening. Yes'm.

AGATHA   (*off-stage*)   Hang up your pretty coat. Have you had your bath?

ROSALIE   (*off-stage*)   Yes, ma'am. This morning.

AGATHA   (*off-stage*)   Well, you better have another one.

(*She is climbing the stairs as* ROSALIE *comes into the room.* MARY, *lying in front of the couch, is hidden from her. Gingerly* ROSALIE *sits down on a chair.*)

MARY   (*softly*) Whooooooo. (ROSALIE *jumps*) Whooooooo. (ROSALIE, *frightened, starts hurriedly for the door.* MARY *sits up, laughs*) You're a goose.

ROSALIE   (*belligerently*) Oh, so it's you. Well, who likes to hear funny noises at night? You could have been a werewolf.

MARY   A werewolf wouldn't want you.

ROSALIE   You know everything, don't you? (MARY *laughs.*

ROSALIE *comes over, stands staring at puzzle*) Isn't it funny about school?

MARY   What's funny about it?

ROSALIE   Don't act like you can come home every night.

MARY   Maybe I can from now on. (*Rolls over on her back luxuriously*) Maybe I'm never going back.

ROSALIE   Am I going back? I don't want to stay home.

MARY   What'll you give to know?

ROSALIE   Nothing. I'll ask Mamma.

MARY   Will you give me a free T. L. if I tell you?

ROSALIE   (*thinks for a moment*) All right. Lois Fisher told Helen that you were very smart.

MARY   That's an old one. I won't take it.

ROSALIE   You got to take it.

MARY   Nope.

ROSALIE   (*laughs*) You don't know, anyway.

MARY   I know what I heard, and I know Grandma phoned your mother in New York to come and get you right away. You're just going to spend the night here. I wish Evelyn could come instead of you.

ROSALIE   But what's happened? Peggy and Helen and Evelyn and Lois went home tonight, too. Do you think somebody's got scarlet fever or something?

MARY   No.

ROSALIE   Do *you* know what it is? How'd you find out? (*No answer*) You're always pretending you know everything. You're just faking. (*Flounces away*) Never mind, don't bother telling me. I think curiosity is very unlady-like, anyhow. I have no concern with your silly secrets.

MARY   Suppose I told you that I just may have said that you were in on it?

ROSALIE   In on what?

MARY   The secret. Suppose I told you that I *may have* said that you told me about it?

ROSALIE   Why, Mary Tilford! You can't do a thing like that. I didn't tell you about anything. (MARY *laughs*) Did you tell your grandmother such a thing?

MARY   Maybe.

ROSALIE   Did you?

MARY   Maybe.

ROSALIE Well, I'm going right up to your grandmother and tell her I didn't tell you anything—whatever it is. You're just trying to get me into trouble and I'm not going to let you. (*Starts for door.*)

MARY Wait a minute, I'll come with you.

ROSALIE What for?

MARY I want to tell her about Helen Burton's bracelet.

ROSALIE (*sits down suddenly*) What about it?

MARY Just that you stole it.

ROSALIE Shut up. I didn't do any such thing.

MARY Yes, you did.

ROSALIE (*tearfully*) You made it up. You're always making things up.

MARY You can't call me a fibber, Rosalie Wells. That's a kind of a dare and I won't take a dare. I guess I'll go tell Grandma, anyway. Then she can call the police and they'll come for you and you'll spend the rest of your life in one of those solitary prisons and you'll get older and older, and when you're very old and can't see anymore, they'll let you out maybe with a big sign on your back saying you're a thief, and your mother and father will be dead and you won't have any place to go and you'll beg on the streets—

ROSALIE I didn't steal anything. I borrowed the bracelet and I was going to put it back as soon as I'd worn it to the movies. I never meant to keep it.

MARY Nobody'll believe that, least of all the police. You're just a common, ordinary thief. Stop that bawling. You'll have the whole house down here in a minute.

ROSALIE You won't tell? Say you won't tell.

MARY Am I a fibber?

ROSALIE No.

MARY Then say: "I apologize on my hands and knees."

ROSALIE I apologize on my hands and knees. Let's play with the puzzle.

MARY Wait a minute. Say: "From now on, I, Rosalie Wells, am the vassal of Mary Tilford and will do and say whatever she tells me under the solemn oath of a knight."

ROSALIE   I won't say that. That's the worse oath there is.
(MARY *starts for the door*) Mary! Please don't—

MARY   Will you swear it?

ROSALIE   (*sniffling*)   But then you could tell me to do anything.

MARY   And you'd have to do it. Say it quick or I'll—

ROSALIE   (*hurriedly*)   From now on, I, Rosalie Wells, am
the vassal of Mary Tilford and will do and say whatever she tells me under the solemn oath of a knight.
(*She gasps, and sits up straight as* MRS. TILFORD *enters.*)

MARY   Don't forget that.

MRS. TILFORD   Good evening, Rosalie, you're looking very
well.

ROSALIE   Good evening, Mrs. Tilford.

MARY   She's getting fatter every day.

MRS. TILFORD   (*abstractedly*)   Then it's very becoming.
(*Door-bell rings*) That must be Joseph. Mary, take
Rosalie into the library. There's some fruit and milk
on the table. Be sure you're both fast asleep by half
past ten. (*Leans down, kisses them both.* ROSALIE *starts
to exit Right, sees* MARY, *stops and hesitates.*)

MARY   Go on, Rosalie. (*Waits until* ROSALIE *reluctantly
exits*) Grandma.

MRS. TILFORD   Yes?

MARY   Grandma, Cousin Joe'll say I've got to go back.
He'll say I really wasn't—

(CARDIN *enters and she runs from the room.*)

CARDIN   Hello, Amelia. (*Looks curiously at the fleeing*
MARY) Mary home, eh?

MRS. TILFORD   (*watching* MARY *as she leaves*)   Hello,
Joseph. Sit down. (*He sits down, looks at her curiously,
waits for her to speak*) Whisky?

CARDIN   Please. How are you feeling? Headaches again?

MRS. TILFORD   (*puts drink on table*)   No.

CARDIN   Those are good powders. Bicarbonate of soda and
water. Never hurt anybody yet.

MRS. TILFORD   Yes. How have you been, Joseph?

CARDIN   My good health is monotonous.

MRS. TILFORD   (*vaguely, sparring for time*)   I haven't seen you the last few weeks. Agatha misses you for Sunday dinners.

CARDIN I've been busy. We're getting the results from the mating-season right about now.

MRS. TILFORD Did I take you away from a patient?

CARDIN No. I was at the hospital.

MRS. TILFORD How's it getting on?

CARDIN Just the same. No money, badly equipped, a lousy laboratory, everybody growling at everybody else—Amelia, you didn't bring me here to talk about the hospital. We're talking like people waiting for the muffins to be passed around. What's the matter with you?

MRS. TILFORD I—I have something to tell you.

CARDIN Well, out with it.

MRS. TILFORD It's a very hard thing to say, Joseph.

CARDIN Hard for you to say to *me?* (*No answer*) Don't be worried about Mary. I guessed that she ran home to tell you about her faint. It was caused by nothing but bad temper and was very clumsily managed, at that. Amelia, she's a terribly spoilt—

MRS. TILFORD I heard about the faint. That's not what is worrying me.

CARDIN (*gently*) Are you in some trouble?

MRS. TILFORD We all are in trouble. Bad trouble.

CARDIN We? Me, you mean? Nothing's the matter with me.

MRS. TILFORD When did you last see Karen?

CARDIN Today. This afternoon.

MRS. TILFORD Oh. Not since seven o'clock?

CARDIN What's happened since seven o'clock?

MRS. TILFORD Joseph, you've been engaged to Karen for a long time. Are your plans any more definite than they were a year ago?

CARDIN You can get ready to buy the wedding present. We'll have the wedding here, if you don't mind. The smell of clean little girls and boiled linen would worry me.

MRS. TILFORD Why has Karen decided so suddenly to make it definite?

CARDIN She has not suddenly decided anything. The

school is pretty well on its feet, and now that Mrs. Mortar is leaving—

MRS. TILFORD   I've heard about their putting Mrs. Mortar out.

CARDIN   Putting her out? Well, maybe. But a nice sum for a trip and a promise that a good niece will support you the rest of your life is an enviable way of being put out.

MRS. TILFORD   (*slowly*)   Don't you find it odd, Joseph, that they want so much to get rid of that silly, harmless woman?

CARDIN   I don't know what you're talking about, but it isn't odd at all. Lily Mortar is not a harmless woman, although God knows she's silly enough. She's a nasty, tiresome, spoilt old bitch. If you're forming a Mortar Welfare Society, you're wasting your time. (*Gets up, puts down his glass*) It's not like you to waste your time. Now, what's it that's really on your mind?

MRS. TILFORD   You must not marry Karen.

CARDIN   (*shocked, he grins*)   You're a very impertinent lady. Why must I— (*imitates her*) not marry Karen?

MRS. TILFORD   Because there's something wrong with Karen—something horrible.

(*The door-bell is heard to ring loud and long.*)

CARDIN   I don't think I can allow you to say things like that, Amelia.

MRS. TILFORD   I have good reason for saying it. (*Breaks off as she hears voices off-stage*) Who is that?

KAREN   (*off-stage*)   Mrs. Tilford, Agatha. Is she in?

AGATHA   (*off-stage*)   Yes'm. Come on in.

MRS. TILFORD   I won't have her here.

CARDIN   (*angrily*)   What are you talking about?

MRS. TILFORD   I won't have her here.

CARDIN   (*picks up his hat*)   Then you don't want me here either. (*Turns to face* KAREN, *who, with* MARTHA, *has rushed in*) Darling, what—?

KAREN   (*stops when she sees him, puts her hand over her eyes*)   Is it a joke, Joe?

MARTHA   (*with great force to* MRS. TILFORD)   We've come to find out what you are doing.

CARDIN (*kissing* KAREN) What is it?

KAREN It's crazy! It's crazy! What did she do it for?

CARDIN What are you talking about? What do you mean?

MRS. TILFORD You shouldn't have come here.

CARDIN What is all this? What's happened?

KAREN I tried to reach you. Hasn't she told you?

CARDIN Nobody's told me anything. I haven't heard anything but wild talk. What is it, Karen? (*She starts to
speak, then dumbly shakes her head*) What's happened,
Martha?

MARTHA (*violently*) An insane asylum has been let loose.
How do we know what's happened?

CARDIN What was it?

KAREN We didn't know what it was. Nobody would talk
to us, nobody would tell us anything.

MARTHA I'll tell you, I'll tell you. You see if you can
make any sense out of it. At dinner-time Mrs. Munn's
chauffeur said that Evelyn must be sent home right
away. At half past seven Mrs. Burton arrived to tell
us that she wanted Helen's things packed and that
she'd wait outside because she didn't want to enter a
place like ours. Five minutes later the Wells's butler
came for Rosalie.

CARDIN What was it?

MARTHA It was a madhouse. People rushing in and out,
the children being pushed into cars—

KAREN (*quiet now, takes his hand*) Mrs. Rogers finally
told us.

CARDIN What? What?

KAREN That—that Martha and I are—in love with each
other. In love with each other. Mrs. Tilford told them.

CARDIN (*for a moment stands staring at her incredulously.
Then he walks across the room, stares out of the window, and finally turns to* MRS. TILFORD) Did you tell
them that?

MRS. TILFORD Yes.

CARDIN Are you sick?

MRS. TILFORD You know I'm not sick.

CARDIN (*snapping the words out*) Then what did you
do it for?

MRS. TILFORD (*slowly*) Because it's true.

KAREN (*incredulously*) You think it's true, then?

MARTHA You fool! You damned, vicious—

KAREN Do you realize what you're saying?

MRS. TILFORD I realize it very well. And—

MARTHA You realize nothing, nothing, nothing.

MRS. TILFORD And that's why I don't think you should have come here. (*Quietly, with a look at* MARTHA) I shall not call you names, and I will not allow you to call me names. It comes to this: I can't trust myself to talk about it with you now or ever.

KAREN What's she talking about, Joe? What's she mean? What is she trying to do to us? What is everybody doing to us?

MARTHA (*softly, as though to herself*) Pushed around. We're being pushed around by crazy people. (*Shakes herself slightly*) That's an awful thing. And we're standing here— (CARDIN *puts his arm around* KAREN, *walks with her to the window. They stand there together*) We're standing here taking it. (*Suddenly with violence*) Didn't you know we'd come here? Were we supposed to lie down and grin while you kicked us around with these lies?

MRS. TILFORD This can't do any of us any good, Miss Dobie.

MARTHA (*scornfully imitating her*) "This can't do any of us any good." Listen, listen. Try to understand this: you're not playing with paper dolls. We're human beings, see? It's our lives you're fooling with. *Our* lives. That's serious business for us. Can you understand that?

MRS. TILFORD (*for the first time she speaks angrily*) I can understand that, and I understand a lot more. *You've* been playing with a lot of children's lives, and that's why I stopped you. (*More calmly*) I know how serious this is for you, how serious it is for all of us.

CARDIN (*bitterly*) I don't think you do know.

MRS. TILFORD I wanted to avoid this meeting because it can't do any good. You came here to find out if I had made the charge. You've found out. Let's end it there.

I don't want you in this house. I'm sorry this had to be done to you, Joseph.

CARDIN I don't like your sympathy.

MRS. TILFORD Very well. There's nothing I mean to do, nothing I want to do. There's nothing anybody can do.

CARDIN (*carefully*) You have already done a terrible thing.

MRS. TILFORD I have done what I had to do. What they are may possibly be their own business. It becomes a great deal more than that when children are involved.

KAREN (*wildly*) It's not true. Not a word of it is true; can't you understand that?

MRS. TILFORD There won't be any punishment for either of you. But there mustn't be any punishment for me, either—and that's what this meeting is. This—this thing is your own. Go away with it. I don't understand it and I don't want any part of it.

MARTHA (*slowly*) So you thought we would go away?

MRS. TILFORD I think that's best for you.

MARTHA There must be something we can do to you, and, whatever it is, we'll find it.

MRS. TILFORD That will be very unwise.

KAREN You are right to be afraid.

MRS. TILFORD I am not afraid, Karen.

CARDIN But you *are* old—and you *are* irresponsible.

MRS. TILFORD (*hurt*) You know that's not true.

KAREN (*goes to her*) I don't want to have anything to do with your mess, do you hear me? It makes me feel dirty and sick to be forced to say this, but here it is: there isn't a single word of truth in anything you've said. We're standing here defending ourselves—and against what? Against a lie. A great, awful lie.

MRS. TILFORD I'm sorry that I can't believe that.

KAREN Damn you!

CARDIN But you can believe this: they've worked eight long years to save enough money to buy that farm, to start that school. They did without everything that young people ought to have. You wouldn't know about that. That school meant things to them: self-respect, and bread and butter, and honest work. Do you know what it is to try so hard for anything? Well, now it's gone. (*Suddenly hits the side of the table with his hand*) What the hell did you do it for?

MRS. TILFORD   (*softly*)   It had to be done.

CARDIN   Righteousness is a great thing.

MRS. TILFORD   (*gently*)   I know how you must feel.

CARDIN   You don't know anything about how I feel. And you don't know how they feel, either.

MRS. TILFORD   I've loved you as much as I loved my own boys. I wouldn't have spared them; I couldn't spare you.

CARDIN   (*fiercely*)   I believe you.

MARTHA   What is there to do to you? What can we do to you? There must be something—something that makes you feel the way we do tonight. You don't want any part of this, you said. But you'll get a part. More than you bargained for. (*Suddenly*) Listen: are you willing to stand by everything you've said tonight?

MRS. TILFORD   Yes.

MARTHA   All right. That's fine. But don't get the idea we'll let you whisper this lie: you made it and you'll come out with it. Shriek it to your town of Lancet. We'll *make* you shriek it—and we'll make you do it in a court room. (*Quietly*) Tomorrow, Mrs. Tilford, you will have a libel suit on your hands.

MRS. TILFORD   That will be very unwise.

KAREN   Very unwise—for you.

MRS. TILFORD   It is you I am thinking of. I am frightened for you. It was wrong of you to brazen it out here to-night; it would be criminally foolish of you to brazen it out in public. That can bring you nothing but pain. I am an old woman, Miss Dobie, and I have seen too many people, out of pride, act on that pride. In the end they punish themselves.

MARTHA   And you feel that you are too old to be punished? That we should spare you?

MRS. TILFORD   You know that is not what I meant.

CARDIN   (*turns from the window*)   So you took a child's word for it?

MARTHA   (*looks at him, shakes her head*)   I knew it, too.

KAREN That is really where you got it? I can't believe—
it couldn't be. Why, she's a child.

MARTHA She's not a child any longer.

KAREN Oh, my God, it all fits so well now. That girl has
hated us for a long time. We never knew why, we never
could find out. There didn't seem to be any reason—

MARTHA There wasn't any reason. She hates everybody
and everything.

KAREN Your Mary's a strange girl, a bad girl. There's
something very awful the matter with her.

MRS. TILFORD I was waiting for you to say that, Miss
Wright.

KAREN I'm telling you the truth. We should have told it
to you long ago. (*Stops, sighs*) It's no use.

MARTHA Where is she? Bring her out here and let us
hear what she has to say.

MRS. TILFORD You cannot see her.

CARDIN Where is she?

MRS. TILFORD I won't have that, Joseph.

CARDIN I'm going to talk to her.

MRS. TILFORD *I won't have her go through with that again.*
(*To* KAREN *and* MARTHA) You came here demanding
explanations. It was I who should have asked them
from you. You attack me, you attack Mary. I've told
you I didn't mean you any harm. I still don't. You claim
that it isn't true; it may be natural that you should say
that, but I *know* that it is true. No matter what you
say, you know very well I wouldn't have acted
until I was absolutely sure. All I wanted was to get
those children away. That has been done. There won't
be any talk about it or about you—I'll see to that. You
have been in my house long enough. Get out.

KAREN (*gets up*) The wicked very young, and the wicked
very old. Let's go home.

CARDIN Sit down. (*To* MRS. TILFORD) When two people
come here with their lives spread on the table for you
to cut to pieces, then the only honest thing to do is to
give them a chance to come out whole. Are you honest?

MRS. TILFORD I've always thought so.

CARDIN Then where is Mary? (*After a moment she moves*

her head to door Right. Quickly CARDIN *goes to the door and opens it*) Mary! Come here.

(*After a moment* MARY *appears, stands nervously near door. Her manner is shy and afraid.*)

MRS. TILFORD   (*gently*) Sit down, dear, and don't be afraid.

MARTHA   (*her lips barely moving*) Make her tell the truth.

CARDIN   (*walking about in front of* MARY) Look: everybody lies all the time. Sometimes they have to, sometimes they don't. I've lied myself for a lot of different reasons, but there was never a time when, if I'd been given a second chance, I wouldn't have taken back the lie and told the truth. You're lucky if you ever get that chance. I'm telling you this because I'm about to ask you a question. Before you answer the question, I want to tell you that if you've l— if you made a mistake, you must take this chance and say so. You won't be punished for it. Do you get all that?

MARY   (*timidly*) Yes, Cousin Joe.

CARDIN   (*grimly*) All right, let's get started. Were you telling your grandmother the truth this afternoon? The exact truth about Miss Wright and Miss Dobie?

MARY   (*without hesitation*) Oh, yes.

(KAREN *sighs deeply,* MARTHA, *her fists closed tight, turns her back to the child.* CARDIN *smiles as he looks at* MARY.)

CARDIN   All right, Mary, that was your chance; you passed it up. (*Pulls up a chair, sits down in front of her*) Now let's find out things.

MRS. TILFORD   She's told you. Aren't you through?

CARDIN   Not by a long shot. You've started something, and I'm going to finish it for you. Will you answer some more questions, Mary?

MARY   Yes, Cousin Joe.

MARTHA   Stop that sick sweet tone.

(MRS. TILFORD *half rises;* CARDIN *motions her back.*)

CARDIN   Why don't you like Miss Dobie and Miss Wright?

MARY   Oh, I do like them. They just don't like me. They never have liked me.

CARDIN How do you know?

MARY They're always picking on me. They're always punishing me for everything that happens. No matter what happens, it's always me.

CARDIN Why do you think they do that?

MARY Because—because they're—because they— (*Stops, turns*) Grandma, I—

CARDIN All right, we'll skip that one. Did you get punished today?

MARY Yes, and it was just because Peggy and Evelyn heard them and so they took it out on me.

KAREN That's a lie.

CARDIN Sssh. Heard what, Mary?

MARY Mrs. Mortar told Miss Dobie that there was something funny about her. She said that she had a funny feeling about Miss Wright, and Mrs. Mortar said that was unnatural. That was why we got punished, just because—

KAREN That was not the reason they got punished.

MRS. TILFORD (*to* MARTHA) Miss Dobie?

MARTHA My aunt is a stupid woman. What she said was unpleasant; it was said to annoy me. It meant nothing more than that.

MARY And, Cousin Joe, she said every time you came to the school Miss Dobie got jealous, and that she didn't want you to get married.

MARTHA (*to* CARDIN) She said that, too. For God's sake, can't you see what's happening? This—this child is taking little things, little family things, and making them have meanings that— (*Stops, suddenly regards* MARY *with a combination of disgust and interest*) Where did you learn so much in so little time?

CARDIN What do you think Mrs. Mortar meant by all that, Mary?

MRS. TILFORD Stop it, Joseph!

MARY I don't know, but it was always kind of funny and she always said things like that and all the girls would talk about it when Miss Dobie went and visited Miss Wright late at night—

KAREN (*angrily*) And we go to the movies at night and

sometimes we read at night and sometimes we drink tea at night. Those are guilty things, too, Mrs. Tilford.

MARY   And there are always funny sounds and we'd stay awake and listen because we couldn't help hearing and I'd get frightened because the sounds were like—

MARTHA   Be still!

KAREN   (*with violence*) No, no. You don't want her still now. What else did you hear?

MARY   Grandma, I—

MRS. TILFORD   (*bitterly to* CARDIN) You are trying to make her name it, aren't you?

CARDIN   (*ignoring her, speaks to* MARY) Go on.

MARY   I don't know; there were just sounds.

CARDIN   But what did you think they were? Why did they frighten you?

MARY   (*weakly*) I don't know.

CARDIN   (*smiles at* MRS. TILFORD) She doesn't know.

MARY   (*hastily*) I saw things, too. One night there was so much noise I thought somebody was sick or something and I looked through the keyhole and they were kissing and saying things and then I got scared because it was different sort of and I—

MARTHA   (*her face distorted, turns to* MRS. TILFORD) That child—that child is sick.

KAREN   Ask her again how she could see us.

CARDIN   How could you see Miss Dobie and Miss Wright?

MARY   I—I—

MRS. TILFORD   Tell him what you whispered to me.

MARY   It was at night and I was leaning down by the keyhole.

KAREN   *There's no keyhole on my door.*

MRS. TILFORD   What?

KAREN   There—is—no—keyhole—on—my—door.

MARY   (*quickly*) It wasn't her room, Grandma, it was the other room, I guess. It was *Miss Dobie's* room. I saw them through the keyhole in Miss Dobie's room.

CARDIN   How did you know anybody was in Miss Dobie's room?

MARY   I told you, I told you. Because we heard them. Everybody heard them—

MARTHA I share a room with my aunt. It is on the first floor at the other end of the house. It is impossible to hear anything from there. (*To* CARDIN) Tell her to come and see for herself.

MRS. TILFORD (*her voice shaken*) What is this, Mary? Why did you say you saw through a keyhole? *Can* you hear from your room—?

MARY (*starts to cry*) Everybody is yelling at me. I don't know what I'm saying with everybody mixing me all up. I did see it! I did see it!

MRS. TILFORD *What* did you see? *Where* did you see it? I want the truth, now. The truth, whatever it is.

CARDIN (*gets up, moves his chair back*) We can go home. We are finished here. (*Looks around*) It's not a pleasant place to be.

MRS. TILFORD (*angrily*) Stop that crying, Mary. Stand up.

(MARY *gets up, head down, still crying hysterically.* MRS. TILFORD *goes and stands directly in front of her.*)

MRS. TILFORD *I want the truth.*

MARY All—all right.

MRS. TILFORD What is the truth?

MARY It was Rosalie who saw them. I just said it was me so I wouldn't have to tattle on Rosalie.

CARDIN (*wearily*) Oh, my God!

MARY It *was* Rosalie, Grandma, she told us all about it. She said she had read about it in a book and she knew. (*Desperately*) You ask Rosalie. You just ask Rosalie. She'll tell you. We used to talk about it all the time. That's the truth, that's the honest truth. She said it was when the door was open once and she told us all about it. I was just trying to save Rosalie, and everybody jumps on me.

MRS. TILFORD (*to* CARDIN) Please wait a minute. (*Goes to library door*) Rosalie!

CARDIN You're giving yourself an awful beating, Amelia, and you deserve whatever you get.

MRS. TILFORD (*stands waiting for* ROSALIE, *passes her hand over her face*) I don't know. I don't know, any more. Maybe it's what I do deserve. (*As Rosalie,*

frightened, appears at the door, making bows to every-
body, she takes the child gently by the hand, brings
her down Center, talking nervously) I'm sorry to keep
you up so late, Rosalie. You must be tired. (*Speaks*
rapidly) Mary says there's been a lot of talk in the
school lately about Miss Wright and Miss Dobie. Is
that true?

ROSALIE   I—I don't know what you mean.

MRS. TILFORD   That things have been said among you
girls.

ROSALIE   (*wide-eyed, frightened*)   What things? I never—
I—I—

KAREN   (*gently*)   Don't be frightened.

MRS. TILFORD   What was the talk about, Rosalie?

ROSALIE   (*utterly bewildered*)   I don't know what she
means, Miss Wright.

KAREN   Rosalie, Mary has told her grandmother that certain things at school have been—er—puzzling you girls.
You, particularly.

ROSALIE   History puzzles me. I guess I'm not very good at
history, and Helen helps me sometimes, if that—

KAREN   No, that's not what she meant. She says that you
told her that you saw certain—certain acts between
Miss Dobie and myself. She says that once, when the
door was open, you saw us kissing each other in a way
that— (*Unable to bear the child's look, she turns her*
back) women don't kiss one another.

ROSALIE   Oh, Miss Wright, I didn't, didn't, I didn't. I
never said such a thing.

MRS. TILFORD   (*grimly*)   That's true, my dear?

ROSALIE   I never saw any such thing. Mary always makes
things up about me and everybody else. (*Starts to*
weep in excitement) I never said any such thing ever.
Why, I never even could have thought of—

MARY   (*staring at her, speaks very slowly*)   Yes, you did,
Rosalie. You're just trying to get out of it. I remember
just when you said it. I remember it, because it was
the day Helen Burton's bracelet was—

ROSALIE   (*stands fascinated and fearful, looking at* MARY)
I never did. I—I— you're just—

MARY   It was the day Helen's bracelet was stolen, and nobody knew who did it, and Helen said that if her mother found out, she'd have the thief put in jail.

KAREN   (*puzzled, as are the others, by the sudden change in* ROSALIE'S *manner*) There's nothing to cry about. You must help us by telling the truth. Why, what's the matter, Rosalie?

MARY   Grandma, there's something I've got to tell you that—

ROSALIE   (*with a shrill cry*) Yes. Yes. I did see it. I told Mary. What Mary said was right. I said it, I said it—
(*Throws herself on the couch, weeping hysterically;* MARTHA *stands leaning against the door;* KAREN, CARDIN *and* MRS. TILFORD *are staring at* ROSALIE; MARY *slowly sits down as the Curtain falls.*)

Act Three

SCENE: *The same as Act One. Living room of the school.*

AT RISE: *The room has changed. It is not dirty, but it is dull and dark and uncared for. The windows are tightly shut, the curtains tightly drawn. KAREN is sitting in a large chair, Right Center, feet flat on floor. MARTHA is lying on the couch, her face buried against the pillows, her back to KAREN. It is a minute or two after the rise of the curtain before either speaks.*

MARTHA   It's cold in here.

KAREN   Yes.

MARTHA   What time is it?

KAREN   I don't know. What's the difference?

MARTHA   None. I was hoping it was time for my bath.

KAREN   Take it early today.

MARTHA   *(laughs)*   Oh, I couldn't do that. I look forward all day to that bath. It's my last touch with the full life. It makes me feel important to know that there's one thing ahead of me, one thing I've *got* to do. You ought to get yourself something like that. I tell you, at five o'clock every day you comb your hair. How's that? It's better for you, take my word. You wake up in the morning and you say to yourself, the day's not entirely empty, life is rich and full; at five o'clock I'll comb my hair.

(They fall back into silence. A moment later the phone rings. Neither of them pays the slightest attention to it. But the ringing becomes too insistent. KAREN rises, takes

the receiver off, goes back to her chair and sits down.)

KAREN   It's raining.

MARTHA   Hungry?

KAREN   No. You?

MARTHA   No, but I'd like to be hungry again. Remember how much we used to eat at college?

KAREN   That was ten years ago.

MARTHA   Well, maybe we'll be hungry in another ten years. It's cheaper this way.

KAREN   What's the old thing about time being more nourishing than bread?

MARTHA   Yeah? Maybe.

KAREN   Joe's late today. What time is it?

MARTHA   (*turns again to lie on her side*) We've been sitting here for eight days asking each other the time. Haven't you heard? There isn't any time any more.

KAREN   It's been days since we've been out of this house.

MARTHA   Well, we'll have to get off these chairs sooner or later. In a couple of months they'll need dusting.

KAREN   What'll we do when we get off?

MARTHA   God knows.

KAREN   (*almost in a whisper*) It's awful.

MARTHA   Let's not talk about it. (*After a moment*) What about eggs for dinner?

KAREN   All right.

MARTHA   I'll make some potatoes with onions, the way you used to like them.

KAREN   It's a week ago Thursday. It never seemed real until the last day. It seems real enough now, all right.

MARTHA   Now and forever after.

KAREN   (*suddenly*) Let's go out.

MARTHA   (*turns over, stares at her*) Where to?

KAREN   We'll take a walk.

MARTHA   Where'll we walk?

KAREN   Why shouldn't we take a walk? We won't see anybody, and suppose we do, what of it? We'll jus—

MARTHA   (*slowly gets up*) Come on. We'll go through the park.

KAREN   They might see us. (*They stand looking at each*

other) Let's not go. (MARTHA *goes back, lies down again*) We'll go tomorrow.

MARTHA (*laughs*) Stop kidding yourself.

KAREN But Joe says we've got to go out. He says that all the people who don't think it's true will begin to wonder if we keep hiding this way.

MARTHA If it makes you feel better to think there *are* such people, go ahead.

KAREN He says we ought to go into town and go shopping and act as though—

MARTHA Shopping? That's a sound idea. There aren't three stores in Lancet that would sell us anything. Hasn't he heard about the ladies' clubs and their meetings and their circulars and their visits and their—

KAREN (*softly*) Don't tell him.

MARTHA (*gently*) I won't. (*There are footsteps in the hall, and the sound of something being dragged*) There's our friend.

(*A* GROCERY BOY *appears lugging a box. He brings it into the room, stands staring at them, giggles a little. Walks toward* KAREN, *stops, examines her. She sits tense, looking away from him. Without taking his eyes from* KAREN, *he speaks.*)

GROCERY BOY I knocked on the kitchen door but nobody answered.

MARTHA You said that yesterday. All right. Thanks. Good-bye.

KAREN (*unable any longer to stand the stare*) Make him stop it.

GROCERY BOY Here are the things. (*Giggles, moves toward* MARTHA, *stands looking at her. Suddenly* MARTHA *thrusts her hand in the air.*)

MARTHA I've got eight fingers, see? I'm a freak.

GROCERY BOY (*giggling*) There's a car comin' here. (*Gets no answer, starts backing out of door, still looking. Familiarly*) Good-bye. (*Exits.*)

MARTHA (*bitterly*) You still think we should go into town?

KAREN I don't know. I don't know about anything any more. (*After a moment*) Martha, Martha, Martha—

MARTHA (*gently*) What is it, Karen?

KAREN What are we going to do? It's all so cold and unreal and— It's like that dark hour of the night when, half awake, you struggle through the black mess you've been dreaming. Then, suddenly, you wake up and you see your own bed or your own nightgown and you know you're back again in a solid world. But now it's all the nightmare; there is no solid world. Oh. Martha, *why* did it happen? *What* happened? What are we doing here like this?

MARTHA Waiting.

KAREN For what?

MARTHA I don't know.

KAREN We've got to get out of this place. I can't stand it any more. .

MARTHA You'll be getting married soon. Everything will be all right then.

KAREN (*vaguely*) Yes.

MARTHA (*looks up at the tone*) What is it?

KAREN Nothing.

MARTHA There mustn't be anything wrong between you and Joe. Never.

KAREN (*without conviction*) Nothing's wrong. (*As footsteps are heard in the hall, her face lights up*) There's Joe now.

(MRS. MORTAR, *small suitcase in hand, stands in the doorway, her face pushed coyly forward.*)

MRS. MORTAR And here I am. Hello, hello.

MARTHA (*she has turned over on her back and is staring at her aunt. She speaks to* KAREN) The Duchess, isn't it? Returned at long last. (*Too jovially*) Come on in. We're delighted to see you. Are you tired from your journey? Is there something I can get you?

MRS. MORTAR (*surprised*) I'm very glad to see you both, and (*looks around*) I'm very glad to see the old place again. How is everything?

MARTHA Everything's fine. We're splendid, thank you. You're just in time for tea.

MRS. MORTAR You know, I should like some tea, if it isn't too much trouble.

MARTHA   No trouble at all. Some small sandwiches and a little brandy?

MRS. MORTAR   (*puzzled finally*) Why, Martha.

MARTHA   Where the hell have you been?

MRS. MORTAR   Around, around. I had a most interesting time. Things—

MARTHA   Why didn't you answer my telegrams?

MRS. MORTAR   Things have changed in the theater—drastically changed, I might say.

MARTHA   *Why didn't you answer my telegrams?*

MRS. MORTAR   Oh, Martha, there's your temper again.

MARTHA   Answer me and don't bother about my temper.

MRS. MORTAR   (*nervously*) I was moving around a great deal. (*Conversationally*) You know, I think it will throw a very revealing light on the state of the new theater when I tell you that the Lyceum in Rochester now has a toilet back stage.

MARTHA   To hell with the toilet in Rochester. Where were you?

MRS. MORTAR   Moving around, I tell you.

KAREN   What difference does it all make now?

MRS. MORTAR   Karen is quite right. Let bygones be bygones. As I was saying, there's an effete something in the theater now, and that accounts for—

MARTHA   (*to* KAREN) Isn't she wonderful? (*To* MRS. MORTAR) Why did you refuse to come back here and testify for us?

MRS. MORTAR   Why, Martha, I didn't refuse to come back at all. That's the wrong way to look at it. I was on a tour; that's a moral obligation, you know. Now don't let's talk about unpleasant things any more. I'll go up and unpack a few things; tomorrow's plenty of time to get my trunk.

KAREN   (*laughs*) Things have changed here, you know.

MARTHA   She doesn't know. She expected to walk right up to a comfortable fire and sit down and she very carefully waited until the whole thing was over. (*Leans forward, speaking to* MRS. MORTAR) Listen, Karen Wright and Martha Dobie brought a libel suit against a woman called Tilford because her grandchild had accused them of having what the judge called "sinful sexual knowledge of one another." (MRS. MORTAR *holds up her hand in protest, and* MARTHA *laughs*) Don't like that, do you? Well, a great part of the defense's case was based on remarks made by Lily Mortar, actress in the toilets of Rochester, against her niece, Martha. And a greater part of the defense's case rested on the telling fact that Mrs. Mortar would not appear in court to deny or explain those remarks. Mrs. Mortar had a moral obligation to the theater. As you probably read in the papers, we lost the case.

MRS. MORTAR I didn't think of it that way, Martha. It couldn't have done any good for all of us to get mixed up in that unpleasant notoriety— (*Sees* MARTHA's *face. Hastily*) But now that you've explained it, why, I do see it your way, and I'm sorry I didn't come back. But now that I am here, I'm going to stand shoulder to shoulder with you. I know what you've gone through, but the body and heart *do* recover, you know. I'll be here working right along with you and we'll—

MARTHA There's an eight o'clock train. Get on it.

MRS. MORTAR Martha.

MARTHA You've come back to pick the bones dry. Well, there aren't even bones anymore. There's nothing here for you.

MRS. MORTAR (*sniffling a little*) How can you talk to me like that?

MARTHA Because I hate you. I've always hated you.

MRS. MORTAR (*gently*) God will punish you for that.

MARTHA He's been doing all right.

MRS. MORTAR When you wish to apologize, I will be temporarily in my room. (*Starts to exit, almost bumps into* CARDIN, *steps back with dignity*) How do you do?

CARDIN (*laughs*) Look who's here. A little late, aren't you?

MRS. MORTAR So it's you. Now, I call *that* loyal. A lot of men wouldn't still be here. They would have felt—

MARTHA Get out of here.

KAREN (*opening door*) I'll call you when it's time for your train.

(MRS. MORTAR *looks at her, exits.*)

CARDIN Now, what do you think brought her back?

KAREN God knows.

MARTHA I know. She was broke.

CARDIN (*pats* MARTHA *on the shoulder*) Don't let her worry you this time, Martha. We'll give her some money and get rid of her. (*Pulls* KAREN *to him*) Been out today, darling?

KAREN We started to go out.

CARDIN (*shakes his head*) Feel all right?

(KAREN *leans over to kiss him. Almost imperceptibly he pulls back.*)

KAREN Why did you do that?

MARTHA Karen.

CARDIN Do what?

KAREN Draw back that way.

CARDIN (*laughs, kisses her*) If we sit around here much longer, we'll all be bats. I sold my place today to Foster.

KAREN You did what?

CARDIN We're getting married this week. Then we're going away—all three of us.

KAREN You can't leave here. I won't have you do this for me. What about the hospital and—

CARDIN Shut up, darling, it's all fixed. We're going to Vienna and we're going quick. Fischer wrote that I can have my old place back.

KAREN No! No! I'm not going to let you.

CARDIN It's already done. Fischer can't pay me much, but it'll be enough for the three of us. Plenty if we live cheap.

MARTHA I couldn't go with you, Joe.

CARDIN Nonsense, Martha, we're all going. We're going to have fun again.

KAREN (*slowly*) You don't want to go back to Vienna.

CARDIN No.

KAREN Then why?

CARDIN Look: I don't want to go to Vienna; I'd rather have stayed here. But then you don't want to go to Vienna; you'd rather have stayed here. Well, to hell with that. We *can't* stay here, and Vienna offers enough to eat and sleep and drink beer on. Now don't object any more, please, darling. All right?

KAREN   All right.

MARTHA   I can't go. It's better for all of us if I don't.

CARDIN   (*puts his arm around her*)   Not now. You stay with us now. Later on, if you want it that way. All right?

MARTHA   (*smiles*)   All right.

CARDIN   Swell. I'll buy you good coffee cakes and take you both to Ischl for a honeymoon.

MARTHA   (*picking up grocery box, she starts for door*)   A big coffee cake with a lot of raisins. It would be nice to like something again. (*Exits.*)

CARDIN   (*with a slightly forced heartiness*)   I'll be going back with a pretty girl who belongs to me. I'll show you off all over the place—to Dr. Engelhardt, and the nurse at the desk, and to the fat gal in the cake shop, and to Fischer. (*Laughs*) The last time I saw him was at the railroad station. He took me back of the baggage car. (*With an imitation of an accent*) "Joseph," he said, "you'll be a good doctor; I would trust you to cut up my Minna. But you're not a great doctor, and you never will be. Go back where you were born and take care of your sick. Leave the fancy work to the others." I came home.

KAREN   You'll be coming home again some day.

CARDIN   No. Let's not talk about it. (*After a moment*) You'll need some clothes?

KAREN   A few. Oh, your Dr. Fischer was so right. This is where you belong.

CARDIN   I need an overcoat and a suit. You'll need a lot of things—heavy things. It's cold there now, much colder than you'd expect—

KAREN   I've done this to you. I've taken you away from everything you want.

CARDIN   But it's lovely in the mountains, and that's where we'll go for a month.

KAREN   They—*they've* done it. They've taken away every chance we had. Everything we wanted, everything we were going to be.

CARDIN   And we've got to stop talking like that. (*Takes*

her by the shoulder) We've got a chance. But it's just one chance, and if we miss it we're done for. It means that we've got to start putting the whole business behind us now. *Now,* Karen. What you've done, you've done—and that's that.

KAREN   What *I've* done?

CARDIN   (*impatiently*) What's been done to you.

KAREN   What did you mean? (*When there is no answer*) What did you mean when you said: "What you've done"?

CARDIN   (*shouting*) Nothing. Nothing. (*Then very quietly*) Karen, there are a lot of people in this world who've had bad trouble in their lives. We're three of those people. We could sit around the rest of our lives and exist on that trouble, until in the end we had nothing else and we'd want nothing else. That's something I'm not coming to and I'm not going to let you come to.

KAREN   I know. I'm sorry. (*After a moment*) Joe, can we have a baby right away?

CARDIN   (*vaguely*) Yes, I guess so. Although we won't have much money now.

KAREN   You used to want one right away. You always said that was the way you wanted it. There's some reason for your changing.

CARDIN   My God, we *can't* go on like this. Everything I say to you is made to mean something else. We don't talk like people any more. Oh, let's get out of here as fast as we can.

KAREN   (*as though she is finishing the sentence for him*) And every word will have a new meaning. You think we'll be able to run away from that? Woman, child, love, lawyer—no words that we can use in safety any more. (*Laughs bitterly*) Sick, high-tragic people. That's what we'll be.

CARDIN   (*gently*) No, we won't, darling. Love is casual—that's the way it should be. We must find that out all over again. We must learn again to live and love like other people.

KAREN   It won't work.

CARDIN   What?

KAREN   The two of us together.

CARDIN   (*sharply*) Stop talking like that.

KAREN   It's true. (*Suddenly*) I want you to say it now.

CARDIN   I don't know what you're talking about.

KAREN   Yes, you do. We've both known for a long time. I knew surely the day we lost the case. I was watching your face in court. It was ashamed—and sad at being ashamed. Say it now, Joe. Ask it now.

CARDIN   I have nothing to ask. Nothing— (*Quickly*) All right. Is it—was it ever—

KAREN   (*puts her hand over his mouth*) No. Martha and I have never touched each other. (*Pulls his head down on her shoulder*) That's all right, darling. I'm glad you asked. I'm not mad a bit, really.

CARDIN   I'm sorry, Karen, I'm sorry. I didn't mean to hurt you, I—

KAREN   I know. You wanted to wait until it was all over, you really never wanted to ask at all. You didn't know for sure; you thought there might be just a little truth in it all. (*With great feeling*) You've been good to me and loyal. You're a fine man. (*Afraid of tears, she pats him, walks away*) Now go and sit down, Joe. I have things to say. They're all mixed up and I must get them clear.

CARDIN   Don't let's talk any more. Let's forget and go ahead.

KAREN   (*puzzled*) Go ahead?

CARDIN   Yes, Karen.

KAREN   You believe me, then?

CARDIN   Of course I believe you. I only had to hear you say it.

KAREN   No, no, no. That isn't the way things work. Maybe you believe me. I'd never know whether you did or not. You'd never know whether you did, either. We couldn't do it that way. Can't you see what would happen? We'd be hounded by it all our lives. I'd be frightened, always, and in the end my own fright would make me—would make me hate you. (*Sees slight movement he makes*) Yes, it would; I know it would. I'd hate you for what I thought I'd done to you. And I'd hate myself, too. It would grow and grow until we'd be ruined

by it. (*Sees him about to speak*) Ah, Joe, you've seen all
that yourself. You knew it first.

CARDIN   (*softly*)   I didn't mean it that way; I don't now.

KAREN   (*smiles*)   You're still trying to spare me, still trying to tell yourself that we might be all right again.
But we won't be all right. Not ever, ever, ever. I don't
know all the reasons why. Look, I'm standing here. I
haven't changed. (*Holds out her hands*) My hands look
just the same, my face is the same, even my dress is
old. We're in a room we've been in so many times before; you're sitting where you always sit; it's nearly
time for dinner. I'm like everybody else. I can have
all the things that everybody has. I can have you and
a baby, and I can go to market, and we can go to the
movies, and people will talk to me and— (*Suddenly
notices the pain in his face*) Oh, I'm sorry. I mustn't
talk like that. That couldn't be true any more.

CARDIN   It could be, Karen. We'll make it be like that.

KAREN   No. That's only what we'd like to have had. It's
what we can't have now. Go home, darling.

CARDIN   (*with force*)   Don't talk like that. No matter
what it is, we can't leave each other. I can't leave you—

KAREN   Joe, Joe. Let's do it now and quick; it will be too
hard later on.

CARDIN   No, no, no. We love each other. (*His voice
breaks*) I'd give anything not to have asked questions,
Karen.

KAREN   It had to be asked sooner or later—and answered.
You're a good man—the best I'll ever know—and you've
been better to me than— But it's no good now, for either
of us; you can see that.

CARDIN   It can be. You say I helped you. Help me now;
help me to be strong and good enough to— (*Goes
toward her with his arms out*) Karen!

KAREN   (*drawing back*)   No, Joe! (*Then, as he stops*)
Will you do something for me?

CARDIN   No. I won't—

KAREN   Will you—will you go away for two days—a day
—and think this all over by yourself—away from me and
love and pity? Will you? And then decide.

CARDIN (*after a long pause*) Yes, if you want, but it won't make any difference. We will—

KAREN Don't say anything. Please go now. (*She sits down, smiles, closes her eyes. For a moment he stands looking at her, then slowly puts on his hat*) And all my heart goes with you.

CARDIN (*at door, leaving*) I'll be coming back. (*Exits, slowly, reluctantly, closing door.*)

KAREN (*a moment after he has gone*) No, you won't. Never, darling. (*Stays as she is until* MARTHA *enters Right.*)

MARTHA (*goes to lamp, lights it*) It gets dark so early now. (*Sits down, stretches, laughs*) Cooking always makes me feel better. Well, I guess we'll have to give the Duchess some dinner. When the hawks descend, you've got to feed 'em. Where's Joe? (*No answer*) Where's Joe?

KAREN Gone.

MARTHA A patient? Will he be back in time for dinner?

KAREN No.

MARTHA (*watching her*) We'll save dinner for him, then. Karen! What's the matter?

KAREN (*in a dull tone*) He won't be back any more.

MARTHA (*speaking slowly and carefully*) You mean he won't be back any more tonight.

KAREN He won't be back at all.

MARTHA (*quickly, walks to* KAREN) What happened? (KAREN *shakes her head*) What happened, Karen?

KAREN He thought that we had been lovers.

MARTHA (*tensely*) I don't believe you.

(*Wearily* KAREN *turns her head away.*)

KAREN All right.

MARTHA (*automatically*) I don't believe it. He's never said a word all these months, all during the trial— (*Suddenly grabs* KAREN *by the shoulder, shakes her*) Didn't you tell him? For God's sake, didn't you tell him it wasn't true?

KAREN Yes.

MARTHA He didn't believe you?

KAREN I guess he believed me.

MARTHA (*angrily*) Then what have you done?

KAREN What had to be done.

MARTHA It's all wrong. It's silly. He'll be back in a little while and you'll clear it all up— (*Realizes why that can't be, covers her mouth with her hand*) Oh, God, I wanted that for you so much.

KAREN Don't. I feel sick to my stomach.

MARTHA (*goes to couch opposite* KAREN, *puts her head in her arms*) What's happened to us? What's really happened to us?

KAREN I don't know. I want to be sleepy. I want to go to sleep.

MARTHA Go back to Joe. He's strong; he'll understand. It's too much for you this way.

KAREN (*irritably*) Stop talking about it. Let's pack and get out of here. Let's take the train in the morning.

MARTHA The train to where?

KAREN I don't know. Some place; any place.

MARTHA A job? Money?

KAREN In a big place we could get something to do.

MARTHA They'd know about us. We've been famous.

KAREN A small town, then.

MARTHA They'd know more about us.

KAREN (*as a child would say it*) Isn't there anywhere to go?

MARTHA No. There'll never be any place for us to go. We're bad people. We'll sit. We'll be sitting the rest of our lives wondering what's happened to us. You think this scene is strange? Well, get used to it; we'll be here for a long time. (*Suddenly pinches* KAREN *on the arm*) Let's pinch each other sometimes. We can tell whether we're still living.

KAREN (*shivers, listlessly gets up, starts making a fire in the fireplace*) But this isn't a new sin they tell us we've done. Other people aren't destroyed by it.

MARTHA They are the people who believe in it, who want it, who've chosen it. We aren't like that. We don't love each other. (*Suddenly stops, crosses to fireplace, stands looking, abstractedly at* KAREN. *Speaks casually*) I don't love you. We've been very close to each other, of course. I've loved you like a friend, the way thousands of women feel about other women.

KAREN (*only half listening*) Yes.

MARTHA Certainly that doesn't mean anything. There's nothing wrong about that. It's perfectly natural that I should be fond of you, that I should—

KAREN (*listlessly*) Why are you saying all this to me?

MARTHA Because I love you.

KAREN (*vaguely*) Yes, of course.

MARTHA I love you that way—maybe the way they said I loved you. I don't know. (*Waits, gets no answer, kneels down next to* KAREN) Listen to me!

KAREN What?

MARTHA *I have loved you the way they said.*

KAREN You're crazy.

MARTHA There's always been something wrong. Always —as long as I can remember. But I never knew it until all this happened.

KAREN (*for the first time looks up, horrified*) Stop it!

MARTHA You're afraid of hearing it; I'm more afraid than you.

KAREN (*puts her hands over her ears*) I won't listen to you.

MARTHA Take your hands down. (*Leans over, pulls* KAREN's *hands away*) You've got to know it. I can't keep it any longer. I've got to tell you how guilty I am.

KAREN (*deliberately*) You are guilty of nothing.

MARTHA I've been telling myself that since the night we heard the child say it; I've been praying I could convince myself of it. I can't, I can't any longer. It's there. I don't know how, I don't know why. But I did love you. I do love you. I resented your marriage; maybe because I wanted you; maybe I wanted you all along; maybe I couldn't call it by a name; maybe it's been there ever since I first knew you—

KAREN (*tensely*) It's a lie. You're telling yourself a lie. We never thought of each other that way.

MARTHA (*bitterly*) No, of course *you* didn't. But who says I didn't? I never felt that way about anybody but you. I've never loved a man— (*Stops. Softly*) I never knew why before. Maybe it's that.

KAREN   (*carefully*) You are tired and sick.

MARTHA   (*as though she were talking to herself*) It's funny; it's all mixed up. There's something in you, and you don't know it and you don't do anything about it. Suddenly a child gets bored and lies—and there you are, seeing it for the first time. (*Closes her eyes*) I don't know. It all seems to come back to *me*. In some way I've ruined your life. I've ruined my own. I didn't even *know*. (*Smiles*) There's a big difference between us now, Karen. I feel all dirty and— (*Puts out her hand, touches* KAREN's *head*) I can't stay with you any more, darling.

KAREN   (*in a shaken, uncertain tone*) All this isn't true. You've never said it; we'll forget it by tomorrow—

MARTHA   Tomorrow? That's a funny word. Karen, we would have had to invent a new language, as children do, without words like tomorrow.

KAREN   (*crying*) Go and lie down, Martha. You'll feel better.

(MARTHA *looks around the room, slowly, carefully. She is very quiet. Exits Right, stands at door for a second looking at* KAREN, *then slowly shuts the door behind her.*)

(KAREN *sits alone without moving. There is no sound in the house until, a few minutes after* MARTHA's *exit, a shot is heard. The sound of the shot should not be too loud or too strong. For a few seconds after the noise has died out,* KAREN *does not move. Then, suddenly, she springs from the chair, crosses the room, pulls open door Right. Almost at the same moment footsteps are heard on the staircase.*)

MRS. MORTAR   What was that? Where is it? (*Enters door Center, frightened, aimlessly moving about*) Karen! Martha! Where are you? I heard a shot. What was— (*Stops as she sees* KAREN *reappear Right. Walks toward her, still talking. Stops when she sees* KAREN's *face*) What—what is it? (KAREN *moves her hands, shakes her head slightly, passes* MRS. MORTAR, *and goes toward window.* MRS. MORTAR *stares at her for a moment, rushes past her through door Right. Left alone,* KAREN *leans against the window.* MRS. MORTAR *re-enters crying. After a minute*) What shall we do? What shall we do?

KAREN (*in a toneless voice*) Nothing.

MRS. MORTAR We've got to get a doctor—right away. (*Goes to phone, nervously, fumblingly starts to dial.*)

KAREN (*without turning*) There isn't any use.

MRS. MORTAR We've got to do something. Oh, it's awful. Poor Martha. I don't know what we can do— (*Puts phone down, collapses in chair, sobs quietly*) You think she's dea—

KAREN Yes.

MRS. MORTAR Poor, poor Martha. I can't realize it's true. Oh, how could she—she was so—I don't know what— (*Looks up, still crying, surprised*) I'm—I'm frightened.

KAREN Don't cry.

MRS. MORTAR I can't help it. How can I help it? (*Gradually the sobs cease, and she sits rocking herself*) I'll never forgive myself for the last words I said to her. But I was good to her, Karen, and you know God will excuse me for that once. I always tried to do everything I could. (*Suddenly*) Suicide's a sin. (*No answer. Timidly*) Shouldn't we call somebody to—

KAREN In a little while.

MRS. MORTAR She shouldn't have done it, she shouldn't have done it. It was because of all this awful business. She would have got a job and started all over again—she was just worried and sick and—

KAREN That isn't the reason she did it.

MRS. MORTAR What—why—?

KAREN (*wearily*) What difference does it make now?

MRS. MORTAR (*reproachfully*) You're not crying.

KAREN No.

MRS. MORTAR What will happen to me? I haven't anything. Poor Martha—

KAREN She was very good to you; she was good to us all.

MRS. MORTAR Oh, I know she was, Karen, and I was good to her too. I did everything I could. I—I haven't any place to go. (*After a few seconds of silence*) I'm afraid. It seems so queer—in the next room. (*Shivers.*)

KAREN Don't be afraid.

MRS. MORTAR It's different for you. You're young.

KAREN Not any more.

(*The sound of the door-bell ringing.* MRS MORTAR *jumps.* KAREN *doesn't move. It rings again.*)

MRS. MORTAR (*nervously*) Who is it? (*The bell rings again*) Shall I answer it? (KAREN *shrugs*) I think we'd better. (*Exits down the hall through Center doors. Returns in a minute followed by* MRS. TILFORD's *maid,* AGATHA, *who stands in the door*) It's a woman. (*No answer*) It's a woman to see you, Karen. (*Getting no answer, she turns to* AGATHA) You can't come in now; we've had a—we've had trouble here.

AGATHA Miss Karen, I've *got* to speak to you.

KAREN (*turns slowly, mechanically*) Agatha.

AGATHA (*goes to* KAREN) Please, Miss Karen. We've tried so hard to get you. I been phoning here all the time. Trying to get you. Phoning and phoning. Please, please let her come in. Just for a minute, Miss Karen. Please—

MRS. MORTAR Who wants to come in here?

AGATHA Mrs. Tilford. (*Looks at* KAREN) Don't you feel well? (KAREN *shakes her head*) You ain't mad at *me?*

MRS. MORTAR That woman can't come in here. She caused all—

KAREN I'm not mad at you, Agatha.

AGATHA Can I—can I get you something?

KAREN No.

AGATHA You poor child. You look like you got a pain somewhere. (*Hesitates, takes* KAREN's *hands*) I only came cause she's so bad off. She's got to see you, Miss Karen, she's just got to. She's been sittin' outside in the car, hoping you'd come out. She can't get Dr. Joe. He—he won't talk to her any more. I wouldn't a come—I always been on your side—but she's sick. If only you could see her, you'd let her come for just a minute.

KAREN I couldn't do that, Agatha.

AGATHA I don't blame you. But I had to tell you. She's old. It's going to kill her.

KAREN (*bitterly*) Kill her? Where is Mrs. Tilford?

AGATHA Outside.

KAREN All right.

AGATHA (*presses* KAREN's *arm*) You always been a good girl. (*Hurriedly exits.*)

MRS. MORTAR· You going to allow that woman to come in here? With Martha lying there? How can you be so feelingless? (*She starts to cry*) I won't stay and see it. I won't have anything to do with it. I'll never let that woman— (*Rushes sobbing from the room.*)

(*A second after,* MRS. TILFORD *appears in the doorway Center. Her face, her walk, her voice have changed. She is feeble.*)

MRS. TILFORD Karen, let me come in.

(*Without turning,* KAREN *bows her head.* MRS. TILFORD *enters, stands staring at the floor.*)

KAREN Why have you come here?

MRS. TILFORD I had to come. (*Stretches out her hand to* KAREN, *who does not turn. She drops her hand*) I know now; I know it wasn't true.

KAREN What?

MRS. TILFORD (*carefully*) I know it wasn't true, Karen.

KAREN (*stares at her, shudders*) You know it wasn't true? I don't care what you know. It doesn't matter any more. If that's what you had to say, you've said it. Go away.

MRS. TILFORD (*puts her hand to her throat*) I've got to tell you.

KAREN I don't want to hear you.

MRS. TILFORD Last Tuesday Mrs. Wells found a bracelet in Rosalie's room. The bracelet had been hidden for several months. We found out that Rosalie had taken the bracelet from another girl, and that Mary— (*Closes her eyes*) that Mary knew that and used it to force Rosalie into saying that she had seen you and Miss Dobie together. I—I've talked to Mary. I've found out. (KAREN *suddenly begins to laugh, high and sharp*) Don't do that, Karen. I have only a little more to say. I've talked to Judge Potter. He will make all arrangements. There will be a public apology and an explanation. The damage suit will be paid to you in full and— and any more that you will be kind enough to take from me. I—I must see that you won't suffer any more.

KAREN   We're not going to suffer any more. Martha is dead. (MRS. TILFORD *gasps, shakes her head as though to shake off the truth, feebly falls into a chair, and covers her face.* KAREN *watches her for a minute*) So you've come here to relieve your conscience? Well, I won't be your confessor. It's choking you, is it? (*Violently*) And you want to stop the choking, don't you? You've done a wrong and you have to right that wrong or you can't rest your head again. You want to be "just," don't you, and you wanted us to help you be just? You've come to the wrong place for help. You want to be a "good" woman again, don't you? (*Bitterly*) Oh, I know. You told us that night you had to do what you did. Now you "have" to do this. A public apology and money paid, and you can sleep again and eat again. That done and there'll be peace for you. You're old, and the old are callous. Ten, fifteen years left for you. But what of me? It's a whole life for me. A whole God-damned life. (*Suddenly quiet, points to door Right*) And what of her?

MRS. TILFORD   (*she is crying*)   You are still living.

KAREN   Yes. I guess so.

MRS. TILFORD   (*with a tremendous effort to control herself*)   I didn't come here to relieve myself. I swear to God I didn't. I came to try—to try anything. I knew there wasn't any relief for me, Karen, and that there never would be again. (*Tensely*) But what I am or why I came doesn't matter. The only thing that matters is you and— You, now.

KAREN   There's nothing for me.

MRS. TILFORD   Oh, let's try to make something for you. You're young and I—I can help you.

KAREN   (*smiles*)   You can help me?

MRS. TILFORD   (*with great feeling*)   Take whatever I can give you. Take it for yourself and use it for yourself. It won't bring me peace, if that's what's worrying you. (*Smiles*) Those ten or fifteen years you talk about! They will be bad years.

KAREN   I'm tired, Mrs. Tilford. (*Almost tenderly*) You will have a hard time ahead, won't you?

MRS. TILFORD   Yes.

KAREN   Mary?

MRS. TILFORD   I don't know.

KAREN   You can send her away.

MRS. TILFORD   No. I could never do that. Whatever she does, it must be to me and no one else. She's—she's——

KAREN   Yes. Your very own, to live with the rest of your life. (*For a moment she watches* MRS. TILFORD's *face*) It's over for me now, but it will never end for you. She's harmed us both, but she's harmed you more, I guess. (*Sits down beside* MRS TILFORD) I'm sorry.

MRS. TILFORD   (*clings to her*)   Then you'll try for yourself.

KAREN   All right.

MRS. TILFORD   You and Joe.

KAREN   No. We're not together anymore.

MRS. TILFORD   (*looks up at her*)   Did I do that, too?

KAREN   I don't think anyone did anything, any more.

MRS. TILFORD   (*makes a half-movement to rise*)   I'll go to him right away.

KAREN   No, it's better now the way it is.

MRS. TILFORD   But he must know what I know, Karen. You must go back to him.

KAREN   (*smiles*)   No, not any more.

MRS. TILFORD   You must, you must— (*Sees her face, hesitates*) Perhaps later, Karen?

KAREN   Perhaps.

MRS. TILFORD   (*after a moment in which they both sit silent*) Come away from here now, Karen. (KAREN *shakes her head*) You can't stay with— (*Moves her hand toward door Right.*)

KAREN   When she is buried, then I will go.

MRS. TILFORD   You'll be all right?

KAREN   I'll be all right, I suppose. Good-bye, now.

(*They both rise.* MRS. TILFORD *speaks, pleadingly.*)

MRS. TILFORD   You'll let me help you? You'll let me try?

KAREN   Yes, if it will make you feel better.

MRS. TILFORD   (*with great feeling*)   Oh, yes, oh, yes, Karen.

(*Unconsciously* KAREN *begins to walk toward the window.*)

KAREN   (*suddenly*)   Is it nice out?

MRS. TILFORD   It's been cold. (KAREN *opens the window*

slightly, sits on the ledge. MRS. TILFORD *with surprise*)
It seems a little warmer, now.

KAREN   It feels very good.

(*They smile at each other.*)

MRS. TILFORD   You'll write me some time?

KAREN   If I ever have anything to say. Good-bye, now.

MRS. TILFORD   You will have. I know it. Good-bye, my dear.

(KAREN *smiles, shakes her head as* MRS. TILFORD *exits. She
    does not turn, but a minute later she raises her hand.*)

KAREN   Good-bye.

Curtain

Days
to Come

FOR
JULIA AND
MAX HELLMAN

Days to Come was first produced at the Vanderbilt Theatre, New York City, on December 15, 1936, with the following cast:

(In the order of their appearance)

HANNAH	CLAIRE WOODBURY
LUCY	MURIEL GALLICK
CORA RODMAN	FRIEDA ALTMAN
HENRY ELLICOTT	NED WEVER
ANDREW RODMAN	WILLIAM HARRIGAN
JULIE RODMAN	FLORENCE ELDRIDGE
THOMAS FIRTH	JOSEPH SWEENEY
LEO WHALEN	BEN SMITH
SAM WILKIE	CHARLES DINGLE
MOSSIE DOWEL	JACK CARR
JOE EASTER	THOMAS FISHER

Produced and directed by HERMAN SHUMLIN

Settings designed by ALINE BERNSTEIN

Act One

Living room of the Rodman house.
Late morning in October.

SCENE: *The living room of the Rodman house in Callom,*
Ohio, two hundred miles from Cleveland. The room is
deep and the Left stage window-wall is curved into
the room. All furniture gives the impression of being
arranged for the entrance doors which are on the Right
Center stage wall. On the backstage wall, on the ex-
treme Right, is a door leading into the library. On the
curved Left stage wall are two high windows. These
windows open on a circular porch and are used as an
entrance by people who know the house well. Between
the windows, and well out on the stage, is a large drum
table. There are chairs on each side of the table. Back
from the table is an antique flat-topped table desk. Left
downstage is a high circular cabinet, unglassed, in
which there are many small figures of animals. Near
the cabinet is a couch. The room is beautiful, simple.
But the objects in the cabinet are too neatly placed and
the effect is rigid and bad.

Left and Right stage directions are always the audi-
ence's Left and Right.

AT RISE: *A large vigorous woman is sitting on the floor in*
front of the window, comfortably arranging flowers in
several bowls. (The bowls and the flowers are on the
porch.) She has on a house dress, but is not in servant's
uniform. LUCY, *in uniform, is dusting. On a chair next*
to HANNAH *is a bowl of half-shelled peas.*

LUCY   (*finishes dusting the animals*) That's enough for them today.

HANNAH   (*hands her a bowl of flowers and laughs*) Did you get your wages this morning? (*No answer*) Huh?

LUCY   (*reluctantly*) Yes.

HANNAH   (*cheerfully*) Then hand it over.

LUCY   I was going to. But Hannah, I got to keep five dollars out of it because I owe somebody the five dollars.

HANNAH   Is the five dollar somebody in this town?

LUCY   No.

HANNAH   Then don't pay 'em. The boys need it— (*Soberly*) and I got a hunch will need it more. (*As* LUCY *gives her the money from her apron pocket*) Thanks, Lucy. You're a nice kid. I'll tell them how it comes from you.

LUCY   But when's it going to be over? Seems funny, don't it?

HANNAH   I'm not laughing. (*She hands* LUCY *another bowl of flowers.* LUCY *takes it to a table near the couch and puts it very carefully in a certain spot*) I don't know when it's going to be over. But I guessed it was going to be. I haven't lived in this house twenty years for nothing. (HANNAH *has been watching* LUCY *place the bowl. She laughs and makes a this-way gesture with her hands*) Uh-uh. Bring it over.

LUCY   (*as if this joke had been played before*) What's the use? Miss Cora will only— (*Makes imitative gestures on the table*) move it right back here.

HANNAH   I know. I like to see her do it.

LUCY   But Aunt Lundee says that all they do is sit around talking and that a man should be at work and that Uncle Jim and the rest should go on back and stop this crazy strike and—

HANNAH   Since when does anybody listen to your Aunt Lundee?

LUCY   I don't know.

HANNAH   (*cheerfully*) Lucy, there were people made to think and people made to listen. I ain't sure either you or Lundee were made to do either.

LUCY   (*pointing to the vase*) Miss Cora's been downtown

already this morning. So was Mrs. Rodman, and when I came out of the butcher store there was Miss Cora standing on one side of the street, looking at Mrs. Rodman in the funniest way, and she didn't call to her, she just stood watching and not saying anything—

HANNAH And *you* just stood watching and not saying anything, too, huh?

LUCY (*hurt*) What's wrong with that now?

HANNAH Nothing. (*Then looks at her, half-seriously, half-teasingly*) As long as you just watch and don't say anything.

(CORA RODMAN *enters from the Center doors. She is a thin, nervous-looking woman of about forty-two. She has a small clay Chinese horse in her hand.* HANNAH *doesn't look up, but* LUCY *watches* CORA *as she crosses to the cabinet with the horse.*)

CORA I brought this down. I'll take the elephant up for my desk. It will make a nice change.

LUCY Yes'm.

CORA (*to* HANNAH) Did you make something sweet?

HANNAH (*to* CORA) Chocolate cake. All over.

CORA (*to* LUCY, *who has picked up carpet sweeper, rags, etc., and is exiting*) Well, don't cut me such a small piece. You didn't bring me enough butter on my tray this morning, and I had a roll left over.

LUCY Yes'm. (*She exits.*)

CORA (*she crosses to flower bowl and, with the motions* LUCY *has imitated, moves it back to its particular spot*) Always seems to be something the matter with the breakfast tray. I read in the morning paper about a thirteen-year-old girl who had a baby in the county hospital. Why don't they watch those things?

HANNAH (*who has smiled maliciously as* CORA *moved the bowl*) Who's going to watch 'em?

CORA It was a very dangerous Caesarian operation. Maybe that always happens when the mother is under age. What's the name of that man who boards with your sister?

HANNAH Now you can go over and ask Doc Morris about

the girl—and he can tell you, the way he did that time about cats, which you never gotten straight.

CORA I asked you what is the name of that man.

HANNAH I don't know which you mean. She's got five boarders regular.

CORA He was walking up and down in front of the factory, the way they've been doing and wasting their time, and I said good morning and he didn't answer. I said it again and he walked to the other side. So I went right up and told him I didn't like rudeness—

HANNAH That's Odave. He's only been here a year. Maybe that's not time enough to fall in love with the Rodman family. (*Thoughtfully*) You know, Miss Cora, they tell me that in places where there's a strike, the men forget sometimes to bow to the boss' sister.

CORA There is never any need for rudeness.

HANNAH She's getting a new boarder. Guess he's moved in by now. Leo Whalen.

CORA (*after a pause*) That's very wrong of your sister. And disloyal of you to let her. He's a bad character—

HANNAH How do you know? You never spoke to him.

CORA I know why he's here. That's enough. He's trying to make trouble and you know it. That's what he came here for—

HANNAH Not my business. She's in the boarding house business and it's open to anybody who don't steal. (*Picks up bowl of peas and starts to exit*) Anyway, she likes him. Lots of people here like him. (*So casually that it has meaning*) Women, too, I guess.

(*She passes* HENRY ELLICOTT *who is entering. He has on a hat and overcoat. He is about forty, good-looking in a worldly kind of way.*)

ELLICOTT Good morning. Did anyone call me, Cora?

CORA (*as he takes off his coat*) A woman called you about a month ago. I told you about that, although I don't see why she called you here.

ELLICOTT You told me about that. Several times.

CORA She hasn't called you since. I think I gave her to understand that you should conduct your affairs at your own house.

ELLICOTT I'm not talking about women, Cora. I'm talking about my office.

CORA *They* did *not* call.

HANNAH (*as* ELLICOTT *crosses to desk*) You be here for lunch? We got a good lunch.

CORA Hannah, will you please allow *me* to invite Mr. Ellicott for lunch?

ELLICOTT You, and you alone, may invite me to lunch.

CORA (*to* HANNAH) *I* have invited Mr. Ellicott to lunch.

(HANNAH *nods, pleased at the effect she has had on* CORA, *then exits.*)

ELLICOTT You put your foot down very firmly on that important matter. Where is Julie? (*He is moving around the room.*)

CORA (*holds out a small box*) Don't move around so. Want one? They're pepsin drops with chocolate. Doctor Morris says they're good for me. I'm going to get a dog this week. I've ordered it. A male this time. Females are too difficult to take care of during, er, during. I was reading only this morning about a thirteen-year-old girl who had a baby. You travel around. Have you ever seen that before?

ELLICOTT I haven't actually seen it. But they tell me that in warm countries—

CORA In *warm* countries. But not in Cleveland. (*He goes to the window, and after a second she says softly*) Julie is out, Henry.

ELLICOTT Where is she?

CORA (*as if she had been waiting for it*) I don't know. I don't spy on Julie.

ELLICOTT (*turns and looks at her*) You've such a pleasant way of saying things. (*Then he looks at his watch and goes to the telephone, dials a number*) This is Mr. Ellicott. Joe still there? (*To* CORA) Andrew around?

CORA I suppose so. I shall have to move my room if he doesn't stop walking up and down in the library all night. I sleep badly enough anyway and if a pin drops it wakes me. I've always been like that—

ELLICOTT (*into phone*) Joe? I've been waiting for you to call. Everything all right? Good. (ANDREW RODMAN *comes in through the library doors. He has a pleasant, serious face. His motions are those of a man who is puzzled and tired. He crosses to the desk and looks at some papers, idly, as he listens to* ELLICOTT *on the phone)* Take them off a few at a time. Then drive Wilkie up to Mr. Rodman's. *(Gets up, to* ANDREW*)* That's good. They'll be off the train about lunch time. The train will come in on the siding. They won't be noticed much.

ANDREW Are these high-jinks necessary? As long as they're coming, let them in at the station.

ELLICOTT There's no sense walking into trouble.

ANDREW *(nods his head)* So you're admitting now that there might be trouble? That they might not see it the way—the way we do?

CORA But why should there be any trouble? We can run the factory when we want to. It's ours. I don't understand why there should be any trouble—

ELLICOTT *(sharply)* I didn't say there'd be any trouble.

CORA *(placatingly to* ANDREW*)* Now you see. Henry says there won't be a bit of trouble.

ELLICOTT *(smiles, obviously irritated)* Andrew, do we have to start this all over again now?

ANDREW No. Don't pay any attention to me. We've made up our minds and that's that.

ELLICOTT And a damn good thing! The loan's o.k. now. But Nelson says you couldn't've gotten a nickel in Cleveland if you hadn't made this decision. He had to swear to them that you wouldn't change your mind again.

CORA See? As long as you have to spend the money anyway, you should have hired these new workers weeks ago. The way Henry and I told you to.

ANDREW I didn't want to do it that way. I don't now.

CORA No, of course you didn't. You thought kind talk and reason would do it. Well, it didn't work, did it? Papa would have known what to do. And without wasting time and money. Papa would have known—

(Her speech is interrupted by JULIE RODMAN *who comes in from the porch windows. She is a very attractive,*

*slim, slightly tired-looking woman of about thirty-two.
She is wearing a sweater and skirt, low shoes, a loose
tweed coat, no hat. Her clothes are expensive and
careless.*)

JULIE (*slowly, as if she didn't expect the room to be full:
as if thinking of something else*) Good morning.

CORA The man was here about the tree planting. I told
him that you always did that. Forgetting about things.

JULIE I did forget. You could have told him about the
planting.

CORA (*smugly*) You know my rules. Not to interfere.

JULIE There are so many rules. It's hard to remember
them all. It's funny to go walking now. The Carlsen
kids were coming from school. (*Smiles*) They had a
bad minute wondering whether to say hello to me.
(ANDREW *has moved on her speech as if he knew what
she meant, and didn't like hearing it. She has gone to
the decanters on the table*) Sherry? It's cold.

ELLICOTT Your walks take you in all directions, don't they?

JULIE (*without answering, turns to* ANDREW, *motions to
sherry glass*) Andy? Do you good.

ANDREW No, darling. (*As he gathers up papers*) I have
work to do before lunch.

ELLICOTT Wilkie should be here soon.

ANDREW (*slowly, at door*) I haven't forgotten.

JULIE (*gently*) You look so tired.

CORA Certainly he looks tired. He's worn himself out for
no reason. Papa would have settled this strike weeks
ago—

ANDREW (*at door, smiles, speaks slowly*) Yes, I suppose
so. Maybe Papa was a better man than I am.

CORA (*gets up, gently to* JULIE) I will see about the
trees. Before my headache gets worse. (JULIE *begins to
protest, but is interrupted by* CORA's *wheeling sharply on*
ELLICOTT *as if she had just thought of something*) Inci-
dentally, I hope you didn't touch my securities for this
loan? You are my lawyer. You must protect me—

ELLICOTT (*smiles*) Certainly. Increased protection, increased fees.

CORA I'm unmarried. It's different with me. I have no one

to support me. It's different when you're not married—

ELLICOTT   Unfortunately, in the business world there is no reward for virginity. (*Sharply, quickly, as he sees the question coming again*) No. Andrew wouldn't let me take your securities. I don't know why—

CORA   (*pleasantly now*) Because I'm his sister.

ELLICOTT   Really? Is that the reason? (*Annoyed at her sudden turn to good nature*) However, when it's cleaned up, you will pay your part of the expenses.

CORA   I don't understand that.

ELLICOTT   Then it's not because I haven't tried to explain it to you. You own as much of the factory as Andy does. As you share the profits, you must share the losses.

CORA   Why should I pay for Andrew's mistakes? If we'd been able to make him do this three weeks ago—

ELLICOTT   You will still be well this side of starvation. You can have two pieces of cake instead of your usual three.

CORA   I shall have to talk the losses business over with Andrew. I don't understand why— (*As if she had just heard him*) And I shall eat just as much as I please. Just as much as I please. (*She closes the door as* ELLICOTT *looks after her.*)

JULIE   (*smiling, watching him*) Cora worries you too much.

ELLICOTT   And you, happily, very little. She seems to be watching you these days— (*As her face changes*) Or am I imagining it? Where have you been, Julie?

JULIE   Walking.

ELLICOTT   In town?

JULIE   I must be getting old. I don't like autumn anymore. The river is full of leaves and it was too cold to walk very far.

ELLICOTT   Weren't you in town?

JULIE   (*very deliberate*) The storm broke the big elm. The heavy branch is lying in the river. There's a big lizard on the branch that looks as if it grew there—

ELLICOTT   You were near the strike office. I saw you. I think Cora saw you, too.

JULIE   (*annoyed*) Really? Were you both hiding?

ELLICOTT   That's the second time you've lied about being in town. Why?

JULIE   Maybe because I like to lie. (*Quietly, looking at him*) Maybe it's because I'm tired of your questions.

ELLICOTT   (*quietly*)   I don't like your being tired. (*After a second*) I'm going down to White Sulphur when things are cleared up here. Are you coming?

JULIE   No.

ELLICOTT   (*suddenly, sharply*)   I want to know where we stand, Julie. It's time for me to know.

JULIE   (*lightly, kindly*)   We stand nowhere. We've always stood nowhere. I knew about you—and you knew about me. (*Quickly*) Staying for lunch?

ELLICOTT   Yes, I knew about you. And what I didn't know our friends told me. (*Carefully*) But I find, more to my surprise than to yours, that you mean something to me. I think you have for a long time.

JULIE   I don't think so. (*Kindly*) Look. It doesn't mean anything to me—and that's where I've got to quit.

ELLICOTT   "And that's where I've got to quit." There isn't a man living who doesn't know about the woman who allows herself anything, but who invents the one rule that will keep her this side of what she thinks is respectable. She'll lie, but not on Thursday. She'll sleep with you, but not immediately after lunch. Usually, it's funny. In your case, for me, it's not so funny. (*Angrily*) What the hell did you expect me to mean to you?

JULIE   (*puts her hand on his arm*)   What did I expect you to mean to me? I don't know. I haven't any excuse, really. I've hoped for a very long time that everybody or anybody would mean something. (*Smiles*) Things start as hopes and end up as habits. (*Earnestly*) Look. Don't let's talk about it. You like civilized conversations about love too much, and I like them too little. One of the things that brings people like you and me together is the understanding that there won't be any talk about it at the end.

ELLICOTT   That's true. And it's too callous for me.

JULIE   (*violently*)   And for me, too. That's why I don't like it. I'm ashamed of its callousness—and I don't want any more of it. I don't mean to hurt you. (*She gets up, smiles, takes off her coat*) I asked you if you were staying for lunch.

ELLICOTT (*after a second, watching her*) Yes, I'm staying. If you ever saw what you wanted, Julie, would you know it?

JULIE (*quickly, unconsciously, very seriously, as if to herself*) Yes. I knew it. I knew about it quick.

ELLICOTT (*suddenly wheels about and takes her arm, tightly*) That's foolish what you're saying. Too foolish to believe. (*Tensely*) And what's more important, it's dangerous. Don't start anything, Julie—

JULIE (*softly*) I don't know what you are talking about.

(*They stand for a second as they are. He does not release her arm until the window-doors open and* THOMAS FIRTH *followed by* LEO WHALEN *appear on the porch. Then he quickly releases her arm and moves away.* FIRTH *taps on the window-wood He is a big, lean, middle-aged American working-man. He is obviously nervous and excited.* WHALEN *is attractive in a simple, clean, undistinguished way. All his movements from this moment until the end of the play show calmness, and are the movements of a man who knows he can take care of himself.*)

FIRTH Mrs. Rodman.

JULIE Oh. (*Then cordially*) Hello, Tom. (*To* WHALEN, *her tone changed and nervous*) Hello, Mr. Whalen. Come in.

ELLICOTT (*to both*) Good morning.

FIRTH I want to see Andrew. I came to see him.

JULIE (*surprised at the tenseness of his tone*) Yes. But come in, won't you? (*Abruptly* FIRTH *steps into the room, standing straight and rigid.* WHALEN *moves in casually*) I thought you were leaving us, Mr. Whalen. I haven't seen you in town the last few days.

WHALEN Leaving? (*Looks at* FIRTH, *smiles*) Not for a while yet.

ELLICOTT (*to* FIRTH) Andrew's busy. Will I do?

FIRTH No.

JULIE (*moves to the wall bell, presses it, speaks nervously to* WHALEN) I thought—I thought perhaps you would come and have dinner with us one night—

WHALEN (*laughs heartily*) The boss asks me for dinner. Well, that's very pleasant. It's never happened to me before. (*Looks at* FIRTH) But strange things happen in this town.

FIRTH Mrs. Rodman, can I see Andrew now?

(LUCY *appears at the door.*)

JULIE Tell Mr. Rodman that Tom Firth is here and wants to see him. (LUCY *disappears. To* WHALEN) Why should that be so strange? We don't get many visitors here and because you and my husband happen to be, well, happen to think differently, is no reason we can't eat together.

WHALEN (*pleasantly*) In my business it's a good reason.

ELLICOTT Julie. Whalen is in the business of hating. It pays well, I imagine.

WHALEN Very well. All labor organizers are racketeers, Mr. Ellicott, as you and I both know from the papers. (*He has started to roll a cigarette. Quickly* JULIE *offers him a box from the table*) But there's no hate *here*. The boss loves the workers, and the workers— (*To* FIRTH) the worker—loves the boss. In other towns I've heard that called something else.

FIRTH Shut up.

(*There is a second's embarrassed silence.* WHALEN, *however, is pleased.*)

JULIE (*to* WHALEN) Old Mrs. Hicks tells me you like our river. That you walk there very often.

WHALEN Yes. You've got a nice river. You've kept it clean.

JULIE (*to* WHALEN) When I first moved here I used to fish in it. Do you like to fish?

WHALEN Yes. Very much. (*To* FIRTH) Maybe Mr. Rodman doesn't want to see you.

FIRTH You don't have to wait.

ELLICOTT (*to* WHALEN) No. I'm sure you're busy—

WHALEN I'll wait. (*To* JULIE) If it's all right.

JULIE (*smiles, warmly, quickly*) It's very all right. (*Still smiling, turns to* ELLICOTT) Mr. Ellicott is too concerned with your time.

FIRTH   You're staying to watch. I don't need you to watch me. You and nobody is going to make me act blind. You and nobody is going to make me hate a man who's been my friend.

ELLICOTT   (*to* JULIE) He *is* in the business of hate. I was right.

WHALEN   (*to* FIRTH) I don't give a damn who you hate and who you love. I'm trying to see that that Christian heart of yours doesn't do too much harm. (*To* ELLICOTT) You were right.

(*On* WHALEN's *words,* FIRTH *moves toward him angrily, and then turns and stands rigidly as* ANDREW *comes into the room.*)

ANDREW   (*slowly*) Hello, Tom. (*Less friendly*) Hello, Mr. Whalen.

FIRTH   Andrew, I went out on strike with the rest. That was my duty. But I stood by you in a lot of ways.

WHALEN   (*unpleasantly*) He did. I can vouch for it.

FIRTH   We've all been trying to see it from both our sides and we've been friends about it—

WHALEN   Ask your question.

FIRTH   He says that a trainload of strikebreakers came through Callom Junction this morning. And I said I didn't believe it. I said you didn't know no more about things like that than we did, and that I knew you—

ANDREW   Tom, I wanted to talk to you this afternoon.

ELLICOTT   (*looking at his watch*) Which would still be wisest. This afternoon.

FIRTH   I'm here. I don't want to wait. Talk to me now. (*After a second's silence, speaks to* WHALEN *over his shoulder*) Read him that fool thing.

WHALEN   (*takes a telegram from his pocket, reads it in a pleasant, unconcerned way*) "Wilkie on way probably fifty sixty of the boys including Gans Easter Malloy which gives you rough idea stop Easter just out of jail with toothache so watch your heart and anything else." That's from a friend of mine in Cleveland. He's a wit.

FIRTH   I don't know about these people he's talking about. And neither do you. That's why I know it's got to be wrong. (*Watches* ANDREW, *gets no answer, then slowly, firmly*) Andrew. It's got to be wrong.

ANDREW   Tom, I've tried to explain. I tried from the first day you came to me. (*Touches a paper on the desk, looks at it*) The figures are here. They're as much yours to see as they are mine.

FIRTH   I don't have to see 'em again.

ANDREW   You don't. But I have to see them again and again and again. We've got to sell the brushes we make.

WHALEN   Some places make what they can sell.

ANDREW   (*sharply*) Yes. They make them cheaper than we do— (*Slowly*) and they make them cheaper because they cost less. You know that Partee cut salaries two years ago—

FIRTH   I know that. I told you to cut us a little. That we'd take a little for you. And I told you to make three, four model brushes, not eighteen—

ANDREW   I can't, against the others.

WHALEN   Then make them the way they make them.

ANDREW   You mean cheaper brushes? Ask Tom what he thinks of that.

FIRTH   We make the best brushes in America.

WHALEN   (*laughs*) There. You've hit on something. That'll pay your rent. You can eat fine on that.

ANDREW   (*to* FIRTH) You tell me a way out, I'll take it. Seven years ago we were making a lot of money. (*Touches the paper*) I can't stay in business losing it this way. We'd be out in another year.

WHALEN   You haven't been answering his questions, Mr. Rodman.

ANDREW   I'm doing my best to answer him. (*After a second*) I knew the cuts had to come. I tried hard to keep them off as long as I could. I thought you'd see that the only way you could stay working and I could stay working was if we took the bad times together. I couldn't do anything else.

FIRTH   And I know we can't live on forty-cent piece work. I told you it was too big a cut. And I told you they wouldn't take it.

ANDREW Do you think I want to cut you that way? It's just for a little while—

FIRTH And who's going to pay our bills for the little while?

ANDREW (*shakes his head*) I know. I don't blame you. But you mustn't blame us, either.

FIRTH (*quickly*) Who's us?

ANDREW Me, I mean. That's the story. I wish I'd known what else to do.

(*Slowly* WHALEN *rises, smiling.* FIRTH *turns and looks at him, looks around the room, and then crosses quickly to* ANDREW *as if he didn't believe the answer had been made.*)

FIRTH All right. We know all that. That's what I been saying to myself, and I ain't got the answer for either of us. (*Hits the table*) But that's something between us to settle. We ain't foreigners. Our people came here with your people, and worked along with them and helped them, too. In twelve when they came and tried to make a union, we threw 'em out. There ain't never been any trouble here, Andrew—

ELLICOTT (*to* ANDREW) It's late.

ANDREW Let him say what he wants to say.

FIRTH I ain't believing that you're bringing foreigners—

ANDREW (*slowly*) You've been out three weeks. The place had to start running again.

FIRTH (*slowly*) You mean you're giving away our jobs. You mean other people are taking our work— (*Breaks off sharply and stands staring at* ANDREW, *shaking his head.*)

WHALEN (*rises, smiles to* JULIE) Sad to grow up, isn't it? (*To* FIRTH) Well, come on. Cry at home. You've wasted enough time now. The world is a bad place and you're a big boy.

ELLICOTT (*to* FIRTH) You could have talked this over with me. It may be all right for you to walk out, but it is also all right for Andrew to keep his own machines going his own way.

FIRTH (*shouting*) And this was his way of keeping 'em going, eh? I could've known you had a hand in it.

ELLICOTT (*sharply*) He's got to start making brushes
again. If you've made up your mind not to make them,
then somebody else has to.

WHALEN No? You're kidding. (*To* ANDREW) Who sold
you the idea Wilkie's boys can run machines? (*Makes
the motion of pointing a pistol*) That's the kind they
meant. That's the kind you'll get run—and they do that
fine. (*To* FIRTH) And be sure you're there to make
speeches about the boat your grandfather came over
on, and God is love, and your heart's breaking. Turn
the other cheek, and crawl back. It hurts less that way,
I guess.

FIRTH (*slowly*) I told the boys we'd be settling it like
friends. I was wrong. (*To* WHALEN) I won't be turning
the other cheek. I won't be crawling back. Nobody
else will either. (*Without turning to look at* ANDREW,
he moves quickly to the window and out.)

ANDREW (*quietly, to* JULIE) He's been a good friend. For
a long time.

ELLICOTT (*slowly, to* WHALEN) We don't want trouble
here. We're sorry that you do want it. But I suppose
that's your job.

WHALEN (*getting up*) Sometimes it is. Sometimes it isn't.
But what you and I want won't make much difference.
When the guns start popping and the skulls start crack-
ing, they won't be thinking about us.

ANDREW (*angrily*) There won't be any guns here—on
either side.

ELLICOTT Unless you have them.

WHALEN I? No, sir. I'm scared to death of them. (*To*
ANDREW, *moving toward the window*) I hope you're
right, Mr. Rodman.

(*As* WHALEN *moves toward the window the front door
bell starts to ring, steadily, loudly. They have all turned,
startled by it.* HANNAH, *calm, quiet, appears in the
door.*)

JULIE What is it, Hannah?

HANNAH Lucy's watching my oven so the things don't
burn.

ANDREW (*looking at her*) Then you answer it, Hannah.

HANNAH   No, Mr. Andrew. If what I heard is right, that's one bell I ain't going to answer. I can't help what other people do, but I don't have to help 'em out.

JULIE   Hannah—

HANNAH   And Lucy can't answer because she's watching my oven so the things don't burn, if she's got the sense. (ELLICOTT, *quickly, angrily, moves past* HANNAH *and out into the hall. To* WHALEN) Like boarding at my sister's?

WHALEN   Sure. It's a good place. (*Smiles at her warmly*) I'm no boarder, I'm charity.

HANNAH   She can afford it. But watch her. She don't always like to get the dust from under things. (*She exits.*)

(WHALEN, *in the first quick motion he has made, moves to* ANDREW's *desk, leans over it, speaks tensely, hurriedly.*)

WHALEN   Rodman. It's hard to believe, but I'm believing it. You don't know— (*He points toward Center doors*) about things like this. I do. This is a nice town. I hate to see it hurt. (*Then quietly*) Give them their sixty-cent hour. Give them their union. They'll be back to work in ten minutes.

ANDREW   They can have any union they want. But I can't pay the salaries. I want to—and I can't. I don't know what you've seen in the past. But there won't be any trouble here. I won't let there be. I hope you won't either.

(ELLICOTT, *followed by* SAMUEL WILKIE, *comes in from the hall.* WILKIE *is of medium height, heavy. He looks like any husky businessman. Directly behind him are* MOSSIE DOWEL *and* JOE EASTER. MOSSIE *is fat and pleasant-looking.* EASTER *is thin, nervous, tough.* MOSSIE *and* EASTER *stand stiffly at the door.*)

WILKIE   Mr. Rodman. I'm Samuel Wilkie. (*He bows to* JULIE) How do you do?

ELLICOTT   (*as* WILKIE *looks at* WHALEN)   This is Mr. Whalen. You'll meet, I think.

WHALEN   (*pleasantly*)   I've heard of Mr. Wilkie.

WILKIE   Seems I've heard of you, too. (*To the others*) We're in the same line, you might say.

WHALEN   You knew my friend Cliff Taylor?

WILKIE   I knew who he was.

WHALEN   (*conversationally to the others*)   Taylor was an organizer. He had his throat cut last year in Gainesville.

WILKIE   They tell me he was a nice guy.

WHALEN   Yeah. And they tell me a side-burn guy did it. He worked for you, I think, and he played with knives a lot.

WILKIE   (*thoughtfully*)   No. I don't think he worked for me. But you can't tell. Lot of people come in and out of the office. Were you in Gainesville?

WHALEN   (*laughs*)   No. (*Touches his throat*) Fortunately, I was in Akron.

WILKIE   Now we're talking. That's the job I wanted. That's money for you. But they pieced it out in New York. You been here long?

WHALEN   About two weeks. I haven't done much. How many men you got?

WILKIE   Fifty-two, three. (WHALEN *says* "um") Yes. That's what I say. I been trying to tell these gentlemen that it isn't enough. Better to spend it now than later. (*Hastily, as he sees* ELLICOTT's *face*) But they're paying, and they should know.

ANDREW   The men with you are good brush makers?

MOSSIE   (*unconsciously*)   Huh?

WILKIE   (*puzzled, turns to look at* WHALEN, *who is smiling*)   Good? Well, we'll hope so.

WHALEN   (*laughs*)   They are also skilled motormen, miners, car loaders, longshoremen—and anything you like. They're the best.

WILKIE   (*laughs*)   Now that's the kind of recommendation we want. (*To* WHALEN) How many men you signed? What kind?

ANDREW   What I need, and what I ordered, were brush workers.

WILKIE   (*looks at him*)   We'll see how it works out.

WHALEN   Hundred and ninety-two men and not bad for a new union. Decent and— (*Looks at* WILKIE) peaceful, the right way.

WILKIE (*heartily*) And that's the way we like it.

WHALEN (*laughs*) Yes. That's the way we like it.

ELLICOTT If you gentlemen are finished with your conference, perhaps, Wilkie—

WHALEN Certainly. I talk too much. (*Moves toward windows, and as he passes* JULIE) And if I promise not to talk at all, may I still walk by your river?

JULIE (*smiles*) Yes. But I hope you will talk. I like to listen.

(*As he exits, he collides with* CORA, *who is coming in from the porch.*)

WHALEN Oh. Sorry.

JULIE This is Mr. Whalen, Cora. (CORA *looks up at him, then lowers her eyes, says "Hum," and marches past him into the room.* WHALEN *looks at her, amazed, then grins and runs off the porch.* JULIE, *violently, to* CORA) Don't ever do that in my house again.

CORA What? What did you say to me?

JULIE I said you were never to do that in my house again.

LUCY (*at door*) Lunch is ready, Mrs. Rodman.

ELLICOTT (*looks at* JULIE, *smiles*) You're very upset, aren't you?

CORA How dare you talk to me that way—

JULIE (*to* ANDREW, *touching his arm*) I'm sorry, Andy.

ANDREW There's nothing to be sorry for, darling. Cora acted like a fool.

CORA (*to* JULIE) So it's *your* house now? My father built it, but it's your house now.

JULIE Please. I'm sorry.

CORA You've thought that all these years. It's very strange that you waited to tell me until something happened about *that* man—

ANDREW (*sharply*) Stop that silly shouting.

JULIE I don't want lunch, Andy. Go in without me.

(*She pats his arm and exits quickly through library door.* CORA *sits down and begins to sniffle.* ANDREW *and* ELLICOTT *stare after* JULIE.)

WILKIE (*after a moment*) Um.

ELLICOTT (*turns*) It's late. You'd better have lunch here, Wilkie. It'll save time.

ANDREW   (*has turned and is looking at* MOSSIE *and* JOE)
Who are these gentlemen, Mr. Wilkie?

WILKIE   Mr. Easter, Mr. Dowel. I'll be staying at the hotel.
They'll be here with you. (*To* ELLICOTT) Thank you.
Can I wash up?

ANDREW   Staying here? Why should they be staying here?
(*To* CORA, *who is sniffling and arranging the figures in
the cabinet*) Please stop that, Cora.

WILKIE   They're here to take good care of you and your
family, Mr. Rodman. You won't have anything to worry
about.

ANDREW   (*carefully*)   I don't think I understand what you
are talking about. Neither I nor my family need any
taking care of.

WILKIE   I hope not. I believe not. But I don't like taking
chances with people who pay my bills.

ANDREW   (*to* ELLICOTT)   What kind of nonsense is this?
(*To* WILKIE) They'll stay at the hotel.

CORA   It's not nonsense. It's not nonsense. I'm paying my
share of this and it's my house, too, and if Julie is going
to have people like that around— (*Motions toward window*) in and out of the house, we will all need protection. She treats that man like—

ELLICOTT   (*sharply*)   Cora.

CORA   I insist on my rights. If you don't care what happens to me, then *I* must care—

WILKIE   (*pleasantly to* ANDREW)   If you'd prefer the boys
stay at the hotel—?

ANDREW   (*wearily*)   My sister needs protection. It makes
no difference. (*Starts slowly for the door.*)

LUCY   (*back at door*)   Lunch is getting cold.

ANDREW   (*at door, over his shoulder to* ELLICOTT)   I don't
want lunch. Go ahead.

ELLICOTT   (*stares after him for a moment. Then to* CORA)
We're a small party. But that will leave more food for
you. Let's go in now. You can take up the hysterics
again after lunch. (CORA *rises, sweeps past him, exits.*
ELLICOTT, *as he starts out, to* WILKIE) Miss Rodman is
a nervous lady.

WILKIE   Yes. They're all nervous, aren't they?

(*Without answering,* ELLICOTT *exits.*)

MOSSIE It's like a society picture, what they were doing. (*Touches his throat*) They talk so high. (*Watches* WILKIE *who is standing in the middle of the room*) You look like you're puzzling something, boss. What's a brush worker? (*He cracks his knuckles.*)

WILKIE (*laughs*) I don't know. Somebody who makes a brush, I guess.

EASTER (*suddenly, as* MOSSIE *cracks knuckles again*) For Christ's sake quit that. You're getting me crazy.

WILKIE (*turns*) Sit down. Both of you. Try to act like you've been in a house with a bathroom before. (*Looks at* EASTER) I don't want to have to worry about your nerves this time. (*He exits.*)

MOSSIE (*sits down near cabinet*) I couldn't follow what they were saying. They talk fast, don't they? (EASTER *has wandered over to desk. Idly he looks at papers on it, examines a few things on it*) They were mad. I got that. But it don't sound bad when you talk high. (*He cracks his knuckles.*)

EASTER I liked it for myself in Cleveland. Fifty of us. What kind of piker job is this? That Wilkie goes crazy when he smells a dollar. Always has.

MOSSIE I don't get what he's doing. The boys sit in the factory and we sit here, huh? What's that for?

EASTER Something he made up. We're going to get a lot extra sitting here.

MOSSIE (*cheerfully*) Well, we're eating on him. (MOSSIE *cracks his knuckles.*)

EASTER Just keep that up for a few days, hear me? I can feed myself. I told him that.

MOSSIE (*laughs*) Yeah. But it tastes better when somebody else buys it.

EASTER There might be street car trouble on the coast next month. I found out. I told him about it. So would he stay and wait and play for big stuff? No. He's got to take this, 'cause they let him smell a dollar bill first.

MOSSIE (*thoughtfully*) Well, he ain't working for us. He don't care about us. Car stuff, huh? Who's going to get it?

EASTER How do I know? (MOSSIE *cracks his knuckles*) Stop it.

MOSSIE Jesus Christ. Passing up street car work. He made enough money in New Orleans to keep him for a year.

EASTER So did you.

MOSSIE And so did you. More'n me, with the dice. I got some of mine yet. I took a little insurance for my mother. That's what you should've done. Instead of that sucker diamond Phil walked you in to—

EASTER (*irritated*) You said that before. (*Looks at his watch*) What do we do? Cook our food in here?

MOSSIE They couldn't invite us to eat inside. We're out here protecting her. (*Cracks his knuckles. During his next speech* EASTER *has idly started to play with a cigarette lighter on the desk. After the second light, it stops working. He picks up a paper-knife and begins fixing it.* MOSSIE *looks down at his hand, smiles*) Everybody's got a habit. That's a good one. Protecting her. Bet there ain't even an inch anymore to protect. But the other one looks good. You can't tell about people like this. They say, in the papers, talking fine, what they wouldn't· do, and then they sneak off and take a shot in bed at the first thing that comes along— (*He has cracked his knuckles again. Quickly,* EASTER *throws the paper-knife at him.* MOSSIE *ducks, the knife misses him and knocks over a vase on a small table. Slowly,* MOSSIE *adjusts his chair, shakes his head, stares at the vase*) Starting it again, huh? When you get time, Joe, you ought to take a rest cure. Ain't natural to be so nervous with knives. (*Shakes his head, looking at the vase*) You certainly ain't neat with other people's things.

Curtain

Act Two

SCENE I

Four weeks later.

AT RISE: MOSSIE DOWEL *is seated and* JOE EASTER *is standing at the table between the windows. They are playing two-handed poker.* MOSSIE *has his chair turned.* WILKIE, *in hat and overcoat, is sitting on the arm of a chair, looking idly out of the window. The radio is playing softly. For a few seconds after the rise of the curtain there are no sounds but the shuffling of cards, the sound of money on the table, the radio.*

EASTER (*after a second, sharply*) All right. All right. Show 'em. Stop flirting with 'em.

(MOSSIE *puts his hand down, smiles, rakes in the center money.* EASTER *puts down his cards, crosses to radio, angrily snaps it off.*)

MOSSIE Funny. Losers never like music. It's good luck for me, on the contrary. (*To* WILKIE) It's after nine. Must be something big keeping you out of bed.

EASTER I guess. It's got to be money to keep him out of those woolen nightgowns.

WILKIE It's pay day, or it should be. That always gives me insomnia. (*They have started to play again*) Ellicott been here?

EASTER Nope.

MOSSIE He's coming. Always is. Looking for Mrs. Rodman with the legs.

EASTER   (*to* WILKIE, *pointing upstairs*)   You think Rodman knows about 'em?

WILKIE   (*unpleasantly*)   What do you know?

MOSSIE   What does he know? He's guessing. He sees it everywhere. It comes from watching the flies go to it on cell doors.

WILKIE   (*sharply, to* EASTER)   I'd get the shakedown out of my head, if I were you.

EASTER   You think I'm crazy? (MOSSIE *cracks his knuckles*) Deal 'em. And stop that cracking. (*He wins a small hand and begins to shuffle the cards. Maliciously, casually to* WILKIE) So things ain't going so good, huh?

MOSSIE   (*cheerfully*)   It's nice and easy here. I like a rest job once in a while.

WILKIE   Another few weeks like this and you'll get a long rest.

MOSSIE   It ain't our fault, Sam.

EASTER   When you got nothing to do, we can't do it for you.

MOSSIE   Finger tried a fight. Eddie tried a fight. I even had Sig chase the old guy Firth's girl around. (*Puzzled*) Any guy'd protect his thirteen-year-old kid.

EASTER   Three sevens.

MOSSIE   But nobody'll fight. No matter what you do, they don't fight. Must be some kind of new religion, maybe. (*Turns up his hand, cracks his knuckles*) Three nines easy.

EASTER   (*through his teeth*)   They *are* running pretty easy the last two days, huh? (*To* WILKIE) I'm crazy for this place. Losing to him and following that dame around.

WILKIE   Just keep on doing it. I'll tell you when you're fit for anything else.

ELLICOTT   (*appears at the Center doors. He looks around the room, then after a second, coldly*)   Good evening. I hear you were looking for me today. You're active on pay day, aren't you?

WILKIE   Yes, sir. (*Pointing to desk*) The account's over there.

ELLICOTT   (*as he passes* MOSSIE *and* JOE)   I'm glad to see that nothing has disturbed your game, gentlemen. (*Picks *up the sheet*) Yes. It's a very full account. Well, you're right to get it while you can. I'm not so sure how many more pay days there are going to be. You do nothing and your bills get bigger.

WILKIE   That's the way it seems to have worked out.

ELLICOTT   The Cincinnati Herald is crying its eyes out tonight over model town being over-run with toughs. None of that helps any. (*Looking at* MOSSIE *and* JOE) Do you think they could have meant these gentlemen and the other friends you brought with you?

WILKIE   I read the papers. (*Looks speculatively at* MOSSIE *and* JOE) They don't look like anything Oscar Wilde would have wanted, do they? But no job's ever paid me enough to have their faces pushed pretty. (*Gets up*) Well, I know I haven't done too much, and I like it less than you. We're in hunting country. You didn't tell me that.

ELLICOTT   What?

WILKIE   The people around here hunt. In the season, I mean. That right?

ELLICOTT   What's that got to do with it?

WILKIE   It's got a lot to do with it. Every man for five miles owns a gun. Flintlocks, maybe, but clean. But they won't use 'em on me. They won't use 'em at all. You know why? Because somebody in Cleveland made a mistake and sent down a smart organizer. He won't let 'em use 'em. There hasn't even been a nose bleed for me to stop. I can't work with nothing.

ELLICOTT   We didn't bargain to cut the plan out for you. That's your business, and you've done a bad job of it.

WILKIE   (*coldly, still pleasantly*) Now, now. It's not all my fault. Even if there had been something to do, I couldn't have done it. Because I'm working for a man who doesn't want me to do anything. I'm working for a man who doesn't want me to work for him. That's a bad set-up, Mr. Ellicott.

ELLICOTT   (*starting to exit, slowly*) You'd better come up and see Mr. Rodman. (*Looks up at him*) As a lawyer, I have found that for my client's own good, it is often wise not to ask his permission on little details.

(WILKIE *has turned to stare at him as he reaches the door and passes* CORA, *who is entering.*)

CORA (*to* ELLICOTT) Don't you ever stay in your own house anymore? There are people who can never stay quietly at home and read a book. (*He exits without answering her*) Good evening. Rain. Rain. Rain. Are there several types of detectives, Mr. Wilkie?

WILKIE Only one kind, Miss Rodman. Lousy.

CORA I mean, very funny things are happening here. Things are missing from the pantry— (*Coquettishly*) Or is that too unimportant work for you?

WILKIE Not at all. I don't seem to be doing much else.

CORA (*goes to cabinet*) On Thursday, I was taking my weekly supply list. Just as a matter of routine. Mrs. Rodman was out—

WILKIE Mrs. Rodman is out a good deal, isn't she?

CORA Yes, Mrs. Rodman always manages to go off by herself. Well, when I looked in the closet I was amazed to find that at least eight or ten dollars' worth of canned goods—

WILKIE (*rises, politely*) Mr. Dowel is a specialist at just such detection. He's at your service, Miss Rodman. I'll be down later and we can lay our trap. (*He exits.*)

MOSSIE (*giggles*) Sure. Who, me? Sure.

CORA I like to see a nice little card game. Do you know that night club singer who got killed in the paper this morning?

MOSSIE No ma'am. I don't know ladies who get into trouble.

EASTER (*motioning to the cards*) Beat the straight.

MOSSIE Easy. (*He rakes in the money as* EASTER *stares at him.*)

CORA (*to* EASTER) My. You were beaten. Are you playing for money?

(HANNAH *enters with a tray of drinks which she puts on the other side of the room.* CORA *watches her as she empties ash trays into a saucer.*)

HANNAH (*slamming ash tray on table, pointing to the floor*) Ain't it *more* trouble to lean over the ash trays to get the ashes on the rug? Pigs.

MOSSIE   My Ma used to say ashes were good for rugs.

HANNAH   Your Ma never saw a rug.

CORA   Hannah. We were just talking about the things that were stolen from the pantry.

HANNAH   Were you now? Anybody in jail?

CORA   It's ridiculous that you shouldn't know where they've disappeared to—

HANNAH   (*has picked up* JOE's *cigarette which is lying on the table, and carefully placed the lighted end nearer the wood*)   Put it like this. It'll burn the table faster.

EASTER   (*angrily, under his breath, as she starts to exit*)   Mind your business.

CORA   Hannah! You haven't been listening to a word I've said— (ANDREW *enters from the rear library door. Goes to desk*)   Henry and Mr. Wilkie are upstairs. Henry's been here three times today. In, out. In, out.

ANDREW   (*as* EASTER *has noisily slammed down his cards*)   Would you play in the other room, please?

MOSSIE   (*softly, not paying any attenion and not moving*)   Yes sir.

CORA   (*as* HANNAH *goes to the door*)   Andrew. It's time for you to know that groceries have been missing from the kitchen. Regularly. Hannah refuses to tell me who's been doing it and I can't allow it to go on. I have asked Mr. Wilkie to take a hand.

HANNAH   (*turning*)   Have you? (*Laughs. The noise of the game, the words, the raking in of the money has become sharp once more.*)

ANDREW   Get out of this room. (*They turn, surprised. Then slowly, without hurry, they gather up their things and move out.*)

CORA   (*after a second*)   Andrew. I was telling you that—

HANNAH   (*crossing to him quickly*)   Miss Cora was telling you that food's been missing. It has. I've been taking it. I wish I could've taken more. (*Motions with her hand toward windows*)   I don't know what you feel, but I don't like to see the boys go hungry. Do what you want about it, Mr. Andrew.

ANDREW   (*slowly, staring at her*)   I don't want to do anything about it, Hannah.

(HANNAH *without answering exits. She passes* JULIE, *in hat and coat, entering. For a fraction,* JULIE *draws back when she sees the room is not empty.*)

CORA   Sometimes I think you're crazy. And sometimes I think you are doing things just to humiliate me.

ANDREW   It's raining, darling.

JULIE   I know. But I'd like a walk anyway.

CORA   I say one thing. You say another. Telling her it's all right to steal. What *right* have you to humiliate me in front of servants?

JULIE   (*gently*)   Cora, do stop nagging at Andy—

CORA   Nagging at him. Nagging at him. He's gone crazy—

ANDREW   I like my wife. Could I ever, anymore, be alone with her? For just a few minutes? And then you can start with me all over again.

CORA   (*at door*)   Certainly you can be alone. I daresay you have a great many things to ask.

JULIE   She has one of her bad headaches. She's upset. (ANDREW *smiles, shakes his head. She looks around the room*) How messy this room looks.

ANDREW   (*comes up to her as he speaks*)   Our friends have been using it as a club. I don't blame you for wanting to go out. (*Leans down, kisses her hair*) But not tonight, Julie. It's cold and it's raining, and—

JULIE   (*slowly*)   I want to go.

ANDREW   (*moves away from her to chair*)   And I'm lonely.

JULIE   (*on the "want to go" she has moved again to the window. On his speech she turns, looks at him, puzzled*)   You? Lonely?

ANDREW   (*smiles*)   Yes. I. Lonely. I always thought loneliness meant alone, without people. It means something else.

JULIE   (*softly*)   That's a late discovery. You're lucky.

ANDREW   (*laughs*)   Why do people always think it's lucky to find out the simple things long after one should have known them?

JULIE   Because each year you can put off knowing about them gives you one more year of peace.

ANDREW   I don't think so. Unless you can put it off forever. (*Smiles*) I think that's what I was trying to do. But

I'm at a mad age to start looking at the world, to start looking at myself. (*Very simply*) It confuses me, Julie. I am mixed up.

JULIE   I know. I've guessed. But I'm no one to help. I'm more mixed up than you.

ANDREW   I've walked up and down this room so much for so many nights, that I'm— (*Angrily*) sick of it and sick of myself. I try to tell myself that I can think things straight, and every night I start the same way—by taking stock of this house. Bums walking in and out, followed by Henry, as undisturbed and as anxious to get down to White Sulphur as always; Hannah, trying to make me into the villain she wants me to be. And Cora. Taking up one unpleasant sentence where she left off the last. (*Softly*) And you. I've missed you.

JULIE   Missed me?

ANDREW   (*looks at her, laughs*) You're embarrassed. Strange. We've lived together so long it seems almost indecent to talk about ourselves. We used to talk about ourselves. Remember?

JULIE   (*smiles*) Yes. When we were young. We belonged to the time when talk was part of the marriage ceremony. Such cynical, smooth talk, about marriage and life and freedom. Not you. Me, I mean.

ANDREW   I suppose. I remember I used to be a little puzzled by it. But that's what we were then. (*Affectionately*) You always hate yesterday, don't you, Julie?

JULIE   Yes. (*She moves again to window and then turns back suddenly*) Andy. We haven't talked about it much. I knew you didn't want to. But the strike, these people here—it's wrong for you. I know it's so wrong for you. Settle it now. It doesn't make any difference who wins—

ANDREW   (*sharply*) I don't care who wins. If it were that simple, it would be fine. But it isn't that simple. (*Leans forward, slowly*) I can't fit the pieces together. That's what is happening to me. I suddenly don't know where my place in the whole thing is. Don't tell me that's one of the things I was lucky to worry about late. That doesn't do any good. I've only loved two things in my whole life: you and this town. Papa never loved it. He just wanted to be boss and get to Carlsbad for the season. But my grandfather loved it. I think the way I do. Remember how I never wanted to go to Europe or to any place else—even when you went? This was my home, these were my people, I didn't want much else. (*With feeling*) But that's been changed, I don't know how. And I don't know where I stand anymore.

JULIE (*softly*) Try to set it right again.

ANDREW I wish I knew how. I worked well because I worked one way, without thinking about any other. They worked one way, without thinking about any other. How do I set that right again? Don't you see? It would be like us. If anything ever happened to us we could come together again and pretend it had never happened. But what good would that be if it had really happened, and we couldn't be the same anymore? (*Laughs suddenly*) Well, I'm not the strong man Papa was, and Cora will be down in a minute to remind me of it.

JULIE (*after a second, she kneels on the floor in front of him*) Andy. Look at me. You've talked because you wanted help. You wanted me to help you, about yourself. I can't do that. I need help myself. It's a mean thing I'm saying: that I can't stay and listen, because I want to talk myself. I want help, too.

ANDREW (*after a second he nods, smiles, pats her head*) Where are you going, Julie? Down by the river in the rain?

JULIE I don't know. Probably the river. I always do. (*Then suddenly, softly*) And perhaps not.

ANDREW (*rises*) Good night, darling.

JULIE (*quietly*) Good night, Andy.

(*He watches her move toward the window and exit. He stands for a moment looking after her as* MOSSIE *opens the library door.*)

MOSSIE Mr. Ellicott says he's waiting for you. (ANDREW, *his eyes on the window, pays no attention to* MOSSIE, *who, after a minute*) Mr. Ellicott's waiting.

(*For a second longer,* ANDREW *stands looking out of the window. Then slowly, without looking at* MOSSIE, *he exits from Center doors.* MOSSIE *comes into the room, idly, pushes the door shut with his foot as he turns on the radio. The radio is playing something banal and loud. Then he sits down—the corner near the cabinet has no light on it—comfortably leans back to listen to the music. After a second,* EASTER *comes slowly in from the library door. He has a pack of cards in his hand and is playing with them. He crosses to the large table and lays out six or seven of them, face-down on the table.*)

MOSSIE Funny how a lot of rich people don't like noise. I like that. I once took piano lessons for two months. (*No answer*) What you doing, Joe?

EASTER (*through his teeth*) Playing solitaire. (*As he leans very close to look at the backs of the cards*) A new way. (*As* MOSSIE *cracks his knuckles*) You doing it worse today. *Stop it.*

MOSSIE (*looks at cabinet*) Screwy. The way she plays with these things. And the other one. Walking up and down, up and down. Tim says she's had him crazy trying to follow her. Bet she's doing it tonight, in the rain. She just went out.

EASTER (*looks up*) Your finger nails need cutting, Mossie.

MOSSIE (*looks at him, laughs*) Yeah. You buying me a manicure?

EASTER That'd be better than having you wear them down making marks on the back of these cards—and it wouldn't cost me as much.

MOSSIE You're nuts.

EASTER (*straightens up*) Put the sixty-five bucks you won over here on the table, Mossie.

MOSSIE *You* got the cards out of *that* drawer. My God, Joe, you don't mean to tell me you think rich people like this would fool around with wrong cards—Jesus, Joe, I been telling you you'd better take a rest cure. Books and milk and just laying in a bed. You're getting too nervous about nothing. You're seeing things. Rodman fixing the cards— (*Laughs, then quietly*) Was it Rodman's dice you made that killing with at Phil's? Joe, you're getting good and batty.

EASTER The cards are scratched. Put that money on the table.

MOSSIE (*slowly, as he cracks his knuckles, turns toward the radio*) You don't want to get so excited, Joe. You don't want to come over here and get the dough, Joe, and I don't blame you. So stay over there and quiet yourself. Sit down and whittle yourself some straight dice.

EASTER (*slowly*) For the last time. Put the money on the table.

MOSSIE (*quietly*) No.

(*As he turns back to the radio,* EASTER, *pressing the spring of his knife, lets it fly through the air.* MOSSIE *screams softly, pushes with his feet from the ground as he topples from the chair. He falls noisily to the floor. For a second* EASTER *stands watching him, listening to the two soft groans. The groans cease and* EASTER *suddenly begins to move. His movements are quick but aimless, as if he didn't know what to do first. He turns out the lamp nearest him, shuts the library door, and moves to Center doors. As he starts to turn the key, the door is violently pushed open by* WILKIE. EASTER *steps back, frightened.*)

WILKIE What's it? (EASTER *looks out in the hall for a second, then quickly closes the door, nods his head toward* MOSSIE *and the chair.* WILKIE *crosses quickly, leans down, looks at* MOSSIE. *Then quickly, he moves toward* EASTER, *grabs the lapel of his coat with one hand as he hits him in the face with the other*) You tough guy. You God damned tough guy.

EASTER (*hoarsely*) I couldn't help it, Sam—he had his gun out.

WILKIE Yeah, out in his pocket. O.K. the hell with you. (*Lets go of his lapels and shoves him.*)

EASTER Sam. Give me some money. Please. Sam. Please.

WILKIE I'll give you money—to get your hair waved for the chair.

EASTER I'm telling you, I'm telling you. What could I do? He tried the gun. I'm telling you— (*Hysterically, as he watches* WILKIE *move toward telephone*) Sam. Sam. What are you doing—

WILKIE I'm trying to think which cop would like to have you most. (*Turning on him violently*) This whole damn job wasn't lousy enough. You got to make it better. That boy scout upstairs you got to spell words in front of is going to like this in his house. I can sit in the office now and knit for a year—until they forget you worked for me. (*Picks up telephone*) Well, I'll take you in myself and make a pretty speech about how I didn't know your record, and the only dope who'll believe that is some guy milking a cow, and I'd never have worked for him anyway. You tough guy.

EASTER   No. No. Sam. No—

WILKIE   (*as he starts to dial*) You son of a bitch. I can't get a nose bleed where I want it, but you've got to start carving— (*His last words have become slower, as if he were thinking. Then he looks up at* EASTER, *and slowly puts the receiver back on the hook. Stands at the table, staring at it, as* EASTER *watches him. After a long silence*) This way you'd hang during the warm weather. My way might keep you alive for the winter—maybe. (*Comes over and stands in front of* EASTER) Take that knife out of him. Take him out and dump him. (*Carefully*) Dump him in the right place—with no fancy work. Do you hear me? (EASTER *nods quickly, and as he starts to move,* WILKIE *jerks him back*) Remember, I don't promise you anything. If it goes wrong, you slob, it goes wrong for you. I'll turn you in myself if I have to—and with plenty of story to keep me in the clear. Do you understand me? (*Waits, gets no answer*) Do you understand me?

EASTER   (*very quietly*) Yes.

Curtain

SCENE II

The same evening. The time is immediately following Scene I.

SETTING: *A bare, clean office-room, the empty side of a store. The office is in an alley. The entrance is Left stage. There is a desk, a few chairs, a filing cabinet, a typewriter, a mimeographing machine, an electric stove.*

AT RISE: WHALEN *is sitting at the desk chair, leaning over to hammer on a box.* FIRTH *is sitting by the window, staring idly out into the alley. Neither of them speaks for a minute after the curtain rises. Then* FIRTH *gets slowly to his feet and goes to the chair on which his hat and raincoat are lying.*

FIRTH Well. Want to come to my house for a bowl of something hot?

WHALEN (*shakes his head, points to a cardboard container on his desk*) Odave treated me to a pint of whisky. It tastes like he made it on the picket line.

FIRTH Bad for your stomach.

WHALEN Don't worry about my stomach. It'll last another few years. (*Waves toward the window*) Worry about the stomachs out there.

FIRTH I been worrying enough.

WHALEN How much we got?

FIRTH Enough, maybe. Hannah brought down canned stuff and Richmondville sent over a pig.

WHALEN That's enough for a month, if you take a little caviar with it.

FIRTH Well, it ain't enough. I don't say anybody's starving, but it's tough to watch kids not get enough. It ain't only my kids, it's kids.

WHALEN Yep!

FIRTH I had a hundred sixty-two dollars left in my savings bank. Clyde needed it. Nobody's got much left. Clyde coughs too much.

WHALEN Didn't anybody ever tell you that Christians aren't supposed to act like Christians?

FIRTH Funny. All the boys had a little something. But we were talking last night how you work all your life to save it, then it runs out fast. Funny.

WHALEN Very funny.

FIRTH (*suddenly, as if he had been thinking of it all along*) I couldn't tell her what they meant. I was so ashamed for the kid. (*Violently*) I'll kill 'em if they ever go near my girl again. I'll kill 'em—

WHALEN (*looks at him, slowly, calmly*) That's just what they want you to do. You boys were hot stuff Thursday. You couldn't take a little pushing around. You got to push back. So what? So it winds up Wilkie gets half his boys sworn in as deputy sheriffs. They're law and order now and you're un-American.

FIRTH There's some things you can't take. Nobody can. Nobody.

WHALEN Speak for yourself. There's not much I can't take, if I have to. (*Slowly*) You gave me your word that you wouldn't fight again, and that you'd keep the boys from fighting.

FIRTH And I've kept my word. But it gets too much—

WHALEN (*wearily*) We've been over all this before. Try to believe that I'm telling you the truth. The longer you're quiet the sooner you'll win. Wilkie's been in this business for a long time. They've all got one gag—to make you fight. And no matter what *they* do to start it, you'll be surprised to read in the paper, and to hear from the police, that *you* started it. (*Slowly, with force*) And once they start a real fight here, you're lost.

FIRTH You don't believe we can take care of ourselves, do you? You don't—

WHALEN No. I don't believe it. There are men in your spot who know what it's about and who can take what's coming. I believe in *their* fighting, but not *you*. Your idea of fighting is not to hit below the waist— (*Laughs*) And that's no good. Now be good. And don't let your kid or anybody else go out alone.

FIRTH (*shakes his head, passes his hand over his face wearily, and begins to put on his coat*) Hannah says Andrew don't like things much. Might be a good sign. He's an easy going man. I don't believe he'd have ever got us into this if it hadn't been for the others.

WHALEN (*smiles*) That's the stuff. That kind of talk will do you a lot of good.

FIRTH (*sighs*) I don't know how much longer we can hold out here, when kids aren't getting enough. (*As he turns he looks at* WHALEN, *who is paying no attention to him*) I wouldn't be the one to know. What do you think?

WHALEN I told you what I thought. Wilkie wants a fight, and as long as we're not giving him one we're sitting not bad. Now go on home. And if they cut your grandmother in half, don't lift a hand. Wait'll they cut her in slices and then maybe, but I don't promise, I'll let you take a sock at one of 'em.

FIRTH That ain't what I meant. That ain't telling me how much longer we can feed. You ain't never told me.

WHALEN (*finally irritated*) And I'm never going to. That may be part of my job, too, but it's not for me. You pick your own minute. You'll get no speeches from me about the beauty of starving for what you think. I don't mind doing it for myself, but I don't do it for other people. (*Gets up*) Because it's a waste of time, and I'm busy. I guess you'll hold out as long as you've got the guts to. That I can't put in you.

FIRTH (*angrily*) We don't need you to tell us about guts—

WHALEN (*smiles*) That's all right. I'm no hero-worshiper.

FIRTH We've got more guts around here than you'll ever see. Our folks have always had. We—

WHALEN (*wearily, goes back to his desk and starts working again on the box*) Go on home and boast to your wife.

(FIRTH *stands watching him. After a second he sighs, moves toward the door.*)

FIRTH (*softly*) I could bring you back something hot.

WHALEN (*affectionately*) Good night, Tom.

FIRTH (*affectionately*) Don't worry about the boys here. We'll be all right when you're crying for a rotten apple.

(*He exits.* WHALEN *watches him, smiling. Then with a few loud hammerings, he finishes with the box and gets up, carrying it to the other side of the room. He goes to a basin, washes his hands, dabs at his face, lights a cigarette, pours himself a drink. He stands smoking as the door opens and* JULIE RODMAN *comes slowly in. She stands away from the door, waiting for him to speak.*)

WHALEN   (*turns, looks at her, then after a moment's silence, says loudly, as if he is talking for somebody outside*)   Please close the door, Mrs. Rodman—unless there is somebody with you.

JULIE   (*closing the door, without turning*)   There is nobody with me. (*She stands waiting for him to speak*) I—I— Can't I come in?

WHALEN   (*slowly, pleasantly*)   I'm guessing. But I want to save you time. You can go back and tell them that I don't want any bribes—and that the gag is too stale.

JULIE   (*crosses to him. Intensely*)   No. No. Really, no. I haven't come for any reason—I mean, any reason except my own. Really, really, Mr. Whalen—

WHALEN   (*picks up two cheap glasses from the window sill*)   Well, whatever your reason, you look cold. Like a drink? (*She nods, shy, embarrassed, watching him*) It's filthy, but it's a drink. (*He hands her a glass, sits down at desk, smiles, pours himself a drink*) Don't listen to the doctors. Cheap whisky is good for you. Why did you come, Mrs. Rodman?

JULIE   I—er—I— (*Looks up at him*)   It won't sound like the truth. I wanted to talk to you. Just talk to you. Not about anything. I just wanted to talk to you—

WHALEN   (*looks at her, then after a pause*)   Well. That sounds too pleasant. Don't you know that you're not supposed to feel friendly enough for a visit and— (*Slowly, seriously*) and that I'm not supposed to let you make the visit?

JULIE   (*rises, softly*)   Yes, I suppose I knew it. I'm sorry. I just wanted to talk to you.

WHALEN   (*kindly*)   What did you want to say?

JULIE   I don't know. Although I've thought about it a lot. (*Turns to him and smiles*) You don't remember, but I do. The first evening you came here, you talked to me.

WHALEN   I do remember. I didn't know who you were.

JULIE   I've walked past your alley often. Tonight I didn't think. I just came in. (*Quickly*) Haven't you ever wanted to talk to somebody you thought knew more about things than you did, and you just hoped the talk would start, and— (*Smiles*) there wouldn't be any questions about why you came?

WHALEN (*pours himself another drink*) Yes. Once. When I was in college. I thought that Lafayette— (*Bows*) Lafayette, of all people—was a fake and I wanted to know about it. But the professor was eating his dinner, and he thought Lafayette was fine. It never seems to work out very well.

JULIE (*without snobbishness*) College?

WHALEN (*laughs*) Yes, ma'am. No, it's not as good as it sounds. I only went to college for seven months. That cost four hundred dollars. (*Bows*) Almost half of what my father could earn in a year. The old story. (*Leans forward, nastily*) My mother sacrificed herself.

JULIE I went to college, too. But it cost more than that. (*Smiles*) And it wasn't any sacrifice for my mother.

WHALEN No? You shouldn't have denied her that. My mother found great happiness in it, crowing over our half-starved neighbors. My mother hated what she was and what she came from. None of that love of beauty stuff in my mother. I was to become a priest.

JULIE (*smiling*) I'd have guessed that.

WHALEN (*smiles*) You would have been wrong. When that failed, she just wanted me to get rich enough to hate what I was and what I came from. (*Leans over to light a cigarette*) I fooled her. I hated her instead. I always had. I kind of liked my father, and that four hundred bucks would have been plenty of carfare for him. He had rheumatism bad and the places where they could pay a gardener were in the suburbs and he had to walk most of the way. He'd come home at night and it would hurt him to take his pants off and he'd sit in a chair and hold them out from his legs so the goods couldn't touch the skin. He wasn't much. But he was nice. Anyway, what for? Four years of dopes and faking that I had as much as they had. I quit. (*Stops, leans over to look at her, then slowly*) What is your reason for coming here?

JULIE (*puts up her hand, as if to detain him, softly*) In

a minute. In a minute. (*Then politely, loudly*) What did you do then?

WHALEN (*sits back, looks at her, then after a second*) Nothing. I hoboed. Once in a while I'd work. But not when I could help it. Then one day, or one month, or one year, I began to get worried. I couldn't understand about things, and it scared hell out of me. (*Laughs, pours himself out a drink, pours her one*) When you don't feel yourself anything, I mean any part of anything, that's when you get scared. I was that way for a long time.

JULIE (*softly*) My husband said he felt that.

WHALEN I imagine he would. Well it took me a long time. I had listened too much to what was wrong with the world from every louse from New Orleans to Seattle. I was sick of it all. I hated the rich. I hated the poor. I couldn't figure either of them. (*Smiles at her*) I'm not bright, but I'm stubborn. And I came out with something. (*Slowly, seriously*) I've been working ever since.

JULIE Then you didn't hate. Not the poor anyway. You loved them.

WHALEN (*laughs*) Love them? No. Do you think you can love the smell that comes from dirty skin, or the scum on dishes, or the holes in the floor with the bugs coming through— (*Sharply*) Or the meanness and the cowardice that comes with poverty? (*Leans forward*) I hate the poor, Mrs. Rodman. But I love what they could be. (*Then lightly*) Do you hate the poor, Mrs. Rodman?

JULIE No. And I don't know what they could be.

WHALEN Not even hate? You've never thought that much about them?

JULIE (*simply*) No. I've never seen many poor people.

WHALEN Some bright Sunday you must lift your hem from the mud and have a try.

JULIE I'd like to.

WHALEN I imagine one of the ladies' charities would be delighted to let you peep over the fence. (*Nastily*) It would not be unpleasant, since the poor *they* will show you will lick your boots—in gratitude for nothing. Or rather for the gift of seeing a handsome, clean lady who can eat three meals every day. The people *they* will show you haven't the— (*Uses the word carefully*) dignity to want those things for themselves. The church has taught them to be grateful that *you* have them. When you have left, with your empty bag of groceries, they will tell themselves that it is easier for a camel to go through the eye of a needle than for a rich lady to enter the Kingdom of God. That has consoled them for a long time.

JULIE (*angrily*) That's not what I am. That's not what I want to see. You have no reason for thinking it is.

WHALEN Perhaps not. But people like me always make symbols of people like you.

JULIE I never wanted to see a selected world: I never knew how to see any other. I think that is one of the reasons I wanted to talk to you.

WHALEN (*laughs mockingly*) Are you in a hurry? Or can I show you my world in fifteen minutes? I'm not a teacher, Mrs. Rodman. (*Looks at her*) And I believe that if one wants to see the world, one knows where to find it. It's all about you. They tell me you've been married here a long time and that they don't know you very well.

JULIE No, they don't. They're a hard people with strangers —as you've probably found out.

WHALEN (*smiles*) Yes.

JULIE But it's really my fault. I've been busy. Busy, like you, finding out. (*Bitterly*) I was finding out about myself. That took all my time.

WHALEN A psychoanalyst?

JULIE (*begins to be angry, then laughs*) No.

WHALEN Oh. I thought that was the rich man's gin. What were you finding out?

JULIE I don't know. When I was young, I guess I was looking for something I could do. Then for something I could be. (*Smiles*) Finally, just for something to want, or to think, or to believe in. I always wanted somebody to show me the way.

WHALEN (*smiles*) Certainly. That's what we all want. It's easy. Were you lucky?

JULIE   Lucky in finding them? No.

WHALEN   (*looks at his watch, begins to put papers away in desk*)   Then you should try for yourself. That works sometimes.

JULIE   No. I decided a long time ago that there were people who had to learn from other people. I'm one of them. (*Gets up, slowly*) That's why I wanted to talk to you.

WHALEN   (*looks up at her, laughs, shakes his head*)   To me? Is that why you came?

JULIE   (*slowly*)   Yes. And I'd like to stay.

WHALEN   (*slowly, puzzled*)   To stay?

JULIE   Sounds crazy, doesn't it? It isn't crazy for me. I know the things you're going to say about a silly, rich woman. But I've thought about it too much, and I know it isn't that. I have no right to come here and talk to you like this—

WHALEN   (*gets up, looks at her*)   What are you talking about, Mrs. Rodman?

JULIE   (*angrily*)   I've told you. I've told you. (*Then softly, quietly*) I want to stay, I want to stay here. I mean, I—

WHALEN   (*there is a second's silence. Then he moves to her quickly, takes her roughly by the arm*)   All right. Now go back and tell Wilkie this isn't a new one either. (*She draws her face away from him, sharply*) Don't look so hurt. What am I supposed to think?

JULIE   I've told you the truth. I don't care what you think. (*He looks at her, drops her arm, moves back to desk, turns to look at her again.*)

WHALEN   Who have you told this nonsense to?

JULIE   (*carefully*)   I haven't told this—this nonsense to anybody.

WHALEN   (*angrily*)   What the hell do you think I am?

JULIE   I don't blame you for anything you think. I know what a fool I've sounded. But it's been the truth. (*Softly*) I've never in my life talked that way before. (*To herself*) I should have known that when I did, I wouldn't be believed.

WHALEN   And if I do believe you, then you are a silly rich woman who doesn't know what to do with her life and who sees the solution for it in the first man she meets who doesn't stutter: sick of your own world, aren't you, and you think I know another? What do you think mine is? A new game to be learned in an evening and played for a week? (*Takes her arm*) I don't like that kind of playing, Mrs. Rodman.

JULIE (*after a second, slowly, carefully*) Maybe what you've said is true. Maybe it isn't. But I'm not playing —and you don't think I am.

WHALEN (*stares at her, as if he were thinking of something else*) You could blow me out of here with this. (*Carefully*) Please. Don't mention your—don't mention your coming here.

JULIE (*softly*) I won't. (*Her face hurt and tight, she begins to move toward the door. As she passes the desk, he stops her.*)

WHALEN I'd like to say something kind. But I'm worrying about my job. (*Smiles*) I'm tired and I've got a lot of work to do.

JULIE (*without turning*) Do you think I'm pretty?

WHALEN (*as he starts to speak, there is the noise of a car outside, and he stops to listen. When he hears nothing more, he smiles*) No. Better than pretty. (*Looks at her, nods*) Yes, that I feel. Sure. I feel a lot of that. You'd be fun. If you ever feel like it, and I'm not working, you bring your maids, and your trunks, and your cars, and—

JULIE (*simply*) No.

WHALEN (*laughs*) All right. (*Pleasantly*) And now, good night.

(*As she walks toward the door, the noise of a car, the grinding of gears, becomes very sharp and close. She stops, and he looks quickly toward the door and window. Then, as if he is wondering whether the noise means anything to her, he looks at her. Quickly, he moves toward the door, jerks it open, runs out, as she draws back into the room. A minute later he returns, stands staring as if unconscious that she was there.*)

JULIE What is it?

WHALEN (*slowly, looking at her*) It's a big night for me. Your friends have been playing tricks.

JULIE What do you mean?

WHALEN   I mean that the dead body of that fat thug who was living in your house has just been planted in the alley.

JULIE   Dead? He's dead? I don't understand—

WHALEN   It's very simple. You heard the car. He was put there to get somebody in trouble. (*Stops, thinks*) Yep. (*Moves quickly to the telephone. Into phone*) Corley? Run next door and get me Tom Firth. Quick. (*Puts phone down. Crosses back to her*) Go out the other end of the alley, Mrs. Rodman. Please don't let anybody see you.

JULIE   But you—

WHALEN   (*quickly, firmly*)   Good night. (*She turns, stares at him, hesitates, and begins to run out of the door. He watches her, shuts the door, moves quickly back to the telephone*) Tom. One of Wilkie's boys is outside in the alley, dead. They planted him there. I don't know. For me or you or anybody else. Listen to me. I'm going to be in jail in a few minutes, sleeping tight. (*Sharply*) Stay where you are and don't worry about me. I don't know what he's going to start, but I know he's going to start something. Stop worrying about me, and listen. (*Very carefully*) No matter what he starts, let him alone. *Don't fight with him.* (*Loudly*) Do you hear me? Let him do what he wants and don't fight with him. (*Pleasantly*) Just get ready to do nothing. That'll take all the guts you've got. No. I'll be all right. Good night. (*He hangs up, sits quietly for a second, then gets up and takes his hat and coat from the floor behind the desk, puts them on, sits down again, turns his chair to face the door, lights a cigarette. A second later there is a loud knocking on the door. He smiles, starts to rise, as the curtain falls.*)

Curtain

SCENE III

Same as Act One.

AT RISE: *The living room of the Rodman house. Some of the lamps have been turned off, as if to keep attention off the room.* WILKIE *has moved a large chair to face the Center doors. A second after the curtain rises, there is the noise of someone descending the hall stairs.* WILKIE *lights a cigarette, slowly, and leans forward.*

WILKIE   Mr. Ellicott.

ELLICOTT   (*coming into the room, putting on his overcoat*) I thought you'd gone home long ago. (*Slowly*) What are you doing here, Wilkie?

WILKIE   (*shakes his head, gets up, waits, then slowly, nodding his head toward card table*)   My man Dowel was found knifed, dead, down near strike headquarters.

ELLICOTT   Oh. (*After a second, puzzled*) But he was here—

WILKIE   (*watching him*)   He went out.

ELLICOTT   (*carefully*)   You think they killed him?

WILKIE   (*looks at him, amused, laughs*)   I think so.

ELLICOTT   Why?

WILKIE   Whalen was there. Any of the others could have been there, too.

ELLICOTT   (*carefully*)   They got into a fight and killed him—

WILKIE   (*smiles*)   Maybe. Or maybe they thought he was snooping around and jumped him.

ELLICOTT   Well?

WILKIE   Well. That gives us a little job of law enforcement to do. The boys we had sworn in as deputy sheriffs last week will have to pass up their crap game, and— (*Smiles broadly*) go to work for justice.

ELLICOTT   (*sharply, irritated*)   What do you intend to do?

WILKIE   Find the guy who put the knife in Mossie, and find the guys he did it for.

ELLICOTT   And where does that lead?

WILKIE Well, we'll hope it leads somewhere. (*Casually*) Is this Judge Alcott a good enough friends of yours that I can count on his not getting up out of bed to issue any silly court orders that could get in my way?

ELLICOTT (*slowly*) Yes.

WILKIE And could you ask your marshal to go home and go to bed?

ELLICOTT (*carefully*) Rodman isn't going to stand for your making any trouble here, Wilkie.

WILKIE I'm not going to make any and I'm going to leave it to you to tell him what's happened and to make him see it right.

ELLICOTT I'll talk to him. (*Starts for door, stops, turns back to look at* WILKIE) You needn't wait. I should think you'd be needed downtown.

WILKIE My boys know what to do. I'm waiting for Mrs. Rodman.

ELLICOTT (*after a second*) Why are you waiting for Mrs. Rodman?

WILKIE Your guess should be pretty good. (*Looks at his watch*) She's taking a long time.

ELLICOTT (*after a second*) Where's Whalen?

WILKIE In jail, I hope.

ELLICOTT You think he—

WILKIE I don't know. I'm only thinking for a little while. It don't hurt to have him in jail while I'm thinking. That—

(*The window doors open and* JULIE *comes quickly in. She looks as if she has been running. She starts for the door, ignores* WILKIE, *speaks to* ELLICOTT.)

JULIE Where's Andy?

WILKIE Mrs. Rodman. (*Sharply, as she does not turn*) Mrs. Rodman. (*Crosses in front of her*) I think Mr. Rodman's gone to bed. But I've been waiting for you. I thought you'd like to talk to me first.

JULIE Yes. I'd like to talk to you. (*To* ELLICOTT) Do you know what's happened? (*He nods, slowly*) Do you know that he had that man's body put in the alley—

ELLICOTT (*sharply*) Julie. Those are dangerous guesses.

JULIE They're not guesses. I was there.

ELLICOTT   I knew where you were. So your adventures
  finally carried you to an unpleasant place at an unpleasant hour? I—

WILKIE   I'd like to talk to Mrs. Rodman. (*Looks toward
  the hall*)   Will you—?

ELLICOTT   (*exiting*)   Yes.

JULIE   (*suddenly, furiously*)   How dare you think you can
  do a thing like this in Mr. Rodman's name?

WILKIE   Mr. Ellicott was right. You are making very dangerous guesses.

JULIE   I am making no guesses. I was there to see and hear.

WILKIE   So you're going to tell your husband where you
  were?

JULIE   (*staring at him*)   Of course. (*She starts again for
  door.*)

WILKIE   I thought you would. That's why I waited. You're
  a noble lady, and I'm frightened of noble ladies. They
  usually land the men they know in cemeteries. (*As she
  opens the door*)   And that's where you're getting ready
  to land Leo Whalen. (*She takes her hand off the door,
  stands without turning*)   You're throwing a monkey-
  wrench, Mrs. Rodman, and it's going to hit both Whalen
  and Mr. Rodman.

JULIE   (*softly, without turning*)   What did you mean
  about—about Whalen?

WILKIE   (*casually, sits down on arm of chair*)   I meant
  several things. Now you tell me that you're going upstairs to tell your husband that Whalen couldn't have
  had anything to do with Mossie, because you were
  with him?

JULIE   Yes.

WILKIE   And that's too bad. Right this minute Whalen's
  probably playing checkers— (*Smiles*)   somewhere. But
  your way, he won't be for long.

JULIE   I don't know what you're talking about.

WILKIE   Then it's because you haven't thought about it.
  (*Pleasantly*)   You see, Mrs. Rodman, *your husband*
  might believe you, *I* might believe you, but the police
  might take your noble gesture not as an alibi— (*Softly,
  as she turns*)   but as a motive. It sounds foolish, since

you and I know better, but they might think that—
(*Makes a mocking gallant stop*) that Mossie caught you
together and Whalen killed him for it. (*She has been
staring at him. Then she moves past him, as if she were
thinking*) That's my guess, and I've been in the business a long time. And even if my guess is wrong—and
there's always a good chance that police will be boobs
—he'll be through anyway. When the strikers found
out he'd been carrying on with the boss's wife—

JULIE (*furiously*) He was not carrying on—

WILKIE (*smiles*) It's going to look like a sell out, and if
he gets out all in one piece he's lucky.

JULIE (*defiance gone from her voice*) Why do you care
what happens to him?

WILKIE I don't. But I'm working for your husband. It's
my job to keep him— (*Slowly*) and his wife out of
trouble. (*Looks at his watch*) For a little while.

JULIE (*sits down slowly, then after a second*) Have you
been telling me the truth? Will he be—

WILKIE Oh, some of it's the truth, and some of it isn't.
(*As he speaks,* CORA *opens the library door and comes
in. She has on a warm woolen robe.*)

CORA (*crossing to bell, ringing it*) My milk and fruit
aren't upstairs. We can't help it if he got killed. Whatever we do now isn't going to do him any good.

WILKIE (*to* JULIE) Yes. He'll be all right.

CORA Henry just told me. He puts everything so badly
that it came as a shock. (HANNAH *appears carrying milk
and a small plate of fruit*) Yes. You forgot it, didn't you?

HANNAH (*looking at* WILKIE, *curiously*) I didn't think
you'd starve. (*Watches* CORA *drink the milk*) Funny
how you drink it just like you need it— (*Motions to
the window*) and those kids down town don't say
anything.

CORA (*hysterical, childish voice*) Take it. Take it. Everything is begrudged me.

HANNAH (*to* JULIE, *gruffly, kindly*) Do you want something Mrs. Rodman?

JULIE (*softly, without looking up*) No, thank you,
Hannah.

(ANDREW *and* ELLICOTT *enter from the Center doors.* AN-
DREW *comes directly into the room,* ELLICOTT *stands at
the door.* JULIE *gets up as if she were going to turn to*
ANDREW, *then slowly turns away again.*)

ANDREW (*to* WILKIE) I'm sorry about Dowel, Wilkie.
(*Then slowly*) But I won't pretend that I am not more
sorry that murder happened in this town. We're not a
tough people here, and we're not used to it.

WILKIE Somebody was tough enough.

ANDREW Yes. That's true, and that shocks me most. But
that means that I pushed them into it, and that I'm
responsible for it. I know these people here.

CORA Do you know that they won't come around to murder us, too?

ANDREW (*to* WILKIE) This murder is for the police. Not
for you and me. Your bill will be paid for the week, of
course. Wilkie, I want you and your people out of here
tonight.

JULIE (*turns quickly*) Yes. Yes. That's right for you,
Andy—

CORA Are you crazy?

ELLICOTT I told you upstairs that the decision wasn't entirely up to you.

ANDREW (*to* ELLICOTT) But my part *is* up to me. (*To*
WILKIE) I know I've been a hard man to work for. I
didn't want you here, and I was right. We can't undo
what's been done. But we can stop any further trouble.

WILKIE (*quietly*) I want the people who did it, Mr.
Rodman.

ANDREW I understand. The police will do that for you.

WILKIE (*pleasantly*) I don't think you do understand. I'm
not talking about Mossie. I'm not crying about that.
That was his job. He got paid for it. But somebody's
been killed and that somebody worked for me. If I'm
going to stay in business I can't let people get the idea
they can slice up my folks. (*Less pleasantly*) And I
won't. I can't make you let me keep this job. But I can't
leave tonight. I'm the police here, Mr. Rodman, and if
I wasn't worrying about finishing a job I was hired for,
I'd have to think of that.

ANDREW   (*with force*)   I won't have any more trouble.

WILKIE   That's just what I'm trying to avoid for you. I want the guns and the knives and the bricks cleaned out, and no more murders. That's what you want too, isn't it? When the guns get put away in a nice, safe spot you and your boys can talk things over. But before I leave here, they're going to be put away. (*Gets up, looks at his watch*) That's the way it'll have to be, Mr. Rodman. No reason why things shouldn't be swell and peaceful. All I want is the guns, and if they don't intend to use 'em, they should be glad to give 'em up.

CORA   That's right. That's the nice way to do it—

ANDREW   (*furiously*)   No. That's not what I want done. No—

HANNAH   You can't let him do that. They can't walk in a house and take anything. Maybe the government can take things, but you— (*Motioning to the others in the room*) you can't take them. Why, you let him go near one of their houses and they'll think you're crazy. You ain't got any rights they haven't got. They could come in here and take from you—

ELLICOTT   Andrew. We want this thing finished. It's gone on for weeks now. We've got to get it over soon—

JULIE   (*to* ELLICOTT)   Andy's right. There's been trouble enough.

CORA   (*to* ANDREW)   I don't know why you're so worried about *them*. You should protect us—

JULIE   (*to* CORA)   What are you talking about? How can you talk that way about people you went to school with, people you've known all your life—

HANNAH   (*bitterly*)   She never liked them. I know. I remember the school days.

ANDREW   (*sharply*)   Stop it. (*To* ELLICOTT)   I won't have any more trouble.

ELLICOTT   He's told you there won't be any trouble—

(*As he speaks, there is the sudden, distant sound of firing. They all turn slowly to stare at the window.* WILKIE *puts his watch back into his pocket, moves toward his overcoat as the firing starts again, this time four or five shots in rapid succession.*)

WILKIE (*shakes his head*) That's too bad. Too bad. (*Starts for door*) Rest easy, Miss Cora, the law will protect you.

(*He exits as they stand stiff and silent. Then suddenly, HANNAH bursts into tears and begins to run from the room. The others do not move until CORA rises, brushes off her robe, starts for the door.*)

CORA It is too bad. Well, all this excitement has made me very tired and nervous. We all get far too worked up about everything. (*As she gets to door*) Mr. Wilkie knows more about these things than we do.

Curtain

Act Three

The same as Act One. Seven-thirty the next morning.

AT RISE: JULIE *is sitting in a chair, wrapped in a coat, her head thrown back. Several of the lamps are still lit, although the dull early light of a rainy morning is beginning to come through. The room is as it was at the end of the second act, but it has the mussed, unaired look of a morning-after living room. A few seconds after the rise of the curtain,* ANDREW, *in an overcoat, opens the Center doors. He comes in slowly, tired. Automatically, he puts the bunch of front door keys back into his pocket.*

JULIE (*without looking up*) It stopped a little while ago. Thank God. (*She shudders, looks up at him*) Are you all right, Andy?

ANDREW (*slowly*) Remember the last time we went riding early in the morning? Well, when we came to the high point on Tucker's Road, I thought that I didn't like to ride much anymore. When you don't know anything about poetry, you know how you feel sometimes when you see things? That's the way I always felt about the high point, because I could look down on the town and that made me happy. It always looks so scrubbed and clean and I thought the way I used to, when I was a kid: that I could stop in any house and have a good breakfast and they'd be glad to see me. (*Violently*) It doesn't look so pretty this morning. And they couldn't be glad to have me for breakfast. (*Turns away, then quickly*) Yes, I'm all right. The partnership of Ellicott and Wilkie practically locked me in the office. They were busy and I'd only have been a nuisance.

JULIE (*again*) It stopped a while ago. Why did it stop? Did you stop it?

ANDREW (*bitterly*) No. Not me. I didn't stop it. (*Slowly*) People got hurt. I guess that's why it stopped.

JULIE (*gets up, starts to turn out lamps*) I've been using guns all my life— (*Turns*) Who got hurt?

ANDREW But the guns sound different when they're not for fun, don't they? I don't know who got hurt. There was some fuss around Corley's house and— (*Softly*) around Firth's.

JULIE (*carefully*) Was Whalen—was Leo Whalen—was he hurt?

ANDREW He's in jail.

JULIE (*sharply*) In jail? What for? Wilkie told me—

ANDREW (*wearily*) I don't know. Something about that fat man. They think he got into a fight with him and— (*Sits down suddenly*) My God, I'm tired.

JULIE He can't— I can't— (*She stands watching him, then turns away as if she had changed her mind.*)

ANDREW I tried to get down to Firth's, but they wouldn't let me.

JULIE (*as if she were thinking of something else*) Maybe it was just a fight. Maybe no one was hurt.

ANDREW Maybe. Maybe.

JULIE (*suddenly, violently*) Why didn't you stop it? Why did you let it go on like this? They talked you into it. Why did you let them?

ANDREW (*smiles*) You make me sound like a child. And you're right.

JULIE You didn't want any of this. Why did you ever have to start it? Then why didn't you stop it?

ANDREW You asked me that before. (*Slowly, with force*) There are a lot of reasons. The reason I tell myself is that I couldn't stop anything. I owe money. A lot of money. (*Bitterly*) I've been borrowing it for a long time. I've borrowed on the factory and on this house

and on how many brushes I thought I could make in
five years—

JULIE   Oh. (*Carefully*) From Henry?

ANDREW   Oh, from everybody. From banks, from dealers—
mostly from Henry.

JULIE   But why did you borrow it? We didn't need it—

ANDREW   Oh, I got pushed and pushed until—until I
couldn't help myself. (*Looks up at her, smiles*) Don't
worry about it. If I were another kind of man, I guess I
wouldn't have let that make any difference.

JULIE   I didn't know any of that. (*After a second*) There
are a lot of things we don't know about each other.

ANDREW   I suppose so, darling. That's the way with most
marriages, I guess.

JULIE   Andy. He can't stay in jail. He had nothing to do
with that man. I was with him last night when it happened. With Whalen.

ANDREW   (*there is a pause. Then he slowly raises his head
to look at her, speaks quietly, carefully*) Then you
shouldn't let him stay in jail, Julie. That's not right.
(*Sharply*) Why are you acting so strange? Why didn't
you say so and get him out? There's nothing to be
ashamed of— (*She looks at him, nods, starts for windows*) Julie! (*She turns*) Never mind. I'll do it. (*He
rises as she watches him go to telephone. Into phone*)
Operator, call Judge Alcott's house. (*To* JULIE) Didn't
you know he'd been arrested?

JULIE   No. I'd been told—

ANDREW   (*through her last words, into phone*) Jim? This
is Andrew Rodman. I want you to let Leo Whalen out
of jail immediately. We—er—I know where he was last
night. I'll be down later and explain. (*Sharply*) Jim. I
don't give a damn what anybody said. Let him out.
(*Wearily*) Yes. Yes. Thanks. No. Everything's all right.

JULIE   Thank you, Andy.

ANDREW   What are you thanking me for? (*As if for himself*) It's not important. You don't have to thank me.

JULIE   (*quietly*) We've been dealing with people shrewder
than we are.

ANDREW   Yes, I suppose so. I suppose that's it.

(*He passes his hand over his eyes. She makes a half motion toward him, changes her mind, turns away. A second later,* FIRTH *appears in the Center doors. He is dirty, bruised and tired-looking. In his hand is a gun. It is hanging at his side, as if he had forgotten it. Through all his speeches, through his exit, he holds the gun, unconscious that he has it. He stands in the doorway as they both look up.*)

FIRTH (*aimlessly*) The front door's open. The rain's coming in. (*Then shakes his head, bewildered*) I don't know what to do with you, Andrew.

JULIE (*in a whisper*) What is it, Tom? What is it?

(ANDREW *is standing by the desk, staring at* FIRTH.)

FIRTH When you can't have a kid, that's bad. It makes a man feel funny, like he can't do anything, and not the way it should be. Specially a big man. You feel like you can't do what you're here for. (*Directly to* ANDREW) Remember once when you were at that college and you came home for Christmas and you came to a meal and after Miriam went up, I told you about it. I cried. Remember? (ANDREW *stares, nods slowly*) They hit her here. (*Puts his hand on the back of his head*) They said she threw a brick. A little kid threw a brick. They broke something.

ANDREW (*horror in his voice*) Where's Morris? Where is he?

FIRTH (*shakes his head as if he were drunk*) It's worse, I guess, when it's an adopted kid. You like it better that way. It makes up for the other thing and you like it better— (*Quietly*) Doc Morris? He's down there, Talking. Telling me what broke. Telling me why it happened. Talking and talking. Talking won't make her live again.

JULIE (*in a whisper*) Oh my God.

ANDREW (*looks up, softly*) They killed her. (*He nods slowly, puts his hand to his mouth, comes to* FIRTH, *takes him by the arm, then lets him go suddenly.*)

FIRTH I don't know what to do. I beat everybody up for a while like crazy, telling myself what I was going to do to you. (*Violently, shaking his finger at* ANDREW)

But I know you. I know you. It's better to tell you. It'll do worse for you. (*Suddenly, quietly*) I can't touch you, Andrew. I'm too tired. (*He sits down, as if he couldn't stand any longer. Then, as if it were an old familiar position between them,* ANDREW *sits opposite him. For a second, neither of them speaks. To* JULIE, *without looking up*) Once she saw you coming home from school and she told me you were pretty and I told her that you weren't half as pretty as her, and not an ounce as pretty as she'd grow to be. She laughed and got red and said she wasn't pretty and that I just liked her— (*Quietly, but with passion*) How can I go home? How can I live? How can I sit and eat with Miriam when only yesterday the kid sat between us—

JULIE (*choking, desperately, to* ANDREW) Do something for him.

ANDREW (*looks up at her in surprise*) What is there to do?

FIRTH There's nothing to do. And I wouldn't let you do it. Ain't it funny how everything's changed? (ANDREW *nods*) I've known you all your life. All my life I worked for your father, or for you. I liked you more—more than anybody except my own, I guess. (*Puzzled*) I guess you can't know anybody. You must have been bad all along.

ANDREW (*leans over to touch his arm, nods*) I must have been.

JULIE Tom, Andrew didn't know. He didn't know anything bad would happen—

FIRTH (*shakes his head*) That does a lot of good. (*Slowly*) If my kid had—had died any other way, you'd been the first I'd come to. I guess I never knew you. I don't understand that.

ANDREW (*simply*) I don't understand it, either.

FIRTH Well, I can't fight anymore. I wouldn't know how. We ain't used to things like last night. Lundee got his hand shot off— (ANDREW *gets up and turns away sharply*) They burnt Carlsen's house all to pieces. We always used to play penny-ante there. We had to drag Berthe out, she was half crazy. She got burnt a little. (*On the next·speech,* WHALEN *appears in the open*

Center doors. EASTER *has him by the arm. All three people see him, and all three stare at him.* FIRTH's *voice becomes defiant, and the next speech is meant for* WHALEN, *but is said directly to* ANDREW) I don't know, but I guess I can speak for most of 'em. We can't fight you when you fight like this. It's our town more'n it's yours. Our folks came and built it. We can't watch it go like this. (*Gets up, wearily, quietly*) You call off your dogs. Keep 'em away from us, so there won't be no more killing. Get 'em out of here. I guess we'll have to go back to work.

EASTER   I picked him up trying to shove in the front door. There wouldn't been any door in a minute. He's in jail.

ANDREW   (*to* EASTER)   Get out of here.

EASTER   Oh. (*Looks at him and begins to exit.*)

WHALEN   (*to* EASTER)   What's Wilkie do? Keep you for the knife work? (*Motions toward hall*) Don't let you in the rough fights, huh? (EASTER *looks at him, exits.* WHALEN *comes into the room, smiles pleasantly*) Somebody got soft and let me out of jail. (*To* FIRTH) They told me where you were. I could have guessed.

FIRTH   They killed my kid.

WHALEN   I got all the news.

FIRTH   I feel bad. I can't fight anymore.

WHALEN   I heard you.

FIRTH   (*angrily*)   It wasn't your kid.

WHALEN   (*angrily*)   Didn't I tell you to give them what they wanted? Didn't I tell you not to fight?

FIRTH   (*quietly*)   You were right.

WHALEN   (*looks at* FIRTH *and then at* RODMAN, *and laughs*) You both look the same kind of surprised. What are you surprised at? What the hell did you think he was after— (*To* ANDREW) Or do you still believe he came down to make brushes for you?

ANDREW   (*slowly*)   No.

WHALEN   (*to* FIRTH)   He wanted you to fight. He's been trying to make you fight for weeks. So as soon as he gets me out of the way for a couple of hours, you give him the fight he's been waiting for.

FIRTH   I couldn't do anything. When they come in talking

and shoving, you don't think. Then they hit my kid— (*As if he hadn't said it before*) My girl's dead.

WHALEN   (*shouting*)   All right. She's dead. What are you trying to do, make Joan of Arc out of her? You wanted to fight—till the time came. Well, here's your time. If they killed my kid, I wouldn't come crawling back to any lousy job—

JULIE   There's been enough trouble. Don't let's make any more.

FIRTH   I don't want any more. We ain't used to this. We're tired. We don't care so much who wins, like you—

WHALEN   (*quietly*)   You *will* care. More than I do. For me, you're only one of a thousand fights. But you've only got one fight. This one. And someday you're going to have to settle it.

FIRTH   There's no use arguing. I'm trying to tell you why and what and you don't understand. (*Gets up, wearily.*)

WHALEN   Your why and what aren't any good to me.

FIRTH   I can't seem to say what I'm getting at. All I'm saying is that it came too quick. We didn't know about the things you know about. Everybody's got to see for themselves, I guess.

WHALEN   You haven't seen anything. They didn't scratch the surface here.

FIRTH   (*nods his head*)   Yeah? Well, maybe you were right, when you said that all the time. Wouldn't make any sense to hold out now. There wouldn't be any spirit to hold out with. I guess I'm worse than anybody, because of my kid. We'll go on back, make the best of it. (*Turns, quietly*) And if the time comes again, we'll be different. We'll know. I don't like him now. He killed my kid. They don't like him, either. We won't forget.

ANDREW   (*with force, to* WHALEN)   That's the truth. He's telling you the truth. They won't forget.

WHALEN   (*to* FIRTH)   He didn't kill your kid. Don't start that, or you'll get the wrong answer again. He hasn't much to do with it. He's got to go his way, and you've got to go yours. And they're not the same way.

FIRTH   (*softly*)   We used to be good friends.

WHALEN   I know. And you're as good as he is. It says so

in the book. Until the time comes. Look. You're on one side. He's on the other. That's lesson number one. Don't let 'em tell you that because your grandfather voted for Jefferson you're any different from some Polack in Pittsburgh whose grandfather couldn't write his name. You're on the same side the Polack is, and that's where you belong.

FIRTH   Well, maybe we'll try again some day.

WHALEN   (*smiles, as if he were pleased*)   I hope so. And the guy they send in my place, you give him a better chance.

FIRTH   (*starts for door*)   You coming? They'd like to see you.

WHALEN   (*shakes his head*)   No. I'm going to be busy for a while.

ANDREW   (*softly*)   Tom, would you let me do anything for you and Miriam and the others?

FIRTH   (*without turning, puzzled*)   What? (*Laughs, then quietly*)   Stay away from downtown, Andrew. For a while. (JULIE, *watching the effect of this on* ANDREW, *moves to him, puts a hand on his sleeve.* FIRTH *speaks to* WHALEN)   Well, if it comes again, I hope they'll be sending you.

WHALEN   (*simply, sincerely*)   I hope so, too. (FIRTH *exits. No one speaks for a second*)   Well, it's time for me to see whether your pink-cheeked policeman is holding me for murder or because I've got two legs. He's having a tough time deciding. (*He has started for door.*)

JULIE   (*quickly*)   Wait. You don't have to go back there. They won't hold you— (*On her speech, he has turned.*)

ANDREW   (*who is still looking at the door, as if he were thinking of* FIRTH)   I've spoken to Judge Alcott. There's no need for you to go back. Everything will be straightened out.

WHALEN   (*carefully*)   Straightened out, Mr. Rodman?

JULIE   (*after a second, softly*)   I've told my husband that I was in your office last night when it happened.

WHALEN   (*has turned to look at* ANDREW, *and then back to* JULIE)   Is that what you are going to say?

JULIE   Yes. (*Not looking at him*)   I wanted to before. But

—but I was told that you weren't in any trouble, and that I'd be doing you harm.

WHALEN (*quietly*) You were told right. (*Looks quickly at them both*) Please. Don't do that. They've got nothing on me, and they know it. A few days of nuisance, maybe, and that's all. That's my job. I don't want trouble for myself, ever, but when it comes it's part of my work.

JULIE (*looking at him*) Why don't you want any help from us? From me?

WHALEN It's not my job to take help from the boss, or— (*Slowly*) the boss's wife. I can't take chances on anybody thinking I do.

(WILKIE *comes in through Center doors.*)

WILKIE Good morning. (*To* ANDREW) Glad to see you here. We were worried about you. (*To* WHALEN) Good morning.

WHALEN Had a good breakfast?

WILKIE Pretty good. I'm like the English, I eat big in the mornings.

WHALEN I thought so. You look like you've been licking the cream.

WILKIE You need some breakfast?

WHALEN (*laughs*) No, thank you. I'm eating on the county. With the marshal.

WILKIE (*looking toward* JULIE, *then back to* WHALEN) That. Oh. That's yokel stuff. They got nothing to hold you on.

WHALEN They held me long enough to make it easy for you.

WILKIE My break this time. Maybe yours the next.

(ELLICOTT *appears in the hall. Comes in, throws his coat and hat on a chair.*)

ELLICOTT (*looking at* JULIE *and* ANDREW, *quietly*) Good morning.

WHALEN (*to* WILKIE) Your spick outside looks like a knife thrower to me. What do you think?

WILKIE (*seriously*) I don't know. Maybe so. You can't keep track of everybody. I don't like to see a man get buried without finding who did it— If you know anything—

WHALEN   (*laughs*) I don't know anything. Some other time. (*Crosses to* JULIE *and says kindly, with meaning*) Don't worry about last night. There's no honor involved in any of it. And if there was it wouldn't be practical to remember it. (*Holds out his hand to her*) Good-bye, Mrs. Rodman.

JULIE   (*touches his hand, speaks softly*)   Good-bye.

WHALEN   (*to* ANDREW) Good-bye.

ANDREW   Good-bye.

(WHALEN *exits.*)

ELLICOTT   (*to* JULIE) You look tired. (*No answer. He looks at his watch*) Almost eight o'clock. I haven't been up this early in a long time.

WILKIE   Does you good sometimes.

JULIE   (*to* ANDREW) What are they talking about? What are they cheerful about?

ANDREW   (*slowly*) I don't know.

JULIE   (*to* ELLICOTT) Did you have a good time? Was it more exciting than being at the club? Is it fun to see a killing?

ELLICOTT   (*sharply*) Stop it. (*After a second*) We've been fighting your husband's battles for him.

ANDREW   Yes. That's quite true. The delicate prince in his ivory tower— (*Carefully*) was carefully protected from the dust and din of battle. You are noble warriors and you've done a noble night's work. (*Sharply to* ELLICOTT) I'll see to it that when the history is written, it won't be mentioned that you were fighting for yourself, too.

ELLICOTT   I knew nothing about the child until Morris told me.

WILKIE   I knew you were going to feel this way, Mr. Rodman. But nobody wanted any trouble. Sometimes these things can't be helped. I understand it's going to be settled now and I'm glad for you, and glad for me. (*Smiles*) I don't like to take money for losing, and for a while—

ANDREW   Send us your bill. We'll mail you a check.

WILKIE   Yes, sir. (*Goes to him, puts out his hand*) Thank you, Mr. Rodman—

ANDREW   (*ignores the hand*)   That's all. Good-bye.

WILKIE   (*looks down at his hand, laughs*)   Well, that's your business. But I want to tell you, I've worked for a lot of men, some of them deacons of the church who were breaking strikes for the good of America, but I never worked for a man before who believed I could come in, run his factory, and break his strike without walking on anybody's toes. You actually believed that. I come in to break strikes. That's my business. It's *not* a tea room business. You ought to have known that. Well, I break your strike and now you're sitting on the right hand of Jesus, crying because it doesn't smell of violets.

ELLICOTT   (*sharply*)   Does this speech go on your bill?

WILKIE   No. I'm giving it free of charge. If you didn't like what I was doing, you should have stopped it. But you didn't stop it, and that doesn't leave you in any place to call names. The boys standing in your shoes need the boys standing in mine. But the next time I have to waste weeks acting like it was a tea party, the next time I have to nurse along a blind man— (*Laughs carefully*) a blind man who calls the turns when they're over—I'm going to charge extra. (*Picks up his hat as he passes* ELLICOTT) There'll be expense items on my bill.

ELLICOTT   You'll get your check.

WILKIE   Good morning.

(*There is a long silence.* ELLICOTT *lights a cigarette, looks at* JULIE, *moves uncomfortably about the room.*)

ELLICOTT   Well, Andy— (*No answer*) What's the matter with you?

ANDREW   (*unpleasantly*)   Very little. I'm over here thinking how I don't like being a murderer. You are fortunate. You don't seem to mind so much.

ELLICOTT   (*angrily*)   I knew nothing about the child. But I did know there had to be trouble. (*Carefully*) And I'm not willing to act the saint about it now.

ANDREW   That's wise for you. I hope the little trouble last night won't keep you from White Sulphur.

ELLICOTT   It won't. I'm going tonight.

ANDREW   I wish you a happy journey, and I hope that your dreams are free.

ELLICOTT (*angrily*) If it makes you feel better to enjoy your conscience, go ahead. There was a lot of truth in what that bum just said.

ANDREW Yes. There was. But did he know that *you* were also his employer? You own so much of me now— (JULIE *has turned to look at them as* ANDREW *breaks off.* ANDREW *sees her, and speaks as if he had been thinking of her all along*) Why were you with Whalen last night?

(ELLICOTT *turns quickly to look at her.*)

JULIE You don't want to hear about it, Andy.

(ANDREW *begins to speak as* LUCY *comes into the room, carrying a small table with breakfast on it. She is followed by* CORA, *in a bathrobe.*)

CORA The noise that's been going on here this morning. (*Puts up a commanding hand*) Now. Please. Please. Don't tell me about last night. I've heard all about it. Lucy had it from Morris' nurse, and insisted upon telling it to me. It's awful. Simply awful. (*Leans over, smells the chocolate pot. Then to* LUCY) Did Hannah make this chocolate? Take it back.

LUCY No, ma'am. I made it. Hannah's out.

CORA Out? At this time of the morning? (*To everybody as* LUCY *exits*) What do you think of that? Out at this time of the morning.

ELLICOTT Do you have to have your breakfast here? In this room?

CORA (*as she starts to eat*) Mind your business. I've had it here for thirty years. I shall continue—

ANDREW (*who has been staring at* JULIE, *paying no attention to* CORA) Julie! Why were you in Whalen's office?

JULIE (*desperately*) Andy, I don't want to— Don't let's talk about it now.

ANDREW Julie. Answer me.

JULIE I wanted to go away with him. I wanted to tell him that.

(ANDREW *rises from his chair, and then, slowly, sits down again.* CORA *puts down her spoon suddenly.*)

ELLICOTT My God, you're a foolish woman.

JULIE (*quietly*) That wasn't foolish. It was what I wanted. It would have been right for me.

CORA (*looking around the room, in a daze*) Is she crazy?

ELLICOTT But he didn't want you to go away with him?

JULIE No.

ANDREW Leave her alone.

CORA (*springing from her chair*) Look at you. So you're just finding out about your wife, are you? Then you're the only one who is. She's been doing this for years.

ELLICOTT Cora. Cora—

CORA (*ignoring the interruption, to* ANDREW) Now she's decided to tell you, finally. (*With great scorn*) "Leave her alone" you tell him. How can he leave her alone? All that's his business, too.

ELLICOTT (*furiously*) Cora, I tell you—

JULIE (*quietly*) Let her say it. She's wanted to for a long time.

CORA Yes. I could have told you about them a long time ago. She's just as much Henry's business as she is yours. Just as much. I knew. I made it my business to know. He's crazy about her. (*Shrieking*) You fool. You fool. All these years—

ANDREW (*he has been staring at her, then as if he were speaking to an insane person*) Control yourself. Get away from my desk. Go back to your breakfast.

CORA (*to* JULIE) You were never fooling me. Never for a minute fooling me.

JULIE I'm glad.

ELLICOTT (*after a long silence, while* CORA *paces around restlessly*) Well, it's a nasty story, Andy. Your best friend and—

CORA And his wife.

ANDREW (*looks up at* ELLICOTT, *smiles*) In what strange ways you think of things. Did you read somewhere that it was wicked to sleep with your best friend's wife? Was it a vulgar book you read it in? Or does the fact that it was *my* wife make it more sinful, and therefore more pleasant?

CORA (*to* JULIE) I knew what you were doing to my brother. I knew every bit of it.

JULIE (*comes toward* ANDREW, *slowly*) I wasn't doing anything to you. Not the way she means. (*She sits down, opposite him*) Andy. I wasn't in love with you when I married you. That was what I did to you. The rest had only to do with me. I didn't want to get married. I didn't want to live here. I wanted to make something for myself, something that would be right for me. I told you all that when we were young. I thought marriage would be all that for me. But it wasn't. (*Gets up*) And when I found it wasn't, I took the wrong way. I knew I should have stopped. But I thought someday I might find somebody who—

ELLICOTT   You found him, didn't you?

JULIE   (*to* ANDREW)   Yes, I found him. It didn't do me any good. I was going to tell you that, Andy. That I thought you ought to know. But the rest—the rest was just me and just exactly as shabby as she's made it sound. (*Leans across the desk, suddenly*) Darling, I told you the truth. I wasn't in love with you when we were married. I'm not in love with you now. But I love you. Not the way I want to. But another way. More than anybody I've ever known.

ANDREW   (*softly*)   Julie. Julie. (*Motioning toward* CORA *and* ELLICOTT)   Don't listen to what they say. I know what you mean. You have done nothing to me.

CORA   No? That's a strange way of looking at it. Done nothing to you. She's broken you, that's what she's done. She's why you owe money— (JULIE *has turned and is staring at her*) to Henry and to everybody else. She's why—

ELLICOTT   (*violently*)   Is that your business, too?

CORA   No, thank you. It's not my money he's lost. But you needn't think I didn't know. I knew where it was going. The year her family lost their money and how her mother had to have the best doctors and how her brother had to go to Paris to study, and how she always had to have trips and clothes, and a year in Europe— (*With scorn*) to make her happy. Thousands and thousands he had to borrow for it—

JULIE   (*suddenly, her voice hysterical*)   I didn't know that. I swear I didn't. We always had so much. Why didn't you tell me?

ANDREW   It wasn't your business. It isn't now. I wanted it
that way. I suppose, underneath, I always knew. I
wanted to keep you. That was my way of trying. You
had nothing to do with it. Nothing at all.

CORA   And didn't it ever occur to you that was *why* Henry
lent you the money. That *she* was the reason he lent
you the money? Why shouldn't he—

ELLICOTT   (*quietly*)   That's not true.

ANDREW   No. It's not true. He made a good investment in
my business. And he protected his investment, last
night.

JULIE   (*in a whisper*)   That's why you couldn't stop—
that's why—

ANDREW   That's the reason I tell myself. It's not a good
one. (*Suddenly starts to laugh. They all watch him.
Then, after a second, he leans on his desk, smiles, talks
to* JULIE) Isn't it strange? The three of us— (*Pointing
to* CORA *and* ELLICOTT) have known each other since
we were born. My sister— (*Bows*) my best friend—
my best friend. We grew up in this town knowing all
about each other. Henry and I, for example, know that
Cora, all her life—

CORA   Be still.

ANDREW   All her life has been, well, slightly ill. Then
Cora and I know all about Henry, the rich and worldly
Henry, and all the very legal manipulating he does with
his money and with his life. They, on the other hand,
Cora and Henry know all about me. They've always
thought me a soft, weak man and they've always had
contempt for me. Hannah shares the secrets of all of us.
That's why Cora can't get rid of her, isn't it, Cora? Ten
years ago you married me and came here, and so you
were one of us, too. Our married life always had an
audience—my sister and my best friend and my cook.
All the things we knew about each other, all the things
that accumulate through a lifetime, or through ten
years, sat quietly, waiting for us, while we lived politely
and tried, like most people, to push them out of sight.
Polite and blind, we lived.

JULIE (*softly*) And then early one morning, it all blew up.

ANDREW You don't understand. It blew up last night. All the things we know were there to know a long time ago. But we were polite. We were doing our best to live happily. Well, there's no need for being polite anymore. You were my wife. (*To* ELLICOTT) You and I and Cora made me a murderer. (*To* CORA) You hate me and I hated you from the day I was old enough to think about you. You hate my wife and you have always hated her. (*To* ELLICOTT) Since we were old enough to play together, you've never had anything but toleration for me—and I've never had anything but contempt for you. That's a lot of hate, isn't it? It was all there before. (*Pleasantly*) It can be said now.

ELLICOTT (*after a moment's silence*) I'm sorry all this had to come now, Andy. That's straight. (*Motioning toward* CORA) And I'm sorry it had to come from Cora.

CORA (*calmly*) I think both of you are drunk.

ELLICOTT (*to* JULIE) Do you want me to stay?

JULIE What? Oh no. (*He looks at her for a second and then exits quickly. After his exit, nobody speaks. Then after a second,* JULIE *says softly*) What do you want me to do, Andy?

ANDREW (*after a second, puzzled*) What do you mean?

JULIE Do you want me to go away? Do you want a divorce?

ANDREW (*quietly, sadly, reproachfully*) Oh, Julie. Even you haven't understood. I'm not sitting here in tears for you or me. A year ago, a month ago, what you told me about you, about us, would have broken my heart. It will again, but not now. Because last night I lost the place and the land where I was born. (*Laughs bitterly*) I can't go downtown, he said. It isn't safe. It isn't safe for *me* to go into that town. You see what I mean. I lost what I thought I was. (*Softly*) I lost Firth his child. (*Suddenly, violently*) Murder is worse than lost love. Murder is worse than a broken heart.

JULIE (*softly*) It is. Yes.

ANDREW They said it would come again. I think they're

right. I'll be hardened to it by then, I guess, and I won't mind what happens. In a little while I'll think about us. About how I lost you, and how I never had you, and how much I loved you. But now it seems so small beside what else has happened here. (*Smiles*) And it seems almost right that it should be this way and that you should have told me this morning. It was right that it should have come. I don't know what you should do, Julie. Go to White Sulphur, if you like.

JULIE   That would be what I deserved.

ANDREW   That's foolish. You don't deserve anything. Go anywhere you like. Or nowhere. Whatever is left here is as much yours as it is mine. *That's* your punishment— if you're looking for it. For the rest of your life, my wife, for all the days to come— (*Laughs*) You can have half of all this. Half of me. I'm sorry for you. (*He has motioned with his arm around the room, toward* CORA. *Suddenly his face is dead and heavy, and he sits down in the desk chair.*)

JULIE   (*turns and stares curiously at* CORA's *cabinet. She rises*) Your animals weren't touched, Cora. They're still all right. (*She exits.*)

CORA   (*after a long silence, she pours herself some chocolate, and speaks timidly*) Things went entirely too far. It comes from everybody getting too excited. Now, you go get some sleep and nothing will seem as bad when you wake up. (*No answer. She takes a bite of toast*) People said a lot of things they didn't mean, Andy. (*Consolingly*) A lot of things they didn't mean. I'm sure of that.

ANDREW   (*doesn't answer for a minute. Then he raises his head and with great force*) Take your breakfast out of here. (*She rises hurriedly, frightened*) Get out. (*As she moves toward the door*) Get out.

Curtain

The
Little Foxes

*"Take us the foxes, the little foxes,
that spoil the vines; for our vines
have tender grapes."*

FOR
ARTHUR KOBER AND
LOUIS KRONENBERGER
WHO HAVE BEEN
MY GOOD FRIENDS

The Little Foxes was first produced at the National **Theatre,** New York City, on February 15, 1939, with the following cast:

('In the order of their appearance)

ADDIE	ABBIE MITCHELL
CAL	JOHN MARRIOTT
BIRDIE HUBBARD	PATRICIA COLLINGE
OSCAR HUBBARD	CARL BENTON REID
LEO HUBBARD	DAN DURYEA
REGINA GIDDENS	TALLULAH BANKHEAD
WILLIAM MARSHALL	LEE BAKER
BENJAMIN HUBBARD	CHARLES DINGLE
ALEXANDRA GIDDENS	FLORENCE WILLIAMS
HORACE GIDDENS	FRANK CONROY

Produced and staged by HERMAN SHUMLIN

Settings designed by HOWARD BAY

Costumes designed by ALINE BERNSTEIN

Scene

The scene of the play is the living room of
the Giddens house, in a small town in the South.

ACT ONE
The Spring of 1900, evening.

ACT TWO
A week later, early morning.

ACT THREE
Two weeks later, late afternoon.

There has been no attempt to write Southern dialect.
It is to be understood that the accents are Southern.

Act One

SCENE: *The living room of the Giddens home, in a small town in the deep South, the spring of 1900. Upstage is a staircase leading to the second story. Upstage, right, are double doors to the dining room. When these doors are open we see a section of the dining room and the furniture. Upstage, left, is an entrance hall with a coatrack and umbrella stand. There are large lace-curtained windows on the left wall. The room is lit by a center gas chandelier and painted china oil lamps on the tables. Against the wall is a large piano. Downstage, right, are a high couch, a large table, several chairs. Against the left back wall are a table and several chairs. Near the window there are a smaller couch and tables. The room is good-looking, the furniture expensive; but it reflects no particular taste. Everything is of the best and that is all.*

AT RISE: ADDIE, *a tall, nice-looking Negro woman of about fifty-five, is closing the windows. From behind the closed dining-room doors there is the sound of voices. After a second, CAL, a middle-aged Negro, comes in from the entrance hall carrying a tray with glasses and a bottle of port. ADDIE crosses, takes the tray from him, puts it on table, begins to arrange it.*

ADDIE (*pointing to the bottle*) You gone stark out of your head?

CAL No, smart lady, I ain't. Miss Regina told me to get out that bottle. (*Points to bottle*) That very bottle for

151

the mighty honored guest. When Miss Regina changes orders like that you can bet your dime she got her reason.

ADDIE (*points to dining room*) Go on. You'll be needed.

CAL Miss Zan she had two helpings frozen fruit cream and she tell that honored guest, she tell him that you make the best frozen fruit cream in all the South.

ADDIE (*smiles, pleased*) Did she? Well, see that Belle saves a little for her. She like it right before she go to bed. Save a few little cakes, too, she like—

(*The dining-room doors are opened and quickly closed again by* BIRDIE HUBBARD. BIRDIE *is a woman of about forty, with a pretty, well-bred, faded face. Her movements, are usually nervous and timid, but now, as she comes running into the room, she is gay and excited.* CAL *turns to* BIRDIE.)

BIRDIE Oh, Cal. (*Closes door*) I want you to get one of the kitchen boys to run home for me. He's to look in my desk drawer and— (*To* ADDIE) My, Addie. What a good supper! Just as good as good can be.

ADDIE You look pretty this evening, Miss Birdie, and young.

BIRDIE (*laughing*) Me, young? (*Turns back to* CAL) Maybe you better find Simon and tell him to do it himself. He's to look in my desk, the left drawer, and bring my music album right away. Mr. Marshall is very anxious to see it because of his father and the opera in Chicago. (*To* ADDIE) Mr. Marshall is such a polite man with his manners and very educated and cultured and I've told him all about how my mama and papa used to go to Europe for the music— (*Laughs. To* ADDIE) Imagine going all the way to Europe just to listen to music. Wouldn't that be nice, Addie? Just to sit there and listen and— (*Turns and steps to* CAL) Left drawer, Cal. Tell him that twice because he forgets. And tell him not to let any of the things drop out of the album and to bring it right in here when he comes back.

(*The dining-room doors are opened and quickly closed by* OSCAR HUBBARD. *He is a man in his late forties.*)

CAL Yes'm. But Simon he won't get it right. But I'll tell him.

BIRDIE Left drawer, Cal, and tell him to bring the blue book and—

OSCAR (*sharply*) Birdie.

BIRDIE (*turning nervously*) Oh, Oscar. I was just sending Simon for my music album.

OSCAR (*to* CAL) Never mind about the album. Miss Birdie has changed her mind.

BIRDIE But, really, Oscar. Really I promised Mr. Marshall. I—

(CAL *looks at them, exits.*)

OSCAR Why do you leave the dinner table and go running about like a child?

BIRDIE (*trying to be gay*) But, Oscar, Mr. Marshall said most specially he *wanted* to see my album. I told him about the time Mama met Wagner, and Mrs. Wagner gave her the signed program and the big picture. Mr. Marshall wants to see that. Very, very much. We had such a nice talk and—

OSCAR (*taking a step to her*) You have been chattering to him like a magpie. You haven't let him be for a second. I can't think he came South to be bored with you.

BIRDIE (*quickly, hurt*) He wasn't bored. I don't believe he was bored. He's a very educated, cultured gentleman. (*Her voice rises*) I just don't believe it. You always talk like that when I'm having a nice time.

OSCAR (*turning to her, sharply*) You have had too much wine. Get yourself in hand now.

BIRDIE (*drawing back, about to cry, shrilly*) What am I doing? I am not doing anything. What am I doing?

OSCAR (*taking a step to her, tensely*) I said get yourself in hand. Stop acting like a fool.

BIRDIE (*turns to him, quietly*) I don't believe he was bored. I just don't believe it. Some people like music and like to talk about it. That's all I was doing.

(LEO HUBBARD *comes hurrying through the dining-room door. He is a young man of twenty, with a weak kind of good looks.*)

LEO Mama! Papa! They are coming in now.

OSCAR   (*softly*) Sit down, Birdie. Sit down now. (BIRDIE *sits down, bows her head as if to hide her face.*)

(*The dining-room doors are opened by* CAL. *We see people beginning to rise from the table.* REGINA GIDDENS *comes in with* WILLIAM MARSHALL. REGINA *is a handsome woman of forty.* MARSHALL *is forty-five, pleasant-looking, self-possessed. Behind them comes* ALEXANDRA GIDDENS, *a very pretty, rather delicate-looking girl of seventeen. She is followed by* BENJAMIN HUBBARD, *fifty-five, with a large jovial face and the light graceful movements that one often finds in large men.*)

REGINA   Mr. Marshall, I think you're trying to console me. Chicago may be the noisiest, dirtiest city in the world but I should still prefer it to the sound of our horses and the smell of our azaleas. I should like crowds of people, and theaters, and lovely women— *Very* lovely women, Mr. Marshall?

MARSHALL   (*crossing to sofa*) In Chicago? Oh, I suppose so. But I can tell you this: I've never dined there with *three* such lovely ladies.

(ADDIE *begins to pass the port.*)

BEN   Our Southern women are well favored.

LEO   (*laughs*) But one must go to Mobile for the ladies, sir. Very elegant worldly ladies, too.

BEN   (*looks at him very deliberately*) Worldly, eh? *Worldly*, did you say?

OSCAR   (*hastily, to* LEO) Your uncle Ben means that worldliness is not a mark of beauty in any woman.

LEO   (*quickly*) Of course, Uncle Ben. I didn't mean—

MARSHALL   Your port is excellent, Mrs. Giddens.

REGINA   Thank you, Mr. Marshall. We had been saving that bottle, hoping we could open it just for you.

ALEXANDRA   (*as* ADDIE *comes to her with the tray*) Oh. May I *really*, Addie?

ADDIE   Better ask Mama.

ALEXANDRA   May I, Mama?

REGINA   (*nods, smiles*) In Mr. Marshall's honor.

ALEXANDRA   (*smiles*) Mr. Marshall, this will be the first taste of port I've ever had.

(ADDIE *serves* LEO.)

MARSHALL   No one ever had their first taste of a better port. (*He lifts his glass in a toast; she lifts hers; they both drink*) Well, I suppose it is all true, Mrs. Giddens.

REGINA   What is true?

MARSHALL   That you Southerners occupy a unique position in America. You live better than the rest of us, you eat better, you drink better. I wonder you find time, or want to find time, to do business.

BEN   A great many Southerners don't.

MARSHALL   Do all of you live here together?

REGINA   Here with me? (*Laughs*) Oh, no. My brother Ben lives next door. My brother Oscar and his family live in the next square.

BEN   But we are a very close family. We've always wanted it that way.

MARSHALL   That is very pleasant. Keeping your family together to share each other's lives. My family moves around too much. My children seem never to come home. Away at school in the winter; in the summer, Europe with their mother—

REGINA   (*eagerly*) Oh, yes. Even down here we read about Mrs. Marshall in the society pages.

MARSHALL   I dare say. She moves about a great deal. And all of you are part of the same business? Hubbard Sons?

BEN   (*motions to* OSCAR) Oscar and me. (*Motions to* REGINA) My sister's good husband is a banker.

MARSHALL   (*looks at* REGINA, *surprised*) Oh.

REGINA   I am so sorry that my husband isn't here to meet you. He's been very ill. He is at Johns Hopkins. But he will be home soon. We think he is getting better now.

LEO   I work for Uncle Horace. (REGINA *looks at him*) I mean I work for Uncle Horace at his bank. I keep an eye on things while he's away.

REGINA   (*smiles*) Really, Leo?

BEN   (*looks at* LEO, *then to* MARSHALL) Modesty in the young is as excellent as it is rare. (*Looks at* LEO *again.*)

OSCAR   (*to* LEO) Your uncle means that a young man should speak more modestly.

LEO   (*hastily, taking a step to* BEN) Oh, I didn't mean, sir—

MARSHALL   Oh, Mrs. Hubbard. Where's that Wagner autograph you promised to let me see? My train will be leaving soon and—

BIRDIE   The autograph? Oh. Well. Really, Mr. Marshall, I didn't mean to chatter so about it. Really I— (*Nervously, looking at* OSCAR) You must excuse me. I didn't get it because, well, because I had—I—I had a little headache and—

OSCAR   My wife is a miserable victim of headaches.

REGINA   (*quickly*) Mr. Marshall said at supper that he would like you to play for him, Alexandra.

ALEXANDRA   (*who has been looking at* BIRDIE) It's not I who play well, sir. It's my aunt. She plays just wonderfully. She's my teacher. (*Rises. Eagerly*) May we play a duet? May we, Mama?

BIRDIE   (*taking* ALEXANDRA's *hand*) Thank you, dear. But I have my headache now. I—

OSCAR   (*sharply*) Don't be stubborn, Birdie. Mr. Marshall wants you to play.

MARSHALL   Indeed I do. If your headache isn't—

BIRDIE   (*hesitates, then gets up, pleased*) But I'd like to, sir. Very much. (*She and* ALEXANDRA *go to the piano.*)

MARSHALL   It's very remarkable how you Southern aristocrats have kept together. Kept together and kept what belonged to you.

BEN   You misunderstand, sir. Southern aristocrats have *not* kept together and have *not* kept what belonged to them.

MARSHALL   (*laughs, indicates room*) You don't call this keeping what belongs to you?

BEN   But we are not aristocrats. (*Points to* BIRDIE *at the piano*) Our brother's wife is the only one of us who belongs to the Southern aristocracy.

(BIRDIE *looks toward* BEN.)

MARSHALL   (*smiles*) My information is that you people have been here, and solidly here, for a long time.

OSCAR   And so we have. Since our great-grandfather.

BEN   (*smiles*) Who was *not* an aristocrat, like Birdie's.

MARSHALL   (*a little sharply*) You make great distinctions.

BEN   Oh, they have been made for us. And maybe they are important distinctions. (*Leans forward, intimately*)

Now you take Birdie's family. When my great-grand-father came here they were the highest-tone plantation owners in this state.

LEO (*steps to* MARSHALL. *Proudly*) My mother's grand-father was *governor* of the state before the war.

OSCAR They owned the plantation, Lionnet. You may have heard of it, sir?

MARSHALL (*laughs*) No, I've never heard of anything but brick houses on a lake, and cotton mills.

BEN Lionnet in its day was the best cotton land in the South. It still brings us in a fair crop. (*Sits back*) Ah, they were great days for those people—even when I can remember. They had the best of everything. (BIRDIE *turns to them*) Cloth from Paris, trips to Europe, horses you can't raise any more, niggers to lift their fingers—

BIRDIE (*suddenly*) We were good to our people. Every-body knew that. We were better to them than—

(MARSHALL *looks up at* BIRDIE.)

REGINA Why, Birdie. You aren't playing.

BEN But when the war comes these fine gentlemen ride off and leave the cotton, *and* the women, to rot.

BIRDIE My father was killed in the war. He was a fine sol-dier, Mr. Marshall. A fine man.

REGINA Oh, certainly, Birdie. A famous soldier.

BEN (*to* BIRDIE) But that isn't the tale I am telling Mr. Marshall. (*To* MARSHALL) Well, sir, the war ends. (BIRDIE *goes back to piano*) Lionnet is almost ruined, and the sons finish ruining it. And there were thousands like them. Why? (*Leans forward*) Because the Southern aris-tocrat can adapt himself to nothing. Too high-tone to try.

MARSHALL Sometimes it is difficult to learn new ways.
(BIRDIE *and* ALEXANDRA *begin to play.* MARSHALL *leans forward, listening.*)

BEN Perhaps, perhaps. (*He sees that* MARSHALL *is listen-ing to the music. Irritated, he turns to* BIRDIE *and* ALEX-ANDRA *at the piano, then back to* MARSHALL) You're right, Mr. Marshall. It is difficult to learn new ways. But maybe that's why it's profitable. *Our* grandfather and *our* father learned the new ways and learned how to make them pay. (*Smiles nastily*) *They* were in trade.

Hubbard Sons, Merchandise. Others, Birdie's family, for example, looked down on them. (*Settles back in chair*) To make a long story short, Lionnet now belongs to *us*. (BIRDIE *stops playing*) Twenty years ago we took over their land, their cotton, and their daughter. (BIRDIE *rises and stands stiffly by the piano.* MARSHALL, *who has been watching her, rises.*)

MARSHALL   May I bring you a glass of port, Mrs. Hubbard?

BIRDIE   (*Softly*) No, thank you, sir. You are most polite.

REGINA   (*Sharply, to* BEN) You are boring Mr. Marshall with these ancient family tales.

BEN   I hope not. I hope not. I am trying to make an important point— (*Bows to* MARSHALL) for our future business partner.

OSCAR   (*to* MARSHALL) My brother always says that it's folks like us who have struggled and fought to bring to our land some of the prosperity of your land.

BEN   Some people call that patriotism.

REGINA   (*laughs gaily*) I hope you don't find my brothers too obvious, Mr. Marshall. I'm afraid they mean that this is the time for the ladies to leave the gentlemen to talk business.

MARSHALL   (*hastily*) Not at all. We settled everything this afternoon. (MARSHALL *looks at his watch*) I have only a few minutes before I must leave for the train. (*Smiles at her*) And I insist they be spent with you.

REGINA   *And* with another glass of port.

MARSHALL   Thank you.

BEN   (*to* REGINA) My sister is right. (*To* MARSHALL) I am a plain man and I am trying to say a plain thing. A man ain't only in business for what he can get out of it. It's got to give him something here. (*Puts hand to his breast*) That's every bit as true for the nigger picking cotton for a silver quarter, as it is for you and me. (REGINA *gives* MARSHALL *a glass of port*) If it don't give him something here, then he don't pick the cotton right. Money isn't all. Not by three shots.

MARSHALL   Really? Well, I always thought it was a great deal.

REGINA   And so did I, Mr. Marshall.

MARSHALL (*leans forward. Pleasantly, but with meaning*)
Now you don't have to convince me that you are the
right people for the deal. I wouldn't be here if you
hadn't convinced me six months ago. You want the mill
here, and I want it here. It isn't my business to find out
why you want it.

BEN To bring the machine to the cotton, and not the cotton to the machine.

MARSHALL (*amused*) You have a turn for neat phrases,
Hubbard. Well, however grand your reasons are, mine
are simple: I want to make money and I believe I'll
make it on you. (*As* BEN *starts to speak, he smiles*) Mind
you, I have no objections to more high-minded reasons.
They are mighty valuable in business. It's fine to have
partners who so closely follow the teachings of Christ.
(*Gets up*) And now I must leave for my train.

REGINA I'm sorry you won't stay over with us, Mr. Marshall, but you'll come again. Any time you like.

BEN (*motions to* LEO, *indicating the bottle*) Fill them up,
boy, fill them up. (LEO *moves around filling the glasses
as* BEN *speaks*) Down here, sir, we have a strange cus-
tom. We drink the *last* drink for a toast. That's to prove
that the Southerner is always still on his feet for the last
drink. (*Picks up his glass*) It was Henry Frick, your
Mr. Henry Frick, who said, "Railroads are the Rembrandts of investments." Well, *I* say, "Southern cotton
mills *will be* the Rembrandts of investment." So I give
you the firm of Hubbard Sons and Marshall, Cotton
Mills, and to it a long and prosperous life. (*They all
pick up their glasses.* MARSHALL *looks at them, amused.
Then he, too, lifts his glass, smiles.*)

OSCAR The children will drive you to the depot. Leo!
Alexandra! You will drive Mr. Marshall down.

LEO (*eagerly, looks at* BEN *who nods*) Yes, sir. (*To* MAR-
SHALL) Not often Uncle Ben lets *me* drive the horses.
And a beautiful pair they are. (*Starts for hall*) Come on,
Zan.

ALEXANDRA May I drive tonight, Uncle Ben, please? I'd
like to and—

BEN   (*shakes his head, laughs*)   In your evening clothes?
Oh, no, my dear.

ALEXANDRA   But Leo always—(*Stops, exits quickly.*)

REGINA   I don't like to say good-bye to you, Mr. Marshall.

MARSHALL   Then we won't say good-bye. You have promised that you would come and let me show you Chicago.
Do I have to make you promise again?

REGINA   (*looks at him as he presses her hand*)   I promise
again.

MARSHALL   (*touches her hand again, then moves to* BIRDIE)
Good-bye, Mrs. Hubbard.

BIRDIE   (*shyly, with sweetness and dignity*)   Good-bye,
sir.

MARSHALL   (*as he passes* REGINA)   Remember.

REGINA   I will.

OSCAR   We'll see you to the carriage. (MARSHALL *exits, followed by* BEN *and* OSCAR. *For a second* REGINA *and* BIRDIE
stand looking after them. Then REGINA *throws up her
arms, laughs happily.*)

REGINA   And there, Birdie, goes the man who has opened
the door to our future.

BIRDIE   (*surprised at the unaccustomed friendliness*)
What?

REGINA   (*turning to her*)   *Our future.* Yours and mine,
Ben's and Oscar's, the children— (*Looks at* BIRDIE's *puzzled face, laughs*)   Our future! (*Gaily*)   You were charming at supper, Birdie. Mr. Marshall certainly thought so.

BIRDIE   (*pleased*)   Why, Regina! Do you think he did?

REGINA   Can't you tell when you're being admired?

BIRDIE   Oscar said I bored Mr. Marshall. (*Then quietly*)
But he admired *you.* He told me so.

REGINA   What did he say?

BIRDIE   He said to me, "I hope your sister-in-law will come
to Chicago. Chicago will be at her feet." He said the
ladies would bow to your manners and the gentlemen
to your looks.

REGINA   Did he? He seems a lonely man. Imagine being
lonely with all that money. I don't think he likes his
wife.

BIRDIE   Not like his wife? What a thing to say.

REGINA   She's away a great deal. He said that several times. And once he made fun of her being so social and high-tone. But that fits in all right. (*Sits back, arms on back of sofa, stretches*) Her being social, I mean. She can introduce me. It won't take long wih an introduction from her.

BIRDIE   (*bewildered*) Introduce you? In Chicago? You mean you really might go? Oh, Regina, you can't leave here. What about Horace?

REGINA   Don't look so scared about everything, Birdie I'm going to live in Chicago. I've always wanted to. And now there'll be plenty of money to go with.

BIRDIE   But Horace won't be able to move around. You know what the doctor wrote.

REGINA   There'll be millions, Birdie, millions. You know what I've always said when people told me we were rich? I said I think you should either be a nigger or a millionaire. In between, like us, what for? (*Laughs. Looks at* BIRDIE) But I'm not going away tomorrow, Birdie. There's plenty of time to worry about Horace when he comes home. If he ever decides to come home.

BIRDIE   Will we be going to Chicago? I mean, Oscar and Leo and me?

REGINA   You? I shouldn't think so. (*Laughs*) Well, we must remember tonight. It's a very important night and we mustn't forget it. We shall plan all the things we'd like to have and then we'll really have them. Make a wish, Birdie, any wish. It's bound to come true now. (BEN *and* OSCAR *enter.*)

BIRDIE   (*laughs*) Well. Well, I don't know. Maybe. (RE-GINA *turns to look at* BEN) Well, I guess I'd know right off what I wanted. (OSCAR *stands by the upper window, waves to the departing carriage.*)

REGINA   (*looks up at* BEN, *smiles. He smiles back at her*) Well, you did it.

BEN   Looks like it might be we did.

REGINA   (*springs up, laughs*) Looks like it! Don't pretend. You're like a cat who's been licking the cream. (*Crosses to wine bottle*) Now we must all have a drink to celebrate.

OSCAR The children, Alexandra and Leo, make a very handsome couple, Regina. Marshall remarked himself what fine young folks they were. How well they looked together!

REGINA (*sharply*) Yes. You said that before, Oscar.

BEN Yes, sir. It's beginning to look as if the deal's all set. I may not be a subtle man—but— (*Turns to them. After a second*) Now somebody ask me how I know the deal is set.

OSCAR What do you mean, Ben?

BEN You remember I told him that down here we drink the *last* drink for a toast?

OSCAR (*thoughtfully*) Yes. I never heard that before.

BEN Nobody's ever heard it before. God forgives those who invent what they need. I already had his signature. But we've all done business with men whose word over a glass is better than a bond. Anyway it don't hurt to have both.

OSCAR (*turns to* REGINA) You understand what Ben means?

REGINA (*smiles*) Yes, Oscar. I understand. I understood immediately.

BEN (*looks at her admiringly*) Did you, Regina? Well, when he lifted his glass to drink, I closed my eyes and saw the bricks going into place.

REGINA And *I* saw a lot more than that.

BEN Slowly, slowly. As yet we have only our hopes.

REGINA Birdie and I have just been planning what we want. I know what I want. What will you want, Ben?

BEN Caution. Don't count the chickens. (*Leans back, laughs*) Well, God would allow us a little daydreaming. Good for the soul when you've worked hard enough to deserve it. (*Pauses*) I think I'll have a stable. For a long time I've had my good eyes on Carter's in Savannah. A rich man's pleasure, the sport of kings, why not the sport of Hubbards? Why not?

REGINA (*smiles*) Why not? What will you have, Oscar?

OSCAR I don't know. (*Thoughtfully*) The pleasure of seeing the bricks grow will be enough for me.

BEN Oh, of course. Our greatest pleasure will be to see the

bricks grow. But we are all entitled to a little side in-
dulgence.

OSCAR Yes, I suppose so. Well, then, I think we might take
a few trips here and there, eh, Birdie?

BIRDIE (*surprised at being consulted*) Yes, Oscar. I'd like
that.

OSCAR We might even make a regular trip to Jekyll Island.
I've heard the Cornelly place is for sale. We might think
about buying it. Make a nice change. Do you good,
Birdie, a change of climate. Fine shooting on Jekyll, the
best.

BIRDIE I'd like—

OSCAR (*indulgently*) What would you like?

BIRDIE Two things. Two things I'd like most.

REGINA Two! I should like a thousand. You are modest,
Birdie.

BIRDIE (*warmly, delighted with the unexpected interest*)
I should like to have Lionnet back. I know you own it
now, but I'd like to see it fixed up again, the way
Mama and Papa had it. Every year it used to get a nice
coat of paint—Papa was very particular about the paint
—and the lawn was so smooth all the way down to the
river, with the trims of zinnias and red-feather plush.
And the figs and blue little plums and the scuppernongs
— (*Smiles. Turns to* REGINA) The organ is still there and
it wouldn't cost much to fix. We could have parties for
Zan, the way Mama used to have for me.

BEN That's a pretty picture, Birdie. Might be a most pleasant way to live. (*Dismissing* BIRDIE) What do you want,
Regina?

BIRDIE (*very happily, not noticing that they are no longer
listening to her*) I could have a cutting garden. Just
where Mama's used to be. Oh, I do think we could be
happier there. Papa used to say that *nobody* had ever
lost their temper at Lionnet, and *nobody* ever would.
Papa would never let anybody be nasty-spoken or mean.
No, sir. He just didn't like it.

BEN What do you want, Regina?

REGINA I'm going to Chicago. And when I'm settled there
and know the right people and the right things to buy—

because I certainly don't now—I shall go to Paris and buy them. (*Laughs*) I'm going to leave you and Oscar to count the bricks.

BIRDIE Oscar. Please let me have Lionnet back.

OSCAR (*to* REGINA) You are serious about moving to Chicago?

BEN She is going to see the great world and leave us in the little one. Well, we'll come and visit you and meet all the great and be proud you are our sister.

REGINA (*gaily*) Certainly. And you won't even have to learn to be subtle, Ben. Stay as you are. You will be rich and the rich don't have to be subtle.

OSCAR But what about Alexandra? She's seventeen. Old enough to be thinking about marrying.

BIRDIE And, Oscar, I have one more wish. Just one more wish.

OSCAR (*turns*) What is it, Birdie? What are you saying?

BIRDIE I want you to stop shooting. I mean, so much. I don't like to see animals and birds killed just for the killing. You only throw them away—

BEN (*to* REGINA) It'll take a great deal of money to live as you're planning, Regina.

REGINA Certainly. But there'll be plenty of money. You have estimated the profits very high.

BEN I have—

BIRDIE (OSCAR *is looking at her furiously*) And you never let anybody else shoot, and the niggers need it so much to keep from starving. It's wicked to shoot food just because you like to shoot, when poor people need it so—

BEN (*laughs*) I have estimated the profits very high—for myself.

REGINA What did you say?

BIRDIE I've always wanted to speak about it, Oscar.

OSCAR (*slowly, carefully*) What are you chattering about?

BIRDIE (*nervously*) I was talking about Lionnet and—and about your shooting—

OSCAR You are exciting yourself.

REGINA (*to* BEN) I didn't hear you. There was so much talking.

OSCAR (*to* BIRDIE) You have been acting very childish, very excited, all evening.

BIRDIE Regina asked me what I'd like.

REGINA What did you say, Ben?

BIRDIE Now that we'll be so rich everybody was saying what they would like, so *I* said what *I* would like, too.

BEN I said— (*He is interrupted by* OSCAR.)

OSCAR (*to* BIRDIE) Very well. We've all heard you. That's enough now.

BEN I am waiting. (*They stop*) I am waiting for you to finish. You and Birdie. Four conversations are three too many. (BIRDIE *slowly sits down.* BEN *smiles, to* REGINA) I said that I had, and I do, estimate the profits very high —for myself, and Oscar, of course.

REGINA (*slowly*) And what does that mean? (BEN *shrugs, looks toward* OSCAR.)

OSCAR (*looks at* BEN, *clears throat*) Well, Regina, it's like this. For forty-nine per cent Marshall will put up four hundred thousand dollars. For fifty-one per cent— (*Smiles archly*) a controlling interest, mind you, we will put up two hundred and twenty-five thousand dollars besides offering him certain benefits that our (*looks at* BEN) local position allows us to manage. Ben means that two hundred and twenty-five thousand dollars is a lot of money.

REGINA I know the terms and I know it's a lot of money.

BEN (*nodding*) It is.

OSCAR Ben means that we are ready with our two-thirds of the money. Your third, Horace's I mean, doesn't seem to be ready. (*Raises his hand as* REGINA *starts to speak*) Ben has written to Horace, I have written, and you have written. He answers. But he never mentions this business. Yet we have explained it to him in great detail, and told him the urgency. Still he never mentions it. Ben has been very patient, Regina. Naturally, you are our sister and we want you to benefit from anything we do.

REGINA And in addition to your concern for me, you do not want control to go out of the family. (*To* BEN) That right, Ben?

BEN   That's cynical. (*Smiles*) Cynicism is an unpleasant way of saying the truth.

OSCAR   No need to be cynical. We'd have no trouble raising the third share, the share that you want to take.

REGINA   I am sure you could get the third share, the share you were saving for me. But that would give you a strange partner. And strange partners sometimes want a great deal. (*Smiles unpleasantly*) But perhaps it would be wise for you to find him.

OSCAR   Now, now. Nobody says we *want* to do that. We would like to have you in and you would like to come in.

REGINA   Yes. I certainly would.

BEN   (*laughs, puts up his hand*) But we haven't heard from Horace.

REGINA   I've given my word that Horace will put up the money. That should be enough.

BEN   Oh, it was enough. I took your word. But I've got to have more than your word now. The contracts will be signed this week, and Marshall will want to see our money soon after. Regina, Horace has been in Baltimore for five months. I know that you've written him to come home, and that he hasn't come.

OSCAR   It's beginning to look as if he doesn't want to come home.

REGINA   Of course he wants to come home. You can't move around with heart trouble at any moment you choose. You know what doctors are like once they get their hands on a case like this—

OSCAR   They can't very well keep him from answering letters, can they? (REGINA *turns to* BEN) They couldn't keep him from arranging for the money if he wanted to—

REGINA   Has it occurred to you that Horace is also a good businessman?

BEN   Certainly. He is a shrewd trader. Always has been. The bank is proof of that.

REGINA   Then, possibly, he may be keeping silent because he doesn't think he is getting enough for his money. (*Looks at* OSCAR) Seventy-five thousand he has to put up. That's a lot of money, too.

OSCAR   Nonsense. He knows a good thing when he hears

it. He knows that we can make *twice* the profit on cotton
goods manufactured here than can be made in the North.

BEN   That isn't what Regina means. (*Smiles*) May I inter-
pret you, Regina? (*To* OSCAR) Regina is saying that
Horace wants *more* than a third of our share.

OSCAR   But he's only putting up a third of the money. You
put up a third and you get a third. What else could he
expect?

REGINA   Well, *I* don't know. I don't know about these
things. It would seem that if you put up a third you
should only get a third. But then again, there's no law
about it, is there? I should think that if you knew your
money was very badly needed, well, you just might say,
I want more, I want a bigger share. You boys have done
that. I've heard you say so.

BEN   (*after a pause, laughs*) So you believe he has deliberately held out? For a larger share? (*Leaning forward*) Well, I don't believe it. But I do believe that's
what *you* want. Am I right, Regina?

REGINA   Oh, I shouldn't like to be too definite. But I could
say that I wouldn't like to persuade Horace unless he did
get a larger share. I must look after his interests. It seems
only natural—

OSCAR   And where would the larger share come from?

REGINA   I don't know. That's not my business. (*Giggles*)
But perhaps it could come off your share, Oscar. (REGINA
and BEN *laugh.*)

OSCAR   (*rises and wheels furiously on both of them as they
laugh*) What kind of talk is this?

BEN   I haven't said a thing.

OSCAR   (*to* REGINA) *You* are talking very big tonight.

REGINA   (*stops laughing*) Am I? Well, you should know
me well enough to know that I wouldn't be asking for
things I didn't think I could get.

OSCAR   Listen. I don't believe you can even get Horace to
come home, much less get money from him or talk quite
so big about what you want.

REGINA   Oh, I can get him home.

OSCAR   Then why haven't you?

REGINA   I thought I should fight his battles for him, before he came home. Horace is a very sick man. And even if *you* don't care how sick he is, I do.

BEN   Stop this foolish squabbling. How can you get him home?

REGINA   I will send Alexandra to Baltimore. She will ask him to come home. She will say that she wants him to come home, and that *I* want him to come home.

BIRDIE   (*suddenly*) Well, of course she wants him here, but he's sick and maybe he's happy where he is.

REGINA   (*ignores* BIRDIE, *to* BEN) You agree that he will come home if she asks him to, if she says that I miss him and want him—

BEN   (*looks at her, smiles*) I admire you, Regina. And I agree. That's settled now and— (*Starts to rise.*)

REGINA   (*quickly*) But before she brings him home, I want to know what he's going to get.

BEN   What do you want?

REGINA   Twice what you offered.

BEN   Well, you won't get it.

OSCAR   (*to* REGINA) I think you've gone crazy.

REGINA   I don't want to fight, Ben—

BEN   I don't either. You won't get it. There isn't any chance of that. (*Roguishly*) You're holding us up, and that's not pretty, Regina, not pretty. (*Holds up his hand as he sees she is about to speak*) But we need you, and I don't want to fight. Here's what I'll do: I'll give Horace forty per cent, instead of the thirty-three and a third he really should get. I'll do that, provided he is home and his money is up within two weeks. How's that?

REGINA   All right.

OSCAR   I've asked before: where is this extra share coming from?

BEN   (*pleasantly*) From you. From your share.

OSCAR   (*furiously*) From me, is it? That's just fine and dandy. That's my reward. For thirty-five years I've worked my hands to the bone for you. For thirty-five years I've done all the things you didn't want to do. And this is what I—

BEN   (*turns slowly to look at* OSCAR. OSCAR *breaks off*) My, my. I am being attacked tonight on all sides. First by my sister, then by my brother. And I ain't a man who likes being attacked. I can't believe that God wants the strong to parade their strength, but I don't mind doing it if it's got to be done. (*Leans back in his chair*) You ought to take these things better, Oscar. I've made you money in the past. I'm going to make you more money now. You'll be a very rich man. What's the difference to any of us if a little more goes here, a little less goes there—it's all in the family. And it will stay in the family. I'll never marry. (ADDIE *enters, begins to gather the glasses from the table.* OSCAR *turns to* BEN) So my money will go to Alexandra and Leo. They may even marry some day and— (ADDIE *looks at* BEN.)

BIRDIE   (*rising*)   Marry—Zan and Leo—

OSCAR   (*carefully*)   That would make a great difference in my feelings. If they married.

BEN   Yes, that's what I mean. Of course it would make a difference.

OSCAR   (*carefully*)   Is that what *you* mean, Regina?

REGINA   Oh, it's too far away. We'll talk about it in a few years.

OSCAR   I want to talk about it now.

BEN   (*nods*)   Naturally.

REGINA   There's a lot of things to consider. They are first cousins, and—

OSCAR   That isn't unusual. Our grandmother and grandfather were first cousins.

REGINA   (*giggles*)   And look at us. (BEN *giggles.*)

OSCAR   (*angrily*)   You're both being very gay with my money.

BEN   (*sighs*)   These quarrels. I dislike them so. (*Leans forward to* REGINA) A marriage might be a very wise arrangement, for several reasons. And then, Oscar has given up something for you. You should try to manage something for him.

REGINA   I haven't said I was opposed to it. But Leo is a wild boy. There were those times when he took a little money from the bank and—

OSCAR   That's all past history—

REGINA   Oh, I know. And I know all young men are wild.

I'm only mentioning it to show you that there are considerations—

BEN   (*irritated because she does not understand that he is trying to keep* OSCAR *quiet*)   All right, so there are. But please assure Oscar that you will think about it very seriously.

REGINA   (*smiles, nods*)   Very well. I assure Oscar that I will think about it seriously.

OSCAR   (*sharply*)   That is not an answer.

REGINA   (*rises*)   My, you're in a bad humor and you shall put me in one. I have said all that I am willing to say now. After all, Horace has to give his consent, too.

OSCAR   Horace will do what you tell him to.

REGINA   Yes, I think he will.

OSCAR   And I have your word that you will try to—

REGINA   (*patiently*)   Yes, Oscar. You have my word that I will think about it. Now do leave me alone. (*There is the sound of the front door being closed.*)

BIRDIE   I—Alexandra is only seventeen. She—

REGINA   (*calling*)   Alexandra? Are you back?

ALEXANDRA   Yes, Mama.

LEO   (*comes into the room*)   Mr. Marshall got off safe and sound. Weren't those fine clothes he had? You can always spot clothes made in a good place. Looks like maybe they were done in England. Lots of men in the North send all the way to England for their stuff.

BEN   (*to* LEO)   Were you careful driving the horses?

LEO   Oh, yes, sir. I was. (ALEXANDRA *has come in on* BEN's *question, hears the answer, looks angrily at* LEO.)

ALEXANDRA   It's a lovely night. You should have come, Aunt Birdie.

REGINA   Were you gracious to Mr. Marshall?

ALEXANDRA   I think so, Mama. I liked him.

REGINA   Good. And now I have great news for you. You are going to Baltimore in the morning to bring your father home.

ALEXANDRA   (*gasps, then delighted*)   Me? Papa said I should come? That must mean— (*Turns to* ADDIE)   Addie, he must be well. Think of it, he'll be back home again. We'll bring him home.

REGINA   You are going alone, Alexandra.

ADDIE   (ALEXANDRA *has turned in surprise*)   Going alone? Going by herself? A child that age! Mr. Horace ain't going to like Zan traipsing up there by herself.

REGINA   (*sharply*)   Go upstairs and lay out Alexandra's things.

ADDIE   He'd expect me to be along—

REGINA   I'll be up in a few minutes to tell you what to pack. (ADDIE *slowly begins to climb the steps. To* ALEXANDRA) I should think you'd like going alone. At your age it certainly would have delighted me. You're a strange girl, Alexandra. Addie has babied you so much.

ALEXANDRA   I only thought it would be more fun if Addie and I went together.

BIRDIE   (*timidly*)   Maybe I could go with her, Regina. I'd really like to.

REGINA   She is going alone. She is getting old enough to take some responsibilities.

OSCAR   She'd better learn now. She's almost old enough to get married. (*Jovially, to* LEO, *slapping him on shoulder*) Eh, son?

LEO   Huh?

OSCAR   (*annoyed with* LEO *for not understanding*)   Old enough to get married, you're thinking, eh?

LEO   Oh, yes, sir. (*Feebly*) Lots of girls get married at Zan's age. Look at Mary Prester and Johanna and—

REGINA   Well, she's not getting married tomorrow. But she is going to Baltimore tomorrow, so let's talk about that. (*To* ALEXANDRA) You'll be glad to have Papa home again.

ALEXANDRA   I wanted to go before, Mama. You remember that. But you said *you* couldn't go, and that *I* couldn't go alone.

REGINA   I've changed my mind. (*Too casually*) You're to tell Papa how much you missed him, and that he must come home now—for your sake. Tell him that you *need* him home.

ALEXANDRA   Need him home? I don't understand.

REGINA   There is nothing for you to understand. You are simply to say what I have told you.

BIRDIE (*rises*) He may be too sick. She couldn't do that—

ALEXANDRA Yes. He may be too sick to travel. I couldn't make him think he had to come home for me, if he is too sick to—

REGINA (*looks at her, sharply, challengingly*) You *couldn't* do what I tell you to do, Alexandra?

ALEXANDRA (*quietly*) No. I couldn't. If I thought it would hurt him.

REGINA (*after a second's silence, smiles pleasantly*) But you are doing this for Papa's own good. (*Takes* ALEXANDRA'S *hand*) You must let me be the judge of his condition. It's the best possible cure for him to come home and be taken care of here. He mustn't stay there any longer and listen to those alarmist doctors. You are doing this entirely for his sake. Tell your papa that I want him to come home, that I miss him very much.

ALEXANDRA (*slowly*) Yes, Mama.

REGINA (*to the others. Rises*) I must go and start getting Alexandra ready now. Why don't you all go home?

BEN (*rises*) I'll attend to the railroad ticket. One of the boys will bring it over. Good night, everybody. Have a nice trip, Alexandra. The food on the train is very good. The celery is so crisp. Have a good time and act like a little lady. (*Exits.*)

REGINA Good night, Ben. Good night, Oscar— (*Playfully*) Don't be so glum, Oscar. It makes you look as if you had chronic indigestion.

BIRDIE Good night, Regina.

REGINA Good night, Birdie. (*Exits upstairs.*)

OSCAR (*starts for hall*) Come along.

LEO (*to* ALEXANDRA) Imagine your not wanting to go! What a little fool you are. Wish it were me. What I could do in a place like Baltimore!

ALEXANDRA (*angrily, looking away from him*) Mind your business. I can guess the kind of things *you* could do.

LEO (*laughs*) Oh no, you couldn't. (*He exits.*)

REGINA (*calling from the top of the stairs*) Come on, Alexandra.

BIRDIE (*quickly, softly*) Zan.

ALEXANDRA I don't understand about my going, Aunt

Birdie. (*Shrugs*) But anyway, Papa will be home again.
(*Pats* BIRDIE's *arm*) Don't worry about me. I can take
care of myself. Really I can.

BIRDIE   (*shakes her head, softly*)   That's not what I'm worried about. Zan—

ALEXANDRA   (*comes close to her*)   What's the matter?

BIRDIE   It's about Leo—

ALEXANDRA   (*whispering*)   He beat the horses. That's why
we were late getting back. We had to wait until they
cooled off. He always beats the horses as if—

BIRDIE   (*whispering frantically, holding* ALEXANDRA's
hands)   He's my son. My own son. But you are
more to me—more to me than my own child. I love you
more than anybody else—

ALEXANDRA   Don't worry about the horses. I'm sorry I told
you.

BIRDIE   (*her voice rising*)   *I am not worrying about the
horses*. I am worrying about *you*. You are *not* going to
marry Leo. I am not going to let them do that to you—

ALEXANDRA   Marry? To Leo? (*Laughs*) I wouldn't marry,
Aunt Birdie. I've never even thought about it—

BIRDIE   But they have thought about it. (*Wildly*) Zan, I
couldn't stand to think about such a thing. You and—
(OSCAR *has come into the doorway on* ALEXANDRA's
speech. He is standing quietly, listening.)

ALEXANDRA   (*laughs*)   But I'm not going to marry. And I'm
certainly not going to marry Leo.

BIRDIE   Don't you understand? They'll make you. They'll
make you—

ALEXANDRA   (*takes* BIRDIE's *hands, quietly, firmly*)   That's
foolish, Aunt Birdie. I'm grown now. Nobody can make
me do anything.

BIRDIE . . I just couldn't stand—

OSCAR   (*sharply*)   Birdie. (BIRDIE *looks up, draws quickly
away from* ALEXANDRA. *She stands rigid, frightened.
Quietly*) Birdie, get your hat and coat.

ADDIE   (*calls from upstairs*)   Come on, baby. Your mama's waiting for you, and she ain't nobody to keep waiting.

ALEXANDRA   All right. (*Then softly, embracing* BIRDIE)

Good night, Aunt Birdie. (*As she passes* OSCAR) Good
night, Uncle Oscar. (BIRDIE *begins to move slowly toward the door as* ALEXANDRA *climbs the stairs.* ALEX-
ANDRA *is almost out of view when* BIRDIE *reaches* OSCAR
in the doorway. As BIRDIE *quickly attempts to pass him,
he slaps her hard, across the face.* BIRDIE *cries out, puts
her hand to her face. On the cry,* ALEXANDRA *turns, begins to run down the stairs*) Aunt Birdie! What happened? What happened? I—

BIRDIE   (*softly, without turning*)   Nothing, darling. Nothing happened. (*Quickly, as if anxious to keep* ALEXANDRA
from coming close) Now go to bed. (OSCAR *exits*) Nothing happened. I only—I only twisted my ankle. (*She
goes out.* ALEXANDRA *stands on the stairs looking after
her as if she were puzzled and frightened.*)

Curtain

Act Two

SCENE: *Same as Act One. A week later, morning.*

AT RISE: *The light comes from the open shutter of the right window; the other shutters are tightly closed.* ADDIE *is standing at the window, looking out. Near the dining-room doors are brooms, mops, rags, etc. After a second,* OSCAR *comes into the entrance hall, looks in the room, shivers, decides not to take his hat and coat off, comes into the room. At the sound of the door,* ADDIE *turns.*

ADDIE (*without interest*) Oh, it's you, Mr. Oscar.

OSCAR What is this? It's not night. What's the matter here? (*Shivers*) Fine thing at this time of the morning. Blinds all closed. (ADDIE *begins to open shutters*) Where's Miss Regina? It's cold in here.

ADDIE Miss Regina ain't down yet.

OSCAR She had any word?

ADDIE (*wearily*) No, sir.

OSCAR Wouldn't you think a girl that age could get on a train at one place and have sense enough to get off at another?

ADDIE Something must have happened. If Zan says she was coming last night, she's coming last night. Unless something happened. Sure fire disgrace to let a baby like that go all that way alone to bring home a sick man with-out—

OSCAR You do a lot of judging around here, Addie, eh? Judging of your white folks, I mean.

ADDIE   (*looks at him, sighs*)   I'm tired. I been up all night watching for them.

REGINA   (*speaking from the upstairs hall*)   Who's downstairs, Addie? (*She appears in a dressing gown, peers down from the landing.* ADDIE *picks up broom, dustpan and brush and exits*) Oh, it's you, Oscar. What are you doing here so early? I haven't been down yet. I'm not finished dressing.

OSCAR   (*speaking up to her*)   You had any word from them?

REGINA   No.

OSCAR   Then something certainly has happened. People don't just say they are arriving on Thursday night, and they haven't come by Friday morning.

REGINA   Oh, nothing has happened. Alexandra just hasn't got sense enough to send a message.

OSCAR   If nothing's happened, then why aren't they here?

REGINA   You asked me that ten times last night. My, you do fret so, Oscar. Anything might have happened. They may have missed connections in Atlanta, the train may have been delayed—oh, a hundred things could have kept them.

OSCAR   Where's Ben?

REGINA   (*as she disappears upstairs*)   Where should he be? At home, probably. Really, Oscar, I don't tuck him in his bed and I don't take him out of it. Have some coffee and don't worry so much.

OSCAR   Have some coffee? There isn't any coffee. (*Looks at his watch, shakes his head. After a second* CAL *enters with a large silver tray, coffee urn, small cups, newspaper*) Oh, there you are. Is everything in this fancy house always late?

CAL   (*looks at him surprised*)   You ain't out shooting this morning, Mr. Oscar?

OSCAR   First day I missed since I had my head cold. First day I missed in eight years.

CAL   Yes, sir. I bet you. Simon he say you had a mighty good day yesterday morning. That's what Simon say. (*Brings* OSCAR ·*coffee and newspaper.*)

OSCAR   Pretty good, pretty good.

CAL (*laughs, slyly*) Bet you got enough bobwhite and squirrel to give every nigger in town a Jesus-party. Most of 'em ain't had no meat since the cotton picking was over. Bet they'd give anything for a little piece of that meat—

OSCAR (*turns his head to look at* CAL) Cal, if I catch a nigger in this town going shooting, you know what's going to happen. (LEO *enters.*)

CAL (*hastily*) Yes, sir, Mr. Oscar. I didn't say nothing about nothing. It was Simon who told me and— Morning, Mr. Leo. You gentlemen having your breakfast with us here?

LEO The boys in the bank don't know a thing. They haven't had any message. (CAL *waits for an answer, gets none, shrugs, moves to door, exits.*)

OSCAR (*peers at* LEO) What you doing here, son?

LEO You told me to find out if the boys at the bank had any message from Uncle Horace or Zan—

OSCAR I told you if they had a message to bring it here. I told you that if they didn't have a message to stay at the bank and do your work.

LEO Oh, I guess I misunderstood.

OSCAR You didn't misunderstand. You just were looking for any excuse to take an hour off. (LEO *pours a cup of coffee*) You got to stop that kind of thing. You got to start settling down. You going to be a married man one of these days.

LEO Yes, sir.

OSCAR You also got to stop with that woman in Mobile. (*As* LEO *is about to speak*) You're young and I haven't got no objections to outside women. That is, I haven't got no objections so long as they don't interfere with serious things. Outside women are all right in their place, but *now* isn't their place. You got to realize that.

LEO (*nods*) Yes, sir. I'll tell her. She'll act all right about it.

OSCAR Also, you got to start working harder at the bank. You got to convince your Uncle Horace you going to make a fit husband for Alexandra.

LEO What do you think has happened to them? Supposed

to be here last night— (*Laughs*) Bet you Uncle Ben's mighty worried. Seventy-five thousand dollars worried.

OSCAR (*smiles happily*) Ought to be worried. Damn well ought to be. First he don't answer the letters, then he don't come home— (*Giggles.*)

LEO What will happen if Uncle Horace don't come home or don't—

OSCAR Or don't put up the money? Oh, we'll get it from outside. Easy enough.

LEO (*surprised*) But *you* don't want outsiders.

OSCAR What do I care who gets my share? I been shaved already. Serve Ben right if he had to give away some of his.

LEO Damn shame what they did to you.

OSCAR (*looking up the stairs*) Don't talk so loud. Don't you worry. When I die, you'll have as much as the rest. You might have yours *and* Alexandra's. I'm not so easily licked.

LEO I wasn't thinking of myself, Papa—

OSCAR Well, you should be, you should be. It's every man's duty to think of himself.

LEO You think Uncle Horace don't want to go in on this?

OSCAR (*giggles*) That's my hunch. He hasn't showed any signs of loving it yet.

LEO (*laughs*) But he hasn't listened to Aunt Regina yet, either. Oh, he'll go along. It's too good a thing. Why wouldn't he want to? He's got plenty and plenty to invest with. He don't even have to sell anything. Eighty-eight thousand worth of Union Pacific bonds sitting right in his safe deposit box. All he's got to do is open the box.

OSCAR (*after a pause. Looks at his watch*). Mighty late breakfast in this fancy house. Yes, he's had those bonds for fifteen years. Bought them when they were low and just locked them up.

LEO Yeah. Just has to open the box and take them out. That's all. Easy as easy can be. (*Laughs*) The things in that box! There's all those bonds, looking mighty fine. (OSCAR *slowly puts down his newspaper and turns to* LEO) Then right next to them is a baby shoe of Zan's and a cheap old cameo on a string, and, *and*—nobody'd believe this—a piece of an old violin. Not even a whole violin. Just a piece of an old thing, a piece of a violin.

OSCAR (*very softly, as if he were trying to control his voice*) A piece of a violin! What do you think of that!

LEO Yes, sirree. A lot of other crazy things, too. A poem, I guess it is, signed with his mother's name, and two old schoolbooks with notes and— (LEO *catches* OSCAR's *look. His voice trails off. He turns his head away.*)

OSCAR (*very softly*) How do you know what's in the box, son?

LEO (*stops, draws back, frightened, realizing what he has said*) Oh, well. Well, er. Well, one of the boys, sir. It was one of the boys at the bank. He took old Manders' keys. It was Joe Horns. He just up and took Manders' keys and, and—well, took the box out. (*Quickly*) Then they all asked me if I wanted to see, too. So I looked a little, I guess, but then I made them close up the box quick and I told them never—

OSCAR (*looks at him*) Joe Horns, you say? He opened it?

LEO Yes, sir, yes, he did. My word of honor. (*Very nervously looking away*) I suppose that don't excuse *me* for looking— (*Looking at* OSCAR) but I did make him close it up and put the keys back in Manders' drawer—

OSCAR (*leans forward, very softly*) Tell me the truth, Leo. I am not going to be angry with you. Did you open the box yourself?

LEO *No, sir, I didn't.* I told you I didn't. No, I—

OSCAR (*irritated, patient*) I am *not* going to be angry with you. (*Watching* LEO *carefully*) Sometimes a young fellow deserves credit for looking round him to see what's going on. Sometimes that's a good sign in a fellow your age. (OSCAR *rises*) Many great men have made their fortune with their eyes. Did you open the box?

LEO (*very puzzled*) No. I—

OSCAR (*moves to* LEO) Did you open the box? It may have been—well, it may have been a good thing if you had.

LEO (*after a long pause*) I opened it.

OSCAR (*quickly*) Is that the truth? (LEO *nods*) Does anybody else know that you opened it? Come, Leo, don't be afraid of speaking the truth to me.

LEO   No. Nobody knew. Nobody was in the bank when I did it. But—

OSCAR   Did your Uncle Horace ever know you opened it?

LEO   (*shakes his head*) He only looks in it once every six months when he cuts the coupons, and sometimes Manders even does that for him. Uncle Horace don't even have the keys. Manders keeps them for him. Imagine not looking at all that. You can bet if I had the bonds, I'd watch 'em like—

OSCAR   If you had them. (LEO *watches him*) If you had them. Then you could have a share in the mill, you and me. A fine, big share, too. (*Pauses, shrugs*) Well, a man can't be shot for wanting to see his son get on in the world, can he, boy?

LEO   (*looks up, begins to understand*) No, he can't. Natural enough. (*Laughs*) But I haven't got the bonds and Uncle Horace has. And now he can just sit back and wait to be a millionaire.

OSCAR   (*innocently*) You think your Uncle Horace likes you well enough to lend you the bonds if he decides not to use them himself?

LEO   Papa, it must be that you haven't had your breakfast! (*Laughs loudly*) Lend me the bonds! My God—

OSCAR   (*disappointed*) No, I suppose not. Just a fancy of mine. A loan for three months, maybe four, easy enough for us to pay it back then. Anyway, this is only April— (*Slowly counting the months on his fingers*) and if he doesn't look at them until Fall, he wouldn't even miss them out of the box.

LEO   That's it. He wouldn't even miss them. Ah, well—

OSCAR   No, sir. Wouldn't even miss them. How could he miss them if he never looks at them? (*Sighs as* LEO *stares at him*) Well, here we are sitting around waiting for him to come home and invest his money in something he hasn't lifted his hand to get. But I can't help thinking he's acting strange. You laugh when I say he could lend you the bonds if he's not going to use them himself. But would it hurt him?

LEO (*slowly looking at* OSCAR)   No. No, it wouldn't.

OSCAR People ought to help other people. But that's not always the way it happens. (BEN *enters, hangs his coat and hat in hall. Very carefully*) And so sometimes you got to think of yourself. (*As* LEO *stares at him,* BEN *appears in the doorway*) Morning, Ben.

BEN (*coming in, carrying his newspaper*)   Fine sunny morning. Any news from the runaways?

REGINA (*on the staircase*)   There's no news or you would have heard it. Quite a convention so early in the morning, aren't you all? (*Goes to coffee urn.*)

OSCAR You rising mighty late these days. Is that the way they do things in Chicago society?

BEN (*looking at his paper*)   Old Carter died up in Senateville. Eighty-one is a good time for us all, eh? What do you think has really happened to Horace, Regina?

REGINA Nothing.

BEN (*too casually*)   You don't think maybe he never started from Baltimore and never intends to start?

REGINA (*irritated*)   Of course they've started. Didn't I have a letter from Alexandra? What is so strange about people arriving late? He has that cousin in Savannah he's so fond of. He may have stopped to see him. They'll be along today some time, very flattered that you and Oscar are so worried about them.

BEN I'm a natural worrier. Especially when I am getting ready to close a business deal and one of my partners remains silent *and* invisible.

REGINA (*laughs*)   Oh, is that it? I thought you were worried about Horace's health.

OSCAR Oh, that too. Who could help but worry? I'm worried. This is the first day I haven't shot since my head cold.

REGINA (*starts toward dining room*)   Then you haven't had your breakfast. Come along. (OSCAR *and* LEO *follow her.*)

BEN Regina. (*She turns at dining-room door*)   That cousin of Horace's has been dead for years and, in any case, the train does not go through Savannah.

REGINA (*laughs, continues into dining room, seats herself*)

Did he die? You're always remembering about people dying. (BEN *rises*) Now I intend to eat my breakfast in peace, and read my newspaper.

BEN   (*goes toward dining room as he talks*)   This is second breakfast for me. My first was bad. Celia ain't the cook she used to be. Too old to have taste anymore. If she hadn't belonged to Mama, I'd send her off to the country.

(OSCAR *and* LEO *start to eat.* BEN *seats himself.*)

LEO   Uncle Horace will have some tales to tell, I bet. Baltimore is a lively town.

REGINA   (*to* CAL)   The grits isn't hot enough. Take it back.

CAL   Oh, yes'm. (*Calling into the kitchen as he exits*)   Grits didn't hold the heat. Grits didn't hold the heat.

LEO   When I was at school three of the boys and myself took a train once and went over to Baltimore. It was so big we thought we were in Europe. I was just a kid then—

REGINA   I find it very pleasant (ADDIE *enters*) to have breakfast alone. I hate chattering before I've had something hot. (CAL *closes the dining-room doors*) Do be still, Leo.

(ADDIE *comes into the room, begins gathering up the cups, carries them to the large tray. Outside there are the sounds of voices. Quickly* ADDIE *runs into the hall. A few seconds later she appears again in the doorway, her arm around the shoulders of* HORACE GIDDENS, *supporting him.* HORACE *is a tall man of about forty-five. He has been good looking, but now his face is tired and ill. He walks stiffly, as if it were an enormous effort, and carefully, as if he were unsure of his balance.* ADDIE *takes off his overcoat and hangs it on the hall tree. She then helps him to a chair.*)

HORACE   How are you, Addie? How have you been?

ADDIE   I'm all right, Mr. Horace. I've just been worried about you.

(ALEXANDRA *enters. She is flushed and excited, her hat awry, her face dirty. Her arms are full of packages, but she comes quickly to* ADDIE.)

ALEXANDRA   Don't tell me how worried you were. We

couldn't help it and there was no way to send a message.

ADDIE   (*begins to take packages from* ALEXANDRA). Yes, sir, I was mighty worried.

ALEXANDRA   We had to stop in Mobile over night. Papa— (*Looks at him*) Papa didn't feel well. The trip was too much for him, and I made him stop and rest— (*As* ADDIE *takes the last package*) No, don't take that. That's father's medicine. I'll hold it. It mustn't break. Now, about the stuff outside. Papa must have his wheel chair. I'll get that and the valises—

ADDIE   (*very happy, holding* ALEXANDRA'S *arms*) Since when you got to carry your own valises? Since when I ain't old enough to hold a bottle of medicine? (HORACE *coughs*) You feel all right, Mr. Horace?

HORACE   (*nods*) Glad to be sitting down.

ALEXANDRA   (*opening package of medicine*) He doesn't feel all right. (ADDIE *looks at her, then at* HORACE) He just says that. The trip was very hard on him, and now he must go right to bed.

ADDIE   (*looking at him carefully*) Them fancy doctors, they give you help?

HORACE   They did their best.

ALEXANDRA   (*has become conscious of the voices in the dining room*) I bet Mama was worried. I better tell her we're here now. (*She starts for door.*)

HORACE   Zan. (*She stops*) Not for a minute, dear.

ALEXANDRA   Oh, Papa, you feel bad again. I knew you did. Do you want your medicine?

HORACE   No, I don't feel that way. I'm just tired, darling. Let me rest a little.

ALEXANDRA   Yes, but Mama will be mad if I don't tell her we're here.

ADDIE   They're all in there eating breakfast.

ALEXANDRA   Oh, are they all here? Why do they *always* have to be here? I was hoping Papa wouldn't have to see anybody, that it would be nice for him and quiet.

ADDIE   Then let your papa rest for a minute.

HORACE   Addie, I bet your coffee's as good as ever. They don't have such good coffee up north. (*Looks at the urn*) Is it as good, Addie? (ADDIE *starts for coffee urn.*)

ALEXANDRA   No. Dr. Reeves said not much coffee. Just now and then. I'm the nurse now, Addie.

ADDIE   You'd be a better one if you didn't look so dirty. Now go and take a bath. Change your linens, get out a fresh dress and give your hair a good brushing—go on—

ALEXANDRA   Will you be all right, Papa?

ADDIE   Go on.

ALEXANDRA   (*on stairs, talks as she goes up*)   The pills Papa must take once every four hours. And the bottle only when—only if he feels very bad. Now don't move until I come back and don't talk much and remember about his medicine, Addie—

ADDIE   Ring for Belle and have her help you and then I'll make you a fresh breakfast.

ALEXANDRA   (*as she disappears*)   How's Aunt Birdie? Is she here?

ADDIE   It ain't right for you to have coffee? It will hurt you?

HORACE   (*slowly*)   Nothing can make much difference now. Get me a cup, Addie. (*She looks at him, crosses to urn, pours a cup*)   Funny. They can't make coffee up north. (ADDIE *brings him a cup*)   They don't like red pepper, either. (*He takes the cup and gulps it greedily*)   God, that's good. You remember how I used to drink it? Ten, twelve cups a day. So strong it had to stain the cup. (*Then slowly*)   Addie, before I see anybody else, I want to know why Zan came to fetch me home. She's tried to tell me, but she doesn't seem to know herself.

ADDIE   (*turns away*)   I don't know. All I know is big things are going on. Everybody going to be high-tone rich. Big rich. You too. All because smoke's going to start out of a building that ain't even up yet.

HORACE   I've heard about it.

ADDIE   And, er (*Hesitates—steps to him*)   And—well, Zan, she going to marry Mr. Leo in a little while.

HORACE   (*looks at her, then very slowly*)   What are you talking about?

ADDIE   That's right. That's the talk, God help us.

HORACE   (*angrily*)   *What's* the talk?

ADDIE I'm telling you. There's going to be a wedding—
(*Angrily turns away*) Over my dead body there is.

HORACE (*after a second, quietly*) Go and tell them I'm
home.

ADDIE (*hesitates*) Now you ain't to get excited. You're
to be in your bed—

HORACE Go on, Addie. Go and say I'm back. (ADDIE *opens
dining-room doors. He rises with difficulty, stands stiff,
as if he were in pain, facing the dining room.*)

ADDIE Miss Regina. They're home. They got here—

REGINA Horace! (REGINA *quickly, rises, runs into the room.
Warmly*) Horace! You've finally arrived. (*As she kisses
him, the others come forward, all talking together.*)

BEN (*in doorway, carrying a napkin*) Well, sir, you had
us all mighty worried. (*He steps forward. They shake
hands.* ADDIE *exits.*)

OSCAR You're a sight for sore eyes.

HORACE Hello, Ben.

(LEO *enters, eating a biscuit.*)

OSCAR And how you feel? Tip-top, I bet, because that's
the way you're looking.

HORACE (*coldly, irritated with* OSCAR's *lie*) Hello, Oscar.
Hello, Leo, how are you?

LEO (*shaking hands*) I'm fine, sir. But a lot better now
that you're back.

REGINA Now sit down. What did happen to you and
where's Alexandra? I am so excited about seeing you
that I almost forgot about her.

HORACE I didn't feel good, a little weak, I guess, and we
stopped over night to rest. Zan's upstairs washing off the
train dirt.

REGINA Oh, I am so sorry the trip was hard on you. I
didn't think that—

HORACE Well, it's just as if I had never been away. All of
you here—

BEN Waiting to welcome you home.

(BIRDIE *bursts in. She is wearing a flannel kimono and her
face is flushed and excited.*)

BIRDIE (*runs to him, kisses him*) Horace!

HORACE   (*warmly pressing her arm*) I was just wondering where you were, Birdie.

BIRDIE   (*excited*) Oh, I would have been here. I didn't know you were back until Simon said he saw the buggy. (*She draws back to look at him. Her face sobers*) Oh, you don't look well, Horace. No, you don't.

REGINA   (*laughs*) Birdie, what a thing to say—

HORACE   (*looking at* OSCAR) Oscar thinks I look very well.

OSCAR   (*annoyed. Turns on* LEO) Don't stand there holding that biscuit in your hand.

LEO   Oh, well. I'll just finish my breakfast, Uncle Horace, and then I'll give you all the news about the bank— (*He exits into the dining room.*)

OSCAR   And what is that costume you have on?

BIRDIE   (*looking at* HORACE) Now that you're home, you'll feel better. Plenty of good rest and we'll take such fine care of you. (*Stops*) But where is Zan? I missed her so much.

OSCAR   I asked you what is that strange costume you're parading around in?

BIRDIE   (*nervously, backing toward stairs*) Me? Oh! It's my wrapper. I was so excited about Horace I just rushed out of the house—

OSCAR   Did you come across the square dressed that way? My dear Birdie, I—

HORACE   (*to* REGINA, *wearily*) Yes, it's just like old times.

REGINA   (*quickly to* OSCAR) Now, no fights. This is a holiday.

BIRDIE   (*runs quickly up the stairs*) Zan! Zannie!

OSCAR   Birdie! (*She stops.*)

BIRDIE   Oh. Tell Zan I'll be back in a little while. (*Whispers*) Sorry, Oscar. (*Exits.*)

REGINA   (*to* OSCAR *and* BEN) Why don't you go finish your breakfast and let Horace rest for a minute?

BEN   (*crossing to dining room with* OSCAR) Never leave a meal unfinished. There are too many poor people who need the food. Mighty glad to see you home, Horace. Fine to have you back. Fine to have you back.

OSCAR   (*to* LEO *as* BEN *closes dining-room doors*) Your

mother has gone crazy. Running around the streets
like a woman—

(*The moment* REGINA *and* HORACE *are alone, they become
awkward and self-conscious.*)

REGINA (*laughs awkwardly*) Well. Here we are. It's been
a long time. (HORACE *smiles*) Five months. You know,
Horace, I wanted to come and be with you in the hospital, but I didn't know where my duty was. Here, or
with you. But you know how much I *wanted* to come.

HORACE That's kind of you, Regina. There was no need
to come.

REGINA Oh, but there was. Five months lying there all by
yourself, no kinfolks, no friends. Don't try to tell me
you didn't have a bad time of it.

HORACE I didn't have a bad time. (*As she shakes her
head, he becomes insistent*) No, I didn't, Regina. Oh, at
first when I—when I heard the news about myself—
but after I got used to that, I liked it there.

REGINA You *liked* it? (*Coldly*) Isn't that strange. You
liked it so well you didn't want to come home?

HORACE That's not the way to put it. (*Then, kindly, as he
sees her turn her head away*) But there I was and I got
kind of used to it, kind of to like lying there and
thinking. (*Smiles*) I never had much time to think before. And time's become valuable to me.

REGINA It sounds almost like a holiday.

HORACE (*laughs*) It was, sort of. The first holiday I've
had since I was a little kid.

REGINA And here I was thinking you were in pain and—

HORACE (*quietly*) I was in pain.

REGINA And instead you were having a holiday! A holiday
of thinking. Couldn't you have done that here?

HORACE I wanted to do it before I came here. I was thinking about us.

REGINA About us? About you and me? Thinking about
you and me after all these years. (*Unpleasantly*) You
shall tell me everything you thought—some day.

HORACE (*there is silence for a minute*) Regina. (*She
turns to him*) Why did you send Zan to Baltimore?

REGINA   Why? Because I wanted you home. You can't make anything suspicious out of that, can you?

HORACE   I didn't mean to make anything suspicious about it. (*Hesitantly, taking her hand*) Zan said you wanted me to come home. I was so pleased at that and touched it made me feel good.

REGINA   (*taking away her hand, turns*)   Touched that I should want you home?

HORACE   (*sighs*)   I'm saying all the wrong things as usual. Let's try to get along better. There isn't so much more time. Regina, what's all this crazy talk I've been hearing about Zan and Leo? Zan and Leo marrying?

REGINA   (*turning to him, sharply*)   Who gossips so much around here?

HORACE   (*shocked*)   Regina!

REGINA   (*annoyed, anxious to quiet him*)   It's some foolishness that Oscar thought up. I'll explain later. I have no intention of allowing any such arrangement. It was simply a way of keeping Oscar quiet in all this business I've been writing you about—

HORACE   (*carefully*)   What has Zan to do with any business of Oscar's? Whatever it is, you had better put it out of Oscar's head immediately. You know what I think of Leo.

REGINA   But there's no need to talk about it now.

HORACE   There is no need to talk about it ever. Not as long as I live. (HORACE *stops, slowly turns to look at her*) As long as I live. I've been in a hospital for five months. Yet since I've been here you have not once asked me about—about my health. (*Then gently*) Well, I suppose they've written you. I can't live very long.

REGINA   (*coldly*)   I've never understood why people have to talk about this kind of thing.

HORACE   (*there is a silence. Then he looks up at her, his face cold*)   You misunderstand. I don't intend to gossip about my sickness. I thought it was only fair to tell you. I was not asking for your sympathy.

REGINA   (*sharply, turns to him*)   What do the doctors think caused your bad heart?

HORACE   What do you mean?

REGINA   They didn't think it possible, did they, that your
fancy women may have—

HORACE   (*smiles unpleasantly*)   Caused my heart to be
bad? I don't think that's the best scientific theory. You
don't catch heart trouble in bed.

REGINA   (*angrily*)   I didn't think you did. I only thought
you might catch a bad conscience—in bed, as you say.

HORACE   I didn't tell them about my bad conscience. Or
about my fancy women. Nor did I tell them that my wife
has not wanted me in bed with her for— (*Sharply*)
How long is it, Regina? (REGINA *turns to him*) Ten
years? Did you bring me home for this, to make me feel
guilty again? That means you want something. But
you'll not make me feel guilty any more. My "thinking"
has made a difference.

REGINA   I see that it has. (*She looks toward dining-room
door. Then comes to him, her manner warm and
friendly*) It's foolish for us to fight this way. I didn't
mean to be unpleasant. I was stupid.

HORACE   (*wearily*)   God knows I didn't either. I came
home wanting so much not to fight, and then all of a
sudden there we were. I got hurt and—

REGINA   (*hastily*)   It's all my fault. I didn't ask about—
about your illness because I didn't want to remind you
of it. Anyway I never believe doctors when they talk
about— (*Brightly*) when they talk like that.

HORACE   (*not looking at her*)   Well, we'll try our best with
each other. (*He rises.*)

REGINA   (*quickly*)   I'll try. Honestly, I will. Horace, Horace, I know you're tired but, but—couldn't you stay down
here a few minutes longer? I want Ben to tell you something.

HORACE   Tomorrow.

REGINA   I'd like to now. It's very important to me. It's very
important to all of us. (*Gaily, as she moves toward dining room*) Important to your beloved daughter. She'll
be a very great heiress—

HORACE   Will she? That's nice.

REGINA   (*opens doors*)   Ben, are you finished breakfast?

HORACE   Is this the mill business I've had so many letters about?

REGINA   (*to* BEN)   Horace would like to talk to you now.

HORACE   Horace would not like to talk to you now. I am very tired, Regina—

REGINA   (*comes to him*)   Please. You've said we'll try our best with each other. I'll try. Really, I will. Please do this for me now. You will see what I've done while you've been away. How I watched your interests. (*Laughs gaily*) And I've done very well too. But things can't be delayed any longer. Everything must be settled this week— (HORACE *sits down*. BEN *enters*. OSCAR *has stayed in the dining room, his head turned to watch them*. LEO *is pretending to read the newspaper*) Now you must tell Horace all about it. Only be quick because he is very tired and must go to bed. (HORACE *is looking up at her. His face hardens as she speaks*) But I think your news will be better for him than all the medicine in the world.

BEN   (*looking at* HORACE)   It could wait. Horace may not feel like talking today.

REGINA   What an old faker you are! You know it can't wait. You know it must be finished this week. You've been just as anxious for Horace to get here as I've been.

BEN   (*very jovial*)   I suppose I have been. And why not? Horace has done Hubbard Sons many a good turn. Why shouldn't I be anxious to help him now?

REGINA   (*laughs*)   Help him! Help him when you need him, that's what you mean.

BEN   What a woman you married, Horace. (*Laughs awkwardly when* HORACE *does not answer*) Well, then I'll make it quick. You know what I've been telling you for years. How I've always said that every one of us little Southern businessmen had great things— (*Extends his arm*)—right beyond our finger tips. It's been my dream: my dream to make those fingers grow longer: I'm a lucky man, Horace, a lucky man. To dream and to live to get what you've dreamed of. That's *my* idea of a lucky man. (*Looks at his fingers as his arm drops slowly*) For thirty years I've cried bring the cotton mills

to the cotton. (HORACE *opens medicine bottle*) Well,
finally I got up nerve to go to Marshall Company in
Chicago.

HORACE   I know all this. (*He takes the medicine.* REGINA
rises, steps to him.)

BEN   Can I get you something?

HORACE   Some water, please.

REGINA   (*turns quickly*)   Oh, I'm sorry. Let me. (*Brings
him a glass of water. He drinks as they wait in silence*)
You feel all right now?

HORACE   Yes. You wrote me. I know all that.

(OSCAR *enters from dining room.*)

REGINA   (*triumphantly*)   But you don't know that in the
last few days Ben has agreed to give us—you, I mean—
a much larger share.

HORACE   Really? That's very generous of him.

BEN   (*laughs*)   It wasn't so generous of me. It was smart
of Regina.

REGINA   (*as if she were signaling* HORACE)   I explained to
Ben that perhaps you hadn't answered his letters because you didn't think he was offering you enough, and
that the time was getting short and you could guess
how much he needed you—

HORACE   (*smiles at her, nods*)   And I could guess that he
wants to keep control in the family.

REGINA   (*to* BEN, *triumphantly*)   Exactly. (*To* HORACE) So
I did a little bargaining for you and convinced my
brothers they weren't the only Hubbards who had a
business sense.

HORACE   Did you have to convince them of that? How
little people know about each other! (*Laughs*) But
you'll know better about Regina next time, eh, Ben?
(BEN, REGINA, HORACE *laugh together.* OSCAR's *face is
angry*) Now let's see. We're getting a bigger share.
(*Looking at* OSCAR) Who's getting less?

BEN   Oscar.

HORACE   Well, Oscar, you've grown very unselfish. What's
happened to you?

(LEO *enters from dining room.*)

BEN (*quickly, before* OSCAR *can answer*) Oscar doesn't mind. Not worth fighting about now, eh, Oscar?

OSCAR (*angrily*) I'll get mine in the end. You can be sure of that. I've got my son's future to think about.

HORACE (*sharply*) Leo? Oh, I see. (*Puts his head back, laughs.* REGINA *looks at him nervously*) I am beginning to see. Everybody will get theirs.

BEN I knew you'd see it. Seventy-five thousand, and that seventy-five thousand will make you a million.

REGINA (*steps to table, leaning forward*) It will, Horace, it will.

HORACE I believe you. (*After a second*) Now I can understand Oscar's self-sacrifice, but what did you have to promise Marshall Company besides the money you're putting up?

BEN They wouldn't take promises. They wanted guarantees.

HORACE Of what?

BEN (*nods*) Water power. Free and plenty of it.

HORACE You got them that, of course.

BEN Cheap. You'd think the Governor of a great state would make his price a little higher. From pride, you know. (HORACE *smiles.* BEN *smiles*) Cheap wages. "What do you mean by cheap wages?" I say to Marshall. "Less than Massachusetts," he says to me, "and that averages eight a week," "Eight a week! By God," I tell him, "*I'd* work for eight a week myself." Why, there ain't a mountain white or a town nigger but wouldn't give his right arm for three silver dollars every week, eh, Horace?

HORACE Sure. And they'll take less than that when you get around to playing them off against each other. You can save a little money that way, Ben. (*Angrily*) And make them hate each other just a little more than they do now.

REGINA What's all this about?

BEN (*laughs*) There'll be no trouble from anybody, white or black. Marshall said that to me. "What about strikes? That's all we've had in Massachusetts for the last three years." I say to him, "What's a strike? I never heard of one. Come South, Marshall. We got good folks and we don't stand for any fancy fooling."

HORACE You're right. (*Slowly*) Well, it looks like you made a good deal for yourselves, and for Marshall, too. (*To* BEN) Your father used to say he made the thousands and you boys would make the millions. I think he was right. (*Rises.*)

REGINA (*they are all looking at* HORACE. *She laughs nervously*) Millions for *us*, too.

HORACE Us? You and me? I don't think so. We've got enough money, Regina. We'll just sit by and watch the boys grow rich. (*They watch* HORACE *tensely as he begins to move toward the staircase. He passes* LEO, *looks at him for a second*) How's everything at the bank, Leo?

LEO Fine, sir. Everything is fine.

HORACE How are all the ladies in Mobile? (HORACE *turns to* REGINA, *sharply*) Whatever made you think I'd let Zan marry—

REGINA Do you mean that you are turning this down? Is it possible that's what you mean?

BEN No, that's not what he means. Turning down a fortune. Horace is tired. He'd rather talk about it tomorrow—

REGINA We can't keep putting it off this way. Oscar must be in Chicago by the end of the week with the money and contracts.

OSCAR (*giggles, pleased*) Yes, sir. Got to be there end of the week. No sense going without the money.

REGINA (*tensely*) I've waited long enough for your answer. I'm not going to wait any longer.

HORACE (*very deliberately*) I'm very tired now, Regina.

BEN (*hastily*) Now, Horace probably has his reasons. Things he'd like explained. Tomorrow will do. I can—

REGINA (*turns to* BEN, *sharply*) I want to know his reasons now! (*Turns back to* HORACE.)

HORACE (*as he climbs the steps*) I don't know them all myself. Let's leave it at that.

REGINA We shall not leave it at that! We have waited for you here like children. Waited for you to come home.

HORACE So that you could invest my money. So that is why you wanted me home? Well, I had hoped— (*Quietly*) If you are disappointed, Regina, I'm sorry. But I must do what I think best. We'll talk about it another day.

REGINA We'll talk about it now. Just you and me.

HORACE (*looks down at her. His voice is tense*) Please, Regina, it's been a hard trip. I don't feel well. Please leave me alone now.

REGINA (*quietly*) I want to talk to you, Horace. I'm coming up. (*He looks at her for a minute, then moves on again out of sight. She begins to climb the stairs.*)

BEN (*softly.* REGINA *turns to him as he speaks*) Sometimes it is better to wait for the sun to rise again. (*She does not answer*) And sometimes, as our mother used to tell you, (REGINA *starts upstairs*) it's unwise for a good-looking woman to frown. (BEN *rises, moves toward stairs*) Softness and a smile do more to the heart of men — (*She disappears.* BEN *stands looking up the stairs. There is a long silence. Then, suddenly,* OSCAR *giggles.*)

OSCAR Let us hope she'll change his mind. Let us hope. (*After a second* BEN *crosses to table, picks up his newspaper.* OSCAR *looks at* BEN. *The silence makes* LEO *uncomfortable.*)

LEO The paper says twenty-seven cases of yellow fever in New Orleans. Guess the flood-waters caused it. (*Nobody pays attention*) Thought they were building the levees high enough. Like the niggers always say: a man born of woman can't build nothing high enough for the Mississippi. (*Gets no answer. Gives an embarrassed laugh.*)

(*Upstairs there is the sound of voices. The voices are not loud, but* BEN, OSCAR, LEO *become conscious of them.* LEO *crosses to landing, looks up, listens.*)

OSCAR (*pointing up*) Now just suppose she don't change his mind? Just suppose he keeps on refusing?

BEN (*without conviction*) He's tired. It was a mistake to talk to him today. He's a sick man, but he isn't a crazy one.

OSCAR (*giggles*) But just suppose he is crazy. What then?

BEN (*puts down his paper, peers at* OSCAR) Then we'll go outside for the money. There's plenty who would give it.

OSCAR And plenty who will want a lot for what they give.

The ones who are rich enough to give will be smart enough to want. That means we'd be working for them, don't it, Ben?

BEN You don't have to tell me the things I told you six months ago.

OSCAR Oh, you're right not to worry. She'll change his mind. She always has. (*There is a silence. Suddenly* REGINA's *voice becomes louder and sharper. All of them begin to listen now. Slowly* BEN *rises, goes to listen by the staircase.* OSCAR, *watching him, smiles. As they listen* REGINA's *voice becomes very loud.* HORACE's *voice is no longer heard*) Maybe. But I don't believe it. I never did believe he was going in with us.

BEN (*turning on him*) What the hell do you expect me to do?

OSCAR (*mildly*) Nothing. You done your almighty best. Nobody could blame you if the whole thing just dripped away right through our fingers. You can't do a thing. But there may be something I could do for us. (OSCAR *rises*) Or, I might better say, Leo could do for us. (BEN *stops, turns, looks at* OSCAR. LEO *is staring at* OSCAR) Ain't that true, son? Ain't it true you might be able to help your own kinfolks?

LEO (*nervously taking a step to him*) Papa, I—

BEN (*slowly*) How would he help us, Oscar?

OSCAR Leo's got a friend. Leo's friend owns eighty-eight thousand dollars in Union Pacific bonds. (BEN *turns to look at* LEO) Leo's friend don't look at the bonds much —not for five or six months at a time.

BEN (*after a pause*) Union Pacific. Uh, huh. Let me understand. Leo's friend would—would lend him these bonds and he—

OSCAR (*nods*) Would be kind enough to lend them to us.

BEN Leo.

LEO (*excited, comes to him*) Yes, sir?

BEN When would your friend be wanting the bonds back?

LEO (*very nervous*) I don't know. I—well, I—

OSCAR (*sharply. Steps to him*) You told me he won't look at them until Fall—

LEO   Oh, that's right. But I—not till Fall. Uncle Horace never—

BEN   (*sharply*)   Be still.

OSCAR   (*smiles at* LEO)   Your uncle doesn't wish to know your friend's name.

LEO   (*starts to laugh*)   That's a good one. Not know his name—

OSCAR   Shut up, Leo! (LEO *turns away slowly, moves to table.* BEN *turns to* OSCAR) He won't look at them again until September. That gives us five months. Leo will return the bonds in three months. And we'll have no trouble raising the money once the mills are going up. Will Marshall accept bonds?

(BEN *stops to listen to sudden sharp voices from above. The voices are now very angry and very loud.*)

BEN   (*smiling*)   Why not? Why not? (*Laughs*) Good. We are lucky. We'll take the loan from Leo's friend—I think he will make a safer partner than our sister. (*Nods toward stairs. Turns to* LEO) How soon can you get them?

LEO   Today. Right now. They're in the safe-deposit box and—

BEN   (*sharply*)   I don't want to know where they are.

OSCAR   (*laughs*)   We will keep it secret from you. (*Pats* BEN's *arm.*)

BEN   (*smiles*)   Good. Draw a check for our part. You can take the night train for Chicago. Well, Oscar (*holds out his hand*), good luck to us.

OSCAR   Leo will be taken care of?

LEO   I'm entitled to Uncle Horace's share. I'd enjoy being a partner—

BEN   (*turns to stare at him*)   You would? You can go to hell, you little— (*Starts toward* LEO.)

OSCAR   (*nervously*)   Now, now. He didn't mean that. I only want to be sure he'll get something out of all this.

BEN   Of course. We'll take care of him. We won't have any trouble about that. I'll see you at the store.

OSCAR   (*nods*)   That's settled then. Come on, son. (*Starts for door.*)

LEO (*puts out his hand*) I was only going to say what a
great day this was for me and— (BEN *ignores his hand.*)

BEN Go on.

(LEO *looks at him, turns, follows* OSCAR *out.* BEN *stands
where he is, thinking. Again the voices upstairs can be
heard.* REGINA's *voice is high and furious.* BEN *looks up,
smiles, winces at the noise.*)

ALEXANDRA (*upstairs*) Mama—Mama—don't . . . (*The
noise of running footsteps is heard and* ALEXANDRA
comes running down the steps, speaking as she comes)
Uncle Ben! Uncle Ben! Please go up. Please make
Mama stop. Uncle Ben, he's sick, he's so sick. How can
Mama talk to him like that—please, make her stop.
She'll—

BEN Alexandra, you have a tender heart.

ALEXANDRA (*crying*) Go on up, Uncle Ben, please—

(*Suddenly the voices stop. A second later there is the
sound of a door being slammed.*)

BEN Now you see. Everything is over. Don't worry. (*He
starts for the door*) Alexandra, I want you to tell your
mother how sorry I am that I had to leave. And don't
worry so, my dear. Married folk frequently raise their
voices, unfortunately. (*He starts to put on his hat and
coat as* REGINA *appears on the stairs.*)

ALEXANDRA (*furiously*) How can you treat Papa like
this? He's sick. He's very sick. Don't you know that? I
won't let you.

REGINA Mind your business, Alexandra. (*To* BEN. *Her
voice is cold and calm*) How much longer can you wait
for the money?

BEN (*putting on his coat*) He has refused? My, that's too
bad.

REGINA He will change his mind. I'll find a way to make
him. What's the longest you can wait now?

BEN I could wait until next week. But I can't wait until
next week. (*He giggles, pleased at the joke*) I could but
I can't. Could and can't. Well, I must go now. I'm very
late—

REGINA (*coming downstairs toward him*) You're not going. I want to talk to you.

BEN I was about to give Alexandra a message for you. I wanted to tell you that Oscar is going to Chicago tonight, so we can't be here for our usual Friday supper.

REGINA (*tensely*) Oscar is going to Chi— (*Softly*) What do you mean?

BEN Just that. Everything is settled. He's going on to deliver to Marshall—

REGINA (*taking a step to him*) I demand to know what— You are lying. You are trying to scare me. *You haven't got the money.* How could you have it? You can't have— (BEN *laughs*) You will wait until I—

(HORACE *comes into view on the landing.*)

BEN You are getting out of hand. Since when do I take orders from you?

REGINA Wait, you— (BEN *stops*) How *can* he go to Chicago? Did a ghost arrive with the money? (BEN *starts for the hall*) I don't believe you. Come back here. (REGINA *starts after him*) Come back here, you— (*The door slams. She stops in the doorway, staring, her fists clenched. After a pause she turns slowly.*)

HORACE (*very quietly*) It's a great day when you and Ben cross swords. I've been waiting for it for years.

ALEXANDRA Papa, Papa, please go back! You will—

HORACE And so they don't need you, and so you will not have your millions, after all.

REGINA (*turns slowly*) You hate to see anybody live now, don't you? You hate to think that I'm going to be alive and have what I want.

HORACE I should have known you'd think that was the reason.

REGINA Because you're going to die and you know you're going to die.

ALEXANDRA (*shrilly*) Mama! Don't— Don't listen, Papa. Just don't listen. Go away—

HORACE Not to keep you from getting what you want. Not even partly that. (*Holding to the rail*) I'm sick of you, sick of this house, sick of my life here. I'm sick of your brothers and their dirty tricks to make a dime. There must be better ways of getting rich than cheating niggers on a pound of bacon. Why should I give you the money? (*Very angrily*) To pound the bones of this town to make dividends for you to spend? You wreck the town, you and your brother, *you* wreck the town and live on it. Not me. Maybe it's easy for the dying to be honest. But it's not my fault I'm dying. (ADDIE *enters, stands at door quietly*) I'll do no more harm now. I've done enough. I'll die my own way. And I'll do it without making the world any worse. I leave that to you.

REGINA   (*looks up at him slowly, calmly*).   I hope you die. I hope you die soon. (*Smiles*) I'll be waiting for you to die.

ALEXANDRA   (*shrieking*) Papa! Don't— Don't listen— Don't—

ADDIE   Come here, Zan. Come out of this room.

(ALEXANDRA *runs quickly to* ADDIE, *who holds her*. HORACE *turns slowly and starts upstairs.*)

Curtain

Act Three

SCENE: *Same as Act One. Two weeks later. It is late after-noon and it is raining.*

AT RISE: HORACE *is sitting near the window in a wheel chair. On the table next to him is a safe-deposit box, and a small bottle of medicine.* BIRDIE *and* ALEXANDRA *are playing the piano. On a chair is a large sewing basket.*

BIRDIE   (*counting for* ALEXANDRA)   One and two and three and four. One and two and three and· four. (*Nods— turns to* HORACE) We once played together, Horace. Remember?

HORACE   (*has been looking out of the window*)   What, Birdie?

BIRDIE   We played together. You and me.

ALEXANDRA   *Papa* used to play?

BIRDIE   Indeed he did. (ADDIE *appears at the door in a large kitchen apron. She is wiping her hands on a towel*) He played the fiddle and very well, too.

ALEXANDRA   (*turns to smile at* HORACE)   I never knew—

ADDIE   Where's your mama?

ALEXANDRA   Gone to Miss Safronia's to fit her dresses.

(ALLIE *nods, starts to exit.*)

HORACE   Addie.

ADDIE   Yes, Mr. Horace.

HORACE   (*speaks as if he had made a sudden decision*)   Tell Cal to get on his things. I want him to go an er-rand.

200

(ADDIE *nods, exits.* HORACE *moves nervously in his chair, looks out of the window.*)

ALEXANDRA (*who has been watching him*) It's too bad it's been raining all day, Papa. But you can go out in the yard tomorrow. Don't be restless.

HORACE I'm not restless, darling.

BIRDIE I remember so well the time we played together, your papa and me. It was the first time Oscar brought me here to supper. I had never seen all the Hubbards together before, and you know what a ninny I am and how shy. (*Turns to look at* HORACE) You said you could play the fiddle and you'd be much obliged if I'd play with you. *I* was obliged to *you*, all right, all right. (*Laughs when he does not answer her*) Horace, you haven't heard a word I've said.

HORACE Birdie, when did Oscar get back from Chicago?

BIRDIE Hasn't he been here yet?

ALEXANDRA (*stops playing*) No. Neither has Uncle Ben since—since that day.

BIRDIE Oh, I didn't know it was *that* bad. Oscar never tells me anything—

HORACE (*smiles, nods*) The Hubbards have had their great quarrel. I knew it would come some day. (*Laughs*) It came.

ALEXANDRA It came. It certainly came all right.

BIRDIE (*amazed*) But Oscar was in such a good humor when he got home, I didn't—

HORACE Yes, I can understand that.

(ADDIE *enters carrying a large tray with glasses, a carafe of elderberry wine and a plate of cookies, which she puts on the table.*)

ALEXANDRA Addie! A party! What for?

ADDIE Nothing for. I had the fresh butter, so I made the cakes, and a little elderberry does the stomach good in the rain.

BIRDIE Isn't this nice! A party just for us. Let's play party music, Zan.

(ALEXANDRA *begins to play a gay piece.*)

ADDIE (*to* HORACE, *wheeling his chair to center*) Come over here, Mr. Horace, and don't be thinking so much.

A glass of elderberry will do more good.

(ALEXANDRA *reaches for a cake.* BIRDIE *pours herself a glass of wine.*)

ALEXANDRA   Good cakes, Addie. It's nice here. Just us. Be nice if it could always be this way.

BIRDIE   (*nods happily*)   Quiet and restful.

ADDIE   Well, it won't be that way long. Little while now, even sitting here, you'll hear the red bricks going into place. The next day the smoke'll be pushing out the chimneys and by church time that Sunday every human born of woman will be living on chicken. That's how Mr. Ben's been telling the story.

HORACE   (*looks at her*)   They believe it that way?

ADDIE   Believe it? They use to believing what Mr. Ben orders. There ain't been so much talk around here since Sherman's army didn't come near.

HORACE   (*softly*)   They are fools.

ADDIE   (*nods, sits down with the sewing basket*)   You ain't born in the South unless you're a fool.

BIRDIE   (*has drunk another glass of wine*)   But we didn't play together after that night. Oscar said he didn't like me to play on the piano. (*Turns to* ALEXANDRA)   You know what he said that night?

ALEXANDRA   Who?

BIRDIE   Oscar. He said that music made him nervous. He said he just sat and waited for the next note. (ALEXANDRA *laughs*)   He wasn't poking fun. He meant it. Ah, well— (*She finishes her glass, shakes her head.* HORACE *looks at her, smiles*)   Your papa don't like to admit it, but he's been mighty kind to me all these years. (*Running the back of her hand along his sleeve*)   Often he'd step in when somebody said something and once— (*She stops, turns away, her face still*)   Once he stopped Oscar from— (*She stops, turns. Quickly*)   I'm sorry I said that. Why, here I am so happy and yet I think about bad things. (*Laughs nervously*)   That's not right, now, is it? (*She pours a drink.* CAL *appears in the door. He has on an old coat and is carrying a torn umbrella.*)

ALEXANDRA   Have a cake, Cal.

CAL (*comes in, takes a cake*) Yes'm. You want me, Mr. Horace?

HORACE What time is it, Cal?

CAL 'Bout ten minutes before it's five.

HORACE All right. Now you walk yourself down to the bank.

CAL It'll be closed. Nobody'll be there but Mr. Manders, Mr. Joe Horns, Mr. Leo—

HORACE Go in the back way. They'll be at the table, going over the day's business. (*Points to the deposit box*) See that box?

CAL (*nods*) Yes, sir.

HORACE You tell Mr. Manders that Mr. Horace says he's much obliged to him for bringing the box, it arrived all right.

CAL (*bewildered*) He know you got the box. He bring it himself Wednesday. I opened the door to him and he say, "Hello, Cal, coming on to summer weather."

HORACE You say just what I tell you. Understand?

(BIRDIE *pours another drink, stands at table.*)

CAL No, sir. I ain't going to say I understand. I'm going down and tell a man he give you something he already know he give you, and you say "understand."

HORACE Now, Cal.

CAL Yes, sir. I just going to say you obliged for the box coming all right. I ain't going to understand it, but I'm going to say it.

HORACE And tell him I want him to come over here after supper, and to bring Mr. Sol Fowler with him.

CAL (*nods*) He's to come after supper and bring Mr. Sol Fowler, your attorney-*at*-law, with him.

HORACE (*smiles*) That's right. Just walk right in the back room and say your piece. (*Slowly*) In front of everybody.

CAL Yes, sir. (*Mumbles to himself as he exits.*)

ALEXANDRA (*who has been watching* HORACE) Is anything the matter, Papa?

HORACE Oh, no. Nothing.

ADDIE Miss Birdie, that elderberry going to give you a headache spell.

BIRDIE   (*beginning to be drunk. Gaily*) Oh, I don't think
so. I don't think it will.

ALEXANDRA   (*as* HORACE *puts his hands to his throat*) Do
you want your medicine, Papa?

HORACE No, no. I'm all right, darling.

BIRDIE Mama used to give me elderberry wine when I
was a little girl. For hiccoughs. (*Laughs*) You know, I
don't think people get hiccoughs any more. Isn't that
funny? (BIRDIE *laughs.* HORACE *and* ALEXANDER *laugh*)
I used to get hiccoughs just when I shouldn't have.

ADDIE   (*nods*) And nobody gets growing pains any more.
That is funny. Just as if there was some style in what
you get. One year an ailment's stylish and the next
year it ain't.

BIRDIE   (*turns*) I remember. It was my first big party, at
Lionnet I mean, and I was so excited, and there I was
with hiccoughs and Mama laughing. (*Softly. Looking
at carafe*) Mama always laughed. (*Picks up carafe*) A
big party, a lovely dress from Mr. Worth in Paris,
France, and hiccoughs. (*Pours drink*) My brother
pounding me on the back and Mama with the elderberry bottle, laughing at me. Everybody was on their
way to come, and I was such a ninny, hiccoughing
away. (*Drinks*) You know, that was the first day I ever
saw Oscar Hubbard. The Ballongs were selling their
horses and he was going there to buy. He passed and
lifted his hat—we could see him from the window—
and my brother, to tease Mama, said maybe we should
have invited the Hubbards to the party. He said Mama
didn't like them because they kept a store, and he said
that was old-fashioned of her. (*Her face lights up*) And
then, and *then*, I saw Mama angry for the first time in
my life. She said that wasn't the reason. She said she
was old-fashioned, but not that way. She said she was
old-fashioned enough not to like people who killed
animals they couldn't use, and who made their money
charging awful interest to poor, ignorant niggers and
cheating them on what they bought. She was very
angry, Mama was. I had never seen her face like that.
And then suddenly she laughed and said, "Look, I've

frightened Birdie out of the hiccoughs." (*Her head drops. Then softly*) And so she had. They were all gone. (*Moves to sofa, sits.*)

ADDIE   Yeah, they got mighty well off cheating niggers. Well, there are people who eat the earth and eat all the people on it like in the Bible with the locusts. Then there are people who stand around and watch them eat it. (*Softly*) Sometimes I think it ain't right to stand and watch them do it.

BIRDIE   (*thoughtfully*)   Like I say, if we could only go back to Lionnet. Everybody's be better there. They'd be good and kind. I like people to be kind. (*Pours drink*) Don't you, Horace; don't you like people to be kind?

HORACE   Yes, Birdie.

BIRDIE   (*very drunk now*)   Yes, that was the first day I ever saw Oscar. Who would have thought— (*Quickly*) You all want to know something? Well, I don't like Leo. My very own son, and I don't like him. (*Laughs, gaily*) My, I guess I even like Oscar more.

ALEXANDRA   Why did you marry Uncle Oscar?

ADDIE   (*sharply*)   That's no question for you to be asking.

HORACE   (*sharply*)   Why not? She's heard enough around here to ask anything.

ALEXANDRA   Aunt Birdie, why did you marry Uncle Oscar?

BIRDIE   I don't know. I thought I liked him. He was kind to me and. I thought it was because he liked me too. But that wasn't the reason— (*Wheels on* ALEXANDRA) Ask why *he* married *me*. I can tell you that: he's told it to me often enough.

ADDIE   (*leaning forward*)   Miss Birdie, don't—

BIRDIE   (*speaking very rapidly, tensely*)   My family was good and the cotton on Lionnet's fields was better. Ben Hubbard wanted the cotton and (*Rises*) Oscar Hubbard married it for him. He was kind to me, then. He used to smile at me. He hasn't smiled at me since. Everybody knew that's what he married me for. (ADDIE *rises*) Everybody but me. Stupid, stupid me.

ALEXANDRA   (*to* HORACE, *holding his hand, softly*).   I see. (*Hesitates*) Papa, I mean—when you feel better couldn't we go away? I mean, by ourselves. Couldn't we find a way to go—

HORACE   Yes, I know what you mean. We'll try to find a way. I promise you, darling.

ADDIE   (*moves to* BIRDIE) Rest a bit, Miss Birdie. You get talking like this you'll get a headache and—

BIRDIE   (*sharply, turning to her*) I've never had a headache in my life. (*Begins to cry hysterically*) You know it as well as I do. (*Turns to* ALEXANDRA) I never had a headache, Zan. That's a lie they tell for me. I drink. All by myself, in my own room, by myself, I drink. Then, when they want to hide it, they say, "Birdie's got a headache again"—

ALEXANDRA   (*comes to her quickly*) Aunt Birdie.

BIRDIE   (*turning away*) Even you won't like me now. You won't like me any more.

ALEXANDRIA   I love you. I'll always love you.

BIRDIE   (*furiously*) Well, don't. Don't love me. Because in twenty years you'll just be like me. They'll do all the same things to you. (*Begins to laugh hysterically*) You know what? In twenty-two years I haven't had a whole day of happiness. Oh, a little, like today with you all. But never a single, whole day. I say to myself, if only I had one more *whole* day, then— (*The laugh stops*) And that's the way you'll be. And you'll trail after them, just like me, hoping they won't be so mean that day or say something to make you feel so bad—only you'll be worse off because you haven't got my Mama to remember— (*Turns away, her head drops. She stands quietly, swaying a little, holding to the sofa.* ALEXANDRA *leans down, puts her cheek on* BIRDIE's *arm.*)

ALEXANDRA   (*to* BIRDIE) I guess we were all trying to make a happy day. You know, we sit around and try to pretend nothing's happened. We try to pretend we are not here. We make believe we are just by ourselves, some place else, and it doesn't seem to work. (*Kisses* BIRDIE's *hand*) Come now, Aunt Birdie, I'll walk you home. You and me. (*She takes* BIRDIE's *arm. They move slowly out.*)

BIRDIE   (*softly as they exit*) You and me.

ADDIE   (*after a minute*) Well. First time I ever heard

Miss Birdie say a word. (HORACE *looks at her*) Maybe it's good for her. I'm just sorry Zan had to hear it. (HORACE *moves his head as if he were uncomfortable*) You feel bad, don't you? (*He shrugs.*)

HORACE   So you didn't want Zan to hear? It would be nice to let her stay innocent, like Birdie at her age. Let her listen now. Let her see everything. How else is she going to know that she's got to get away? I'm trying to show her that. I'm trying, but I've only got a little time left. She can even hate me when I'm dead, if she'll only learn to hate and fear this.

ADDIE   Mr. Horace—

HORACE   Pretty soon there'll be nobody to help her but you.

ADDIE   (*crossing to him*)   What can I do?

HORACE   Take her away.

ADDIE   How can I do that? Do you think they'd let me just go away with her?

HORACE   I'll fix it so they can't stop you when you're ready to go. You'll go, Addie?

ADDIE   (*after a second, softly*)   Yes, sir. I promise. (*He touches her arm, nods.*)

HORACE   (*quietly*)   I'm going to have Sol Fowler make me a nice will. They'll make trouble, but you make Zan stand firm and Fowler'll do the rest. Addie, I'd like to leave you something for yourself. I always wanted to.

ADDIE   (*laughs*)   Don't you do that, Mr. Horace. A nigger woman in a white man's will! I'd never get it nohow.

HORACE   I know. But upstairs in the armoire drawer there's seventeen hundred dollars bills. It's money left from my trip. It's in an envelope with your name. It's for you.

ADDIE   Seventeen hundred dollar bills! My God, Mr. Horace, I won't know how to count up that high. (*Shyly*) It's mighty kind and good of you. I don't know what to say for thanks—

CAL   (*appears in doorway*)   I'm back. (*No answer*) I'm back.

ADDIE   So we see.

HORACE   Well?

CAL   Nothing. I just went down and spoke my piece. Just

like you told me. I say, "Mr. Horace he thank you mightily for the safe box arriving in good shape and he say you come right after supper to his house and bring Mr. Attorney-at-law Sol Fowler with you." Then I wipe my hands on my coat. Every time I ever told a lie in my whole life, I wipe my hands right after. Can't help doing it. Well, while I'm wiping my hands, Mr. Leo jump up and say to me, "What box? What you talking about?"

HORACE (*smiles*) Did he?

CAL And Mr. Leo say he got to leave a little early cause he got something to do. And then Mr. Manders say Mr. Leo should sit right down and finish up his work and stop acting like somebody made him Mr. President. So he sit down. Now, just like I told you, Mr. Manders was mighty surprised with the message because he knows right well he brought the box— (*Points to box, sighs*) But he took it all right. Some men take everything easy and some do not.

HORACE (*puts his head back, laughs*) Mr. Leo was telling the truth; he *has* got something to do. I hope Manders don't keep him too long. (*Outside there is the sound of voices.* CAL *exits.* ADDIE *crosses quickly to* HORACE, *puts basket on table, begins to wheel his chair toward the stairs. Sharply*) No. Leave me where I am.

ADDIE But that's Miss Regina coming back.

HORACE (*nods, looking at door*) Go away, Addie.

ADDIE (*hesitates*) Mr. Horace. Don't talk no more today. you don't feel well and it won't do no good—

HORACE (*as he hears footsteps in the hall*) Go on. (*She looks at him for a second, then picks up her sewing from table and exits as* REGINA *comes in from hall.* HORACE's *chair is now so placed that he is in front of the table with the medicine.* REGINA *stands in the hall, shakes umbrella, stands it in the corner, takes off her cloak and throws it over the banister. She stares at* HORACE.)

REGINA (*as she takes off her gloves*) We had agreed that you were to stay in your part of this house and I in mine. This room is *my* part of the house. Please don't come down here again.

HORACE   I won't.

REGINA   (*crosses toward bell-cord*)   I'll get Cal to take you upstairs.

HORACE   (*smiles*)   Before you do I want to tell you that after all, we have invested our money in Hubbard Sons and Marshall, Cotton Manufacturers.

REGINA   (*stops, turns, stares at him*)   What are you talking about? You haven't seen Ben— When did you change your mind?

HORACE   I didn't change my mind. *I* didn't invest the money. (*Smiles*) It was invested for me.

REGINA   (*angrily*)   What—?

HORACE   I had eighty-eight thousand dollars' worth of Union Pacific bonds in that safe-deposit box. They are not there now. Go and look. (*As she stares at him, he points to the box*) Go and look, Regina. (*She crosses quickly to the box, opens it*) Those bonds are as negotiable as money.

REGINA   (*turns back to him*)   What kind of joke are you playing now? Is this for my benefit?

HORACE   I don't look in that box very often, but three days ago, on Wednesday it was, because I had made a decision—

REGINA   I want to know what you are talking about.

HORACE   (*sharply*)   Don't interrupt me again. Because I had made a decision, I sent for the box. The bonds were gone. Eighty-eight thousand dollars gone. (*He smiles at her.*)

REGINA   (*after a moment's silence, quietly*)   Do you think I'm crazy enough to believe what you're saying?

HORACE   (*shrugs*)   Believe anything you like.

REGINA   (*stares at him, slowly*)   Where did they go to?

HORACE   They are in Chicago. With Mr. Marshall, I should guess.

REGINA   What did they do? Walk to Chicago? Have you really gone crazy?

HORACE   Leo took the bonds.

REGINA   (*turns sharply then speaks softly, without conviction*)   I don't believe it.

HORACE   (*leans forward*)   I wasn't there but I can guess what happened. This fine gentleman, to whom you were willing to marry your daughter, took the keys and opened the box. You remember that the day of the fight Oscar went to Chicago? Well, he went with my bonds that his son Leo had stolen for him. (*Pleasantly*) And for Ben, of course, too.

REGINA   (*slowly, nods*)   When did you find out the bonds were gone?

HORACE   Wednesday night.

REGINA   I thought that's what you said. Why have you waited three days to do anything? (*Suddenly laughs*) This *will* make a fine story.

HORACE   (*nods*)   Couldn't it?

REGINA   (*still laughing*)   A fine story to hold over their heads. How could they be such fools? (*Turns to him.*)

HORACE   But I'm not going to hold it over their heads.

REGINA   (*the laugh stops*)   What?

HORACE   (*turns his chair to face her*)   I'm going to let them keep the bonds—as a loan from you. An eighty-eight-thousand-dollar loan; they should be grateful to you. They will be, I think.

REGINA   (*slowly, smiles*)   I see. You are punishing me. But I won't let you punish me. If you won't do anything, I will. Now. (*She starts for door.*)

HORACE   You won't do anything. Because you can't. (RE-GINA *stops*) It won't do you any good to make trouble because I shall simply say that I lent them the bonds.

REGINA   (*slowly*)   You would do that?

HORACE   Yes. For once in your life I am tying your hands. There is nothing for you to do. (*There is silence. Then she sits down.*)

REGINA   I see. You are going to lend them the bonds and let them keep all the profit they make on them, and there is nothing I can do about it. Is that right?

HORACE   Yes.

REGINA   (*softly*)   Why did you say that I was making this gift?

HORACE I was coming to that. I am going to make a new will, Regina, leaving you eighty-eight thousand dollars in Union Pacific bonds. The rest will go to Zan. It's true that your brothers have borrowed your share for a little while. After my death I advise you to talk to Ben and Oscar. They won't admit anything and Ben, I think, will be smart enough to see that he's safe. Because I knew about the theft and said nothing. Nor will I say anything as long as I live. Is that clear to you?

REGINA (*nods, softly, without looking at him*) You will not say anything as long as you live.

HORACE That's right. And by that time they will probably have replaced your bonds, and then they'll belong to you and nobody but us will ever know what happened. (*Stops, smiles*) They'll be around any minute to see what I am going to do. I took good care to see that word reached Leo. They'll be mighty relieved to know I'm going to do nothing and Ben will think it all a capital joke on you. And that will be the end of that. There's nothing you can do to them, nothing you can do to me.

REGINA You hate me very much.

HORACE No.

REGINA Oh, I think you do. (*Puts her head back, sighs*) Well, we haven't been very good together. Anyway, I don't hate you either. I have only contempt for you. I've always had.

HORACE From the very first?

REGINA I think so.

HORACE I was in love with *you*. But why did *you* marry *me*?

REGINA I was lonely when I was young.

HORACE *You* were lonely?

REGINA Not the way people usually mean. Lonely for all the things I wasn't going to get. Everybody in this house was so busy and there was so little place for what I wanted. I wanted the world. Then, and then— (*Smiles*) Papa died and left the money to Ben and Oscar.

HORACE And you married me?

REGINA Yes, I thought— But I was wrong. You were a small-town clerk then. You haven't changed.

HORACE (*nods, smiles*) And that wasn't what you wanted.

REGINA No. No, it wasn't what I wanted. (*Pauses, leans back, pleasantly*) It took me a little while to find out I had made a mistake. As for you—I don't know. It was almost as if I couldn't stand the kind of man you were— (*Smiles, softly*) I used to lie there at night, praying you wouldn't come near—

HORACE Really? It was as bad as that?

REGINA (*nods*) Remember when I went to Doctor Sloan and I told you he said there was something the matter with me and that you shouldn't touch me any more?

HORACE I remember.

REGINA But you believed it. I couldn't understand that. I couldn't understand that anybody could be such a soft fool. That was when I began to despise you.

HORACE (*puts his hand to his throat, looks at the bottle of medicine on table*) Why didn't you leave me?

REGINA I told you I married you for something. It turned out it was only for this. (*Carefully*) This wasn't what I wanted, but it was something. I never thought about it much but if I had (HORACE *puts his hand to his throat*) I'd have known that you would die before I would. But I couldn't have known that you would get heart trouble so early and so bad. I'm lucky, Horace. I've always been lucky. (HORACE *turns slowly to the medicine*) I'll be lucky again. (HORACE *looks at her. Then he puts his hand to his throat. Because he cannot reach the bottle he moves the chair closer. He reaches for the medicine, takes out the cork, picks up the spoon. The bottle slips and smashes on the table. He draws in his breath, gasps.*)

HORACE Please. Tell Addie— The other bottle is upstairs. (REGINA *has not moved. She does not move now. He stares at her. Then, suddenly as if he understood, he raises his voice. It is a panic-stricken whisper, too small to be heard outside the room*) Addie! Addie! Come— (*Stops as he hears the softness of his voice. He makes a sudden, furious spring from the chair to the stairs, taking the first few steps as if he were a desperate runner.*

*On the fourth step he slips, gasps, grasps the rail, makes
a great effort to reach the landing. When he reaches
the landing, he is on his knees. His knees give way, he
falls on the landing, out of view.* REGINA *has not turned
during his climb up the stairs. Now she waits a second.
Then she goes below the landing, speaks up.*)

REGINA   Horace. Horace. (*When there is no answer, she
turns, calls*) Addie! Cal! Come in here. (*She starts up
the steps.* ADDIE *and* CAL *appear. Both run toward the
stairs*) He's had an attack. Come up here. (*They run
up the steps quickly.*)

CAL   My God. Mr. Horace—

(*They cannot be seen now.*)

REGINA   (*her voice comes from the head of the stairs*)   Be
still, Cal. Bring him in here.

(*Before the footsteps and the voices have completely died
away,* ALEXANDRA *appears in the hall door, in her rain-
cloak and hood. She comes into the room, begins to
unfasten the cloak, suddenly looks around, sees the
empty wheel chair, stares, begins to move swiftly as
if to look in the dining room. At the same moment* ADDIE
runs down the stairs. ALEXANDRA *turns and stares up at*
ADDIE.)

ALEXANDRA   Addie! What?

ADDIE   (*takes* ALEXANDRA *by the shoulders*)   I'm going for
the doctor. Go upstairs. (ALEXANDRA *looks at her, then
quickly breaks away and runs up the steps.* ADDIE *exits.
The stage is empty for a minute. Then the front door
bell begins to ring. When there is no answer, it rings
again. A second later* LEO *appears in the hall, talking
as he comes in.*)

LEO   (*very nervous*)   Hello. (*Irritably*) Never saw any use
ringing a bell when a door was open. If you are going
to ring a bell, then somebody should anwer it. (*Gets
in the room, looks around, puzzled, listens, hears no
sound*) Aunt Regina. (*He moves around restlessly*)
Addie. (*Waits*) Where the hell— (*Crosses to the bell
cord, rings it impatiently, waits, gets no answer, calls*)
Cal! Cal! (CAL *appears on the stair landing.*)

CAL   (*his voice is soft, shaken*) Mr. Leo. Miss Regina says you stop that screaming noise.

LEO   (*angrily*) Where is everybody?

CAL   Mr. Horace he got an attack. He's bad. Miss Regina says you stop that noise.

LEO   Uncle Horace— What— What happened? (CAL *starts down the stairs, shakes his head, begins to move swiftly off.* LEO *looks around wildly*) But when— You seen Mr. Oscar or Mr. Ben? (CAL *shakes his head. Moves on.* LEO *grabs him by the arm*) Answer me, will you?

CAL   No, I ain't seen 'em. I ain't got time to answer you. I got to get things. (CAL *runs off.*)

LEO   But what's the matter with him? When did this happen— (*Calling after* CAL) You'd think Papa'd be some place where you could find him. I been chasing him all afternoon.

(OSCAR *and* BEN *come quickly into the room.*)

LEO   Papa, I've been looking all over town for you and Uncle Ben—

BEN   Where is he?

OSCAR   Addie just told us it was a sudden attack, and—

BEN   (*to* LEO) Where is he? When did it happen?

LEO   Upstairs. Will you listen to me, please? I been looking for you for—

OSCAR   (*to* BEN) You think we should go up? (BEN, *looking up the steps, shakes his head.*)

BEN   I don't know. I don't know.

OSCAR   (*shakes his head*) But he was all right—

LEO   (*yelling*) *Will you listen to me?*

OSCAR   (*sharply*) What is the matter with you?

LEO   I been trying to tell you. I been trying to find you for an hour—

OSCAR   Tell me what?

LEO   Uncle Horace knows about the bonds. He knows about them. He's had the box since Wednesday—

BEN   (*sharply*) Stop shouting! What the hell are you talking about?

LEO   (*furiously*) I'm telling you he knows about the bonds. Ain't that clear enough—

OSCAR (*grabbing* LEO's *arm*) You God-damn fool! Stop screaming!

BEN Now what happened? Talk quietly.

LEO You heard me. Uncle Horace knows about the bonds. He's known since 'Wednesday.

BEN (*after a second*) How do you know that?

LEO Because Cal comes down to Manders and says the box came O.K. and—

OSCAR (*trembling*) That might not mean a thing—

LEO (*angrily*) No? It might not, huh? Then he says Manders should come here tonight and bring Sol Fowler with him. I guess that don't mean a thing either.

OSCAR (*to* BEN) Ben— What— Do you think he's seen the—

BEN (*motions to the box*) There's the box. (*Both* OSCAR *and* LEO *turn sharply.* LEO *makes a leap to the box*) You ass. Put it down. What are you going to do with it, eat it?

LEO I'm going to— (*Starts.*)

BEN (*furiously*) Put it down. Don't touch it again. Now sit down and shut up for a minute.

OSCAR Since Wednesday. (*To* LEO) You said he had it since Wednesday. Why didn't he say something— (*To* BEN) I don't understand—

LEO (*taking a step*) I can put it back. I can put it back before anybody knows.

BEN (*who is standing at the table, softly*) He's had it since Wednesday. Yet he hasn't said a word to us.

OSCAR Why? Why?

LEO What's the difference why? He was getting ready to say plenty. He was going to say it to Fowler tonight—

OSCAR (*angrily*) Be still. (*Turns to* BEN, *looks at him, waits.*)

BEN (*after a minute*) I don't believe that.

LEO (*wildly*) You don't believe it? What do I care what *you* believe? I do the dirty work and then—

BEN (*turning his head sharply to* LEO) I'm remembering that. I'm remembering that, Leo.

OSCAR What do you mean?

LEO You—

BEN (*to* OSCAR) If you don't shut that little fool up, I'll show you what I mean. For some reason he knows, but he don't say a word.

OSCAR   Maybe he didn't know that *we*—

BEN   (*quickly*) That *Leo*— He's no fool. Does Manders know the bonds are missing?

LEO   How could I tell? I was half crazy. I don't think so. Because Manders seemed kind of puzzled and—

OSCAR   But we got to find out— (*He breaks off as* CAL *comes into the room carrying a kettle of hot water.*)

BEN   How is he, Cal?

CAL   I don't know, Mr. Ben. He was bad. (*Going toward stairs.*)

OSCAR   But when did it happen?

CAL   (*shrugs*) He wasn't feeling bad early. (ADDIE *comes in quickly from the hall*) Then there he is next thing on the landing, fallen over, his eyes tight—

ADDIE   (*to* CAL) Dr. Sloan's over at the Ballongs. Hitch the buggy and go get him. (*She takes the kettle and cloths from him, pushes him, runs up the stairs*) Go on. (*She disappears.* CAL *exits.*)

BEN   Never seen Sloan anywhere when you need him.

OSCAR   (*softly*) Sounds bad.

LEO   He would have told *her* about it. Aunt Regina. He would have told his own wife—

BEN   (*turning to* LEO) Yes, he might have told her. But they weren't on such pretty terms and maybe he didn't. Maybe he didn't. (*Goes quickly to* LEO) Now, listen to me. If she doesn't know, it may work out all right. If she does know, you're to say he lent you the bonds.

LEO   Lent them to me! Who's going to believe that?

BEN   Nobody.

OSCAR   (*to* LEO) Don't you understand? It can't do no harm to say it—

LEO   Why should I say he lent them to me? Why not to you? (*Carefully*) Why not to Uncle Ben?

BEN   (*smiles*) Just because he didn't lend them to me. Remember that.

LEO   But all he has to do is say he didn't lend them to me—

BEN   (*furiously*). But for some reason, he doesn't seem to be talking, does he?

(*There are footsteps above. They all stand looking at the stairs.* REGINA *begins to come slowly down.*)

BEN   What happened?

REGINA   He's had a bad attack.

OSCAR   Too bad. I'm sorry we weren't here when—when Horace needed us.

BEN   When *you* needed us.

REGINA   (*looks at him*)   Yes.

BEN   How is he? Can we—can we go up?

REGINA   (*shakes her head*)   He's not conscious.

OSCAR   (*pacing around*)   It's that—it's that bad? Wouldn't you think Sloan could be found quickly, just once, just once?

REGINA   I don't think there is much for him to do.

BEN   Oh, don't talk like that. He's come through attacks before. He will now.

(REGINA *sits down. After a second she speaks softly.*)

REGINA   Well. We haven't seen each other since the day of our fight.

BEN   (*tenderly*)   That was nothing. Why, you and Oscar and I used to fight when we were kids.

OSCAR   (*hurriedly*)   Don't you think we should go up? Is there anything we can do for Horace—

BEN   You don't feel well. Ah—

REGINA   (*without looking at them*)   No, I don't. (*Slight pause*) Horace told me about the bonds this afternoon. (*There is an immediate shocked silence.*)

LEO   The bonds. What do you mean? What bonds? What—

BEN   (*looks at him furiously. Then to* REGINA)   The Union Pacific bonds? *Horace's* Union Pacific bonds?

REGINA   Yes.

OSCAR   (*steps to her, very nervously*)   Well. Well what— what about them? What—what could he say?

REGINA   He said that Leo had stolen the bonds and given them to you.

OSCAR   (*aghast, very loudly*)   That's ridiculous, Regina, absolutely—

LEO   I don't know what you're talking about. What would I— Why—

REGINA   (*wearily to* BEN)   Isn't it enough that he stole them from me? Do I have to listen to this in the bargain?

OSCAR   You are talking—

LEO   I didn't steal anything. I don't know why—

REGINA   (*to* BEN)   Would you ask them to stop that, please? (*There is silence for a minute.* BEN *glowers at* OSCAR *and* LEO.)

BEN   Aren't we starting at the wrong end, Regina? What did Horace tell you?

REGINA   (*smiles at him*)   He told me that Leo had stolen the bonds.

LEO   I didn't steal—

REGINA   Please. Let me finish. Then he told me that he was going to pretend that he had lent them to you (LEO *turns sharply to* REGINA, *then looks at* OSCAR, *then looks back at* REGINA) as a present from me—to my brothers. He said there was nothing I could do about it. He said the rest of his money would go to Alexandra. That is all. (*There is a silence.* OSCAR *coughs,* LEO *smiles slyly.*)

LEO   (*taking a step to her*)   I told you he had lent them— I could have told you—

REGINA   (*ignores him, smiles sadly at* BEN)   So I'm very badly off, you see. (*Carefully*) But Horace said there was nothing I could do about it as long as he was alive to say he had lent you the bonds.

BEN   You shouldn't feel that way. It can all be explained, all be adjusted. It isn't as bad—

REGINA   So you, at least, are willing to admit that the bonds were stolen?

BEN   (OSCAR *laughs nervously*)   I admit no such thing. It's possible that Horace made up that part of the story to tease you— (*looks at her*) Or perhaps to punish you. Punish you.

REGINA   (*sadly*)   It's not a pleasant story. I feel bad, Ben, naturally. I hadn't thought—

BEN   Now you shall have the bonds safely back. That was the understanding, wasn't it, Oscar?

OSCAR   Yes.

REGINA   I'm glad to know that. (*Smiles*) Ah, I had greater hopes—

BEN   Don't talk that way. That's foolish. (*Looks at his watch*) I think we ought to drive out for Sloan ourselves. If we can't find him we'll go over to Senateville for Doctor Morris. And don't think I'm dismissing this other business. I'm not. We'll have it all out on a more appropriate day.

REGINA   (*looks up, quietly*)   I don't think you had better go yet. I think you had better stay and sit down.

BEN   We'll be back with Sloan.

REGINA   Cal has gone for him. I don't want you to go.

BEN   Now don't worry and—

REGINA   You will come back in this room and sit down. I have something more to say.

BEN   (*turns, comes toward her*)   Since when do I take orders from you?

REGINA   (*smiles*)   You don't—yet. (*Sharply*) Come back, Oscar. You too, Leo.

OSCAR   (*sure of himself, laughs*)   My dear Regina—

BEN   (*softly, pats her hand*)   Horace has already clipped your wings and very wittily. Do I have to clip them, too? (*Smiles at her*) You'd get farther with a smile, Regina. I'm a soft man for a woman's smile.

REGINA   I'm smiling, Ben. I'm smiling because you are quite safe while Horace lives. But I don't think Horace will live. And if he doesn't live I shall want seventy-five per cent in exchange for the bonds.

BEN   (*steps back, whistles, laughs*)   Greedy! What a greedy girl you are! You want so much of everything.

REGINA   Yes. And if I don't get what I want I am going to put all three of you in jail.

OSCAR   (*furiously*)   You're mighty crazy. Having just admitted—

BEN   And on what evidence would you put Oscar and Leo in jail?

REGINA   (*laughs, gaily*)   Oscar, listen to him. He's getting ready to swear that it was you and Leo! What do you say to that? (OSCAR *turns furiously toward* BEN) Oh, don't be angry, Oscar. I'm going to see that he goes in with you.

BEN   Try anything you like, Regina. (*Sharply*) And now

we can stop all this and say good-bye to you. (ALEXAN-
DRA *comes slowly down the steps*) It's his money and
he's obviously willing to let us borrow it. (*More pleasantly*) Learn to make threats when you can carry them
through. For how many years have I told you a good-
looking woman gets more by being soft and appealing?
Mama used to tell you that. (*Looks at his watch*)
Where the hell is Sloan? (*To* OSCAR) Take the buggy
and— (*As* BEN *turns to* OSCAR, *he sees* ALEXANDRA. *She
walks stiffly. She goes slowly to the lower window, her
head bent. They all turn to look at her.*)

OSCAR (*after a second, moving toward her*) What? Alexandra— (*She does not answer. After a second,* ADDIE
*comes slowly down the stairs, moving as if she were
very tired. At foot of steps, she looks at* ALEXANDRA, *then
turns and slowly crosses to door and exits.* REGINA *rises.*
BEN *looks nervously at* ALEXANDRA, *at* REGINA.)

OSCAR (*as* ADDIE *passes him, irritably to* ALEXANDRA). Well,
what is— (*Turns into room—sees* ADDIE *at foot of steps*)
—what's (BEN *puts up a hand, shakes his head*) My
God, I didn't know—who *could* have known—I didn't
know he was that sick Well, well—I— (REGINA *stands
quietly, her back to them.*)

BEN (*softly, sincerely*) Seems like yesterday when he first
came here.

OSCAR (*sincerely, nervously*) Yes, that's true. (*Turns to*
BEN) The whole town loved him and respected him.

ALEXANDRA (*turns*) Did you love him, Uncle Oscar?

OSCAR Certainly, I— What a strange thing to ask! I—

ALEXANDRA Did you love him, Uncle Ben?

BEN (*simply*) He had—

ALEXANDRA (*suddenly starts to laugh very loudly*) And
you, Mama, did you love him, too?

REGINA I know what you feel, Alexandra, but please try
to control yourself.

ALEXANDRA (*still laughing*) I'm trying, Mama. I'm trying
very hard.

BEN Grief makes some people laugh and some people cry.
It's better to cry, Alexandra.

ALEXANDRA   (*the laugh has stopped. Tensely moves toward* REGINA)   What was Papa doing on the staircase?
(BEN *turns to look at* ALEXANDRA.)

REGINA   Please go and lie down, my dear. We all need time to get over shocks like this. (ALEXANDRA *does not move.* REGINA's *voice becomes softer, more insistent*) Please go, Alexandra.

ALEXANDRA   No, Mama. I'll wait. I've got to talk to you.

REGINA   Later. Go and rest now.

ALEXANDRA   (*quietly*) I'll wait, Mama. I've plenty of time.

REGINA   (*hesitates, stares, makes a half shrug, turns back to* BEN)   As I was saying. Tomorrow morning I am going up to Judge Simmes. I shall tell him about Leo.

BEN   (*motioning toward* ALEXANDRA)   Not in front of the child, Regina. I—

REGINA   (*turns to him. Sharply*)   I didn't ask her to stay. Tomorrow morning I go to Judge Simmes—

OSCAR   And what proof? What proof of all this—

REGINA   (*turns sharply*)   None. I won't need any. The bonds are missing and they are with Marshall. That will be enough. If it isn't, I'll add what's necessary.

BEN   I'm sure of that.

REGINA   (*turns to* BEN)   You can be quite sure.

OSCAR   We'll·deny—

REGINA   Deny your heads off. You couldn't find a jury that wouldn't weep for a woman whose brothers steal from her. And you couldn't find twelve men in this state you haven't cheated and who hate you for it.

OSCAR   What kind of talk is this? You couldn't do anything like that! We're your own brothers. (*Points upstairs*) How can you talk that way when upstairs not five minutes ago—

REGINA   (*slowly*)   There are people who can't go back, who must finish what they start. I am one of those people, Oscar. (*After a slight pause*) Where was I? (*Smiles at* BEN) Well, they'll convict you. But I won't care much if they don't. (*Leans forward, pleasantly*) Because by that time you'll be ruined. I shall also tell my story to Mr. Marshall, who likes me, I think, and who will not want to be involved in your scandal. A respectable firm like Marshall and Company. The deal would be off in an hour. (*Turns to them angrily*) And you know it. Now I don't want to hear any more from any of you. *You'll do no more bargaining in this house.* I'll take my seventy-five per cent and we'll forget the story forever. That's cne way of doing it, and the way I prefer. You know me well enough to know that I don't mind taking the other way.

BEN (*after a second, slowly*)   None of us has ever known you well enough, Regina.

REGINA   You're getting old, Ben. Your tricks aren't as smart as they used to be. (*There is no answer. She waits, then smiles*) All right. I take it that's settled and I get what I asked for.

OSCAR (*furiously to* BEN)   Are you going to let her do this—

BEN (*turns to look at him, slowly*)   You have a suggestion?

REGINA (*puts her arms above her head, stretches, laughs*) No, he hasn't. All right. Now, Leo, I have forgotten that you ever saw the bonds. (*Archly, to* BEN *and* OSCAR) And as long as you boys both behave yourselves, I've forgotten that we ever talked about them. You can draw up the necessary papers tomorrow. (BEN *laughs.* LEO *stares at him, starts for door. Exits.* OSCAR *moves toward door angrily.* REGINA *looks at* BEN, *nods, laughs with him. For a second,* OSCAR *stands in the door, looking back at them. Then he exits.*)

REGINA   You're a good loser, Ben. I like that.

BEN (*he picks up his coat, then turns to her*)   Well, I say to myself, what's the good? You and I aren't like Oscar. We're not sour people. I think that comes from a good digestion. Then, toc, one loses today and wins tomorrow. I say to myself, years of planning and I get what I want. Then I don't get it. But I'm not discouraged. The century's turning, the world is open. Open for people like you and me. Ready for us, waiting for us. After all this is just the beginning. There are hundreds of Hubbards sitting in rooms like this throughout the country. All their names aren't Hubbard, but they are all Hubbards and they will own this country some day. We'll get along.

REGINA (*smiles*) I think so.

BEN Then, too, I say to myself, things may change. (*Looks at* ALEXANDRA) I agree with Alexandra. What is a man in a wheel chair doing on a staircase? I ask myself that.

REGINA (*looks up at him*) And what do you answer?

BEN I have no answer. But maybe some day I will. Maybe never, but maybe some day. (*Smiles. Pats her arm*) when I do, I'll let you know. (*Goes toward hall.*)

REGINA When you do, write me. I will be in Chicago. (*Gaily*) Ah, Ben, if Papa had only left me his money.

BEN I'll see you tomorrow.

REGINA Oh, yes. Certainly. You'll be sort of working for me now.

BEN (*as he passes* ALEXANDRA, *smiles*) Alexandra, you're turning out to be a right interesting girl. (*Looks at* REGINA) Well, good night all. (*He exits.*)

REGINA (*Sits quietly for a second, stretches, turns to look at* ALEXANDRA) What do you want to talk to me about, Alexandra?

ALEXANDRA (*slowly*) I've changed my mind. I don't want to talk. There's nothing to talk about now.

REGINA You're acting very strange. Not like yourself. You've had a bad shock today. I know that. And you loved Papa, but you must have expected this to come some day. You knew how sick he was.

ALEXANDRA I knew. We all knew.

REGINA It will be good for you to get away from here. Good for me, too. Times heals most wounds, Alexandra. You're young, you shall have all the things I wanted. I'll make the world for you the way I wanted it to be for me. (*Uncomfortably*) Don't sit there staring. You've been around Birdie so much you're getting just like her.

ALEXANDRA (*nods*) Funny. That's what Aunt Birdie said today.

REGINA (*nods*) Be good for you to get away from all this. (ADDIE *enters.*)

ADDIE   Cal is back, Miss Regina. He says Dr. Sloan will be coming in a few minutes.

REGINA   We'll go in a few weeks. A few weeks! That means two or three Saturdays, two or three Sundays. (*Sighs*) Well, I'm very tired. I shall go to bed. I don't want any supper. Put the lights out and lock up. (ADDIE *moves to the piano lamp, turns it out*) You go to your room, Alexandra. Addie will bring you something hot. You look very tired. (*Rises. To* ADDIE) Call me when Dr. Sloan gets here. I don't want to see anybody else. I don't want any condolence calls tonight. The whole town will be over.

ALEXANDRA   Mama, I'm not coming with you. I'm not going to Chicago.

REGINA   (*turns to her*) You're very upset, Alexandra.

ALEXANDRA   (*quietly*) I mean what I say. With all my heart.

REGINA   We'll talk about it tomorrow. The morning will make a difference.

ALEXANDRA   It won't make any difference. And there isn't anything to talk about. I am going away from you. Because I want to. Because I know Papa would want me to.

REGINA   (*puzzled, careful, polite*) You *know* your papa wanted you to go away from me?

ALEXANDRA   Yes.

REGINA   (*softly*) And if I say no?

ALEXANDRA   (*looks at her*) Say it Mama, say it. And see what happens.

REGINA   (*softly, after a pause*) And if I make you stay?

ALEXANDRA   That would be foolish. It wouldn't work in the end.

REGINA   You're very serious about it, aren't you? (*Crosses to stairs*) Well, you'll change your mind in a few days.

ALEXANDRA   You only change your mind when you want to. And I won't want to.

REGINA   (*going up the steps*) Alexandra, I've come to the end of my rope. Somewhere there has to be what I want, too. Life goes too fast. Do what you want; think what you want; go where you want. I'd like to keep you with me, but I won't make you stay. Too many people used to make me do too many things. No, I won't make you stay.

ALEXANDRA You couldn't, Mama, because I want to leave here. As I've never wanted anything in my life before. Because now I understand what Papa was trying to tell me. (*Pause*) All in one day: Addie said there were people who ate the earth and other people who stood around and watched them do it. And just now Uncle Ben said the same thing. Really, he said the same thing. (*Tensely*) Well, tell him for me, Mama, I'm not going to stand around and watch you do it. Tell him I'll be fighting as hard as he'll be fighting (*rises*) some place where people don't just stand around and watch.

REGINA Well, you have spirit, after all. I used to think you were all sugar water. We don't have to be bad friends. I don't want us to be bad friends, Alexandra. (*Starts, stops, turns to* ALEXANDRA) Would you like to come and talk to me, Alexandra? Would you—would you like to sleep in my room tonight?

ALEXANDRA (*takes a step toward her*) Are you afraid, Mama? (REGINA *does not answer. She moves slowly out of sight.* ADDIE *comes to* ALEXANDRA, *presses her arm.*)

The Curtain Falls

Watch on the Rhine

FOR
HERMAN SHUMLIN
THANKS AND
AFFECTION

Watch on the Rhine was first produced at the Martin Beck Theatre, New York City, on April 1, 1941, with the following cast:

(*In the order of their appearance*)

ANISE	EDA HEINEMANN
JOSEPH	FRANK WILSON
FANNY FARRELLY	LUCILE WATSON
DAVID FARRELLY	JOHN LODGE
MARTHE DE BRANCOVIS	HELEN TRENHOLME
TECK DE BRANCOVIS	GEORGE COULOURIS
SARA MÜLLER	MADY CHRISTIANS
JOSHUA MÜLLER	PETER FERNANDEZ
BODO MÜLLER	ERIC ROBERTS
BABETTE MÜLLER	ANNE BLYTH
KURT MÜLLER	PAUL LUKAS

Produced and staged by HERMAN SHUMLIN

Setting designed by JO MIELZINER

Costumes designed by HELENE PONS

Scene

The scene of the play is the living room
of the Farrelly country house, about twenty miles
from Washington.
The time is late spring, 1940.

ACT ONE
Early on a Wednesday morning.

ACT TWO
Ten days later.

ACT THREE
A half hour later.

Act One

SCENE: *The living room of the Farrelly house, about twenty miles from Washington, D. C., on a warm spring morning.*

Center stage are large French doors leading to an elevated open terrace. On the terrace are chairs, tables, a large table for dining. Some of this furniture we can see; most of it is on the left side of the terrace, beyond our sight. Left stage is an arched entrance, leading to the oval reception hall. We can see the main staircase as it goes off to the back of the hall. Right stage is a door leading to a library. The Farrelly house was built in the early nineteenth century. It has space, simplicity, style. The living room is large. Up stage right is a piano; down stage left, a couch; down stage right, a couch and chairs; up stage a few smaller chairs. Four or five generations have furnished this room and they have all been people of taste. There are no styles, no periods; the room has never been refurnished. Each careless aristocrat has thrown into the room what he or she liked as a child, what he or she brought home when grown up. Therefore the furniture is of many periods: the desk is English, the couch is Victorian, some of the pictures are modern, some of the ornaments French. The room has too many things in it: vases, clocks, miniatures, boxes, china animals. On the right wall is a large portrait of a big kind-faced man in an evening suit of 1900. On another wall is a large, very ugly landscape. The room is crowded. But it is cool and clean and its fabrics and woods are in soft colors.

AT RISE: ANISE, *a thin Frenchwoman of about sixty, in a*

231

dark housekeeper's dress, is standing at a table sorting mail. She takes the mail from a small basket, holds each letter to the light, reads each postal card, then places them in piles. On the terrace, JOSEPH, *a tall, middle-aged Negro butler, wheels a breakfast wagon. As he appears,* FANNY FARRELLY *comes in from the hall. She is a handsome woman of about sixty-three. She has on a fancy, good-looking dressing-gown.*

Left and right are the audience's left and right.

FANNY   (*stops to watch* ANISE. *Sees* JOSEPH *moving about on terrace. Calls*)   Joseph! (*To* ANISE) Morning.

ANISE   (*continues examining mail*)   Good morning, Madame.

JOSEPH   (*comes to terrace door*)   Yes'm?

FANNY   Everybody down?

JOSEPH   No'm. Nobody. I'll get your tea. (*He returns to breakfast wagon on terrace.*)

FANNY   Mr. David isn't down yet? But he knows he is to meet the train.

JOSEPH   (*comes in from the terrace with the cup of tea*)   He's got plenty of time, Miss Fanny. The train ain't in till noon.

FANNY   Breakfast is at nine o'clock in this house and will be until the day after I die. Ring the bell.

JOSEPH   It ain't nine yet, Miss Fanny. It's eight-thirty.

FANNY   Well, put the clocks up to nine and ring the bell.

JOSEPH   Mr. David told me not to ring it any more. He says it's got too mean a ring, that bell. It disturbs folks.

FANNY   That's what it was put there for. I like to disturb folks.

JOSEPH   Yes'm.

FANNY   You slept well, Anise. You were asleep before I could dismantle myself.

ANISE   I woke several times during the night.

FANNY   Did you? Then you were careful not to stop snoring. We must finally get around to rearranging your room. (ANISE *hands her three or four letters*) Even when you don't snore, it irritates me. (FANNY *opens a letter, begins to read it. After a minute*) What time is it?

ANISE It is about eight-thirty. Joseph just told you.

FANNY I didn't hear him. I'm nervous. Naturally. My mail looks dull. (*Reading the letter*) Jenny always tells you a piece of gossip three times, as if it grew fresher with the telling. Did you put flowers in their rooms?

ANISE Certainly.

FANNY David ought to get to the station by eleven-thirty.

ANISE (*patiently*) The train does not draw in until ten minutes past noon.

FANNY But it might come in early. It's been known.

ANISE Never. Not in the Union Station in Washington, the District of Columbia.

FANNY (*irritably*) But it might. It might. Don't argue with me about everything. What time is it?

ANISE It's now twenty-seven minutes before nine. It will be impossible to continue telling you the time every three minutes from now until Miss Sara arrives. I think you are having a nervous breakdown. Compose yourself.

FANNY It's been twenty years. Any mother would be nervous. If your daughter were coming home and you hadn't seen her, and a husband, *and* grandchildren—

ANISE I do not say that it is wrong to be nervous. I, too, am nervous. I say only that you are.

FANNY Very well. I heard you. *I* say that I am. (*She goes back to reading her letter. Looks up*) Jenny's still in California. She's lost her lavallière again. Birdie Chase's daughter is still faire l'amouring with that actor. Tawdry, Jenny says it is. An actor. Fashions in sin change. In my day, it was Englishmen. I don't understand infidelity. If you love a man, then why? If you don't love him, then why stay with him? (*Without turning, she points over her head to Joshua Farrelly's portrait*) Thank God, I was in love. I thought about Joshua last night. Three grandchildren. He would have liked that. I hope I will. (*Points to other letters*) Anything in anybody else's mail?

ANISE Advertisements for Mr. David and legal things. For our Count and Countess, there is nothing but what seems an invitation to a lower-class embassy tea and letters asking for bills to get paid.

FANNY   That's every morning. (*Thoughtfully*) In the six
weeks the Balkan nobility have been with us, they seem
to have run up a great many bills.

ANISE   Yes. *I* told you that. Then there was a night-letter
for Mr. David.

(*A very loud, very unpleasant bell begins to ring.*)

FANNY   (*through the noise*)   Really? From whom?

ANISE   From her. I took it on the telephone, and—

(*Bell drowns out her voice.*)

FANNY   Who is "her"? (*Bell becomes very loud*) Go tell
him to stop that noise—

ANISE   (*goes toward terrace, calling*) Joseph! Stop that
bell. Miss Fanny says to stop it.

JOSEPH   (*calls*) Miss Fanny said to start it.

FANNY   (*shouts out to him*)   I didn't tell you to hang yourself with it.

JOSEPH   (*appears on terrace*)   I ain't hung. Your breakfast
is ready. (*Disappears.*)

FANNY   (*to* ANISE)   Who is "her"?

ANISE   That Carter woman from Lansing, Michigan.

FANNY   Oh, my. Is she back in Washington again? What
did the telegram say?

ANISE   It said the long sickness of her dear Papa had termi-
nated in full recovery.

FANNY   That's too bad.

ANISE   She was returning, and would Mr. David come for
dinner a week from Thursday? "Love," it said, "to you
and your charming mother." (*To* FANNY) That's you. I
think Miss Carter from Lansing, Michigan, was unwise
in attending the illness of her Papa.

FANNY   I hope so. Why?

ANISE   (*shrugs*)   There is much winking of the eyes going
on between our Countess and Mr. David.

FANNY   (*eagerly*)   I know that. Anything new happen?

ANISE   (*too innocently*)   Happen? I don't know what you
mean?

FANNY   You know damn well what I mean.

ANISE   *That?* Oh, no, I don't think that.

JOSEPH   (*appears in the door*)   The sausage cakes is
shrinking.

FANNY   (*rises. To* ANISE)   I want everybody down here immediately. Is the car ready? (ANISE *nods*) Did you order a good dinner? (*Shrieks*) David! Oh.

(DAVID FARRELLY, *a pleasant-looking man of thirty-nine, comes in from the entrance hall, almost bumps into* FANNY.)

DAVID   Good morning, everybody.

ANISE   (*to* FANNY)   Everything is excellent. You have been asking the same questions for a week. You have made the kitchen very nervous.

DAVID   (*to* JOSEPH)   Why did you ring that air-raid alarm again?

JOSEPH   Ain't me, Mr. David. I don't like no noise. Miss Fanny told me.

FANNY   Good morning, David.

DAVID   (*to* JOSEPH)   Tell Fred to leave the car. I'll drive to the station.

JOSEPH   (*nods*)   Yes, sir. (*Exits.*)

DAVID   (*to* FANNY, *half amused, half annoyed, as he begins to read his mail*)   Mama, I think we'll fix up the chicken-house for you as a playroom. We'll hang the room with bells and you can go into your second childhood in the proper privacy.

FANNY   I find it very interesting. You sleep soundly, you rise at your usual hour—although your sister, whom you haven't seen in years, is waiting at the station—

DAVID   She is not waiting at the station. (*Laughs*) The train does not come in until ten minutes past twelve.

FANNY   (*airily*)   It's almost that now.

ANISE   (*turns to look at her*)   Really, Miss Fanny, contain yourself. It is twenty minutes before nine.

DAVID   And I have *not* slept soundly. And I've been up since six o'clock.

FANNY   The Balkans aren't down yet. Where are they?

DAVID   I don't know.

ANISE   There's nothing in your mail, Mr. David. Only the usual advertisements.

DAVID   And for me, that is all that is ever likely to come— here.

ANISE   (*haughtily, as she starts toward hall*)   I cannot, of course, speak for Miss Fanny. *I* have never opened a letter in my life.

DAVID   I know. You don't have to. For you they fly open.

FANNY   (*giggles*)   It's true. You're a snooper, Anise. (ANISE *exits.* FANNY *talks as* ANISE *moves out*) I rather admire it. It shows an interest in life.)*She looks up at Joshua's portrait*) You know, I've been lying awake most of the night wondering what Papa would have thought about Sara. He'd have been very pleased, wouldn't he? I always find myself wondering what Joshua would have felt.

DAVID   Yes. But maybe it would be just as well if you didn't expect me to be wondering about it, too. I wasn't married to him, Mama. He was just my father.

FANNY   My. You got up on the wrong side of the bed. (*She moves past him. Points to the mail which he is still opening*) The bills are for our noble guests. Interesting, how many there are every morning. How much longer are they going to be with us?

DAVID   (*without looking at her*)   I don't know.

FANNY   It's been six weeks. Now that Sara and her family are coming, even this house might be a little crowded— (*He looks up at her. Quickly*) Yes. I know I invited them. I felt sorry for Marthe, and Teck rather amused me. He plays good cribbage, and he tells good jokes. But that's not enough for a lifetime guest. If you've been urging her to stay, I wish you'd stop it. They haven't any money; all right, lend them some—

DAVID   I have been urging them to stay?

FANNY   I'm not so old I don't recognize flirting when I see it.

DAVID   But you're old enough not to be silly.

FANNY   I'm not silly. I'm charming.

(MARTHE DE BRANCOVIS, *an attractive woman of thirty-one or thirty-two, enters.*)

MARTHE   Good morning, Fanny. Morning, David.

FANNY   Good morning, Marthe.

DAVID   (*warmly*)   Good morning.

MARTHE   Fanny, darling, couldn't you persuade yourself to let me have a tray in bed and some cotton for my ears?

DAVID Certainly not. My father ate breakfast at nine; and whatever my father did . . .

FANNY (*carefully, to* DAVID) There was a night-letter for you from that Carter woman in Lansing, Michigan. She is returning and you are to come to dinner next Thursday. (*As she exits on terrace*) C-A-R-T-E-R. (*Pronounces it carefully*) Lansing, Michigan.

DAVID (*laughs*) I know how to spell Carter, but thank you. (FANNY *exits.* DAVID *looks up at* MARTHE) Do you understand my mother?

MARTHE Sometimes.

DAVID Miss Carter was done for your benefit.

MARTHE (*smiles*) That means she has guessed that I would be jealous. And she has guessed right.

DAVID (*looks at her*) Jealous?

MARTHE I know I've no right to be, but I am. And Fanny knows it.

DAVID (*carelessly*) Don't pay any attention to Mama. She has a sure instinct for the women I like, and she begins to hammer away early. Marthe— (*Goes to decanter on side-table*) I'm going to have a drink. I haven't had a drink before breakfast since the day I took my bar examination. (*Pours himself a drink, gulps it down*) What's it going to be like to stand on a station platform and see your sister after all these years? I'm afraid, I guess.

MARTHE Why?

DAVID I don't·know. Afraid she won't like me— (*Shrugs*) We were very fond of each other, but it's been a long time.

MARTHE I remember Sara. Mama brought me one day when your father was stationed in Paris. I was about six and Sara about fifteen and you were—

DAVID You were a pretty little girl.

MARTHE Do you really remember me? You never told me before.

FANNY (*yelling from the terrace*) David! Come to breakfast.

DAVID (*as if he had not been listening*) You know, I've never met Sara's husband. Mama. did. I think the first day Sara met him, in Munich. Mama didn't like the

marriage much in those days—and Sara didn't care, and
Mama didn't like Sara not caring. Mama cut up about
it, bad.

MARTHE   Why?

DAVID   Probably because they didn't let her arrange it.
Why does Mama ever act badly? She doesn't remember
ten minutes later.

MARTHE   Wasn't Mr. Müller poor?

DAVID   Oh, Mama wouldn't have minded that. If they'd
only come home and let her fix their lives for them—
(*Smiles*) But Sara didn't want it that way.

MARTHE   You'll have a house full of refugees—us and—

DAVID   Are you and Teck refugees? I'm not sure I know
what you're refugees from.

MARTHE   From Europe.

DAVID   From what Europe?

MARTHE   (*smiles, shrugs*)   I don't know. I don't know myself, really. Just Europe. (*Quickly, comes to him*) Sara
will like you. I like you. (*Laughs*) That doesn't make
sense, does it?

(*On her speech,* TECK DE BRANCOVIS *appears in the hall.
He is a good-looking man of about forty-five. She stops
quickly.*)

TECK   (*to* MARTHE *and* DAVID)   Good morning.

(*The bell gives an enormous ring.*)

DAVID   (*goes to terrace*)   Good morning, Teck. For years
I've been thinking they were coming for Mama with a
net. I'm giving up hope. I may try catching her myself.
(*Disappears, calling*) Mama? Stop that noise.

TECK   I wonder if science has a name for women who enjoy noise? (*Goes to table, picks up his mail*) Many mistaken people, Marthe, seem to have given you many
charge accounts.

MARTHE   The Countess de Brancovis. That still does it. It
would be nice to be able to pay bills again—

TECK   Do not act as if I refused to pay them. I did not
sleep well last night. I was worried. We have eighty-
seven dollars in American Express checks. (*Pleasantly,
looking at her*) That's all we have, Marthe.

MARTHE   (*shrugs*)   Maybe something will turn up. It's due.

TECK   (*carefully*)   David? (*Then, as she turns to look at him*) The other relatives will arrive this morning?

MARTHE   Yes.

TECK   (*points to porch*)   I think Madame Fanny and Mr. David may grow weary of accents and charity guests. Or is the husband of the sister a rich one?

MARTHE   No. He's poor. He had to leave Germany in '33.

TECK   A Jew?

MARTHE   No. I don't think so.

TECK   Why did he have to leave Germany?

MARTHE   (*still reading*)   Oh, I don't know, Teck. He's an anti-Nazi.

TECK   A political?

MARTHE   No, I don't think so. He was an engineer. I don't know. I don't know much about him.

TECK   Did you sleep well?

MARTHE   Yes. Why not?

TECK   Money does not worry you?

MARTHE   It worries me very much. But I just lie still now and hope. I'm glad to be here. (*Shrugs*) Maybe something good will happen. We've come to the end of a road. That's been true for a long time. Things will have to go one way or the other. Maybe they'll go well, for a change.

TECK   I have not come to the end of any road.

MARTHE   (*looks at him*)   No? I admire you.

TECK   I'm going into Washington tonight. Phili has a poker gave every Wednesday evening. He has arranged for me to join it.

MARTHE   (*after a pause*)   Have you been seeing Phili?

TECK   Once or twice. Why not? Phili and I are old friends. He may be useful. I do not want to stay in this country forever.

MARTHE   You can't leave them alone. Your favorite dream, isn't it, Teck? That they will let you play with them again? I don't think they will, and I don't think you should be seeing Phili, or that you should be seen at the Embassy.

TECK (*smiles*) You have political convictions now?

MARTHE I don't know what I have. I've never liked Nazis, as you know, and you should have had enough of them. They seem to have had enough of you, God knows. It would be just as well to admit they are smarter than you are and let them alone.

TECK (*looking at her carefully, after a minute*) That is interesting.

MARTHE What is interesting?

TECK I think you are trying to say something to me. What is it?

MARTHE That you ought not to be at the Embassy, and that it's insane to play cards in a game with Von Seitz with eighty-seven dollars in your pocket. I don't think he'd like your not being able to pay up. Suppose you lose?

TECK I shall try not to lose.

MARTHE But if you do lose and can't pay, it will be all over Washington in an hour. (*Points to terrace*) They'll find out about it, and we'll be out of here when they do.

TECK I think I want to be out of here. I find that I do not like the picture of you and our host.

MARTHE (*carefully*) There is no picture, as you put it, to like or dislike.

TECK Not yet? I am glad to hear that. (*Comes toward her slowly*) Marthe, you understand that I am not really a fool? You understand that it is unwise to calculate me that way?

MARTHE (*slowly, as if it were an effort*) Yes, I understand that. And I understand that I am getting tired. Just plain tired. The whole thing's too much for me. I've always meant to ask you, since you played on so many sides, why we didn't come out any better. I've always wanted to ask you what happened. (*Sharply*) I'm tired, see? And I just want to sit down. Just to sit down in a chair and stay.

TECK (*carefully*) Here?

MARTHE I don't know. Any place—

TECK You have thus arranged it with David?

MARTHE I've arranged nothing.

TECK But you are trying, eh? (*He comes close to her*) I think not. I would not like that. Do not make any arrangements, Marthe. I may not allow you to carry them through. (*Smiles*) Come to breakfast now. (*He passes her, disappears on the terrace. She stands still and thoughtful. Then she, too, moves to the terrace, disappears.* JOSEPH *appears on the terrace, carrying a tray toward the unseen breakfast table. The stage is empty. After a minute, there are sounds of footsteps in the hall.* SARA MÜLLER *appears in the doorway, comes toward the middle of the room as if expecting to find somebody, stops, looks around, begins to smile. Behind her in the doorway, are three children; behind them,* KURT MÜLLER. *They stand waiting, watching* SARA. SARA *is forty-one or forty-two, a good-looking woman, with a well-bred, serious face. She is very badly dressed. Her dress is too long, her shoes were bought a long time ago and have no relation to the dress, and the belt of her dress has become untied and is hanging down. She looks clean and dowdy. As she looks around the room, her face is gay and surprised. Smiling, without turning, absently, she motions to the children and* KURT. *Slowly, the children come in.* BODO MÜLLER, *a boy of nine, comes first. He is carrying coats. Behind him, carrying two cheap valises, is* JOSHUA MÜLLER, *a boy of fourteen. Behind him is* BABETTE MÜLLER, *a pretty little girl of twelve. They are dressed for a much colder climate. They come forward, look at their mother, then move to a couch. Behind them is* KURT MÜLLER, *a large, powerful, German-looking man of about forty-seven. He is carrying a shabby valise and a brief-case. He stands watching* SARA. JOSHUA *puts down the valises, goes to his father, takes the valise from* KURT, *puts it neatly near his, and puts the brief-case near* KURT. BABETTE *goes to* SARA, *takes a package from her, places it near the valise. Then she turns to* BODO, *takes the coats he is carrying, puts them neatly on top of the valises. After a second,* KURT *sits down. As he does so, we see that his movements are slow and careful, as if they are made with effort.*)

BABETTE   (*points to a couch near which they are standing. She has a slight accent*)   Is it allowed?

KURT   (*smiles. He has an accent*)   Yes. It is allowed. (BAB-ETTE *and* BODO *sit stiffly on the couch.*)

JOSHUA   (*nervously. He has a slight accent*)   But we did not sound the bell—

SARA   (*idly, as she wanders around the room, her face excited*)   The door isn't locked. It never was. Never since I can remember.

BODO   (*softly, puzzled*)   The entrance of the home is never locked. So.

KURT   (*looks at him*)   You find it curious to believe there are people who live and do not need to watch, eh, Bodo?

BODO   Yes, Papa.

KURT   (*smiles*)   You and I.

JOSHUA   (*smiles*)   It is strange. But it must be good, I think.

KURT   Yes.

SARA   Sit back. Be comfortable. I—I wonder where Mama and David— (*Delighted, sees portrait of Joshua Farrelly, points to it*)   And that was my Papa. That was the famous Joshua Farrelly. (*They all look up at it. She wanders around the room*)   My goodness, isn't it a fine room? I'd almost forgotten— (*Picks up a picture from the table*)   And this was my grandmother. (*Very nervously*)   Shall I go and say we're here? They'd be having breakfast, I think. Always on the side terrace in nice weather. I don't know. Maybe— (*Picks up another picture*)   "To Joshua and Fanny Farrelly. With admiration. Alfonso, May 7, 1910." I had an ermine boa and a pink coat. I was angry because it was too warm in Madrid to wear it.

BODO   Alfons von Spanien? Der hat immer Bilder von sich verschenkt. Ein schlectes Zeichen für einen Mann.

JOSHUA   Mama told you it is good manners to speak the language of the country you visit. Therefore, speak in English.

BODO   I said he seemed always to give his photograph. I said that is a bad flag on a man. Grow fat on the poor people and give pictures of the face. (JOSHUA *sits down.*)

SARA   I remember a big party and cakes and a glass of

champagne for me. I was ten, I guess— (*Suddenly laughs*) That was when Mama said the first time a king got shot at, he was a romantic, but the fifth time he was a comedian. And when my father gave his lecture in Madrid, he repeated it—right in Madrid. It was a great scandal. You know, Alfonso was always getting shot at or bombed.

BODO (*shrugs*) Certainement.

JOSHUA Certainement? As-tu perdu la tête?

BABETTE Speak in English, please.

KURT (*without turning*) You are a terrorist, Bodo?

BODO (*slowly*) No.

JOSHUA Then since when has it become *natural* to shoot upon people?

BODO Do not give me lessons. It is neither right nor natural to shoot upon people. I know that.

SARA (*looks at* BABETTE, *thoughtfully*) An ermine boa. A boa is a scarf. I should like to have one for you, Babbie. Once, in Prague, I saw a pretty one. I wanted to buy it for you. But we had to pay our rent. (*Laughs*) But I almost bought it.

BABETTE Yes, Mama. Thank you. Tie your sash, Mama.

SARA (*thoughtfully*) Almost twenty years.

BODO You were born here, Mama?

SARA Upstairs. And I lived here until I went to live with your father. (*Looks out beyond terrace*) Your Uncle David and I used to have a garden, behind the terrace. I wonder if it's still there. I like a garden. I've always hoped we'd have a house some day and settle down— (*Stops, nervously, turns to stare at* KURT, *who is looking at her*) I am talking so foolish. Sentimental. At my age. Gardens and ermine boas. I haven't wanted anything—

KURT (*comes toward her, takes her hand*) Sara. Stop it. This is a fine room. A fine place to be. Everything is so pleasant and full of comfort. This will be a good piano on which to play again. And it is all so clean. I like that. Now, you shall not be a baby. You must enjoy your house, and not be afraid that you hurt me with it. Yes?

BABETTE Papa, tie Mama's sash, please.

SARA (*shyly smiles at him as he leans down to tie the belt*) Yes, of course. It's strange, that's all. We've never been in a place like this together—

KURT That does not mean, and should not mean, that we do not remember how to enjoy what comes our way. We are on a holiday.

JOSHUA A holiday? But for how long? And what plans afterward?

KURT (*quietly*) We will have plans when the hour arrives to make them. (ANISE *appears from the hall. She starts into the room, stops, bewildered. The* MÜLLERS *have not seen her. Then, as* SARA *turns,* ANISE *speaks. As she speaks, the children rise.*)

ANISE What? What?

SARA (*softly*) Anise. It's me. It's Sara.

ANISE (*coming forward slowly*) What? (*Then as she approaches* SARA, *she begins to run toward her*) Miss Sara! Miss Sara! (*They reach each other, both laugh happily.* SARA *kisses* ANISE) I would have known you. Yes, I would. I would have known— (*Excited, bewildered, nervous, she looks toward* KURT) How do you do, sir? How do you do? (*Turns toward the children*) How do you do?

JOSHUA Thank you, Miss Anise. We are in good health.

SARA (*very happily*) You look the same. I think you look the same. Just the way I've always remembered. (*To the others*) This is the Anise I have told you about. She was here before I was born.

ANISE But how— Did you just come in? What a way to come home! And after all the plans we've made! But you were to come on the twelve o'clock train, and Mr. David was to meet you—

BABETTE The twelve o'clock train was most expensive. We could not have come with that train. We liked the train we came on. It was most luxurious.

ANISE (*very nervously, very rattled*) But Madame Fanny will have a fit. I will call her— She will not be able to contain herself. She—

SARA (*softly*) I wanted a few minutes. I'm nervous about coming home, I guess.

BODO   (*conversationally*)   You are French, Madame Anise?

ANISE   Yes, I am from the Bas Rhin. (*She looks past* SARA, *and bobs her head idiotically at* KURT) Sara's husband. That is nice. That is nice.

BODO   Yes. Your accent is from the North. That is fine country. We were in hiding there once. (BABETTE *quickly pokes him.*)

ANISE   Hiding? You— (*Turns nervously to* KURT) But here we stand and talk. You have not had your breakfast, sir!

BABETTE   (*simply, eagerly*)   It would be nice to have breakfast.

ANISE   Yes, of course— I will go and order it.

SARA   (*to the children*)   What would you like for breakfast?

BABETTE   (*surprised*)   What would we like? Why, Mama, we will have anything that can be spared. If eggs are not too rare or too expensive—

ANISE   (*amazed*)   Rare? Why— Oh, I—I must call Miss Fanny now. It is of a necessity. (*Excited, rushing toward terrace, calling*) Miss Fanny. Miss Fanny. (*Back to* SARA) Have you forgotten your Mama's nature? She cannot bear not knowing things. Miss Fanny! What a way to come home! After twenty years and nobody at the station—

FANNY'S VOICE   Don't yell at me. What is the matter with you?

ANISE   (*excitedly, as* FANNY *draws near*) She's here. They're here. Miss Sara. She's here, I tell you. (FANNY *comes up to her, stares at her, then looks slowly around until she sees* SARA.)

SARA   (*softly*)   Hello, Mama.

FANNY   (*after a long pause, softly, coming toward her*) Sara. Sara, darling. You're here. You're really here. (*She reaches her, takes her arms, stares at her, smiles*) Welcome. Welcome. Welcome to your house. (*Slowly*) You're not young, Sara.

SARA   (*smiles*)   No, Mama. I'm forty-one.

FANNY   (*softly*)   Forty-one. Of course. (*Presses her arms again*) Oh, Sara, I'm— (*Then quickly*) You look more

like Papa now. That's good. The years have helped you.
(*Turns to look at* KURT) Welcome to this house, sir.

KURT   (*warmly*)   Thank you, Madame.

FANNY   (*turns to look at* SARA *again, nervously pats her
arm. Nods, turns again to stare at* KURT. *She is nervous
and chatty*)   You are a good-looking man, for a German.
I didn't remember you that way. I like a good-looking
man. I always have.

KURT   (*smiles*)   I like a good-looking woman. I always
have.

FANNY   Good. That's the way it should be.

BODO   (*to* SARA)   Ist das Grossmama?

FANNY   (*looks down*)   Yes. I am your grandmother. Also,
I speak German, so do not talk about me. I speak languages very well. But there is no longer anybody to
speak with. Anise has half forgotten her French, which
was always bad; and I have nobody with whom to speak
my Italian or German or—Sara, it's very good to have you
home. I'm chattering away, I—

JOSHUA   Now you have us, Madame. We speak ignorantly,
but fluently, in German, French, Italian, Spanish—

KURT   And boastfully in English.

BODO   There is never a need for boasting. If we are to fight
for the good of all men, it is to be accepted that we must
be among the most advanced.

ANISE   My God.

FANNY   (*to* SARA)   Are these your *children?* Or are they
dressed up midgets?

SARA   (*laughs*)   These are my children, Mama. This, Babette. (BABETTE *bows*) This, Joshua. (JOSHUA *bows*) This
is Bodo. (BODO *bows.*)

FANNY   Joshua was named for Papa. You wrote me. (*Indicates picture of Joshua Farrelly*) You bear a great
name, young man.

JOSHUA   (*smiles, indicates his father*)   My name is Müller.

FANNY   (*looks at him, laughs*)   Yes. You look a little like
your grandfather. (*To* BABETTE) And so do you. You are
a nice-looking girl. (*To* BODO) You look like nobody.

BODO   (*proudly*)   I am not beautiful.

FANNY   (*laughs*)   Well, Sara, well. Three children. You

have done well. (*To* KURT) You, too, sir, of course. Are
you quite recovered? Sara wrote that you were in Spain
and—

BODO Did Mama write that Papa was a great hero? He
was brave, he was calm, he was expert, he was resource-
ful, he was—

KURT (*laughs*) My biographer. And as unprejudiced as
most of them.

SARA Where is David? I am so anxious— Has he changed
much? Does he . . .

FANNY (*to* ANISE) Don't stand there. Go and get him
right away. Go get David. (*As* ANISE *exits*) He's out having breakfast with the titled folk. Do you remember
Marthe Randolph? I mean, do you remember Hortie
Randolph, her mother, who was my friend? Can you
follow what I'm saying? I'm not speaking well today.

SARA (*laughs*) Of course I remember Marthe and Hortie.
You and she used to scream at each other.

FANNY Well, Martha, her daughter, married Teck de
Brancovis. *Count* de Brancovis. He was fancy when she
married him. Not so fancy now, I suspect. Although still
chic and tired. You know what I mean, the way they
are in Europe. Well, they're here.

SARA What's David like now? I—

FANNY Like? Like? I don't know. He's a lawyer. You
know that. Papa's firm. He's never married. You know
that, too—

SARA Why hasn't he married?

FANNY Really, I don't know. I don't think he likes his own
taste. Which is very discriminating of him. He's had a
lot of girls, of course, one more ignorant and silly than
the other— (*Goes toward terrace, begins to scream*)
And where is he? David! David!

ANISE'S VOICE He's coming, Miss Fanny. He's coming. Contain yourself. He was down at the garage getting ready
to leave—

FANNY I don't care where he is. Tell him to come.—
David! (*Suddenly points to picture of Joshua*) That's
my Joshua. Handsome, eh? We were very much in love.
Hard to believe of people nowadays, isn't it?

SARA   Kurt and I love each other.

FANNY   Oh. You do? I daresay. But there are ways and ways of loving.

SARA   How dare you, Mama—

KURT   (*laughs*)   Ladies, ladies.

SARA   (*giggles*)   Why, I almost got mad then. You know, I don't think I've been mad since I last saw you.

BODO   My! You and Mama must not get angry. Anger is protest. And so you must direction it to the proper channels and then harness it for the good of other men. That is correct, Papa?

FANNY   (*peers down at him*)   If you grow up to talk like that, and stay as ugly as you are, you are going to have one of those successful careers on the lecture platform. (JOSHUA *and* BABETTE *laugh.*)

JOSHUA   (*to* BODO)   Ah. It is a great pleasure to hear Grandma talk with you.

BODO   (*to* FANNY, *tenderly*)   We will not like each other. (KURT *has wandered to the piano. Standing, he touches the keys in the first bars of a Mozart Rondo.*)

FANNY   You are wrong. I think we are rather alike; if that is so, let us at least remember to admire each other. (DAVID *comes running in from the entrance hall. At the door he stops, stares at* SARA.)

DAVID   (*to* SARA)   Sara. Darling—

SARA   (*wheels, goes running toward him. She moves into his arms. He leans down, kisses her with great affection*)   David. David.

DAVID   (*softly*)   It's been a long, long time. I got to thinking it would never happen. (*He leans down, kisses her hair. After a minute, he smiles, presses her arm.*)

SARA   (*excited*)   David, I'm excited. Isn't it strange? To be here, to see each other— But I am forgetting. This is my husband. These are my children. Babette, Joshua, Bodo. (*They all three advance, stand in line to shake hands.*)

BODO   (*shaking hand*)   How do you do, Uncle David?

DAVID   How do you do, Bodo? (DAVID *shakes hands with* JOSHUA) Boys can shake hands. But so pretty a girl must be kissed. (*He kisses* BABETTE. *She smiles, very pleased, and crosses to the side of* SARA.)

BABETTE Thank you. Fix your hairpin, Mama. (SARA *shoves back a falling hairpin.*)

DAVID (*crossing to* KURT) I'm happy to meet you, sir, and to have you here.

KURT Thank you. Sara has told me so much from you. You have a devoted sister.

DAVID (*very pleased*) Have I? Still? That's mighty good to hear. (ANISE *comes in from the library.*)

ANISE Your breakfast is coming. Shall I wash the children, Miss Sara?

JOSHUA (*amazed*) Wash us? Do people wash each other?

SARA No, but the washing is a good idea. Go along now, and hurry. (*All three start for the hall*) And then we'll all have a fine, big breakfast again. (*The children exit.*)

FANNY Again? Don't you usually have a good breakfast?

KURT (*smiles*) No, Madame. Only sometimes.

SARA (*laughs*) Oh, we do all right, usually. (*Very happily, very gaily*) Ah, it's good to be here. (*Puts her arm in* DAVID's) We were kids. Now we're all grown up! I've got children, you're a lawyer, and a fine one, I bet—

FANNY The name of Farrelly on the door didn't, of course, hurt David's career.

DAVID (*smiles*) Sara, you might as well know Mama thinks of me only as a monument to Papa and a not very well-made monument at that. I am not the man Papa was.

SARA (*to* FANNY, *smiles*) How do you know he's not?

FANNY (*carefully*) I beg your pardon. That is the second time you have spoken disrespectfully of your father. (SARA *and* DAVID *laugh.* FANNY *turns to* KURT) I hope you will like me.

KURT I hope so.

SARA (*pulls him to the couch, sits down with him*) Now I want to hear about you— (*Looks at him, laughs*) I'm awfully nervous about seeing you. Are you, about me?

DAVID Yes. I certainly am.

SARA (*looks around*) I'm like an idiot. I want to see everything right away. The lake, and my old room—and I want to talk and ask questions . . .

KURT (*laughs*) More slow, Sara. It is most difficult to have twenty years in a few minutes.

SARA   Yes, I know, but— Oh, well. Kurt's right. We'll say it all slowly. It's just nice being back. Haven't I fine children?

DAVID   Very fine. You're lucky. I wish I had them.

FANNY   How could you have them? All the women you like are too draughty, if you know what I mean. I'm sure that girl from Lansing, Michigan, would be sterile. Which is as God in his wisdom would have it.

SARA   Oh. So you have a girl?

DAVID   I have no girl. This amuses Mama.

FANNY   He's very attractive to some women. (*To* KURT) Both my children are attractive, whatever else they're not. Don't you think so? (*Points to* DAVID) He's flirting with our Countess now, Sara. You will see for yourself.

DAVID   (*sharply*) You are making nervous jokes this morning, Mama. And they're not very good ones.

FANNY   (*gaily*) I tell the truth. If it turns out to be a joke, all the better.

SARA   (*affectionately*) Ah, Mama hasn't changed. And that's good, too.

FANNY   Don't mind me, Sara. I, too, am nervous about seeing you. (*To* KURT) You'll like it here. You are an engineer?

KURT   Yes.

FANNY   Do you remember the day we met in München? The day Sara brought you to lunch? I thought you were rather a clod and that Sara would have a miserable life. I think I was wrong. (*To* DAVID) You see? I always admit when I'm wrong.

DAVID   You are a woman who is noble in all things, at all times.

FANNY   Oh, you're mad at me. (*To* KURT) As I say, you'll like it here. I've already made some plans. The new wing will be for you and Sara. The old turkey-house we'll fix up for the children. A nice, new bathroom, and we'll put in their own kitchen, and Anise will move in with them—

SARA   That's kind of you, Mama. But—but—we won't make any plans for a while— (*Very quietly*) A good, long vacation; God knows Kurt needs it—

FANNY A vacation? You'll be staying here, of course. You don't have to worry about work—engineers can always get jobs, David says, and he's already begun to inquire—

KURT I have not worked as an engineer since many years, Madame.

DAVID Haven't you? I thought— Didn't you work for Dornier?

KURT Yes. Before '33.

FANNY But you have worked in other places. A great many other places, I should say. Every letter of Sara's seemed to have a new postmark.

KURT (*smiles*) We move most often.

DAVID You gave up engineering?

KURT I gave it up? (*shrugs*) One could say it that way.

FANNY What do you do?

SARA Mama, we—

KURT It is difficult to explain.

DAVID (*after a slight pause*) If you'd rather not.

FANNY No, I—I'm trying to find out something. (*To* KURT) May I ask it, sir?

KURT Let me help you, Madame. You wish to know whether not being an engineer buys adequate breakfasts for my family. It does not. I have no wish to make a mystery of what I have been doing; it is only that it is awkward to place neatly. (*Smiles, motions with his hand*) It sounds so big: it is so small. I am an Anti-Fascist. And that does not pay well.

FANNY Do you mind questions?

SARA Yes.

KURT (*sharply*) Sara. (*To* FANNY) Perhaps I shall not answer them. But I shall try.

FANNY Are you a radical?

KURT You would have to tell me what that word means to you, Madame.

FANNY (*after a slight pause*) That is just. Perhaps we all have private definitions. We all are Anti-Fascists, for example—

SARA Yes. But Kurt works at it.

FANNY What kind of work?

KURT Any kind. Anywhere.

FANNY   (*sharply*)   I will stop asking questions.

SARA   (*very sharply*)   That would be sensible, Mama.

DAVID   Darling, don't be angry. We've been worried about you, naturally. We knew so little, except that you were having a bad time.

SARA   I didn't have a bad time. We never—

KURT   Do not lie for me, Sara.

SARA   I'm not lying. I didn't have a bad time, the way they mean. I—

FANNY   (*slowly*)   You had a bad time just trying to live, didn't you? That's obvious, Sara, and foolish to pretend it isn't. Why wouldn't you take money from us? What kind of nonsense—

SARA   (*slowly*)   We've lived the way we wanted to live. I don't know the language of rooms like this any more. And I don't want to learn it again.

KURT   Do not bristle about it.

SARA   I'm not bristling. (*To* FANNY) I married because I fell in love. You can understand that.

FANNY   (*slowly*)   Yes.

SARA   For almost twelve years, Kurt went to work every morning and came home every night, and we lived modestly, and happily— (*Sharply*) As happily as people could in a starved Germany that was going to pieces—

KURT   Sara, please. You are angry. I do not like it that way. I will try to find a way to tell you with quickness. Yes. (SARA *turns, looks at him, starts to speak, stops*) I was born in a town called Fürth. (*Pauses. Looks up, smiles*) There is a holiday in my town. We call it Kirchweih. It was a gay holiday with games and music and a hot white sausage to eat with the wine. I grow up, I move away—to school, to work—but always I come back for Kirchweih. It is for me, the great day of the year. (*Slowly*) But after the war, that day begins to change. The sausage is made from bad stuff, the peasants come in without shoes, the children are too sick— (*Carefully*) It is bad for my people, those years, but always I have hope. In the festival of August, 1931, more than a year before the storm, I give up that hope. On that day, I see twenty-seven men murdered in a Nazi street fight. I cannot stay by now and watch. My time has come to move. I say with Luther, "Here I stand. I can do nothing else. God help me. Amen."

SARA It doesn't pay well to fight for what we believe in. But I wanted it the way Kurt wanted it. (*Shrugs*) They don't like us in Europe; I guess they never did. So Kurt brought us home. You've always said you wanted us. If you don't, I will understand.

DAVID Darling, of course we want you—

FANNY (*rises*) I am old. And made of dry cork. And bad-mannered. Please forgive me.

SARA (*goes quickly to* FANNY) Shut up, Mama. We're all acting like fools. I'm glad to be home. That's all I know. So damned glad.

DAVID And we're damned glad to have you. Come on. Let's walk to the lake. We've made it bigger and planted the island with blackberries— (*She smiles and goes to him. Together they move out the hall entrance.*)

FANNY (*after a silence*) They've always liked each other. We're going to have Zwetschgen-Knoedel for dinner. You like them?

KURT Indeed.

FANNY I hope you like decent food.

KURT I do.

FANNY That's a good sign in a man.

MARTHE (*coming in from the terrace. Stops in the doorway*) Oh, I'm sorry, Fanny. We were waiting. I didn't want to interrupt the family reunion. I—

FANNY This is my son-in-law, Herr Müller. The Countess de Brancovis.

KURT AND MARTHE (*together*) How do you do?

MARTHE And how is Sara, Herr Müller? I haven't seen her since I was a little girl. She probably doesn't remember me at all. (TECK *comes in from the hall. She turns*) This is my husband, Herr Müller.

KURT How do you do?

TECK How do you do, sir? (KURT *bows. They shake hands*) Would it be impertinent for one European to make welcome another?

KURT (*smiles*) I do not think so. It would be friendly.

BODO   (*appears at the hall door*) Papa— (*Sees* TECK *and* MARTHE, *bows*) Oh, good morning. Miss Anise says you are the Count and Countess. Once before we met a Count and Countess. They had a small room bordering on ours in Copenhagen. They were more older than you, and more poor. We shared with them our newspaper.

MARTHE   (*laughs*) It wasn't us, but it might have been. What's your name?

TECK   (*laughs*) We hope you will be as kind to us.

BODO   My name is Bodo. It's a strange name. No? (*To* KURT) Papa, this is the house of great wonders. Each has his bed, each has his bathroom. The arrangement of it, that is splendorous.

FANNY   (*laughs*) You are a fancy talker, Bodo.

KURT   Oh, yes. In many languages.

BODO   (*to* FANNY) Please to correct me when I am wrong. Papa, the plumbing is such as you have never seen. Each implement is placed on the floor, and all are simultaneous in the same room. You will therefore see that being placed most solidly on the floor allows of no rats, rodents or crawlers, and is most sanitary. (*To the others*) Papa will be most interested. He likes to know how each thing of everything is put together. And he is so fond of being clean—

KURT   (*laughs. To* FANNY) I am a hero to my children. It bores everybody but me.

TECK   It is most interesting, Herr Müller. I thought I had a good ear for the accents of your country. But yours is most difficult to place. It is Bayrisch? Or is it—

BODO   That's because Papa has worked in so many—

KURT   (*quickly*) German accents are the most difficult to identify. I, myself, when I try, am usually incorrect. It would be particularly difficult with me because I speak other languages. Yours would be Roumanian?

MARTHE   (*laughs*) My God, is it that bad?

KURT   (*smiles*) I am showing off. I know the Count de Brancovis is Roumanian.

TECK   (*heartily*) So? We have met before? I thought so, but I cannot remember—

KURT   No, sir. We have not met before. I read your name in the newspapers.

TECK   (*to* KURT)   Strange. I was sure I had met you. I was in the Paris Legation for many years, and I thought perhaps—

KURT   Oh, no. If it is possible to believe, I am the exile who is not famous. (*To* FANNY) I have been thinking with pleasure, Madame Fanny, of breakfast on your porch. (*He points to the picture of Joshua Farrelly*) Your husband once wrote: "I am getting older now and Europe seems far away. Fanny and I will have an early breakfast on the porch and then I shall drive the bays into Washington." (*Remembering*) And then he goes on: "Henry Adams tells me he has been reading Karl Marx. I shall have to tell him my father made me read Marx many years ago and that, since he proposes to exhibit himself to impress me, will spoil Henry's Sunday."

FANNY   (*laughs, delighted. Takes* KURT's *arm*)   And so it did. I had forgotten that. I am pleased with you. I shall come and serve you food myself. I had forgotten Joshua ever wrote it. (*They start out of the terrace doors together, followed by* BODO.)

KURT   (*as they disappear*)   I try to impress you. I learned it last night. (FANNY *laughs. They disappear.*)

TECK   (*smiles*)   He is a clever man. A quotation from Joshua Farrelly is a sure road to Fanny's heart. Where did you say Herr Müller was from?

MARTHE   Germany.

TECK   I know that. (*Goes to a valise. He leans over, stares at it, looks at the labels, pushes the lock. The lock opens; he closes it. Then he turns and, as he speaks, picks up the brief-case*) What part of Germany?

MARTHE   I don't know. And I never knew you were an expert on accents.

TECK   I never knew it either. Are you driving into Washington with David this morning?

MARTHE   I was going to. But he may not be going to the office, now that Sara's here. I was to have lunch with Sally Tyne. (TECK *puts down the brief-case*) What are you doing?

TECK   Wondering why luggage is unlocked and a shabby brief-case is so carefully locked.

MARTHE   You're very curious about Mr. Müller.

TECK   Yes. And I do not know why. Something far away . . . I am curious about a daughter of the Farrellys' who marries a German who has bullet scars on his face and broken bones in his hands.

MARTHE   (*sharply*) Has he? There are many of them now, I guess.

TECK   So there are. But this one is in this house. (*He goes to the bell cord, pulls it. She watches him nervously.*)

MARTHE   Is it—is he any business of yours?

TECK   What is my business? Anything might be my business now.

MARTHE   Yes—unfortunately. You might inquire from your friend Von Seitz. They always know their nationals.

TECK   (*pleasantly, ignoring the sharpness with which she has spoken*) Oh, yes, I will do that, of course. But I do not like to ask questions without knowing the value of the answers.

MARTHE   Teck. This man is a little German Sara married years ago. I remember Mama talking about it. He was nothing then and he isn't now. They've had a tough enough time already without—

TECK   Have you— Have you been sleeping with David?

MARTHE   (*stops, stares at him, then simply*) No. I have not been. And that hasn't been your business for a good many years now.

TECK   You like him?

MARTHE   (*nervously*) What's this for, Teck?

TECK   Answer me, please.

MARTHE   I— (*She stops.*)

TECK   Yes? Answer me.

MARTHE   I do like him.

TECK   What does he feel about you?

MARTHE   I don't know.

TECK   But you are trying to find out. You have made plans with him?

MARTHE   Of course not. I—

TECK   But you will try to make him have plans. I have recognized it. Well, we have been together a long— (JOSEPH *enters,* TECK *stops*) Joseph, Miss Fanny wishes you to take the baggage upstairs.

JOSEPH   Yes, sir. I was going to. (*He begins to pick up the baggage.* MARTHE *has turned sharply and is staring at* TECK. *Then she rises, watches* JOSEPH *pick up the baggage, turns again to look at* TECK.)

TECK   As I was saying. It is perhaps best that we had this talk.

MARTHE   (*she stops, waits for* JOSEPH *to move off. He exits, carrying the valises*) Why did you do that? Why did you tell Joseph that Fanny wanted him to take the baggage upstairs?

TECK   Obviously it is more comfortable to look at baggage behind closed doors.

MARTHE   (*very sharply*) What kind of silliness is this now? Leave these people alone— (*As he starts to exit*) I won't let you—

TECK   What? (*As he moves again, she comes after him.*)

MARTHE   I said I won't let you. You are not—

TECK   How many times have you seen me angry? (MARTHE *looks up, startled*) You will not wish to see another. Run along now and have lunch with something you call Sally Tyne. But do not make plans with David. You will not be able to carry them out. You will go with me, when I am ready to go. You understand. (*He exits during his speech. The last words come as he goes through the door, and as the curtain falls.*)

Act Two

SCENE: *The same as Act One, about ten days later. During the act it will begin to grow dark; but the evening is warm and the terrace doors are open.*

AT RISE: SARA *is sitting on the couch, crocheting.* FANNY *and* TECK *are sitting at a small table playing cribbage.* BODO *is sitting near them, at a large table, working on a heating pad. The cord is torn from the bag, the bag is ripped open.* ANISE *sits next to him, anxiously watching him. Outside on the terrace,* JOSHUA *is going through baseball motions, coached by* JOSEPH. *From time to time they move out of sight, reappear, move off again.*

FANNY *(playing a card)* One.

BODO *(after a minute, to* TECK*)* The arrangement of this heating pad grows more complex.

TECK *(smiles, moves on the cribbage board)* And the more wires you remove, the more complex it will grow.

BODO *(points to bag)* Man has learned to make man comfortable. Yet all cannot have the comforts. *(To* ANISE*)* How much did this cost you?

ANISE It cost me ten dollars. And you have made a ruin of it.

BODO That is not yet completely true. *(To* FANNY*)* Did I not install for you a twenty-five-cent button-push for your radio?

TECK *(playing a card)* Two and two. *(Moves pegs on the cribbage board.)*

FANNY Yes, you're quite an installer.

BODO (*to* TECK) As I was wishing to tell you, Count de Brancovis, comfort and plenty exist. Yet all cannot have them it. Why?

TECK I do not know. It has worried many men. Why?

ANISE (*to* BODO) Yes, why?

BODO (*takes a deep breath, raises his finger as if about to lecture*) Why? (*Considers a moment, then deflates himself*) I am not as yet sure.

ANISE I thought not.

FANNY (*turns to look at* JOSHUA *and* JOSEPH *on the terrace*) Would you mind doing that dancing some place else?

JOSEPH (*looking in*) Yes'm. That ain't dancing. I'm teaching Josh baseball.

FANNY Then maybe he'd teach you how to clean the silver.

JOSEPH I'm a good silver-cleaner, Miss Fanny.

FANNY But you're getting out of practice.

JOSEPH (*after a moment's thought*) Yes'm. I see what you mean. (*He exits.*)

FANNY (*playing a card*) Three.

JOSHUA It is my fault. I'm crazy about baseball.

BODO Baseball players are among the most exploited people in this country. I read about it.

FANNY You never should have learned to read.

BODO Their exploited condition is foundationed on the fact that—

JOSHUA (*bored*) All right, all right. I still like baseball.

SARA Founded, Bodo, not foundationed.

JOSHUA He does it always. He likes long words. In all languages.

TECK How many languages do you children speak?

BODO Oh, we do not really know any very well, except German and English. We speak bad French and—

SARA And bad Danish and bad Czech.

TECK You seem to have stayed close to the borders of Germany. Did Herr Müller have hopes, as so many did, that National Socialism would be overthrown on every tomorrow?

SARA   We have not given up that hope. Have you, Count
de Brancovis?

TECK   I never had it.

JOSHUA   (*pleasantly*)   Then it must be most difficult for
you to sleep.

TECK   I beg your pardon?

SARA   Schweig doch, Joshua!

FANNY   (*to* TECK)   Sara told Joshua to shut up. (*Playing a
card*) Twelve.

TECK   I have offended you, Mrs. Müller. I am most sorry.

SARA   (*pleasantly*)   No, sir, you haven't offended me. I
just don't like polite political conversations any more.

TECK   (*nods*)   All of us, in Europe, had too many of them.

SARA   Yes. Too much talk. By this time all of us must know
where we are and what we have to do. It's an indul-
gence to sit in a room and discuss your beliefs as if
they were a juicy piece of gossip.

FANNY   You know, Sara, I find it very pleasant that Kurt,
considering his history, doesn't make platform speeches.
He hasn't tried to convince anybody of anything.

SARA   (*smiles*)   Why should he, Mama? You are quite old
enough to have your own convictions—or Papa's.

FANNY   (*turns to look at her*)   I am proud to have Papa's
convictions.

SARA   Of course. But it might be well to have a few new
ones, now and then.

FANNY   (*peers over at her*)   Are you criticizing me?

SARA   (*smiles*)   Certainly not.

BABETTE   (*comes running in from the right entrance door.
She has on an apron and she is carrying a plate. She
goes to* FANNY)   Eat it while it's hot. Grandma.

(FANNY *peers down, takes the fork, begins to eat.* ANISE
and BODO *both rise, move to* FANNY, *inspect the plate.*)

FANNY   (*to them*)   Go away.

ANISE   It is a potato pancake.

FANNY   And the first good one I've eaten in many, many
years. I love a good potato pancake.

BODO   I likewise.

BABETTE   I am making a great number for dinner. Move
away, Bodo.

TECK (*playing a card*) Fifteen and two.

ANISE (*who has followed* BODO *back to the table, leans over to look at the heating pad*) You've ruined it! I shall sue you.

JOSHUA I told you not to let him touch it.

SARA (*laughs*) I remember you were always saying that, Anise—that you were going to sue. That's very French. I was sick once in Paris, and Babbie stayed up for a whole night and day and finished a dress I was making for a woman in the Rue Jacob. I told her to tell the woman she'd done it—I thought perhaps the woman would give her a candy or something—and anyway, I was very proud of her work. But no. The woman admitted the dress was well done, but said she was going to sue because I hadn't done it myself. Fancy that.

FANNY (*slowly*) You sewed for a living?

SARA Not a very good one. But Babbie and I made a little something now and then. Didn't we, darling?

FANNY (*sharply*) Really, Sara, were these—these things necessary? Why couldn't you have written?

SARA (*laughs*) You've asked me that a hundred times in the last week.

JOSHUA (*gently*) I think it is only that Grandma feels sorry for us. Grandma has not seen much of the world.

FANNY Don't you start giving me lectures, Joshua. I'm fond of you. And of you, Babbie. (*To* ANISE) Are there two desserts for dinner? And are they sweet?

ANISE Yes.

FANNY (*turns to* BODO) I wish I were fond of you.

BODO You are. (*Happily*) You are very fond of me.

FANNY (*playing a card*) Twenty-five.

BABETTE This is for you, Grandma. I'm making a bed-jacket. It is nice lace. Papa brought it to me from Spain and I mean for you to have it.

FANNY (*kisses* BABETTE) Thank you, darling. A sequence and three. A pair and five. (*To* TECK, *as they finish the cribbage game*) There. That's two dollars off. I owe you eight-fifty.

TECK Let us carry it until tomorrow. You shall give it to me as a going-away token.

FANNY   (*too pleased*) You're going away?

TECK   (*laughs*) Ah, Madame Fanny. Do not sound *that* happy.

FANNY   Did I? That's rude of me. When are you going?

TECK   In a few days, I think. (*Turns to look at* SARA) We're too many refugees, eh, Mrs. Müller?

SARA   (*pleasantly*) Perhaps.

TECK   Will you be leaving, also?

SARA   I beg your pardon?

TECK   I thought perhaps you, too, would be moving on. Herr Müller does not give me the feeling of a man who settles down. Men who have done his work, seldom leave it. Not for a quiet country house.

(*All three children look up.*)

SARA   (*very quietly*) What work do you think my husband has done, Count de Brancovis?

TECK   Engineering?

SARA   (*slowly*) Yes. Engineering.

FANNY   (*very deliberately to* TECK) I don't know what you're saying. They shall certainly not be leaving—ever. Is that understood, Sara?

SARA   Well, Mama—

FANNY   There are no wells about it. You've come home to see me die and you will wait until I'm ready.

SARA   (*laughs*) Really, Mama, that isn't the reason I came home.

FANNY   It's a good enough reason. I shall do a fine death. I intend to be a great deal of trouble to everybody.

ANISE   I daresay.

FANNY   I shall take to my bed early and stay for years. In great pain.

ANISE   I am sure of it. You will duplicate the disgrace of the birth of Miss Sara.

SARA   (*laughs*) Was I born in disgrace?

ANISE   It was not your fault. But it was disgusting. Three weeks before you were to come—all was excellent, of course, in so healthy a woman as Madame Fanny—a great dinner was given here and, most unexpectedly, attended by a beautiful lady from England.

FANNY   Do be still. You are dull and fanciful—

ANISE   Mr. Joshua made the great error of waltzing the beauty for two dances, Madame Fanny being unfitted for the waltz and under no circumstances being the most graceful of dancers.

FANNY   (*her voice rising*)   Are you crazy? I danced magnificently.

ANISE   It is well you thought so. A minute did not elapse between the second of the waltzes and a scream from Madame Fanny. She was in labor. Two hundred people, and if we had left her alone, she would have remained in the ballroom—

FANNY   How you invent! How you invent!

ANISE   Do not call to me that I am a liar. For three weeks you are in the utmost agony—

FANNY   And so I was. I remember it to this day—

ANISE   (*to* SARA, *angrily*)   Not a pain. Not a single pain. She would lie up there in state, stealing candy from herself. Then, when your Papa would rest himself for a minute at the dinner or with a book, a scream would dismantle the house—it was revolting. (*Spitefully to* FANNY) And now the years have passed I may disclose to you that Mr. Joshua knew you were going through the play-acting—

FANNY   (*rises*)   He did not. You are a malicious—

ANISE   Once he said to me, "Anise, it is well that I am in love. This is of a great strain and her great-uncle Freddie was not right in the head, neither."

FANNY   (*screaming*)   You will leave this house— You are a liar, a woman of—

SARA   Mama, sit down.

ANISE   I will certainly leave this house. I will—

SARA   (*sharply*)   Both of you. Sit down. And be still.

ANISE   She has intimated that I lie—

FANNY   (*screaming*)   Intimated! Is that what I was doing— (ANISE *begins to leave the room*) All right. I beg your pardon. I apologize.

(ANISE *turns.*)

SARA   Both of you. You are acting like children.

BODO   Really, Mama. You insult us.

ANISE   I accept your apology. Seat yourself.

(*They both sit down.*)

FANNY   (*after a silence*)   I am unloved.

BABETTE   I love you, Grandma.

FANNY   Do you, Babbie?

JOSHUA   And I.

FANNY   (*nods, very pleased. To* BODO)   And you?

BODO   *I* loved you the primary second I saw you.

FANNY   You are a charlatan.

ANISE   As for me, I am fond of all the living creatures. It is true that the children cause me greater work, which in turn more greatly inconveniences the feet. However, I do not complain. I believe in children.

FANNY   Rather like believing in the weather, isn't it? (DAVID *and* KURT *come in from the terrace. Both are in work clothes, their sleeves rolled up*) Where have you been?

DAVID   Oh, we've been helping Mr. Chabeuf spray the fruit trees.

ANISE   Mr. Chabeuf says that Herr Müller has the makings of a good farmer. From a Frenchman that is a large thing to say.

KURT   (*who has looked around the room, looked at* TECK, *strolled over to* BODO)   Mr. Chabeuf and I have an excellent time exchanging misinformation. My father was a farmer. I have a wide knowledge of farmer's misinformation.

FANNY   This is good farm land. Perhaps, in time—

DAVID   (*laughs*)   Mama would give you the place, Kurt, if you guaranteed that your great-grandchildren would die here.

KURT   (*smiles*)   I would like to so guarantee.

TECK   A farmer. That is very interesting. Abandon your ideals, Herr Müller?

KURT   Ideals? (*Carefully*) Sara, heisst das auf deutsch "Ideale"?

SARA   Yes.

KURT   Is that what I have now? I do not like the word. It gives to me the picture of a small, pale man at a seaside resort. (*To* BODO) What are you doing?

BODO Preparing an elderly electric pad for Miss Anise. I am confused.

KURT (*wanders toward the piano*) So it seems.

BODO Something has gone wrong with the principle on which I have been working. It is probably that I will ask your assistance.

KURT (*bows to him*) Thank you. Whenever you are ready. (*Begins to pick out notes with one hand.*)

FANNY We shall have a little concert tomorrow evening. In honor of Babbie's birthday. (*To* KURT) Kurt, you and I will play "The Clock Symphony." Then Joshua and I will play the duet we've learned, and Babbie will sing. And I shall finish with a Chopin Nocturne.

DAVID (*laughs*) I thought you'd be the last on the program.

TECK Where is Marthe?

FANNY She'll be back soon. She went into town to do an errand for me. (*To* DAVID) Did you buy presents for everybody?

DAVID I did.

SARA (*smiles, to* BABETTE) We always did that here. If somebody had a birthday, we all got presents. Nice, isn't it?

DAVID (*to* ANISE) I shall buy you an electric pad. You will need it.

ANISE Indeed.

FANNY Did you buy me a good present?

DAVID Pretty good. (*Pats* BABETTE's *head*) The best present goes to Babbie; it's *her* birthday.

FANNY Jewelry?

DAVID No, not jewelry.

FANNY Oh. Not jewelry.

DAVID Why?

FANNY (*too casually*) I just asked you.

TECK (*gets up*) It was a natural mistake, David. You see, Mrs. Mellie Sewell told your mother that she had seen you and Marthe in Barstow's. And your mother said you were probably buying her a present, or one for Babbie.

DAVID (*too sharply*) Yes.

TECK (*laughs*) Yes what?

DAVID (*slowly*) Just yes.

FANNY (*too hurriedly*) Mellie gets everything wrong.
She's very anxious to meet Marthe because she used to
know Francie Cabot, her aunt. Marthe's aunt, I mean,
not Mellie's.

SARA (*too hurriedly*) She really came to inspect Kurt and
me. But I saw her first. (*She looks anxiously at* DAVID,
*who has turned his back on the room and is facing the
terrace*) You were lucky to be out, David.

DAVID Oh, she calls every Saturday afternoon, to bring
Mama all the Washington gossip of the preceding week.
She gets it all wrong, you understand, but that doesn't
make any difference to either Mama or her. Mama then
augments it, wits it up, Papa used to say—

FANNY Certainly. I sharpen it a little. Mellie has no sense
of humor.

DAVID So Mama sharpens it a little, and delivers it tomorrow afternoon to old lady Marcy down the road.
Old lady Marcy hasn't heard a word in ten years, so
she unsharpens it again, and changes the names. By
Wednesday afternoon—

TECK (*smiles*) By Wednesday afternoon it will not be
you who were in Barstow's, and it will be a large diamond pin with four sapphires delivered to Gaby Deslys.

DAVID (*turns, looks at him*) Exactly.

FANNY (*very nervously*) Francie Cabot, Marthe's aunt,
you understand— (*To* KURT) Did you ever know Paul
von Seitz, a German?

KURT I have heard of him.

FANNY (*speaking very rapidly*) Certainly. He was your
Ambassador to somewhere, I've forgotten. Well, Francie
Cabot married him. I could have. Any American, not
crippled, whose father had money— He was crazy
about me. I was better-looking than Francie. Well, years
later when he was your Ambassador—my father was,
too, as you probably know—not your Ambassador, of
course, ours—but I am talking about Von Seitz.

DAVID (*laughs to* KURT) You can understand how it goes.
Old lady Marcy is not entirely to blame.

FANNY Somebody asked me if I didn't regret not marrying him. I said, "Madame, je le regrette tous les jours et j'en suis heureuse chaque soir." (FANNY *turns to* DAVID) That means I regret it every day and am happy about it every night. You understand what I meant, by *night?* Styles in wit change so.

DAVID I understood it, Mama.

JOSHUA We, too, Grandma.

BABETTE (*approvingly*) It was most witty.

BODO I do not know that I understood. You will explain to me, Grandma?

SARA Later.

FANNY (*turns to look at* TECK) You remember the old Paul von Seitz?

TECK (*nods*) He was stationed in Paris when I first was there.

FANNY Of course. I always forget you were a diplomat.

TECK It is just as well.

FANNY There's something insane about a Roumanian diplomat. Pure insane. I knew another one, once. He wanted to marry me, too.

SARA (*laughs*) All of Europe.

FANNY Not all. Some. Naturally. I was rich, I was witty, my family was of the best. I was handsome, unaffected—

DAVID And noble and virtuous and kind and elegant and fashionable and simple—it's hard to remember everything you were. I've often thought it must have been boring for Papa to have owned such perfection.

FANNY (*shrieks*) What! Your father bored with me! Not for a second of our life—

DAVID (*laughs*) Oh God, when will I learn?

BODO Do not shriek, Grandma. It is an unpleasant sound for the ear.

FANNY Where was I? Oh, yes. What I started out to say was— (*She turns, speaks carefully to* TECK) Mellie Sewell told me, when you left the room, that she had heard from Louis Chandler's child's governess that you had won quite a bit of money in a poker game with Sam Chandler and some Germans at the Embassy.

(KURT, *who has been playing the piano, stops playing very abruptly.* TECK *turns to look at him*) *That's* how I thought of Von Seitz. His nephew Philip was in on the game.

DAVID   (*looks at* TECK) It must have been a big game. Sam Chandler plays in big games.

TECK   Not big enough.

DAVID   Have you known Sam long?

TECK   For years. Every Embassy in Europe knew him.

DAVID   (*sharply*) Sam and Nazis must make an unpleasant poker game.

(KURT *begins to play a new melody.*)

TECK   (*who has not looked away from* KURT) I do not play poker to be amused.

DAVID   (*irritably*) What's Sam selling now?

TECK   Bootleg munitions. He always has.

DAVID   You don't mind?

TECK   Mind? I have not thought about it.

FANNY   Well, you ought to think about it. Sam Chandler has always been a scoundrel. All the Chandlers are. They're cousins of mine. Mama used to say they never should have learned to walk on two feet. They would have been more comfortable on four.

TECK   Do you know the young Von Seitz, Herr Müller? He was your military attaché in Spain.

KURT   He was the German government attaché in Spain. I know his name, of course. He is a famous artillery expert. But the side on which I fought was not where he was stationed, Count de Brancovis.

ANISE   (BABETTE *and* JOSHUA *begin to hum the song* KURT *is playing.* SARA *begins to hum*) It is time for the bath and the change of clothes. I will give you five more minutes—

FANNY   What is the song?

TECK   It was a German soldier's song. They sang it as they straggled back in '18. I remember hearing it in Berlin. Were you there then, Herr Müller?

KURT   (*the playing and the humming continue*) I was not in Berlin.

TECK   But you were in the war, of course?

KURT   Yes. I was in the war.

FANNY   You didn't think then you'd live to see another war.

KURT   Many of us were afraid we would.

FANNY   What are the words?

SARA   The Germans in Spain, in Kurt's Brigade, wrote new words for the song.

KURT   This was what you heard in Berlin, in 1918. (*Begins to sing.*)

"Wir zieh'n Heim, wir zieh'n Heim,
Mancher kommt nicht mit,
Mancher ging verschütt,
Aber Freunde sind wir stets."
    (*in English.*)
"We come home. We come home.
Some of us are gone, and some of us are lost, but
    we are friends:
Our blood is on the earth together.
Some day. Some day we shall meet again.
Farewell."

(*Stops singing*) At a quarter before six on the morning of November 7th, 1936, eighteen years later, five hundred Germans walked through the Madrid streets on their way to defend the Manzanares River. We felt good that morning. You know how it is to be good when it is needed to be good? So we had need of new words to say that. I translate with awkwardness, you understand. (*Begins to sing.*)

"And so we have met again.
The blood did not have time to dry.
We lived to stand and fight again.
This time we fight for people.
This time the bastards will keep their hands away.
Those who sell the blood of other men, this time,
They keep their hands away.
For us to stand.
For us to fight.
This time no farewell, no farewell."

(*Music dies out. There is silence for a minute*) We did not win. (*Looks up, gently*) It would have been a different world if we had.

SARA   Papa said so years ago. Do you remember, Mama? "For every man who lives without freedom, the rest of us must face the guilt."

FANNY   Yes. "We are liable in the conscience-balance for the tailor in Lodz, the black man in our South, the peasant in—" (*Turns to* TECK. *Unpleasantly*) Your country, I think.

ANISE   (*rises*) Come. Baths for everybody. (*To* BODO) Gather the wires. You have wrecked my cure.

BODO   If you would allow me a few minutes more—

ANISE   Come along. I have been duped for long enough. Come Joshua. Babette. Baths.

JOSHUA   (*starts out after* ANISE. BABETTE *begins to gather up her sewing*) My tub is a thing of glory. But I do not like it so prepared for me and so announced by Miss Anise. (*He exits.*)

BODO   (*to* ANISE) You are angry about this. I do not blame you with my heart or my head. I admit I have failed. But Papa will repair it, Anise. Will you not, Papa? In a few minutes—

TECK   (*to* BODO) Your father is an expert electrician?

BODO   Oh yes, sir.

TECK   And as good with radio—

(BODO *begins to nod.*)

KURT   (*sharply*) Count de Brancovis. Make your questions to me, please. Not to my children.

(*The others look up, surprised.*)

TECK   (*pleasantly*) Very well, Herr Müller.

ANISE   (*as she exits with* BODO) Nobody can fix it. You have made a pudding of it.

BODO   (*as he follows her*) Do not worry. In five minutes tonight, you will have a pad far better— (*As* BODO *reaches the door he bumps into* MARTHE *who is carrying large dress boxes*) Oh. Your pardon. Oh, hello. (*He disappears.*)

MARTHE   (*gaily*) Hello. (*To* FANNY) I waited for them. I was afraid they wouldn't deliver this late in the day. (*To* SARA) Come on, Sara. I can't wait to see them.

SARA   What?

MARTHE   Dresses. From Fanny. A tan linen, and a dark

green with wonderful buttons, a white net for Babbie,
and a suit for you, and play dresses for Babbie, and a
dinner dress in gray to wear for Babbie's birthday—
gray should be good for you, Sara—all from Savitt's.
We sneaked the measurements, Anise and I—

SARA (*she goes toward* FANNY) How nice of you, Mama.
How very kind of you. And of you, Marthe, to take so
much trouble— (*She leans down, kisses* FANNY) You're
a sweet woman, Mama.

DAVID That's the first time Mama's ever heard that word.
(*He takes the boxes from* MARTHE, *puts them near the
staircase.* MARTHE *smiles at him, touches his hand, as*
TECK *watches them.*)

FANNY (*giggles*) I have a bottom sweetness, if you understand what I mean.

DAVID I have been too close to the bottom to see it.

FANNY That should be witty. I don't know why it isn't.

(BABETTE *goes over to stare at the boxes.*)

SARA From Savitt's. Extravagant of you. They had such
lovely clothes. I remember my coming-out dress—
(*Goes to* KURT) Do you remember the black suit with
the braid, and the Milan hat? Not the *first* day we met,
but the picnic day? (*He smiles up at her*) Well, they
were from Savitt's. That was over twenty years ago—
I've known you a long time. Me, in an evening dress.
Now you'll have to take me into Washington. I want to
show off. Next week, and we'll dance, maybe— (*Sees
that he is not looking at her*) What's the matter, darling?
(*No answer. Slowly he turns to look at her*) What's the
matter, Kurt? (*Takes his arms, very unhappily*) What
have I done? It isn't that dresses have ever mattered to
me, it's just that—

KURT Of course, they have mattered to you. As they
should. I do not think of the dresses. (*Draws her to
him*) How many years have I loved that face?

SARA (*her face very happy*) So?

KURT So. (*He leans down, kisses her, as if it were important.*)

SARA (*pleased, unembarrassed*) There are other people
here.

MARTHE   (*slowly*) And good for us to see.

TECK   Nostalgia?

MARTHE   No. Nostalgia is for something you have known.
(FANNY *coughs.*)

BABETTE   (*comes to* FANNY) Grandma, is it allowed to
look at my dresses?

FANNY   Of course, child. Run along.

BABETTE   (*picks up the boxes, goes toward the hall entrance, stops near* FANNY) I love dresses, I have a great
fondness for materials and colors. Thank you, Grandma.
(*She runs out of the room.*)

(JOSEPH *appears in the doorway.*)

JOSEPH   There is a long-distance operator with a long-
distance call for Mr. Müller. She wants to talk with him
on the long-distance phone.

KURT   Oh— Excuse me, please—

(KURT *rises quickly.* SARA *turns sharply to look at him.*
TECK *looks up.* KURT *goes quickly out.* TECK *watches him
go.* SARA *stands staring after him.*)

MARTHE   (*laughs*) I feel the same way as Babbie. Come
on, Sara. Let's try them on.

(SARA *does not turn.*)

TECK   You also have a new dress?

MARTHE   (*looks at him*) Yes. Fanny was kind to me, too.

TECK   You are a very generous woman, **Madame Fanny.**
Did you also give her a sapphire bracelet from
Barstow's?

FANNY   I beg your—

DAVID   (*slowly*) No. I gave Marthe the bracelet. And I
understand that it is not any business of yours.

(FANNY *rises.* SARA *turns.*)

FANNY   Really, David—

DAVID   Be still, Mama.

TECK   (*after a second*) Did you tell him that, Marthe?

MARTHE   Yes.

TECK   (*looks up at her*) I shall not forgive you for that.
(*Looks at* DAVID) It is a statement which no man likes
to hear from another man. You understand that? (*Playfully*) That is the type of thing about which we used to
play at duels in Europe.

DAVID (*comes toward him*) We are not so musical comedy here. And you are not in Europe.

TECK Even if I were, I would not suggest any such action. I would have reasons for not wishing it.

DAVID It would be well for you not to suggest *any* action. And the reason for *that* is you might get hurt.

TECK (*slowly*) That would not be my reason. (*To* MARTHE) Your affair has gone far enough—

MARTHE (*sharply*) It is not an affair—

TECK I do not care what it is. The time has come to leave here. Go upstairs and pack your things. (*She does not move.* DAVID *turns toward her*) Go on, Marthe.

MARTHE (*to* DAVID) I am not going with him. I told you that.

DAVID I don't want you to go with him.

FANNY (*carefully*) Really, David, aren't you interfering in all this a good deal—

DAVID (*carefully*) Yes, Mama. I am.

TECK (*to* MARTHE) When you are speaking to me, please say what you have to say to me.

MARTHE (*comes to him*) You are trying to frighten me. But you are not going to frighten me any more. I will say it to you: I am not going with you. I am never going with you again.

TECK (*softly*) If you do not fully mean what you say, or if you might change your mind, you are talking unwisely, Marthe.

MARTHE I know that.

TECK Shall we talk about it alone?

MARTHE You can't make me go, can you, Teck?

TECK No, I can't make you.

MARTHE Then there's no sense talking about it.

TECK Are you in love with him?

MARTHE Yes.

FANNY (*sharply*) Marthe! What is all this?

MARTHE (*sharply*) I'll tell *you* about it in a minute.

DAVID You don't have to explain anything to anybody.

TECK (*ignores him*) Is he in love with you?

MARTHE I don't think so. You won't believe it, because you can't believe anything that hasn't got tricks to it,

But David hasn't much to do with this. I told you I would leave some day, and I remember where I said it—(*Slowly*)—and why I said it.

TECK   I also remember. But I did not believe you. I have not had much to offer you these last years. But if now we had some money and could go back—

MARTHE   No. I don't like you, Teck. I never have.

TECK   And I have always known it.

FANNY   (*stiffly*) I think your lack of affections should be discussed with more privacy. Perhaps—

DAVID   Mama—

MARTHE   There is nothing to discuss. Strange. I've talked to myself about this scene for almost fifteen years. I knew a lot of things to say to you and I used to lie awake at night or walk along the street and say them. Now I don't want to. I guess you only want to talk that way, when you're not sure what you can do. When you're sure, then what's the sense of saying it? "This is why and this is why and this—" (*Very happily*) But when you know you can do it, you don't have to say anything; you can just go. And I'm going. There is nothing you can do. I would like you to believe that now.

TECK   Very well, Marthe. I think I made a mistake. I should not have brought you here. I believe you now.

MARTHE   (*after a pause, she looks at* DAVID) I'll move into Washington, and—

DAVID   Yes. Later. But I'd like you to stay here for a while, with us, if you wouldn't mind.

SARA   It would be better for you, Marthe—

FANNY   It's very interesting that I am not being consulted about this. (*To* MARTHE) I have nothing against you, Marthe. I am sorry for you, but I don't think—

MARTHE   Thank you, Sara, David. But I'd rather move in now. (*Turns, comes toward* FANNY) But perhaps I have something against you. Do you remember my wedding?

FANNY   Yes.

MARTHE   Do you remember how pleased Mama was with herself? Brilliant Mama, handsome Mama—everybody thought so, didn't they? A seventeen-year-old daughter, marrying a pretty good title, about to secure herself in a world that Mama liked—she didn't ask me what I liked. And the one time I tried to tell her, she frightened me— (*Looks up*) Maybe I've always been frightened. All my life.

TECK Of course.

MARTHE (*to* FANNY, *as if she had not heard* TECK) I remember Mama's face at the wedding—it was *her* wedding, really, not mine.

FANNY (*sharply*) You are very hard on your mother.

MARTHE Nineteen hundred and twenty-five. No, I'm not hard on her. I only tell the truth. She wanted a life for me, I suppose. It just wasn't the life I wanted for myself. (*Sharply*) And that's what you have tried to do. With your children. In another way. Only Sara got away. And that made you angry—until so many years went by that you forgot.

FANNY I don't usually mind people saying anything they think, but I find that—

MARTHE I don't care what you mind or don't mind. I'm in love with your son—

FANNY (*very sharply*) That's unfortunate—

MARTHE And I'm sick of watching you try to make him into his father. I don't think you even know you do it any more and I don't think he knows it any more, either. And that's what's most dangerous about it.

FANNY (*very angrily*) I don't know what you are talking about.

DAVID I think you do. (*Smiles*) You shouldn't mind hearing the truth—and neither should I.

FANNY (*worried, sharply*) David! What does all this nonsense mean? I—

MARTHE (*to* FANNY) Look. That pretty world Mama got me into was a tough world, see? I'm used to trouble. So don't try to interfere with me, because I won't let you. (*She goes to* DAVID) Let's just have a good time. (*He leans down, takes both her hands, kisses them. Then slowly, she turns away, starts to exit. To* TECK) You will also be going today?

TECK Yes.

MARTHE   Then let us make sure we go in different directions, and do not meet again. Good-bye, Teck.

TECK   Good-bye, Marthe. You will not believe me, but I tried my best, and I am now most sorry to lose you.

MARTHE   Yes. I believe you. (*She moves out. There is silence for a minute.*)

FANNY   Well, a great many things have been said in the last few minutes.

DAVID   (*crosses to bell cord. To* TECK) I will get Joseph to pack for you.

TECK   Thank you. Do not bother. I will ring for him when I am ready. (KURT *comes in from the study door.* SARA *turns, stares at him, waits. He does not look at her*) It will not take me very long. (*He starts for the door, looking at* KURT.)

SARA   What is it, Kurt?

KURT   It is nothing of importance, darling— (*He looks quickly at* TECK, *who is moving very slowly.*)

SARA   Don't tell me it's nothing. I know the way you look when—

KURT   (*sharply*) I said it was of no importance. I must get to California for a few weeks. That is all.

SARA   I—

TECK   (*turns*) It is in the afternoon newspaper, Herr Müller. (*Points to paper on table*) I was waiting to find the proper moment to call it to your attention. (*He moves toward the table, as they all turn to watch him. He picks up the paper, turns it over, begins to read*) "Zurich, Switzerland: The Zurich papers today reprinted a despatch from the *Berliner Tageblatt* on the capture of Colonel Max Freidank. Freidank is said—(SARA *begins to move toward him*)—to be the chief of the Anti-Nazi Underground Movement. Colonel Friedank has long been an almost legendary figure. The son of the famous General Freidank, he was a World War officer and a distinguished physicist before the advent of Hitler." That is all.

SARA   Max—

KURT   Be still, Sara.

TECK   They told me of it at the Embassy last night. They

also told me that with him they had taken a man who called himself Ebber, and a man who called himself Triste. They could not find a man called Gotter. (*He starts again toward the door*) I shall be a lonely man without Marthe. I am also a very poor one. I should like to have ten thousand dollars before I go.

DAVID (*carefully*) You will make no loans in this house.

TECK I was not speaking of a loan.

FANNY (*carefully*) God made you not only a scoundrel but a fool. That is a dangerous combination.

DAVID (*suddenly leaps toward* TECK) Damn you, you—

KURT (*suddenly pounds on the top of the piano, as* DAVID *almost reaches* TECK) Leave him alone. (*Moves quickly to stop* DAVID) Leave him alone! *David! Leave him alone!*

DAVID (*angrily to* KURT) Keep out of it. (*Starts toward* TECK *again*) I'm beginning to see what Marthe meant. Blackmailing with your wife— You—

KURT (*very sharply*) He is not speaking of his wife. Or you. He means me. (*Looks at* TECK) Is that correct?

(SARA *moves toward* KURT. DAVID *draws back, bewildered.*)

TECK Good. It was necessary for me to hear you say it. You understand that?

KURT I understand it.

SARA (*frightened, softly*) Kurt—

DAVID What is all this about? What the hell are you talking about?

TECK (*sharply for the first time*) Be still. (*To* KURT) At your convenience. Your hands are shaking, Herr Müller.

KURT (*quietly*) My hands were broken; they are bad when I have fear.

TECK I am sorry. I can understand that. It is not pleasant. (*Motions toward* FANNY *and* DAVID) Perhaps you would like a little time to— I will go and pack, and be ready to leave. We will all find that more comfortable, I think. You should get yourself a smaller gun, Herr Müller. That pistol you have been carrying is big and awkward.

KURT You saw the pistol when you examined our bags?

TECK You knew that?

KURT Oh, yes. I have the careful eye, through many years

of needing it. And then you have not the careful eye. The pistol was lying to the left of a paper package and when you leave, it is to the right of the package.

SARA Kurt! Do you mean that—

KURT (*sharply*) Please, darling, do not do that.

TECK It is a German Army Luger?

KURT Yes.

TECK Keep it in your pocket, Herr Müller. You will have no need to use it. And, in any case, I am not afraid of it. You understand that?

KURT (*slowly*) I understand that you are not a man of fears. That is strange to me, because I am a man who has so many fears.

TECK (*laughs, as he exits*) Are you? That is most interesting. (*He exits.*)

DAVID (*softly*) What is this about, Kurt?

KURT He knows who I am and what I do and what I carry with me.

SARA (*carefully*) What about Max?

KURT The telephone was from Mexico. Ilse received a cable. Early on the morning of Monday, they caught Ebber and Triste. An hour after they took Max in Berlin. (*She looks up at him, begins to shake her head. He presses her arm*) Yes. It is hard.

FANNY (*softly*) You said he knew who you were and what you carried with you. I don't understand.

KURT I am going to tell you: I am an outlaw. I work with many others in an illegal organization. I have so worked for seven years. I am on what is called a desired list. But I did not know I was worth ten thousand dollars. My price has risen.

DAVID (*slowly*) And what do you carry with you?

KURT Twenty-three thousand dollars. It has been gathered from the pennies and the nickels of the poor who do not like Fascism, and who believe in the work we do. I came here to bring Sara home and to get the money. I had hopes to rest here for a while, and then—

SARA (*slowly*) And I had hopes someone else would take it back and you would stay with us— (*Shakes her head, then*) Max is not dead?

KURT No. The left side of his face is dead. (*Softly*) It was a good face.

SARA (*to* FANNY *and* DAVID, *as if she were going to cry*) It was a very good face. He and Kurt—in the old days— (*To* KURT) After so many years. If Max got caught, then nobody's got a chance. Nobody. (*She suddenly sits down.*)

DAVID (*points upstairs*) He wants to sell what he knows to you? Is that right?

KURT Yes.

FANNY Wasn't it careless of you to leave twenty-three thousand dollars lying around to be seen?

KURT No, it was not careless of me. It is in a locked briefcase. I have thus carried money for many years. There seemed no safer place than Sara's home. It was careless of you to have in your house a man who opens baggage and blackmails.

DAVID (*sharply*) Yes. It was very careless.

FANNY But you said you knew he'd seen it—

KURT Yes. I knew it the first day we were here. What was I to do about it? He is not a man who steals. This is a safer method. I knew that it would come some other way. I have been waiting to see what the way would be. That is all I could do.

DAVID (*to* FANNY) What's the difference? It's been done (*To* KURT) If he wants to sell to you, he must have another buyer. Who?

KURT The Embassy. Von Seitz, I think.

DAVID You mean he has told Von Seitz about you and—

KURT No. I do not think he has told him anything. As yet. It would be foolish of him. He has probably only asked most guarded questions.

DAVID But you're here. You're in this country. They can't do anything to you. They wouldn't be crazy enough to try it. Is your passport all right?

KURT Not quite.

FANNY Why not? Why isn't it?

KURT (*wearily, as if he were bored*) Because people like me are not given visas with such ease. And I was in a hurry to bring my wife and my children to safety. (*Sharply*) Madame Fanny, you must come to understand it is no longer the world you once knew.

DAVID It doesn't matter. You're a political refugee. We don't turn back people like you. People who are in danger. You will give me your passport and tomorrow morning I'll see Barens. We'll tell him the truth— (*Points to the door*) Tell de Brancovis to go to hell. There's not a damn thing he or anybody else can do.

SARA (*looks up at* KURT, *who is staring at her*) You don't understand, David.

DAVID There's a great deal I don't understand. But there's nothing to worry about.

SARA Not much to worry about as long as Kurt is in this house. But he's not going to—

KURT The Count has made the guess that—

SARA That you will go back to get Ebber and Triste and Max. Is that right, Kurt? Is that right?

KURT Yes, darling, I will try. They were taken to Sonnenburg. Guards can be bribed— It has been done once before at Sonnenburg. We will try for it again. I must go back, Sara. I must start.

SARA Of course, you must go back. I guess I was trying to think it wouldn't come. But— (*To* FANNY *and* DAVID) Kurt's got to go back. He's got to go home. He's got to buy them out. He'll do it, too. You'll see. (*She stops, breathes*) It's hard enough to get back. Very hard. But if they knew he was coming— They want Kurt bad. Almost as much as they wanted Max— And then there are hundreds of others, too— (*She gets up, comes to him. He holds her, puts his face in her hair. She stands holding him, trying to speak without crying. She puts her face down on his head*) Don't be scared, darling. You'll get back. You'll see. You've done it before— you'll do it again. Don't be scared. You'll get Max out all right. (*Gasps*) And then you'll do his work, won't you? That's good. That's fine, You'll do a good job, the way you've always done. (*She is crying very hard. To* FANNY) Kurt doesn't feel well. He was wounded and he

gets tired— (*To* KURT) You don't feel well, do you?
(*Slowly. She is crying too hard now to be heard clearly*)
Don't be scared, darling. You'll get home. Don't worry,
you'll get home. Yes, you will.

(*The curtain falls.*)

Act Three

SCENE: *The same. A half hour later.*

AT RISE: FANNY *is sitting in a chair.* KURT *is at the piano, his head resting on one hand. He is playing softly with the other hand.* SARA *is sitting very quietly on the couch.* DAVID *is pacing on the terrace.*

FANNY (*to* DAVID) David, would you stop that pacing, please? (DAVID *comes in*) And would you stop that one-hand piano playing? Either play, or get up.

(KURT *gets up, crosses to the couch, sits.* SARA *looks at him, gets up, crosses to the decanters, begins to make a drink.*)

SARA (*to* DAVID) A drink?

DAVID What? Yes, please. (*To* KURT) Do you intend to buy your friends out of jail?

KURT I intend to try.

FANNY It's all very strange to me. I thought things were so well run that bribery and—

KURT (*smiles*) What a magnificent work Fascists have done in convincing the world that they are men from legends.

DAVID They have done very well for themselves—unfortunately.

KURT Yes. But not by themselves. Does it make us all uncomfortable to remember that they came in on the shoulders of the most powerful men in the world? Of course, And so we would prefer to believe they are men from the planets. They are not. Let me reassure you. They are smart, they are sick, and they are cruel. But given men who know what they fight for— (*Shrugs*) I will console you. A year ago last month, at three o'clock in the morning, Freidank and I, with two elderly pistols, raided the home of the Gestapo chief in Konstanz, got what we wanted, and the following morning Friedank was eating his breakfast three blocks away, and I was over the Swiss border.

FANNY (*slowly*) You are brave men.

KURT *I* do not tell you the story to prove we are remarkable, but to prove they are *not*.

(SARA *brings him a drink. Gives one to* DAVID.)

SARA (*softly, touching* KURT's *shoulder*)   Kurt loves Max.

KURT Always since I came here I have a dream: that he will come into this room some day. How he would like it here, eh, Sara? He loves good food and wine, and you have books— (*Laughs happily*) He is fifty-nine years of age. And when he was fifty-seven, he carried me on his back, seven miles across the border. I had been hurt— That takes a man, does it not?

FANNY (*to* KURT) You look like a sick man to me.

KURT No. I'm only tired. I do not like to wait. It will go. It is the waiting that is always most bad for me.

DAVID (*points upstairs*) Damn him! He's doing it deliberately.

KURT It is then the corruption begins. Once in Spain I waited for two days until the planes would exhaust themselves. I think then why must our side fight always with naked hands. The spirit and the hands. All is against us but ourselves.

SARA You will not think that when the time comes. It will go.

KURT Of a certainty.

FANNY But does it have to go on being your hands?

KURT For each man, his own hands. He has to sleep with them.

DAVID (*uncomfortably, as if he did not like to say it*) That's right. I guess it's the way all of us should feel. But—but you have a family. Isn't there somebody else who hasn't a wife and children—

KURT   Each could have his own excuse. Some love for the first time, some have bullet holes, some have fear of the camps, some are sick, many are getting older. (*Shrugs*) Each could find a reason. And many find it. My children are not the only children in the world, even to me.

FANNY   That's noble of you, of course. But they are your children, nevertheless. And Sara, she—

SARA   Mama—

KURT   (*after a slight pause*)   One means always in English to insult with that word noble?

FANNY   Of course not, I—

KURT   It is not noble. It is the way I must live. Good or bad, it is what I am. (*Turns deliberately to look at* FANNY) And what I am is not what you wanted for your daughter, twenty years ago or now.

FANNY   You are misunderstanding me.

KURT   (*smiles*)   For our girl, too, we want a safe and happy life. And it is thus I try to make it for her. We each have our way. I do not convert you to mine.

DAVID   You are very certain of your way.

KURT   (*smiles*)   I seem so to you? Good.

(JOSEPH *appears in the hall doorway. He is carrying valises and overcoats.*)

JOSEPH   What'll I do with these, Miss Fanny?

FANNY   They're too large for eating, aren't they? What were you thinking of doing with them?

JOSEPH   I mean, it's Fred's day off.

DAVID   All right. You drive him into town.

JOSEPH   Then who's going to serve at dinner?

FANNY   (*impatiently*)   Belle can do it alone tonight.

JOSEPH   No she can't. Belle's upstairs packing with Miss Marthe. My, there's quite a lot of departing, ain't there?

FANNY   (*very impatiently*)   All right, then cook can bring in dinner.

JOSEPH   I wouldn't ask her to do that, if I were you. She's mighty mad: the sink pipe is leaking again. You just better wait for your dinner till I get back from Washington.

FANNY   (*shouting*)   We are not cripples and we were eating dinner in this house before you arrived to show us how to use the knife and fork. (JOSEPH *laughs*) Go on. Put his things in the car. I'll ring for you when he's ready.

JOSEPH You told me the next time you screamed to remind you to ask my pardon.

FANNY You call that screaming?

JOSEPH Yes'm.

FANNY Very well. I ask your pardon. (*Waves him away*) Go on!

JOSEPH Yes'm. (*Exits.*)

(TECK *appears in the door. He is carrying his hat and the brief-case we have seen in Act One.* SARA, *seeing the brief-case, looks startled, looks quickly at* KURT. KURT *watches* TECK *as he comes toward him.* TECK *throws his hat on a chair, comes to the table at which* KURT *is sitting, puts the brief-case on the table.* KURT *puts out his hand, puts it on the brief-case, leaves it there.*)

TECK (*smiles at the gesture*) Nothing has been touched, Herr Müller. I brought it from your room, for your convenience.

FANNY (*angrily*) Why didn't you steal it? Since you do not seem to—

TECK That would have been very foolish of me, Madame Fanny.

KURT Very.

TECK I hope I have not kept you waiting too long. I wanted to give you an opportunity to make any explanations—

DAVID (*angrily*) Does your price include listening to this tony conversation?

TECK (*turns to look at him*) My price will rise if I have to spend the next few minutes being interrupted by your temper. I will do my business with Herr Müller. And you will understand, I will take from you no interruptions, no exclamations, no lectures, no opinions of what I am or what I am doing.

KURT (*quietly*) You will not be interrupted.

TECK (*sits down at table with* KURT) I have been curious about you, Herr Müller. Even before you came here. Because Fanny and David either knew very little about you, which was strange, or wouldn't talk about you, which was just as strange. Have you ever had come to you one of those insistent half-memories of some person or some place?

KURT   (*quietly, without looking up*) You had such a half-memory of me?

TECK   Not even a memory, but something. The curiosity of one European for another, perhaps.

KURT   A most sharp curiosity. You lost no time examining—(*Pats the case*)—this. You are an expert with locks?

TECK   No, indeed. Only when I wish to be.

FANNY   (*angrily, to* TECK) I would like you out of this house as quickly as—

TECK   (*turns to her*) Madame Fanny, I have just asked Mr. David not to do that. I must now ask you. (*Leans forward to* KURT) Herr Müller, I got one of the desired lists from Von Seitz, without, of course, revealing anything to him. As you probably know, they are quite easy to get. I simply told him that we refugees move in small circles and I might come across somebody on it. If, however, I have to listen to any more of this from any of you, I shall go immediately to him.

KURT   (*to* DAVID *and* FANNY) Please allow the Count to do this in his own way. It will be best.

TECK   (*takes a sheet of paper from his pocket*) There are sixty-three names on this list. I read them carefully, I narrow the possibilities and under "G" I find Gotter. (*Begins to read*) "Age, forty to forty-five. About six feet. One hundred seventy pounds. Birthplace unknown to us. Original occupation unknown to us, although he seems to know Munich and Dresden. Schooling unknown to us. Family unknown to us. No known political connections. No known trade-union connections. Many descriptions, few of them in agreement and none of them of great reliability. Equally unreliable, though often asked for, were Paris, Copenhagen, Brussels police descriptions. Only points on which there is agreement: married to a foreign woman, either American or English; three children; has used name of Gotter, Thomas Bodmer, Karl Francis. Thought to have left Germany in

1933, and to have joined Max Freidank shortly after. Worked closely with Freidank, perhaps directly under his orders. Known to have crossed border in 1934—February, May, June, October. Known to have again crossed border with Max Friedank in 1935—August, twice in October, November, January—"

KURT (*smiles*) The report is unreliable. It would have been impossible for God to have crossed the border that often.

TECK (*looks up, laughs. Then looks back at list*) "In 1934, outlaw radio station announcing itself as Radio European, begins to be heard. Station was located in Düsseldorf: the house of a restaurant waiter was searched, and nothing was found. Radio heard during most of 1934 and 1935. In an attempt to locate it, two probable Communists killed in the tool-house of a farm near Bonn. In three of the broadcasts, Gotter known to have crossed border immediately before and after. Radio again became active in early part of 1936. Active attempt made to locate Freidank. Gotter believed to have then appeared in Spain with Madrid Government army, in one of the German brigades, and to have been a brigade commander under previously used name of Bodmer. Known to have stayed in France the first months of 1938. Again crossed German border some time during week when Hitler's Hamburg radio speech interrupted and went off the air." (*Looks up*) That was a daring deed, Herr Müller. It caused a great scandal. I remember. It amused me.

KURT It was not done for that reason.

TECK "Early in 1939, informer in Konstanz reported Gotter's entry, carrying money which had been exchanged in Paris and Brussels. Following day, home of Konstanz Gestapo chief raided for spy list by two men—" (KURT *turns to look at* FANNY *and* DAVID, *smiles*) My God, Herr Müller, that job took two good men.

SARA (*angrily*) Even you admire them.

TECK Even I. Now I conclude a week ago that you are Gotter, Karl Francis—

KURT Please. Do not describe me to myself again.

TECK And that you will be traveling home—(*Points to brief-case*)—with this. But you seem in no hurry, and so I must wait. Last night when I heard that Freidank has been taken, I guess that you will now be leaving. Not for California. I will tell you free of charge, Herr Müller, that they have got no information from Freidank or the others.

KURT Thank you. But I was sure they would not. I know all three most well. They will take what will be given them.

TECK (*looks down. Softly*) There is a deep sickness in the German character, Herr Müller. A pain-love, a death-love—

DAVID (*very angrily*) Oh, for God's sake, spare us *your* moral judgments.

FANNY (*very sharply*) Yes. They are sickening. Get on!

KURT Fanny and David are Americans and they do not understand our world—as yet. (*Turns to* DAVID *and* FANNY) All Fascists are not of one mind, one stripe. There are those who give the orders, those who carry out the orders, those who watch the orders being carried out. Then there are those who are half in, half hoping to come in. They are made to do the dishes and clean the boots. Frequently they come in high places and wish now only to survive. They come late: some because they did not jump in time, some because they were stupid, some because they were shocked at the crudity of the *German* evil, and preferred their own evils, and some because they were fastidious men. For those last, we may well some day have pity. They are lost men, their spoils are small, their day is gone. (*To* TECK) Yes?

TECK (*slowly*) Yes. You have the understanding heart. It will get in your way some day.

KURT (*smiles*) I will watch it.

TECK We are both men in trouble, Herr Müller. The world, ungratefully, seems to like your kind even less than it does mine. (*Leans forward*) Now. Let us do business. You will not get back if Von Seitz knows you are going.

KURT   You are wrong. Instead of crawling a hundred feet an hour in deep night, I will walk across the border with as little trouble as if I were a boy again on a summer walking trip. There are many men they would like to have. I would be allowed to walk directly to them— until they had all the names and all the addresses. (*Laughs, points his finger at* TECK) *Roumanians* would pick me up ahead of time. *Germans* would not.

TECK   (*smiles*)   Still the national pride?

KURT   Why not? For that which is good.

FANNY   (*comes over, very angrily, to* TECK)   I have not often in my life felt what I feel now. Whatever you are, and however you became it, the picture of a man selling the lives of other men—

TECK   Is very ugly, Madame Fanny. I do not do it without some shame, and therefore I must sink my shame in large money. (*Puts his hand on the brief-case*) The money is here. For ten thousand, you go back to save your friends, nobody will know that you go, and I will give you my good wishes. (*Slowly, deliberately,* KURT *begins to shake his head.* TECK *waits, then carefully*) No?

KURT   This money is going home with me. It was not given to me to save my life, and I shall not so use it. It is to save the lives and further the work of more than I. It is important to me to carry on that work and to save the lives of three valuable men, and to do that with all speed. But— (*Sharply*) Count de Brancovis, the first morning we arrived in this house, my children wanted their breakfast with great haste. That is because the evening before we had been able only to buy milk and buns for them. If I would not touch this money for them, I would not touch it for you. (*Very sharply*) It goes back with me. The way it is. And if it does not get back, it is because I will not, get back.

(*There is a long pause.* SARA *gets up, turns away.*)

TECK   Then I do not think you will get back. You are a brave one, Herr Müller, but you will not get back.

KURT   (*as if he were very tired*)   I will send to you a postal card and tell you about my bravery.

DAVID (*coming toward* KURT) Is it true that if this swine talks, you and the others will be—

SARA (*very softly*) Caught and killed. Of course. If they're lucky enough to get killed quickly. (*Quietly, points to the table*) You should have seen his hands in 1935.

FANNY (*violently, to* DAVID) We'll give him the money. For God's sake, let's give it to him and get him out of here.

DAVID (*to* SARA) Do you want Kurt to go back?

SARA Yes. I do.

DAVID All right. (*Goes to her, lifts her face*) You're a good girl.

KURT That is true. Brave and good, my Sara. She is everything. She is handsome and gay and— (*Puts his hand over his eyes.* SARA *turns away.*)

DAVID (*after a second, comes to stand near* TECK) If we give you the money, what is to keep you from selling to Von Seitz?

TECK I do not like your thinking I would do that. But—

DAVID (*tensely*) Look here. I'm sick of what you'd like or wouldn't like. And I'm sick of your talk. We'll get this over with now, without any more fancy talk from you, or as far as I am concerned, you can get out of here without my money and sell to any buyer you can find. I can't take much more of you at any cost.

TECK (*smiles*) It is your anger which delays us. I was about to say that I understood your fear that I would go to Von Seitz, and I would suggest that you give me a small amount of cash now and a check dated a month from now. In a month, Herr Müller should be nearing home, and he can let you know. And if you should not honor the check because Herr Müller is already in Germany, Von Seitz will pay a little something for a reliable description. I will take my chance on that. You will now say that I could do that in any case—and that is the chance you will take.

DAVID (*looks at* KURT, *who does not look up*) Is a month enough? For you to get back?

KURT (*shrugs·*) I do not know.

DAVID (*to* TECK) Two months from today. How do you want the cash and how do you want the check?

TECK *One month from today.* That I will not discuss. One month. Please decide now.

DAVID (*sharply*) All right. (*To* TECK) How do you want it?

TECK Seventy-five hundred dollars in a check. Twenty-five hundred in cash.

DAVID I haven't anywhere near that much cash in the house. Leave your address and I'll send it to you in the morning.

TECK (*laughs*) Address? I have no address, and I wish it now. Madame Fanny has cash in her sitting-room safe.

FANNY Have you investigated that, too?

TECK (*laughs*) No. You once told me you always kept money in the house.

DAVID (*to* FANNY) How much have you got upstairs?

FANNY I don't know. About fifteen or sixteen hundred.

TECK Very well. That will do. Make the rest in the check.

DAVID Get it, Mama, please. (*He starts toward the library door.* FANNY *starts for the hall exit.*)

FANNY (*turns, looks carefully at* TECK) Years ago, I heard somebody say that being Roumanian was not a nationality, but a profession. The years have brought no change.

KURT (*softly*) Being a Roumanian aristocrat is a profession.

(FANNY *exits. After her exit, there is silence.* KURT *does not look up,* SARA *does not move.*)

TECK (*awkwardly*) The new world has left the room. (*Looks up at them*) I feel less discomfort with you. We are Europeans, born to trouble and understanding it.

KURT My wife is not a European.

TECK Almost. (*Points upstairs*) They are young. The world has gone well for most of them. For us— (*Smiles*) The three of us—we are like peasants watching the big frost. Work, trouble, ruin— (*Shrugs*) But no need to call curses at the frost. There it is, it will be again, always—for us.

SARA (*gets up, moves to the window, looks out*) You

mean my husband and I do not have angry words for you. What for? We know how many there are of you. They don't, yet. My mother and brother feel shocked that you are in their house. For us—we have seen you in so many houses.

TECK I do not say you *want* to understand me, Mrs. Müller. I say only that you do.

SARA Yes. You are not difficult to understand.

KURT (*slowly gets up, stands stiffly. They he moves toward the decanter table*) A whiskey?

TECK No, thank you. (*He turns his head to watch* KURT *move. He turns back.*)

KURT Sherry?

TECK (*nods*) Thank you, I will.

KURT (*as he pours*) You, too, wish to go back to Europe.

TECK Yes.

KURT But they do not much want you. Not since the Budapest oil deal of '31.

TECK You seem as well informed about me as I am about you.

KURT That must have been a conference of high comedy, that one. Everybody trying to guess whether Kessler was working for Fritz Thyssen, and what Thyssen *really* wanted—and whether this "National Socialism" was a smart blind of Thyssen's, and where was Wolff—I should like to have seen you and your friends. It is too bad: you guessed an inch off, eh?

TECK More than an inch.

KURT And Kessler has a memory? (*Almost playfully*) I do not think Von Seitz would pay you money for a description of a man who has a month to travel. But I think he would pay you in a visa and a cable to Kessler. I think you want a visa almost as much as you want money. Therefore, I conclude you will try for the money here, and the visa from Von Seitz. (*He comes toward the table carrying the sherry glass*) I cannot get anywhere near Germany in a month and you know it. (*He is about to place the glass on the table*) I have been bored with this talk of paying you money. If they are willing to try you on this fantasy, I am not. Whatever made you think I would take such a chance? Or *any* chance? You are a gambler. But you should not gamble with your life. (TECK *has turned to stare at him, made a half motion as if to rise. As he does so, and on the words, "gamble with your life," KURT drops the glass, hits TECK in the face. Struggling, TECK makes a violent effort to rise. KURT throws himself on TECK, knocking him to the floor. As TECK falls to the ·floor, KURT hits him on the side of the head. At the fourth blow, TECK does not move. KURT rises, takes the gun from his pocket, begins to lift TECK from the floor. As he does so, JOSHUA appears in the hall entrance. He is washed and ready for dinner. As he reaches the door, he stops, sees the scene, stands quietly as if he were waiting for orders. KURT begins to balance TECK, to balance himself. To* JOSHUA) Hilf mir. (JOSHUA *comes quickly to* KURT) Mach die Tür auf! (JOSHUA *runs toward the doors, opens them, stands waiting*) Bleib da! Mach die Tür zu! (KURT *begins to move out through the terrace. When he is outside the doors,* JOSHUA *closes them quickly, stands looking at his mother.*)

SARA There's trouble.

JOSHUA Do not worry. I will go up now. I will pack. In ten minutes all will be ready. I will say nothing. I will get the children ready— (*He starts quickly for the hall, turns for a second to look toward the terrace doors. Then almost with a sob*) This was a nice house.

SARA (*softly*) We're not going this time, darling. There's no need to pack.

JOSHUA (*stares at her, puzzled*) But Papa—

SARA Go upstairs, Joshua. Take Babbie and Bodo in your room, and close the door. Stay there until I call you. (*He looks at her,* SARA *sits down*) There's nothing to be frightened of, darling. Papa is all right. (*Then very softly*) Papa is going home.

JOSHUA To Germany?

SARA Yes.

JOSHUA Oh. Alone?

SARA Alone. (*Very softly*) Don't say anything to the children. He will tell them himself.

JOSHUA   I won't.

SARA   (*as he hesitates*) I'm all right. Go upstairs now. (*He moves slowly out, she watches him, he disappears. For a minute she sits quietly. Then she gets up, moves to the terrace doors, stands with her hands pressed against them. Then she crosses, picks up the overturned chair, places it by the table, picks up the glass, puts it on the table. As if without knowing what she is doing, she wipes the table with her handkerchief.*)

(*FANNY comes in from hall. After a second, DAVID comes in from library. Stops, looks around room.*)

DAVID   Where is he? Upstairs?

SARA   No. They went outside.

FANNY   Outside? They went outside. What are they doing, picking a bouquet together?

SARA   (*without turning*) They just went outside.

DAVID   (*looks at her*) What's the matter, Sara?

(*SARA shakes her head. Goes to the desk, opens the telephone book, looks at a number, begins to dial the telephone.*)

FANNY   Eleven hundred, eleven hundred and fifty, twelve, twelve-fifty—

DAVID   For God's sake, stop counting that money.

FANNY   All right. I'm nervous. And I don't like to think of giving him too much.

SARA   It's very nice of you and Mama. All that money— (*Into the telephone*) Hello. What time is your next plane? Oh. To— South. To El Paso, or—Brownsville. Yes.

DAVID   (*to FANNY*) Is Joseph ready?

FANNY   I don't know. I told him I'd call him.

SARA   To Brownsville? Yes. Yes. That's all right. At what time? Yes. No. The ticket will be picked up at the airport. (*DAVID begins to cross to the bell cord. She looks up*) No. David. Don't call Joseph. *David! Please!* (*He draws back, stares at her. Looking at him, she goes on with the conversation*) Ritter. R-I-T-T-E-R. From Chicago. Yes. Yes. (*She hangs up, walks away.*)

DAVID   Sara! What's happening? What is all this? (*She does not answer*) Where is Kurt? What— (*He starts for the terrace door.*)

SARA David. *Don't go out.*

FANNY (*rises*) Sara! What's happening—

SARA For seven years now, day in, day out, men have crossed the German border. They are always in danger. They always may be going in to die. Did you ever see the face of a man who never knows if this day will be the last day? (*Softly*) Don't go out on the terrace, David. Leave Kurt alone.

FANNY (*softly*) Sara! What is—

SARA (*quietly*) For them, it may be torture, and it may be death. Some day, when it's all over, maybe there'll be a few of them left to celebrate. There aren't many of Kurt's age left. He couldn't take a chance on them. They wouldn't have liked it. (*Suddenly, violently*) He'd have had a bad time trying to explain to them that because of this house and this nice town and my mother and my brother, he took chances with their work and with their lives. (*Quietly*) Sit down, Mama. I think it's all over now. (*To* DAVID) There's nothing you can do about it. It's the way it had to be.

DAVID Sara—

FANNY Do you mean what I think you— (*She sits down.*)

SARA (*she turns, looks out toward the doors. After a pause*) He's going away tonight and he's never coming back any more. (*In a sing-song*) Never, never, never. (*She looks down at her hands, as if she were very interested in them*) I don't like to be alone at night. I guess everybody in the world's got a time they don't like. Me, it's right before I go to sleep. And now it's going to be for always. All the rest of my life. (*She looks up as* KURT *comes in from the terrace*) I've told them. There is an eight-thirty plane going as far south as Brownsville. I've made you a reservation. In the name of Ritter.

KURT (*stands looking at her*) Liebe Sara! (*Then he goes to the table at which* FANNY *is sitting. To* FANNY) It is hard for you, eh? (*He pats her hand*) I am sorry.

FANNY (*without knowing why, she takes her hand away*) Hard? I don't know. I— I don't— I don't know what I want to say.

KURT (*looks at the hand she has touched, then turns to*

look at DAVID)   Before I come in, I stand and think. I
say, I will make Fanny and David understand. I say,
how can I? Does one understand a killing? No. To
hell with it, I say. I do what must be done. I have long
sickened of words when I see the men who live by
them. What do you wish to make them understand, I
ask myself. Wait. Stand here. Just stand here. What are
you. thinking? Say it to them just as it comes to you.
And this is what came to me. When you kill in a war,
it is not so lonely; and I remember a cousin I have not
seen for many years; and a melody comes back and I
begin to make it with my fingers; a staircase in a house
in Bonn years ago; an old dog who used to live in our
town; Sara in a hundred places— Shame on us. Thousands of years and we cannot yet make a world. Like a
child I am. I have stopped a man's life. (*Points to the
place on the couch where he had been sitting opposite*
TECK)   I sit here. I listen to him. You will not believe—
but I pray that I will not have to touch him. Then I
know I will have to, I know that if I do not, it is only
that I pamper myself, and risk the lives of others. I
want you from the room. I know what I must do.
(*Loudly*)   All right. Do I now pretend sorrow? Do I
now pretend it is not I who act thus? No. I do it. I have
done it. I will do it again. And I will keep my hope that
we may make a world in which all men can die in bed.
I have a great hate for the violent. They are the sick
of the world. (*Softly*)   Maybe I am sick now, too.

SARA   You aren't sick. Stop that. It's late. You must go soon.

KURT   (*he puts out his hands, she touches them*)   I am
going to say good-bye now to my children. Then I am
going to take your car— (*Motions with his head*)   I
will take him with me. After that, it is up to you. Two
ways: You can let me go and keep silent. I believe I can
hide him and the car. At the end of two days, if they
have not been found, you will tell as much of the truth
as is safe for you to say. Tell them the last time you saw
us we were on our way to Washington. You did not
worry at the absence, we might have rested there. Two
crazy foreigners fight, one gets killed, you know noth-

ing of the reason. I will have left the gun, there will be no doubt who did the killing. If you will give me those two days, I think I will be far enough away from here. If the car is found before then—(*Shrugs*) I will still try to move with speed. And all that will make you, for yourselves, part of a murder. For the world, I do not think you will be in bad trouble. (*He pauses*) There is another way. You can call your police. You can tell them the truth. I will not get home. (*To* SARA) I wish to see the children now. (*She goes out into the hall and up the stairs. There is silence.*)

FANNY What are you thinking, David?

DAVID I don't know. What are you thinking?

FANNY Me? Oh, I was thinking about my Joshua. I was thinking that a few months before he died, we were sitting out there. (*Points to terrace*) He said, "Fanny, the Renaissance American is dying, the Renaissance man is dying." I said what do you mean, although I knew what he meant, I always knew. "A Renaissance man," he said, "is a man who wants to know. He wants to know how fast a bird will fly, how thick is the crust of the earth, what made Iago evil, how to plow a field. He knows there is no dignity to a mountain, if there is no dignity to man. You can't put that in a man, but when it's *really* there, and he will fight for it, put your trust in him."

DAVID (*gets up, smiles, looks at* FANNY) You're a smart woman sometimes. (SARA *enters with* JOSHUA. *To* KURT) Don't worry about things here. My soul doesn't have to be so nice and clean. I'll take care of it. You'll have your two days. And good luck to you.

FANNY You go with my blessing, too. I like you. (BODO *enters.*)

SARA See? I come from good stock. (KURT *looks at* DAVID. *Then he begins to smile. Nods to* DAVID. *Turns, smiles at* FANNY.)

FANNY Do you like me?

KURT I like you, Madame, very much.

FANNY Would you be able to cash that check?

KURT (*laughs*) Oh, no.

FANNY   Then take the cash. I, too, would like to contribute to your work.

KURT   (*slowly*) All right. Thank you. (*He takes the money from the table, puts it in his pocket.*)

BODO   (*to* KURT) You like Grandma? I thought you would, with time. I like her, too. Sometimes she dilates with screaming, but— Dilates is correct? (BABETTE *enters.* JOSHUA *stands away from the others, looking at his father.* KURT *turns to look at him.*)

JOSHUA   Alles in Ordnung?

KURT   Alles in Ordnung.

BODO   What? What does that mean, all is well? (*There is an awkward silence.*)

BABETTE   (*as if she sensed it*) We are all clean for dinner. But nobody else is clean. And I have on Grandma's dress to me—

FANNY   (*very nervously*) Of course. And you look very pretty. You're a pretty little girl, Babbie.

BODO   (*looks around the room*) What is the matter? Everybody is acting like such a ninny. I got that word from Grandma.

KURT   Come here. (*They look at him. Then slowly* BABETTE *comes toward him, followed by* BODO. JOSHUA *comes more slowly, to stand at the side of* KURT's *chair*) We have said many good-byes to each other, eh? We must now say another. (*As they stare at him, he smiles, slowly, as if it were difficult*) This time, I leave you with good people to whom I believe you also will be good. (*Half playfully*) Would you allow me to give away my share in you, until I come back?

BABETTE   (*slowly*) If you would like it.

KURT   Good. To your mother, her share. My share, to Fanny and David. It is all I have to give. (*Laughs*) There. I have made a will, eh? Now. We will not joke. I have something to say to you. It is important for me to say it.

JOSHUA   (*softly*) You are talking to us as if we were children.

KURT   (*turns to look at him*) Am I, Joshua? I wish you were children. I wish I could say love your mother, do not eat too many sweets, clean your teeth— (*Draws*

BODO *to him*) I cannot say these things. You are not children. I took it all away from you.

BABETTE We have had a most enjoyable life, Papa.

KURT (*smiles*) You are a gallant little liar. And I thank you for it. I have done something bad today—

FANNY (*shocked, sharply*) Kurt—

SARA Don't, Mama. (BODO *and* BABETTE *have looked at* FANNY *and* SARA, *puzzled. Then they have turned again to look at* KURT.)

KURT It is not to frighten you. In a few days, your mother and David will tell you.

BODO You could not do a bad thing.

BABETTE (*proudly*) You could not.

KURT (*shakes his head*) Now let us get straight together. The four of us. Do you remember when we read "Les Misérables"? Do you remember that we talked about it afterward and Bodo got candy on Mama's bed?

BODO I remember.

KURT Well. He stole bread. The world is out of shape we said, when there are hungry men. And until it gets in shape, men will steal and lie and—(*A little more slowly*)—kill. But for whatever reason it is done, and whoever does it—you understand me—it is all bad. I want you to remember that. Whoever does it, it is bad. (*Then very gaily*) But you will live to see the day when it will not have to be. All over the world, in every place and every town, there are men who are going to make sure it will not have to be. They want what I want: a childhood for every child. For my children, and I for theirs. (*He picks* BODO *up, rises*) Think of that. It will make you happy. In every town and every village and every mud hut in the world, there is always a man who loves children and who will fight to make a good world for them. And now good-bye. Wait for me. I shall try to come back for you. (*He moves toward the hall, followed by* BABETTE, *and more slowly, by* JOSHUA) Or you shall come to me. At Hamburg, the boat will come in. It will be a fine, safe land— I will be waiting on the dock. And there will be the three of you and Mama and Fanny and David. And I will have ordered an extra big dinner and we will show them what our Germany can be like— (*He has put* BODO *down. He leans down, presses his face in* BABETTE'S *hair. Tenderly, as her mother has done earlier, she touches his hair.*)

JOSHUA   Of course. That is the way it will be. Of course. But—but if you should find yourself delayed— (*Very slowly*) Then I will come to you. Mama.

SARA   (*she has turned away*) I heard you, Joshua.

KURT   (*he kisses* BABETTE) Gute Nacht, Liebling!

BABETTE   Gute Nacht, Papa. Mach's gut!

KURT   (*leans to kiss* BODO) Good night, baby.

BODO   Good night, Papa. Mach's gut! (BABETTE *runs up the steps. Slowly* BODO *follows her.*)

KURT   (*kisses* JOSHUA) Good night, son.

JOSHUA   Good night, Papa. Mach's gut! (*He begins to climb the steps.* KURT *stands watching them, smiling. When they disappear, he turns to* DAVID.)

KURT   Good-bye, and thank you.

DAVID   Good-bye, and good luck.

KURT   (*he moves to* FANNY) Good-bye. I have good children, eh?

FANNY   Yes, you have. (KURT *kisses her hand.*)

KURT   (*slowly, he turns toward* SARA) Men who wish to live have the best chance to live. I wish to live. I wish to live with you. (*She comes toward him.*)

SARAH   For twenty years. It is as much for me today— (*Takes his arms*) Just once, and for all my life. (*He pulls her toward him*) Come back for me, darling. If you can. (*Takes brief case from table and gives it to him.*)

KURT   (*simply*) I will try. (*He turns*) Good-bye, to you all. (*He exits. After a second, there is the sound of a car starting. They sit listening to it. Gradually the noise begins to go off into the distance. A second later,* JOSHUA *appears.*)

JOSHUA   Mama— (*She looks up. He is very tense*) Bodo cries. Babette looks very queer. I think you should come.

SARA   (*gets up, slowly*) I'm coming.

JOSHUA   (*to* FANNY *and* DAVID. *Still very tense*) Bodo talks so fancy, we forget sometimes he is a baby. (*He waits for* SARA *to come up to him. When she reaches him, she takes his hand, goes up the steps, disappears.* FANNY *and* DAVID *watch them.*)

FANNY (*after a minute*) Well, here we are. We're shaken out of the magnolias, eh?

DAVID Yes. So we are.

FANNY Tomorrow will be a hard day. But we'll have Babbie's birthday dinner. And we'll have music afterward. You can be the audience. I think you'd better go up to Marthe now. Be as careful as you can. She'd better stay here for a while. I daresay I can stand it.

DAVID (*turns, smiles*) Even your graciousness is ungracious, Mama.

FANNY I do my best. Well, I think I shall go and talk to Anise. I like Anise best when I don't feel well. (*She begins to move off.*)

DAVID Mama. (*She turns*) We are going to be in for trouble. You understand that?

FANNY I understand it very well. We will manage. You and I. I'm not put together with flour paste. And neither are you—I am happy to learn.

DAVID Good night, Mama. (*As she moves out, the curtain falls.*)

Another
Part of the Forest

FOR
MY GOOD FRIEND
GREGORY ZILBOORG

Kermit Bloomgarden presents Lillian Hellman's New
Play *Another Part of the Forest*

CAST

(In the order of their appearance)

REGINA HUBBARD	PATRICIA NEAL
JOHN BAGTRY	BARTLETT ROBINSON
LAVINIA HUBBARD	MILDRED DUNNOCK
CORALEE	BEATRICE THOMPSON
MARCUS HUBBARD	PERCY WARAM
BENJAMIN HUBBARD	LEO GENN
JACOB	STANLEY GREENE
OSCAR HUBBARD	SCOTT MCKAY
SIMON ISHAM	OWEN COLL
BIRDIE BAGTRY	MARGARET PHILLIPS
HAROLD PENNIMAN	PAUL FORD
GILBERT JUGGER	GENE O'DONNELL
LAURETTE SINCEE	JEAN HAGEN

The play was directed by MISS HELLMAN.

The settings were designed by JO MIELZINER.

*Opened at the Fulton Theatre on
the night of November 20, 1946.*

Scene

ACT ONE

A Sunday morning in June 1880,
the Alabama town of Bowden,
the side portico of the Hubbard house.

ACT TWO

The next evening,
the living room of the Hubbard house.

ACT THREE

Early the next morning,
the side portico of the Hubbard house.

Throughout the play, in the stage directions,
left and right mean audience's
left and right.

Act One

SCENE: *The side portico of the Hubbard house, a Sunday morning in the summer of 1880 in the Alabama town of Bowden. The portico leads into the living room by back center French doors. On the right side of the portico is an old wing of the house. An exterior staircase to this wing leads to an upper porch off which are the bedrooms of the house and behind the staircase are the back gardens and the kitchen quarters. Under the second-story porch is a door leading to the dining room of the house, and a back door leading to the kitchen. The other side of the portico leads to a lawn which faces the town's main street. The main part of the house, built in the 1850's, is Southern Greek. It is not a great mansion but it is a good house built by a man of taste from whom* MARCUS HUBBARD *bought it after the Civil War. There is not much furniture on the portico: two chairs and a table at one end, one comfortable chair and a table at the other end. Twin heads of Aristotle are on high pedestals. There is something too austere, too pretended Greek about the portico, as if it followed one man's eccentric taste and was not designed to be comfortable for anyone else.*

As the curtain rises, REGINA HUBBARD, *a handsome girl of twenty, is standing looking down at* JOHN BAGTRY. REGINA *has on a pretty negligee thrown over a nightgown. Her hair is pinned high, as if she had pinned it up quickly.* JOHN BAGTRY *is a man of thirty-six with a sad, worn face. He is dressed in shabby riding shirt and Confederate Cavalry pants.*

REGINA   (*after a long silence*) Where were you going?

JOHN   (*he has a soft, easy voice*) And what you doing awake so early?

REGINA   Watching for you. But you tried not to hear me when I called you. I called you three times before you turned.

JOHN   I didn't think this was the place or the hour for us to be meeting together. (*Looks around nervously*) We'll be waking your folks. You out here in your wrapper! That would make a pretty scandal, honey—

REGINA   (*impatiently*) Nobody's awake. And I don't care. Why didn't you—

JOHN   (*quickly, gaily*) Oh, your Mama's up all right. I saw her and your Coralee going into nigger church. I bowed to her—

REGINA   (*softly*) Why didn't you meet me last night?

JOHN   (*after a second*) I couldn't. And I didn't know how to send word.

REGINA   Why couldn't you? Plantation folks giving balls again? Or fancy dress parties?

JOHN   (*smiles*) I haven't been to a party since I was sixteen years old, Regina. The Bacons gave the last ball I ever remember, to celebrate the opening of the war and say good-by to us—

REGINA   You've told me about it. Why couldn't you come last night?

JOHN   I couldn't leave Aunt Clara and Cousin Birdie. They wanted to sit out and talk after supper, and I couldn't.

REGINA   (*slowly*) They wanted to talk? And so they made you stay?

JOHN   No, they didn't *make* me. They're lonely, Regina, and I'm not with them much, since you and I—

REGINA   Why should you be with them? When I want to meet you, I go and do it.

JOHN   Things are different with us. Everything is bad. This summer is the worst, I guess, in all the years. They are lonely—

REGINA It's not the first time you didn't come. And you
    think I shouldn't be angry, and take you back the next
    day. It would be better if you lied to me where you
    were. This way it's just insulting to me. Better if you
    lied.

JOHN Lie? Why would I lie?

REGINA Better if you said you were with another woman.
    But not meeting me because of those two mummies—

JOHN (*softly*) I like them, Regina. And they don't go
    around raising their voices in anger on an early Sunday
    day.

REGINA I don't want you to tell me about the differences
    in your family and mine.

JOHN (*stares at her*) I've never done that. Never.

REGINA That's what you always mean when you say I'm
    screaming.

JOHN (*sharply*) I mean no such thing. I said only that I
    stayed with Aunt Clara and Cousin Birdie last night.
    And I'll do it again. (*Desperately*) Look, honey, I didn't
    mean not to come to meet you. But I've lived on them
    for fifteen years. They're good to me. They share with
    me the little they got, and I don't give back anything to
    them—

REGINA (*tensely*) I'm getting sick of them. They've got to
    know about you and me some day soon. I think I'm go-
    ing to sashay right up to that sacred plantation grass and
    tell them the war's over, the old times are finished, and
    so are they. I'm going to tell them to stay out of my
    way—

JOHN (*sharply*) They've never mentioned you, Regina.

REGINA That's good breeding: to know about something
    and not talk about it?

JOHN I don't know about good breeding.

REGINA (*turns to him*) They think they do. Your Cousin
    Birdie's never done more than say good morning in all
    these years—when she knows full well who I am and
    who Papa is. Knows full well he could buy and sell Lion-
    net on the same morning, its cotton and its women with
    it—

JOHN I would not like to hear anybody talk that way again. No, I wouldn't.

REGINA (*pleadingly, softly*) I'm sorry, I'm sorry, I'm sorry. I give you my apology. I'm sorry, darling.

JOHN We shouldn't be—

REGINA (*runs to him, takes his arm*) I'm never going to be mean again, never going to talk mean— Look, honey, I was mad about last night because I wanted to tell you about my plan. I've been thinking about it for months, and I've got Papa almost ready for it. But I can't tell it to you tonight because Papa makes me read to him every Sunday. But late tomorrow night, after Papa's music—it's over early—please, darling, tomorrow night— tomorrow night— (*She clings to him.*)

JOHN (*turns to her*) Regina, we mustn't. We mustn't any more. It's not right for you, honey, we're a scandal now. I'm no good for you. I'm too old, I'm—

REGINA (*clinging to him, impatient*) Why do you say that? A man at thirty-six talking that way? It comes from hanging around this town and your kinfolk.

JOHN I was only good once—in a war. Some men shouldn't ever come home from a war. You know something? It's the only time I was happy.

REGINA (*draws away from him, wearily*) Oh, don't tell me that again. You and your damn war. Wasn't it silly to be happy when you knew you were going to lose?

JOHN You think it is silly? You think we all were? Of course you do. In this house you couldn't think anything else. (*She draws back*) And now *I'm* sorry. That was most rude. It's late, honey.

REGINA (*quickly*) You haven't even asked me about my plan.

JOHN I have a plan, too. I have a letter from Cod Carter. He's in Brazil. He's fighting down there, he says—

(LAVINIA HUBBARD *and* CORALEE *appear from around the portico, as if coming from street.* JOHN *stares at them, draws back nervously.* REGINA *watches him, amused.* LA- VINIA HUBBARD *is a woman of about fifty-eight, stooped, thin, delicate-looking. She has a sweet, high voice and a distracted, nervous way of speaking.* CORALEE *is a sturdy*

Negro woman of about forty-five. She is holding a para-
sol over LAVINIA. JOHN *steps forward.* CORALEE *folds par-*
asol, stares at REGINA's *costume, exits under porch to*
kitchen.)

LAVINIA (*as if this were an ordinary morning scene*)
Morning, Captain Bagtry. Been for a nice little stroll?

JOHN (*quickly*) Morning, Mrs. Hubbard. No, ma'am. I
was just riding by and glimpsed Miss Regina—

LAVINIA (*nods*) That's nice. Coralee and I been to our
church. The colored folks said a prayer for me and a
little song. It's my birthday.

JOHN Congratulations, ma'am. I sure give you my good
wishes.

LAVINIA Thank you, sir. And later I'm going back to the
second service. And I know a secret: they're going to
give me a cake. Ain't that lovely of them, and me un-
deserving? (*Looks up at him*) I always go to the colored
church. I ain't been to a white church in years. Most
people don't like my doing it, I'm sure, but I got my
good reasons—

REGINA All right, Mama.

LAVINIA There's got to be one little thing you do that you
want to do, all by yourself you want to do it.

REGINA (*sharply*) All right, Mama.

LAVINIA (*hurries toward the doors of the living room*)
Oh. Sorry. (*At the door of living room, looks back at*
JOHN) I remember you and your cousins the day you left
town for war. I blew you a kiss. Course we were living
in our little house then and you didn't know. But I blew
you all a kiss.

JOHN (*very pleased*) I'm glad to know it, ma'am. It was
a great day. A hot day— You know something, ma'am?
It was my birthday, too, that day. I was sixteen, and my
cousins not much older. My birthday. Isn't that a coincidence, ma'am?

REGINA Why?

JOHN (*lamely*) Because it's your Mama's birthday today.

LAVINIA And you know something else, Captain Bagtry?

Tomorrow's my wedding anniversary day. Your birthday, my birthday, and a wedding anniversary day.

REGINA (*very sharply*) All right, Mama.

(MARCUS HUBBARD *opens the door of his bedroom and appears on the upper porch. He is a strong-looking man of
sixty-three, with a soft voice of tone and depth. He
speaks slowly, as if he put value on the words.*)

MARCUS Who's speaking on the porch?

(*At the sound of his voice* LAVINIA *hurries into the house.*
JOHN *draws back into the living-room doors.* REGINA
comes forward.)

REGINA I'm down here, Papa.

MARCUS Morning, darling. Waiting for me?

REGINA Er. Mama's just been to church.

MARCUS Of course—where else would she go? Wait. Have
your first coffee with me. (*He exits into his room.*)

REGINA (*amused at* JOHN'S *nervous movements, takes his
arm*) I want you to meet Papa. Not now. But soon.

JOHN I know your Papa. I'm in and out of your store—

REGINA I want you to come *here*. I guess no Bagtry ever
been inside our house. But would your Aunt Clara and
your Cousin Birdie allow you to come, do you reckon?

JOHN Allow me? I didn't think that was the way it was. I
thought your Papa didn't want anybody here—

REGINA He doesn't. But I'll find a way. Will you meet me
tomorrow night, same place? Darling, darling, please.
Please. (*She pulls him toward her. He hesitates for a
second. Then he takes her in his arms, kisses her with
great feeling. She smiles.*) Meet me?

JOHN (*softly*) I always do. No matter what I say or
think, I always do.

(*He kisses her again. Then he runs off. She stands for
a minute staring after him. Then, from the street side
of the lawn,* BENJAMIN HUBBARD *appears. He is followed
by* JACOB *carrying a small valise and three boxes.* JACOB
is a tall, thin Negro of about thirty. BEN *is thirty-five:
a powerful, calm man with a quiet manner.*)

REGINA (*amused*) Morning, Ben. Have a good trip?

BEN Was that Bagtry?

REGINA He said that was his name.

BEN   What you doing having men on the porch, you in your wrapper?

REGINA   (*gaily*) Isn't it a pretty wrapper? Came from Chicago.

BEN   (*pointing to boxes*) And so did these, on the mail train. They got your name on 'em. Belong to you?

REGINA   (*giggling*) Writing can't lie. Specially writing in ink.

MARCUS   (*reappears on balcony, calls down*) Coffee ready for me, darling?

REGINA   (*gaily, smiling at* BEN) Going in to brew it my- self, honey.

(*She disappears into house.* MARCUS *comes forward on the porch, sees* BEN *and* JAKE.)

MARCUS   (*stares at* JAKE) Jake, takes the boxes in. (JAKE *starts in*) And put Mr. Benjamin's valise out of your hand. (JAKE *hesitates, looks puzzled.* BEN *stares up at* MARCUS. *Then* JAKE *puts valise down, exits*) How was the world of fashion, Benjamin?

BEN   I was only in it for twenty-four hours.

MARCUS   Ah. That isn't long enough.

BEN   You ordered me back.

MARCUS   What for?

BEN   (*looks up, smiles*) The pleasure of it, I think.

MARCUS   (*giggles*) Certainly. But what did I call the pleasure?

BEN   You said the books needed checking, and I was to be back to do them today.

MARCUS   (*thinks*) Books? I wouldn't let you touch the books in my library, Benjamin. Certainly you know that.

BEN   (*annoyed*) Books for the store. *Store. Bookkeeping. Accounts.*

MARCUS   Oh. But why today?

BEN   I don't know, Papa. I'd like to have stayed in Mobile. I had some business—

MARCUS   (*clucks*) But I brought you back on a Sunday to look at store books. Now, why did I do that? I must have had some reason. I'll think of it later. (*He looks down, realizes* BEN *isn't going to answer*) What business did you have, Ben?

BEN   I wanted to invest two thousand dollars in Birmingham Coal, Incorporated. It will bring fifty thousand some day. There's coal there, and they're sending down men from the North with money for it— But I couldn't raise it. And you wouldn't lend it to me.

MARCUS   That why you went? That foolish old scheme of yours? I had hoped you went to Mobile for a lady.

BEN   No, sir. I have no lady.

MARCUS   I believe you. But certainly you went to the concert last night?

BEN   No, I didn't. I told you: I was trying to borrow the two thousand you wouldn't let me have.

MARCUS   Well, you must hear a good concert before you die.

(LAVINIA *and* CORALEE *enter from kitchen door*.)

MARCUS   (*starts into his room*)   Carry in your own valise, son. It is not seemly for a man to load his goods on other men, black or white.

(BEN *looks up, half annoyed, half amused. He picks up his valise, starts toward door as* CORALEE *appears, carrying breakfast tray.* LAVINIA *follows her.* BEN *watches them as* CORALEE *puts tray on table.* LAVINIA, *knowing that* MARCUS *is on the balcony, but not knowing whether she should speak to him, helps* CORALEE *by aimlessly fussing about with the tray*.)

LAVINIA   (*to* BEN)   Morning, son.

BEN   Morning, Mama.

LAVINIA   Pleasant trip?

BEN   No, unsuccessful.

LAVINIA   That's good, I'm sure. I mean— Morning, Marcus.

MARCUS   Coralee. I'll be right down. Lavinia, send everybody else to the dining room for breakfast. Go on, Lavinia.

(*He disappears.* LAVINIA *spills coffee*.)

CORALEE   (*quickly*)   All right, Miss Viney. No harm. Go on in and have your breakfast before there's trouble.

LAVINIA   I was only trying—

(LAVINIA *goes into living room as* MARCUS *comes down-*

stairs carrying a book. He goes immediately to table.
CORALEE *pours coffee.*)

MARCUS   Who is down for breakfast?

CORALEE   I don't know.

LAVINIA   (*reappears in living-room doorway*)   Oh, Marcus,
Colonel Isham is calling. Can he come out?

MARCUS   If he is capable of walking.

(COLONEL ISHAM, *a man of sixty-five, appears in the doorway.*)

MARCUS   Colonel Isham.

ISHAM   You will forgive this too early visit?

MARCUS   You're in town for church?

ISHAM   I've come to see you. I was asked to come to see
you.

MARCUS   To talk about bad cotton?

ISHAM   No sir. I don't mix with a man's Sunday breakfast
to talk about cotton. I come to talk about your son
Oscar.

MARCUS   Then you will need coffee.

ISHAM   Thank you, no. Two nights ago—

MARCUS   People like you don't drink coffee with people
like me?

ISHAM   I've had coffee. Now, Mr. Hubbard—

MARCUS   Then come again when you haven't had it.

(*There is a pause. Slowly* ISHAM *comes to the table.*
MARCUS *smiles, pours a cup of coffee, hands it to* ISHAM,
who takes it and sits down.)

ISHAM   Thank you. I have come here for your sake, Mr.
Hubbard. There is dangerous feeling up in my town
this morning—

MARCUS   Colonel, I hate conversations for my sake. Sunday
is my day of study. I don't wish to sound rude but please
say quickly what you have come about.

ISHAM   (*smiles*)   Mr. Hubbard, I'm too old to frighten.

MARCUS   (*smiles*)   And I should be a daring man to try it.
You, one of our great heroes. Commanding the first
Alabama troops at—

ISHAM   (*sharply*)   I am not interested in talking to you
about the War Between the States, or about your per-
sonal war on the people of this state— Now, please

listen to me. Two nights ago Sam Taylor in Roseville was badly beaten up. Last night fourteen people identified the night riders as the Cross boys, from over the line, and your son Oscar.

MARCUS   (*shouts into the house*)   Benjamin. Rope Oscar and bring him out here immediately. I told you fifteen years ago you were damn fools to let Klansmen ride around, carrying guns—

ISHAM   Were you frightened of our riding on you? I came here to tell you to make your son quit. He can thank me he's not swinging from a rope this minute. You have good reason to know there's not a man in this county wouldn't like to swing up anybody called Hubbard. I stopped my friends last night but I may not be able to stop them again. Tell him what patriots do is our business. But he's got no right to be riding down on anybody—

(BEN, *followed by* OSCAR, *appears in the dining-room doorway.* OSCAR *looks frightened, decides to be cute.*)

OSCAR   *Rope* me out. I can stand up, Papa. Never felt my Saturday night liquor that bad—

ISHAM   (*ignoring* OSCAR, *to* MARCUS)   Taylor is a good man. He's got no money for treatment, got no job now, won't get one again.

MARCUS   (*to* OSCAR)   Colonel Isham has just saved you from a lynching party. Should I thank him?

OSCAR   (*terrified*)   Lynching! What did— Colonel Isham— I—

ISHAM   I don't want to speak with you.

MARCUS   Who does?

OSCAR   But what did I—

MARCUS   Do I have to tell you that if you ever put on those robes again, or take a gun to any man— (*Takes roll of bills from his pocket, throws it to* BENJAMIN) Count out five hundred dollars, Benjamin.

OSCAR   (*very nervous*)   You mean Taylor? I wasn't riding with the Klan boys. No, I wasn't. I was thinking about it, but—

BEN   No, he couldn't have been with them. He took me

to the Mobile train, and the train was late, so we sat talking. He couldn't have got up to Roseville.

ISHAM You say you're willing to swear to that, Mr. Benjamin? You sure you're willing to go against fourteen people identifying your brother—?

BEN Oh, Oscar looks like anybody.

MARCUS (*smiles*) Give the money to Colonel Isham, Benjamin. Go away, Oscar. (*Oscar exits through dining-room door*) Please use the money for Taylor.

ISHAM We'll take care of him, Hubbard. Good day, sir.

MARCUS You won't take care of him, because you can't. Learn to be poor, Isham, it has more dignity. Tell Taylor there will be a check each month. Tell him that my other son, Benjamin, wishes to make amends. Ben has a most charitable nature.

(ISHAM *hesitates, decides, takes the money, looks at it.*)

ISHAM There is no need for so much. A hundred would be more proper.

MARCUS Good day, Colonel. Don't give me lectures on propriety.

(ISHAM *starts to speak, changes his mind, exits left toward street. There is a pause.* BEN *looks at* MARCUS, *drops the roll of money on* MARCUS's *table.*)

BEN (*smiles*) You didn't like my story about Oscar?

MARCUS Not much. Very loyal of you, however.

BEN I like it.

MARCUS Good. It's yours. Keep it. You must have one of your usual involved reasons for wanting it.

BEN Five hundred dollars is a lot of money to a man who allows himself six dollars for a trip to Mobile.

MARCUS Perhaps you're stingy.

BEN You can't be much else on a salary of twenty dollars a week.

MARCUS Is that all I pay you? Ah, well, you'll be better off when I—if and when I die. But I may not die; did I tell you, Benjamin?

(REGINA, OSCAR *and* LAVINIA *appear from the living room.* REGINA *hurries to* MARCUS.)

REGINA Forgive me, darling. I forgot your coffee.

(OSCAR *is carrying a cup of coffee and a roll.* LAVINIA, *who never sees anything, bumps into him.* OSCAR *turns on her angrily.*)

OSCAR Goodness sake, Mama. Watch where you going.

REGINA Oscar's in a bad humor this morning. Oscar's got one of those faces shows everything.

LAVINIA (*to everybody—nobody pays any attention*) I'm sorry. I'm sure I didn't mean to—

MARCUS Oscar has good reason for being in a bad humor. He owes me five hundred dollars.

(OSCAR's *hand begins to shake on the cup. He rattles the spoon and saucer.*)

BEN For God's sake sit down and stop rattling that cup.

OSCAR Papa, you can't mean that— Ben told you where I was. I wasn't even—

MARCUS (*to* REGINA) You look charming. New?

REGINA No. But I *did* buy a few new dresses.

MARCUS A few? I saw the boxes coming in.

OSCAR Seven dresses. Seven, I counted them.

REGINA Can you count up to seven now? And more coming next week, Papa.

MARCUS What are you going to do with them, honey?

REGINA (*hesitates, then gaily*) Could we go for a walk?

BEN You buying these clothes out of your allowance?

REGINA (laughs) Aren't you silly? How could I? There's a fur piece and a muff that cost three hundred dollars alone. They're charming, Papa, wait till you see them—

OSCAR (*delighted at the diversion in the conversation*) You really gone crazy? Nobody's ever worn furs in this climate since old lady Somers put that bear rug around her and jumped out the porch.

REGINA I won't jump out the porch.

BEN I will have to O.K. the bills, so would you tell me how much you've spent?

REGINA (*airily*) I don't know. I didn't even ask.

OSCAR (*shrilly*) Didn't even ask? Didn't even ask? You gone real crazy, acting like Miss Vanderbilt, whatever her name is—rich people up North don't act that way. They watch their money, and their father's money.

REGINA Oh, that's not true. Those people in Chicago, just

the other day, gave their daughter a hundred-thousand-dollar check for a trousseau—

BEN (*looks at her*) A trousseau? So that's what you're buying? I saw Horace Giddens in Mobile last evening, and he was mighty disappointed you haven't answered his letter about coming up for another visit here.

OSCAR Hey, he wouldn't be bad for you, Regina—

BEN He's in love with you. That was obvious when he was here. It's good society, that family, and rich. Solid, quiet rich.

OSCAR And you'd get to like him. A lot of people get married not liking each other. Then, after marriage, they still don't like each other much, I guess—

BEN (*sharply*) Are you still drunk?

LAVINIA (*comes to life*) A wedding? That would be nice. I hope you make your plans right quick, Regina, because—

MARCUS (*very slowly*) What is all this, Regina?

LAVINIA I didn't say anything. I was twisting my handkerchief—

REGINA It's nothing, Papa, nothing. You know Ben. You know he wants me to marry money for him. I'm not even thinking about Giddens. I don't like him.

BEN Certainly I want you to marry money. More than that— (*She wheels around to stare at him*) You're twenty years old. You ought to be settled down. You been worrying us. (*Pleased at the nervousness* REGINA *is showing*) Isn't that so, Mama? Hasn't Regina been worrying you?

LAVINIA I really don't know, son. I really couldn't say.

OSCAR Well, I could say she's been worrying me. Many's the time I thought of taking action. Sashaying around as open as—

REGINA (*to* OSCAR) Oh, shut up. (*To* MARCUS) Papa. You can't blame me if Ben thinks up one of his plans to annoy you, and Oscar chimes in like he always does. I bought the clothes because I—because I want to take a little trip. That's all, Papa.

MARCUS A trip?

REGINA All right. I'll send back the dresses. I don't know

what all this talk's about. (*Comes to him*) Spoiling your Sunday. Come on, darling. Let's take our lunch and go on a picnic, just you and me. We haven't done that in a long time.

MARCUS   No, not for a long time. (*To* BEN) Something amuses you?

BEN   Yes. You and Regina.

MARCUS   (*to* BEN *and* OSCAR)   The two of you have contrived to give me a bad morning. (*To* OSCAR) And you have cost me five hundred dollars. How much you drawing at the store?

OSCAR   (*nervous but determined*)   I was going to talk to you about that, Papa. I'm drawing sixteen a week. It ain't enough, Papa, because, well, I'm getting on and I want a little life of my own. I was going to ask you if you couldn't sort of make a little advance against a little raise—

MARCUS   You'll get eleven a week hereafter. Five dollars will go to repay me for the five hundred.

OSCAR   My God, Papa. You can't— Eleven a week! My God, Papa— That wasn't what I meant. You misunderstood me 'cause I wasn't talking clear. I wanted a little *raise*, not a—

MARCUS   (*to* BEN, *sharply*)   Put aside your plans for your sister's future. Spend with profit your time today going over the store books. (*Then amused*) You'll find we are short of cash. Call in some cotton loans or mortgages. (*Giggles*) Then go to church.

LAVINIA   (*delighted*)   Want to come with me, Benjamin? I'm going to my church, because they're saying a prayer for my birthday. (*To* MARCUS) It's my birthday, Marcus.

MARCUS   Congratulations, Lavinia.

LAVINIA   Thank you. (*Comes to* MARCUS) We were going to talk today. You promised, Marcus—

MARCUS   I promised to talk? Talk about what?

LAVINIA   (*amazed, worried*)   Talk about what? You know, Marcus. You promised last year, on my last birthday. You said you were too busy that day, but this year you said—

MARCUS I'm still busy, my dear. Now you run and tell
Belle to make us up a fine picnic basket. (*To* REGINA)
And a good bottle of wine. I'll get it myself.

LAVINIA But, Marcus, I been waiting since last year—

MARCUS Get the lunch now. (*She hesitates, looks frightened, goes toward kitchen door. To* REGINA) I'll bring
my Aristotle. You'll read in English, I'll follow you in
Greek. Shall we walk or drive?

REGINA (*smiling*) Let's walk. You get the wine and your
books. I'll change my clothes— (*He nods, smiles, goes
into house. She stops to look at* BEN, *smiles*) You never
going to learn, Ben. Been living with Papa for thirty-five
years, and never going to learn.

OSCAR Regina, you got a few hundred dollars to lend me?
Wouldn't take me long to pay it back—

BEN Learn what, honey?

OSCAR Papa's sure hard on me. It's unnatural. If a stranger
came in he'd think Papa didn't like me, his own son.

REGINA (*turns to* OSCAR) You want some money? If you
had any sense, you'd know how to get it; just tell Papa
Ben don't want you to have it. You'll get it. (*To* BEN)
You ain't smart for a man who wants to get somewhere.
You should have figured out long ago that Papa's going
to do just whatever you tell him not to do, unless *I* tell
him to do it. (*Pats his shoulder*) Goodness gracious,
that's been working for the whole twenty years I been
on earth.

BEN (*to* REGINA) You are right, and you're smart. You
must give me a full lecture on Papa some day; tell me
why he's so good to you, how you manage, and so on.

REGINA (*laughs*) I'm busy now, taking him on a picnic.

BEN Oh, not now. Too hot for lectures. We'll wait for
a winter night. Before the fire. I'll sit opposite you and
you'll talk and I'll listen. And I'll think many things,
like how you used to be a beauty but at fifty years your
face got worn and sour. Papa'll still be living, and he'll
interrupt us, the way he does even now: he'll call from
upstairs to have you come and put him to bed. And
you'll get up to go, wondering how the years went by—
(*Sharply*) Because, as you say, he's most devoted to

you, and he's going to keep you right here with him, all his long life.

REGINA (*angrily*) He's not going to keep me here. And don't you think he is. I'm going away. I'm going to Chicago— (BEN *gets up, stares at her.* OSCAR *looks up. She catches herself*) Oh, well, I guess you'd have to know. But I wanted him to promise before you began any interfering— I'm going for a trip, and a nice long trip. So you're wrong, honey.

BEN (*slowly*) He's consented to the trip?

REGINA (*giggles*) No. But he will by the time the picnic's over.

OSCAR Chicago? You sure got Mama's blood. Little while now, and you're going to be just as crazy as Mama.

REGINA (*to* BEN) And the trip's going to cost a lot of money. I got books from hotels, and I know. But you'll be working hard in the store and sending it on to me—

BEN You could always come home occasionally and go on another picnic. (*Comes up to her*) This time I don't think so. Papa didn't just get mad about you and Horace Giddens. Papa got mad about you and any man, or any place that ain't near him. I wouldn't like to be in the house, for example, the day he ever hears the gossip about you and Bagtry— (*Sharply*) Or is Bagtry going to Chicago—

REGINA (*tensely, softly*) Be still, Ben.

OSCAR And everybody sure is gossiping. Laurette even heard it up in Roseville. I said there's nothing between you. I wouldn't believe it. But if ever I thought there was I'd ride over to Lionnet, carrying a gun. I sure would—

REGINA (*carefully*) And the day you do I'll be right behind you. It'll be your last ride, darling.

OSCAR (*backing away*) All right, all right, I was joking. Everybody's talking so wild today—

REGINA (*turns back to* BEN) Look, Ben, don't start anything. I'll get you in trouble if you do.

BEN I believe you.

REGINA Wish me luck. I got a hard day's work ahead.

(*She goes up steps to upper porch and into her room.*)

OSCAR (*yawns*) Where she going?

BEN Try to keep awake. Why did you beat up Sam Taylor?

OSCAR (*after a second, sulkily*) He's a no-good carpet-bagger.

BEN (*wearily*) All right. Let's try again. Why did you beat up Sam Taylor?

OSCAR He tried to make evening appointments with Laurette. He tried it twice. I told him the first time, and I told her too.

BEN Is Laurette the little whore you've been courting?

OSCAR (*slowly, tensely*) Take that back, Ben. Take back that word. (BEN *laughs.* OSCAR *advances toward him, very angry*) I don't let any man—

BEN Now listen to me, you clown. You put away your gun and keep it away. If those fools in your Klan want to beat up niggers and carpetbaggers, you let 'em do it. But you're not going to make this country dangerous to me, or dangerous to the business. We had a hard enough time making them forget Papa made too much money out of the war, and I ain't ever been sure they forgot it.

OSCAR Course they haven't forgot it. Every time anybody has two drinks, or you call up another loan, there's plenty of talk, and plenty of hints I don't understand. (*Rises*) If I had been old enough to fight in the war, you just bet I'd been right there, and not like you, bought off. I'm a Southerner. And when I see an old carpetbagger or upstart nigger, why, I feel like taking revenge.

BEN For what? Because Papa got rich on them? (*Very sharply*) Put away that gun, sonny, and keep it put away, you hear me?

OSCAR (*frightened*) All right, all right. I want to thank you. I forgot. For saying that I was talking to you on the train. Thanks, Ben.

BEN I wasn't lying for you. I was trying to save five hundred dollars.

OSCAR (*hurt*) Oh. Guess I should have known. (*Sighs*) How'm I ever going to pay it back? I'm in a mess. I—

Ben, help me, will you? I'm deeply and sincerely in love.

BEN   Go give yourself a cooling sponge bath.

OSCAR   I want to marry Laurette. I was going to ask Papa to advance me a little money, so we could ship on down to New Orleans. He's going to leave money when he dies, plenty of it. I just want a little of mine now, and I'll go away—

BEN   He won't leave much. Not at this rate. He's spent forty thousand on nothing in the last six months.

OSCAR   My God, forty thousand and us slaving away in the store! And that's the way it's always going to be. I'm telling you: I'm taking Laurette and I'm going. Laurette's a fine girl. Hasn't looked at another man for a year.

BEN   Well, she better take them up again if you're going away. *You* can't earn a living.

(JAKE *appears from the living room.*)

JAKE   Mr. Ben, a lady who says she doesn't want to say her name, she would like to speak with you. She's in the front hall, waiting.

BEN   Who? Who is it?

JAKE   Miss Birdie Bagtry.

(BEN *and* OSCAR *turn in surprise.*)

BEN   (*after a minute*) Wants to see *me?* (JAKE *nods vigorously*) Bring her out.

(JAKE *exits.*)

OSCAR   Now what do you think of that? What's she want to come here for? To see *you?* (*Giggles*) What you been up to, boy?

BEN   Maybe she's come to look at you. Didn't you tell me she once gave you a glass of lemonade?

OSCAR   Did she?

BEN   I don't know. I only know that you told me so.

OSCAR   Then I guess it happened.

BEN   That doesn't necessarily follow.

OSCAR   Well, it was true. I was pushing a lame horse past Lionnet. I was lame myself from something or other—

BEN   Laurette Sincee?

OSCAR   I told you once, stop that. I am in love with Laurette, deeply and sincerely.

BEN   Better you'd stayed for the lemonade and fallen in love with Lionnet's cotton-fields.

OSCAR   Oh, this girl's supposed to be awfully silly. Melty-mush-silly. (*Smiles*) That's what Laurette calls people like that. Melty-mush-silly.

BEN   She's witty, Laurette, eh? (JAKE *appears in the living-room door followed by a slight, pretty, faded-looking girl of twenty. Her clothes are seedy, her face is worn and frightened*) Good morning, ma'am.

OSCAR   (*with charm*) Well, hello there, Miss Birdie!

BIRDIE   (*bows*) Mr. Benjamin. And morning to you. Mr. Oscar. (*Nervously*) We haven't seen you in many a long day. You haven't been hunting lately?

OSCAR   Oh, my time's been taken up with so many things, haven't had much chance.

BIRDIE   (*nods*) I know, you gentlemen in business. Please, you all, forgive my coming to your house, particularly on this day of privacy. I'll just take a few minutes and—

OSCAR   Excuse me, Miss Birdie. Hope you'll come again. (*He starts toward room.*)

BEN   Wait inside, Oscar. (OSCAR *turns to stare at him, then shrugs, disappears. To* BIRDIE) Please.

BIRDIE   (*sits down*) Yes, sir. Thank you.

BEN   Can I get you coffee?

BIRDIE   No, sir. Thank you. You see, I only got a few minutes before Mama begins wondering. I'm sorry to worry you here, but I couldn't come to see you in the store, because then the whole town would know, wouldn't they? And my Mama and Cousin John would just about— (*Giggles nervously*) Isn't that so, Mr. Benjamin?

BEN   Isn't what so?

BIRDIE   (*very nervous*) About knowing. I must apologize for disturbing— Oh, I said that before. It's not good manners to take up all your time saying how sorry I am to take up all your time, now is it? (*Giggles*) Oh, and I'm doing that again, too. Mama says I say everything in a question. Oh.

BEN   What do you want to talk to me about, Miss Birdie?

BIRDIE   Yes. (*Rises. Desperately*) Mr. Benjamin, we're having a mighty bad time. It can't go on. It got so bad that last month Mama didn't want to do it, but she did it, and it was just awful for her.

BEN   (*after a second, politely*) Did what?

BIRDIE Went all the way to Natchez, just to keep from going to our kinfolk in Mobile. Course they're so poor now they couldn't have done anything anyway, but just to keep them from knowing she went all the way to Natchez.

BEN   Really?

BIRDIE Yes, sir, all the way by herself. But they said they just couldn't. They said they'd like to, for Papa's dead sake and Grandpapa's, but they just couldn't. Mama said she didn't want it for anybody's sake, not like that, not for those reasons—well, you know Mama, Mr. Benjamin.

BEN   No, I don't.

BIRDIE Oh. Well, I don't blame her, although . . . No, when everything else is gone, Mama says you at least got pride left. She did it to save me, Mr. Benjamin, the trip, I mean. I was such a ninny, being born when I did, and growing up in the wrong time. I'm much younger than my brothers. I mean I am younger, if they were living. But it didn't do any good.

BEN   I beg your pardon?

BIRDIE The trip to Natchez. It didn't do any good.

BEN   What kind of good didn't it do? (*She looks puzzled*) Why did your Mama make the trip?

BIRDIE To borrow money on the cotton. Or on the land— (*softly*)—or even to sell the pictures, or the silver. But they said they couldn't: that everybody was raising cotton that nobody else wanted. I don't understand that. I thought people always wanted cotton.

BEN   They will again in fifty years.

BIRDIE (*after a pause*) Oh. Fifty years. (*Smiles sadly*) Well, I guess we can't wait that long. The truth is, we can't pay or support our people, Mr. Benjamin, we can't— Well, it's just killing my Mama. And my Cousin John, he wants to go away.

BEN   Where does he want to go?

BIRDIE Away from here. (*Tense, very frightened*) Forgive

me. Would you, I mean your father and you, would you
lend money on our cotton, or land, or—

BEN Your Cousin John, does he want to go to New York or
Chicago, perhaps? Has he spoken of going to Chicago?

BIRDIE Oh dear, no. There's no war going on in Chicago.

BEN I beg your pardon?

BIRDIE A war. He wants to go back to war. Mama says she
can even understand that. She says there isn't any life
for our boys any more.

BEN I see. Where will Captain Bagtry find a war?

BIRDIE There's something going on in Brazil, John says. He
looked it up in the paper, and he's got a map.

BEN Brazil. Is there a nice war going on in Brazil?

BIRDIE Yes. I think so. (*Eagerly*) You see, that was one of
the things Mama was going to do with the money. Pay
all our people and give John the carfare. He can earn a
lot in Brazil, he can be a general. (*Pauses, breathes*)
Now about the loan, Mr. Benjamin—

BEN You will inherit Lionnet?

BIRDIE Me? Er. Yes. You mean if Mama were to— You
mustn't believe those old stories. Mama's not so sick
that a little good care and— (*Very embarrassed*) I'm
sorry.

BEN You don't want your Mama to know you've come
here?

BIRDIE Oh, no, no. She'd never forgive me, rather die—

BEN (*laughs*) To think you had come to us.

BIRDIE I didn't mean that. I am so sorry. I didn't—

BEN You have not offended me, ma'am. I only ask because
as I understand it you don't own Lionnet, your Mama
does. But you don't want her to know about the loan.
And so who would sign for it?

BIRDIE (*stares at him*) I would. Oh. You mean you can't
sign for what you don't own. Oh. I see. I hadn't thought
of that. Oh. That's how much of a ninny I am. Forgive
me for bothering you. I shouldn't have. I'm sorry I just
ruined your Sunday morning. Good day, sir.

BEN (*goes to dining-room door*) Oscar, Oscar, I know
you want to walk Miss Bagtry home.

BIRDIE Oh, no. Thank you. I—

OSCAR   (*calling, offstage*)   I have an appointment. I'm late.

BIRDIE   (*embarrassed*)   Please, sir—

BEN   (*to* BIRDIE)   How much of a loan were you thinking about?

BIRDIE   Five thousand dollars. It would take that much to pay your people and buy seed and pay debts and— But I guess I was as foolish about that as—

BEN   You know, of course, that all loans from our company are made by my father. I only work for him. Yours is good cotton and good land. But you don't own it. That makes it hard. It's very unusual, but perhaps I could think of some way to accommodate you. A promise from you, in a letter—

BIRDIE   (*delighted*)   Oh. Oh. Of course, I'd make the promise.

BEN   Why don't you talk to my father yourself? I'll tell him what it's all about, and you come back this afternoon—

BIRDIE   (*backing away*)   Oh, no. I couldn't say all that to-day again. I just couldn't— (*Softly*) That's silly. Of course I could. What time will I come?

BEN   I have a pleasanter idea. Come tomorrow evening. Once a month my father has a music evening with musicians from Mobile to play on the violin, and flatter him. He's always in a good humor after his music. Come in then, Miss Birdie, and please invite Captain Bagtry to escort you.

BIRDIE   You really think there's any chance? Your Papa would— And my Mama wouldn't ever have to find out?

BEN   (*bows*)   I will do my best for you before you come.

BIRDIE   (*after a second, with determination*)   Thank you very much. I will be most pleased to come. Imagine having a concert right in your own house! I just love music. (OSCAR *appears in the door, stares angrily at* BEN) Thank you for your courtesy in offering to walk me back, Mr. Oscar. And thank you, Mr. Benjamin. (BIRDIE *smiles happily, moves quickly off.*)

OSCAR   (*comes close to* BEN, *softly, very angry*)   What the hell's the matter with you? Bossing me around, ruining my day?

BEN   (*softly*)   Be nice to the girl. You hear me?

OSCAR   I'm taking her home. That's enough. Damned little ninny.

BEN   I was thinking of trying to do you a favor. I was thinking if something works right for me, I'd lend you the five hundred to pay Papa back.

OSCAR   Squee, Ben! If you only could. What would you be doing it for?

BEN   Because I want you to be nice to this girl. Flatter her, talk nice. She's kind of pretty.

OSCAR   Pretty? I can't stand 'em like that.

BEN   I know. Virtue in woman offends you. Now go on. Be charming. Five hundred possible dollars' charming.

OSCAR   (*smiles*)   All right.

(*He runs off. After a minute* MARCUS, *carrying three books and a bottle of wine, appears on the porch.*)

MARCUS   (*reading*)   "The customary branches of education number four. Reading and writing." You know *those,* Benjamin, I think. "Gymnastic exercise"—(MARCUS *laughs*)—"and music." Aristotle. *You* don't know any music, Benjamin.

BEN   I've been too busy, Papa.

MARCUS   At what?

BEN   Working all my life for you. Doing a lot of dirty jobs. And then watching you have a wild time throwing the money around. But when I ask you to lend me a little . . .

MARCUS   You're a free man, Benjamin. A free man. You don't like what I do, you don't stay with me. (*Holding up the book*) I do wish you would read a little Aristotle, take your mind off money.

(REGINA *comes down the steps, in a new dress, carrying a parasol and a steamer rug.*)

BEN   (*looks at her*)   Oh. Before I forget. I invited Miss Birdie Bagtry and her cousin to come here tomorrow night.

MARCUS   To come here? What do you mean?

BEN   I thought you'd like having the quality folk here. (*Smiles*) Come here to beg a favor of you.

MARCUS   (*stares at him, giggles*)   You teasing me?

BEN   No. The girl just left here. She wants us to lend

money on the cotton. Her Mama didn't know, and mustn't know. But Miss Birdie doesn't own the place—

MARCUS   Then what kind of nonsense is that?

BEN   Maybe it's not nonsense. Take a note from her. If she dies before her mother—

MARCUS   (*sharply*) Who said anything about dying? You're very concerned with people dying, aren't you?

BEN   (*laughs*) You hate that word. (*Quickly*) Her mother could get out of it legally, maybe, but I don't think she would. Anyway, the old lady is sick, and it's worth a chance. Make it a short loan, call it in a few years. They've wrecked the place and the money won't do 'em much good. I think the time would come when you'd own the plantation for almost nothing. (*Looks up at* REGINA) A loan would make them happy and make us money. Make the Bagtrys grateful to us—

REGINA   (*softly*) Course I don't know anything about business, Papa, but could I say something, please? I've been kind of lonely here with nobody nice having much to do with us. I'd sort of like to know people of my own age, a girl my own age, I mean—

MARCUS   (*to* BEN) How much does she want?

BEN   (*hesitates for a minute*) Ten thousand.

MARCUS   On Lionnet? Ten thousand is cheap. She's a fool.

BEN   (*smiles*) Yes, I think she's a fool.

MARCUS   (*giggles*) Well, the one thing I never doubted was your making a good business deal. Kind of cute of you to think of their coming here to get it, too. Bagtrys in this house, begging. Might be amusing for an hour.

REGINA   (*quickly*) Can't invite 'em for an hour. Papa. And we've got to be nice to them. Otherwise I just wouldn't want to see him come unless we'd be awful nice and polite.

MARCUS   They'll think we're nice and polite for ten thousand.

REGINA   (*laughs, in a high good humor*) I guess. But you be pleasant to them—

MARCUS   Why, Regina? Why are you so anxious?

REGINA   Papa, I told you. I been a little lonesome. No peo-

ple my age ever coming here— I do think people like
that sort of want to forgive you, and be nice to us—

MARCUS (*sharply, angrily*) Forgive me?

REGINA (*turns away, little-girl tearful*) I'm mighty sorry.
What have I done? Just said I'd like to have a few people to listen to your old music. Is that so awful to want?

MARCUS (*quickly, pleadingly*) Come on, darling. (*Shouts*)
Lavinia, *where* is the basket? Lavinia! Coralee! (*To RE-
GINA*) Come on now, honey. It's been a long time since
you been willing to spend a Sunday with me. If I was
sharp, I'm sorry. Don't you worry. I'll be charming to
the visiting gentry.

BEN Miss Birdie got a fear of asking you for the loan and
of her cousin, John, knowing about it. Might be better
if you just gave your consent, Papa, and didn't make her
tell the story all over again. I can do the details.

(LAVINIA *appears with a basket.* MARCUS *takes it from her,
peers in it.*)

MARCUS (*to* REGINA) That's mighty nice-looking. We'll
have a good lunch. (*To* BEN) I don't want to hear the
woes of Lionnet and Mistress Birdie. Most certainly you
will do the details. Be kind of pleasant owning Lionnet.
It's a beautiful house. Very light in motive, very well
conceived—

LAVINIA You going now, Marcus? Marcus! You promised
you'd talk to me. Today—

MARCUS I'm talking to you, Lavinia.

EAVINIA Last year this morning, you promised me it
would be today—

MARCUS (*gently*) I'm going out now, Lavinia.

LAVINIA I've fixed you a mighty nice lunch, Marcus, the
way you like it. I boiled up some crabs right fast, and—

MARCUS I'm sure. Thank you. (*He starts to move off.*)

LAVINIA (*comes running to him*) Please, Marcus, I won't
take up five minutes. Or when you come back? When
you come back, Marcus?

MARCUS Another day, my dear.

LAVINIA It can't be another day, Marcus. It was to be on
my birthday, this year. When you sat right in that chair,
and I brought my Bible and you swore—

MARCUS Another day.

LAVINIA It ought to be today. If you swear to a day, it's got to be that day— (*Very frightened*) Tomorrow then. Tomorrow wouldn't hurt so much, because tomorrow is just after today— I've *got* to go this week, because I had a letter from the Reverend—

REGINA Oh, Mama. Are you talking that way again?

LAVINIA (*shaking, wildly*) Tomorrow, Marcus? Tomorrow, tomorrow.

MARCUS (*to Ben*) Ben, get Coralee.

LAVINIA Tomorrow— (BEN *exits. She grabs* MARCUS's *arm*) Promise me tomorrow, Marcus. Promise me. I'll go get my Bible and you promise me—

MARCUS (*very sharply*) Stop that nonsense. Get hold of yourself. I've had enough of that! I want no more.

LAVINIA (*crying*) I'm not making any trouble. You know that, Marcus. Just promise me tomorrow.

MARCUS Stop it! I've had enough. Try to act like you're not crazy. Get your self in hand. (*He exits.*)

REGINA (*as Coralee appears*) Never mind, Mama. Maybe you'll be coming away with me. Would you like that? There are lots of churches in Chicago—

CORALEE All right, Miss Regina. Don't tease her now.

REGINA (*gaily, as she goes off*) I'm not teasing.

(*After a pause,* LAVINIA *sits down.*)

LAVINIA Now I'm going to pretend. You ready?

CORALEE (*as if this had happened a thousand times before*) All right.

LAVINIA He didn't say any of those things. He said he would speak with me sure thing— (*Her voice rises*) No man breaks a Bible promise, and you can't tell me they do. You know I got my correspondence with the Reverend. He wants me to come and I got my mission and my carfare. In his last letter, the Reverend said if I was coming I should come, or should write him and say I couldn't ever come. "Couldn't ever come—" Why did he write that?

CORALEE I don't know.

LAVINIA Your people are my people. I got to do a little humble service. I lived in sin these thirty-seven years,

Coralee. (*Rocks herself*) Such sin I couldn't even tell you.

CORALEE You told me.

LAVINIA Now I got to finish with the sin. Now I got to do my mission. And I'll be— I'll do it nice, you know I will. I'll gather the little black children round, and I'll teach them good things. I'll teach them how to read and write, and sing the music notes and—

CORALEE (*wearily*) Oh, Miss Viney. Maybe it's just as well. Maybe they'd be scared of a white teacher coming among them.

LAVINIA (*after a pause*) Scared of me?

CORALEE (*turns*) No, ma'am. You're right. News of you has gone ahead.

LAVINIA Course they could have many a better teacher. I know mighty little, but I'm going to try to remember better. (*Quietly*) And the first thing I'm going to remember is to speak to Marcus tomorrow. Tomorrow. (*Turns pleadingly to* CORALEE) I was silly to speak today. And I did it wrong. Anyway, he didn't say I *couldn't* go, he just said— (*Stops suddenly*) My goodness, it's such a little thing to want. Just to go back where you were born and help little colored children to grow up knowing how to read books and— (*Giggles*) You'll be proud of me. I'll remember things to teach them. You remember things when you're happy. And I'm going to be happy. You get to be fifty-nine, you don't be happy then, well, you got to find it. I'm going to be a very happy, happy, happy, happy— I'm going, Coralee. (*She suddenly stops, looks down in her lap.*)

CORALEE Nice and cool in your room. Want to lie down? (LAVINIA *doesn't answer*) Want to play a little on the piano? Nobody's inside. (*No answer. She waits, then very gently*) All right, if you don't want to. I tell you what. Come on in the kitchen and rest yourself with us. (LAVINIA *gets up,* CORALEE *takes her arm, they start out as*

Curtain Falls

Act Two

SCENE: *The living room of the* HUBBARD *house. This is the room we have seen through the French doors of the first act, and now we are looking at the room as if we were standing in the French doors of the portico. A large bay window is center stage, leading to a porch that faces the first-act portico. Right stage is a door leading to the dining room. Left stage is an open arch leading to the entrance hall and main staircase. The furniture is from the previous owner but* MARCUS *has cleared the room of the ornaments and the ornamented. Right stage is a round table and three chairs. Left stage is a sofa and chair. Right, upstage, is a desk. Left, upstage, is a piano. Right, upstage, is a long table. Center of the room, before the columns of the porch, are a table and chairs. The room is simpler, more severe, than many rooms of the 1880's. A Greek vase, glass-enclosed, stands on a pedestal; a Greek statue sits on the table; Greek battle scenes are hung on the walls.*

As the curtain rises, BEN *and* OSCAR *are sitting at table, stage right. They each have a glass of port and the port decanter is in front of them.* MARCUS, PENNIMAN *and* JUGGER *are standing at a music stand, looking down at a music score.* PENNIMAN *is a tall, fattish man.* JUGGER *looks like everybody.* PENNIMAN *looks up from the score, hums, drains his glass, looks at the empty glass, and crosses to* BEN *and* OSCAR. MARCUS *is intent on the score.*

PENNIMAN (*meaning the score*) Very interesting. Harmonically fresh, eh, Mr. Benjamin?

BEN I know nothing of music.

JUGGER Why do people always sound so proud when they announce they know nothing of music?

PENNIMAN (*quickly, as* OSCAR *fills his glass*) A fine port, and a mighty good supper. I always look forward to our evening here. I tell my wife Mrs. Hubbard is a rare housekeeper.

BEN You like good port, Mr. Penniman?

PENNIMAN Yes, sir, and don't trust the man who don't.

(OSCAR *goes off into gales of laughter. This pleases* PENNIMAN *and he claps* OSCAR *on the shoulder.* MARCUS *looks up, annoyed, taps bow on music stand.* PENNIMAN *and* OSCAR *stop laughing,* PENNIMAN *winks at* OSCAR, *carries his glass back to music stand.* JAKE *comes from the hall entrance carrying two chairs, a lamp, and passes through to porch.* LAVINIA *hurries in from the dining room. Her hair is mussy, her dress spotted. She looks around the room, smiles at everybody. When nobody notices her, she crosses to* MARCUS, *leans over to examine the score, nods at what she reads.*)

LAVINIA Oh, it's nice, Marcus. Just as nice as anybody could have. It's going to be a cold collation. Is that all right?

MARCUS (*who is in a good humor*) Yes, certainly. What's that?

LAVINIA A cold collation? That's what you call food when you have guests. A cold collation.

PENNIMAN (*looks toward the dining room, delighted*) More food? After that fine supper—

LAVINIA This is a special night. Guests. Isn't that pleasant? My, we haven't had guests— I don't think I remember the last time we had guests—

MARCUS (*looks at her*) All right, Lavinia.

LAVINIA There'll be a dish of crabs, of course. And a dish of crawfish boiled in white wine, the way Belle does. And a chicken salad, and a fine strong ham we've been saving. (*Stops*) Oh. I'm worrying you gentlemen—

PENNIMAN (*lifting his glass*) Worrying us? You, the honor of Rose County, and the redeemer of this family.

(JUGGER *and* MARCUS *look up sharply.* BEN *laughs.* MARCUS *reaches over and takes* PENNIMAN's *glass, carries it to table.*)

MARCUS I am awaiting your opinion.

PENNIMAN (*who has the quick dignity of a man with too much port*) The judgment of music, like the inspiration for it, must come slow and measured, if it comes with truth.

OSCAR (*to* BEN) Talks like a Christmas tree, don't he?

LAVINIA It's your third composition, isn't it, Marcus? Oh, I'm sure it's lovely. Just lovely.

MARCUS (*looks at her—softly*) How would you know, Lavinia?

LAVINIA (*hurt*) I can read notes, Marcus. Why, I taught you how to read music. Don't you remember, Marcus? (*She goes toward* BEN *and* OSCAR) I did. Yes, I did.

BEN (*amused*) Of course you did.

PENNIMAN (*hurriedly*) I would say this: It is done as the Greeks might have imposed the violin upon the lute. (*Hums*) Right here. Close to Buxtehude— (*Inspiration*) Or, the Netherland Contrapuntalists. Excellent.

(OSCAR *pours himself another port,* LAVINIA *has wandered to the piano, mumbling to herself.*)

MARCUS (*very pleased, to* PENNIMAN) You like it?

PENNIMAN I like it very much. And if you would allow us, I would like to introduce it in Mobile during the season. Play it first at the school, say, then, *possibly—*

MARCUS That would make me very happy. And what do you think of it, Mr. Jugger?

JUGGER (*slowly*) Penniman speaks for me. He always does.

PENNIMAN (*quickly*) Come. We'll try it for you. I am most anxious to hear it. (*Points to* MARCUS's *violin, coyly*) I daresay you know the solo part you have written for yourself?

MARCUS Well, I—yes. (*Very pleased*) I had hoped you would want to try it tonight. I— (JUGGER *picks up his violin, starts for portico.* MARCUS *turns to him*) Mr. Jugger. Would *you* like to try it now?

JUGGER (*turns, looks at* MARCUS, *seems about to say something, changes his mind*). I would like to try.

PENNIMAN But where *is* my cello? Goodness God—

JUGGER (*sharply, at door of portico*) It's out here. When will you learn that it's hard to mislay a cello? (PENNIMAN *giggles, trips out to porch.*)

LAVINIA (*suddenly plays a few notes on the piano*) See? I told you, Marcus. *That's* it. I told you I could read music just as good as I used to—

MARCUS Is there something disturbing you this evening, Lavinia? More than usual?

(REGINA *enters from the hall. She is dressed up, very handsome. They all turn to stare at her. She smiles, goes to* MARCUS.)

MARCUS (*softly*) You're a beautiful girl.

OSCAR Looks like the decorated pig at the county fair.

REGINA (*wheels around for* MARCUS) It's my Chicago dress. *One* of my Chicago dresses. (REGINA *notices* LAVINIA) Oh, Mama, it's late. Do go and get dressed.

LAVINIA I'm dressed, Regina.

REGINA You can't look like that. Put on a nice silk—

LAVINIA I only have what I have—

REGINA Put on your nice dress, Mama. It will do for tonight. We must order you new things. You can't go to Chicago looking like a tired old country lady—

LAVINIA (*wheels around*) *Chicago?* I'm not going to Chicago. Where I'm going I don't need clothes or things of the world. I'm going to the poor, and it wouldn't be proper to parade in silk— Marcus! You tell Regina where I'm going. *Tell her where I'm going.* You tell her right now. You—

REGINA All right, Mama. Now don't you fret. Go upstairs and get dressed up for the high-toned guests. (*She leads* LAVINIA *to the hall*) Don't you worry now. Go on up, honey. Coralee's waiting for you. (*She comes back into room. To* MARCUS) Whew! I'm sorry. I should have known. I hope she isn't going to act queer the rest of the evening.

MARCUS   There's always that chance.

REGINA   Well, don't let's worry. (*Gaily*) I'll see to everything. I'd better have a look in the kitchen, and more chairs— Let's have the very good champagne, Papa?

PENNIMAN   (*from portico*)   Mr. Hubbard—

MARCUS   (*takes keys from his pocket, throws them to* BEN) Wine as good as Regina's dress. And count the bottles used. I don't want to find that Oscar has sold them again.

BEN   (*to* REGINA)   So your picnic was successful? When do you leave for Chicago?

REGINA   (*gaily*)   In ten days, two weeks. (*Comes to him*) Going to miss me?

BEN   Yes. Very much.

MARCUS   What's the matter? What's the matter, Regina?

REGINA   (*gaily, leaving* BEN)   Matter? Nothing. (*Calls into dining room as she exits*) Two more chairs, Jake—

OSCAR   Now just tell me how I'm going to get word to Laurette that I can't meet her till later tonight, just somebody tell me that.

MARCUS   (*very sharply to* BEN)   I told you to get the wine.

(BEN *looks at him, smiles as if he understood why* MARCUS *was angry, exits through dining-room door.* MARCUS *stands staring at him. Then goes to piano, looks through scores.* OSCAR *moves nervously toward* MARCUS.)

OSCAR   (*desperately*)   Papa, I'm in trouble. You see, I had an appointment with a lady from out of town, Roseville, I mean.

MARCUS   What were they doing?

OSCAR   Who?

MARCUS   Regina and Ben when they were standing together— (*Breaks off, turns sharply away.*)

OSCAR   Oh, you know Ben..Always up to something. Yesterday, trying to marry off Regina, tonight trying to press me on the Bagtry girl.

MARCUS   (*looks up*)   Oh, come. Ben's not a fool. You and a Bagtry is a very comic idea.

OSCAR   I know, but Ben's figured they're so hard up for money they might even have me. It all fits in with this mortgage you're giving them, or somthing. He's got his eye on the cotton— (*Giggles*) And Ben's eye goes in a

lot of directions, mostly around corners. It's true, Papa.
He made me take the girl home yesterday—

MARCUS (*looks at* OSCAR) The mortgage, and then the
girl and you. Interesting man, Benjamin.

OSCAR (*pleadingly*) Papa, like I say. I've got a friend
who's waiting for me right now. I want you to meet her.
You see, I'm deeply and sincerely in love. Deeply and sincerely. She's a fine girl. But *Ben* cries her down. *Ben*
don't want me to be happy.

MARCUS Isn't that too bad. Your own brother. It's a shame.

OSCAR Course she's of the lower classes, and that doesn't
fit in with Ben's plans for us to marry money for him.
But the lower classes don't matter to me; I always say
it's not how people were born but what they are—

MARCUS You always say that, eh? Well, some people are
democrats by choice, and some by necessity. You, by
necessity.

OSCAR Could I go fetch her here— (*Desperately*) tonight?
Could I, Papa?

MARCUS What is this, a night at the circus?

OSCAR (*slyly, as a last chance*) I think it would just about
finish Mr. Ben to have a member of the lower classes,
sort of, mixing with the gentry, here. I thought it would
sort of, sort of amuse you, and well, you could meet her
at the same time. Be a good joke on Ben, sort of—

MARCUS (*slowly*) Is this Laurette that, that little, er—
little thing from Roseville you been steaming about?

OSCAR She's not, Papa. Oh, maybe she was a little wild
before I met her, but— She was left an orphan and she
· didn't know what else to do, starving and cold, friend-
less.

MARCUS (*shudders*) Oh God, shut up. (*Hesitates, then
laughs*) All right, go and get her, if you like. Er. Does
she come dressed? I wouldn't like her here, er, unrobed.

OSCAR (*hurt but happy*) Aw, she's a fine woman, Papa,
don't talk like that. And she loves music. She wants to
learn just about everything—

MARCUS Don't bring her as a student, Oscar.

OSCAR Oh, no. No, I wouldn't. She won't say a word. She
admires you, Papa—

MARCUS   For what?

OSCAR   Well, just about, well, just for everything, I guess— (MARCUS *makes a dismissive gesture, goes on porch as* REGINA *comes into room.* OSCAR *sees Regina, smiles*) I'll be back in a few minutes. Going across the square to get Laurette, bring her here.

REGINA   (*starts toward him, as* BEN *comes in carrying champagne bottles*)   Here? That girl— What's the matter with you? You're doing nothing of the kind. Come back here. You can't bring that—

OSCAR   Can't I? Well, just ask Papa. *He* wants her to meet my folks.

REGINA   (*turns to* BEN)   Ben, stop him. He can't bring her here tonight— Stop him! (*But* OSCAR *has disappeared*) Get him, Ben!

BEN   What am I supposed to do, shoot him? I'm too old to run down streets after men in love.

REGINA   He *can't* bring her here. You know what John will think. I saw him this afternoon: I had to beg him to come tonight. He doesn't know why Birdie wants him to come, but— Ben, he'll think we meant to do it, planned to insult them—

BEN   Yes, I'm sure he will.

(*The music on the porch begins.*)

REGINA   What's the matter with Papa? Why did he let Oscar—

BEN   (*smiles*)   You're going to learn some day about Papa. It's not as easy as you think, Regina. (*They stand looking out to the porch, listening to the music*) He gave those clowns five thousand last month for something they call their music school. Now that they are playing his composition he should be good for another five thousand—

REGINA   (*turns, softly, amazed*)   Did he? Really? (*Shakes her head*) Well, anyway, he's promised me plenty for—

BEN   To marry Bagtry? Enough to support you the rest of your life, you and your husband? I'm taking a vacation the day he finds out about your marriage plans.

REGINA   (*angrily, nervous*)   I don't know what you're talking about. Marry— What are you saying—? I— (*Turns*

to him, tensely) Leave me alone, Ben. Leave me alone.
Stop making trouble. If you dare say *anything* to Papa
about John, I'll—

BEN (*very sharply*) Don't threaten me. I'm sick of
threats.

REGINA (*angry*) You'll be much sicker of them if you—
(*Then, softly*) Ben, don't. I'm in love with John.

BEN (*softly*) But he's not in love with you.

(LAVINIA *comes into room, followed by* CORALEE, *who is
pulling at her, trying to button her dress.* REGINA *turns
away from* BEN.)

LAVINIA Don't bother with the lower buttons. (*Timidly*)
Am I proper now, daughter? (REGINA *doesn't answer
her.* LAVINIA *points out to porch, meaning the music*)
You know, I've made myself cheer up. I know you were
just teasing about Chicago, Regina, and I know full well
I've never been good about teasing. What do people do
now, curtsy or shake hands? I guess it's just about the
first guests we had since the suspicion on your Papa.

REGINA Now, Mama. Please don't talk about any of that
tonight. Don't talk at all about the war, or anything that
happened. Please remember, Mama. Do you hear?

CORALEE (*quickly*) She won't. You all have been teasing
her, and she's tired.

(CORALEE *goes to* BEN, *takes the champagne bottles from
the table.* JAKE *comes in from the dining room carrying
a tray of glasses and a punch bowl.*)

LAVINIA Could I try the nice punch, Coralee?

CORALEE You certainly can. (JAKE *exits.* BEN *starts to the
table. As if such courtesy were unusual,* CORALEE *stares
at him*) Thank you, Mr. Ben.

(CORALEE *exits.* BEN *pours three glasses of punch.*)

LAVINIA Regina, when you don't frown you look like my
Grandmama—(*as* BEN *brings her a glass of punch, and
moves on to* REGINA)—the one who taught me to read
and write. And 'twas mighty unusual, a lady to know
how to read and write, up in the piney woods.

BEN (*laughs*) Now, that's a safer subject, Mama. Tell the
Bagtrys about our kinfolk in the piney woods. (*He lifts
his glass to* REGINA) To you, honey.

REGINA   (*smiles*) And to you, *honey*.

(*On the porch the music comes to an end.* REGINA, *who has not, of course, been paying any attention, starts to applaud. She turns to* LAVINIA, *indicates* MARCUS *on porch.*)

LAVINIA   But I didn't hear it. I wasn't paying any attention.

(MARCUS *comes into room.*)

REGINA   (*goes to him*) It's brilliant of you, Papa.

MARCUS   I'm glad you liked it. Come along. We're about to start—(*laughs*)—the better-known classics.

BEN   Won't you wait for our guests?

MARCUS   Certainly not, I resent their thinking they can stroll in late on my music.

REGINA   (*placatingly*) You're right, darling. *We'll* come out.

(MARCUS *goes to porch.* REGINA *follows.* BEN *follows her.* LAVINIA *puts down her glass, follows* BEN. REGINA *and* BEN *sit down,* LAVINIA *sits down. Then musicians tune up.* MARCUS, PENNIMAN, *and* JUGGER *begin to play a divertimento by Leopold Mozart, a trio of violin, viola, and cello. Then the hall door opens and closes. On the porch,* REGINA *and* BEN *both turn, turn back again. After a second,* OSCAR *appears in the living room pulling* LAURETTE SINCEE. LAURETTE *is about twenty, pig-face cute, a little too fashionably dressed. She stands in the door, admiring the room.*)

LAURETTE   Squee!

OSCAR   (*proud and excited*) Not bad, eh? (*Looks toward portico*) We got to talk soft.

LAURETTE   This *is* nice. You born here, Oskie?

OSCAR   No. Like I told you. Right after the war Papa bought—(*giggles*)—or something, this house from old man Reed. Like it?

LAURETTE   Squee. Who wouldn't?

OSCAR   Well, maybe, some day—

LAURETTE   Ah, go on, Oskie. Go on.

OSCAR   You just wait and see.

LAURETTE   (*points to portico*) What's that?

OSCAR   What?

LAURETTE   The noise?

OSCAR   That's music, honey.

LAURETTE Oh.

OSCAR When you speak to Papa, tell him how much you like music. Tell him how fine he plays.

LAURETTE What's he playing?

OSCAR The violin.

LAURETTE Ain't that a coincidence? I had a beau who said he played the violin. A Frenchman, much older than me. Had to leave his very own country because of the revolution.

OSCAR (*winces*) I don't like to hear about him, Laurette, him or any other men. I am deeply and sincerely in love with you.

LAURETTE (*pleasantly, but without too much interest*) Are you really, Oskie?

OSCAR Laurette, I'm going to ask Papa for a loan. Then we'll go on down to New Orleans. Would you, Laurette—

LAURETTE You've asked me the same question for the last year, twenty times. But you never yet asked your Papa for the loan.

OSCAR I'v been waiting for the right opportunity. I want you to be my *wife*, honey. I am deeply and—

LAURETTE We can't eat on deeply and sincerely.

OSCAR No, I know. But this is the big night, don't you see? (*Laughs happily*) I never thought he'd let you come here. I mean—I mean a chance like this. And he's in a good humor about something. Now, darling, be very very—well, er. I tell you: you speak with him about what *he* likes. Tell him how much you think of music, not new music, mind you, but—and tell him how you stay awake reading.

LAURETTE I've always been a reader. But I can't talk about it. What's there to say?

OSCAR And he's fond of Mozart. Talk about Mozart.

LAURETTE I can't do that.

OSCAR Well, just try to please him. So much depends on it. We could have our own little place in New Orleans—

LAURETTE What kind of place?

OSCAR I'd find a job. You bet I would, and with you behind me to encourage and love me, with you to fight for, I'd forge ahead.

LAURETTE   (*looks at him, puzzled*)   Oh. Well, I'd certainly like to go to New Orleans. I know a girl there. She has an embroidery shop on Royal Street. I'm good at embroidery. It's what I always wanted to do. Did I ever tell you that? Always wanted to do embroidery.

OSCAR   Did you?

LAURETTE   Yep. instead of whoring. I just wanted to do fancy embroidery.

OSCAR   (*loudly, in a hurt cry*)   Don't, Laurette, don't talk that way! (BEN *and* REGINA, *on the porch, look into room.* REGINA *coughs loudly*) We better go out now.

LAURETTE   Why did your papa let me come tonight?

OSCAR   Don't let him worry you, honey. Just take it nice and easy. Pretend nobody knows anything about you, pretend you're just as good as them—

LAURETTE   (*stares at him*)   *Pretend?* Pretend I'm as good as anybody called Hubbard? Why, my Pa died at Vicksburg. He didn't stay home bleeding the whole state of Alabama with money tricks, and suspected of worse. You think I been worried for that reason?

OSCAR   (*desperately*)   No, no. I— For God's sake don't talk like that—

LAURETTE   You may be the rich of this country, but everybody knows how. Why, the Frenchman, I used to eat dinner with, and his sister, the Countess. What you mean, boy, your folks—?

OSCAR   I didn't mean anything bad. Haven't I just said I wanted to *marry* you? I think you're better than anybody.

LAURETTE   I'm not better than anybody, but I'm as good as piney wood crooks.

OSCAR   (*puts his hand over her mouth, looks toward porch*)   Stop, *please*. We've got to go outside. *Please*—

LAURETTE   (*good-natured again*)   Sometimes you bring out the worst in my nature, Oskie, and make me talk foolish. Squee, it's the truth—I am a little twitchy about coming here and meeting your folks. That's why I'm talking so brave. I ain't been in a place like this before. . . . (*Pats him*) All right, I'll be very good and nice. I would like to go to New Orleans.

(OSCAR *takes her in his arms. The front bell rings, but they don't hear it.*)

OSCAR   Course you would, with me. You love me, honey? (*He leans down to kiss her*) Tell me you love me.

LAURETTE   Now, Oskie, you know this ain't the place or the time for mush—

(BEN *rises at the sound of the bell. As* BEN *comes from the porch,* JAKE *brings in the* BAGTRYS. *As they enter,* OSCAR *is kissing* LAURETTE, *she is giggling, trying to push him away. The* BAGTRYS *stop in the doorway as they see the scene.* BEN *comes to meet them, crosses stage. As he passes* OSCAR *and* LAURETTE, *he shoves* OSCAR.)

BEN   Excuse me. (*As* LAURETTE *jumps away,* REGINA *comes in from porch, tapping* LAVINIA *on the arm as she comes.* BEN *speaks to* BIRDIE) My apologies. We don't always arrange this scene for our guests.

(BIRDIE *smiles nervously.* JOHN *stares at* LAURETTE.)

OSCAR   We were just, I was, we were—

REGINA   (*sharply*)   All right. (*Goes quickly to* BIRDIE) I am happy to have you here, Miss Birdie.

(BIRDIE *curtsies, puts out her hand, smiles warmly.* LAVINIA *enters room.*)

JOHN   (*bows to* REGINA, BEN, OSCAR, *then speaks to* LAURETTE). Hello, Laurette.

LAURETTE   Hello, John.

JOHN   (*turns to* BIRDIE)   Birdie, this is Miss Sincee.

LAURETTE   Finely, thank you.

(BIRDIE *bows.*)

LAVINIA   (*hears* LAURETTE *speak and so hurries to her*) An honor to have you here, Miss Birdie—

REGINA   (*sharply*)   *This* is Miss Birdie, Mama.

LAVINIA   (*who is shaking hands with* LAURETTE, *looks bewildered*)   Oh. Sorry. I—

(OSCAR *bumps into* LAVINIA, *who is coming toward* BIRDIE.)

BIRDIE   I'm sorry we're late. I just couldn't seem to get dressed—

REGINA   Do come out now for the music.

(*They move out together.* LAVINIA *speaks to* BIRDIE.)

LAVINIA   Come, ma'am. And you, Miss— (*Brightly, to* BIRDIE.) Is the other lady your sister?

LAURETTE (*annoyed, shoves* OSCAR) What's the matter with you?

OSCAR Oh. Mama, this is Miss Laurette Sincee. She's a visitor in town.

LAVINIA Who's she visiting?

BEN Us.

(BEN *reaches the porch door, stands aside to let* LAVINIA *pass him. She looks puzzled, passes on to porch.* LAURETTE, OSCAR, REGINA, JOHN, *are now seated on the porch.* LAVINIA *sits near them.* BIRDIE *and* BEN *stand for a minute listening to the music.*)

BIRDIE Nice. To have a special night, just to play music— I've heard your father is a very cultured gentleman. Have you been able, did he, speak of the matter that I—

BEN Yes. We will make the loan.

BIRDIE (*turns radiant—softly*) Oh, what fine news! You can't imagine how worried I've been. I am very grateful to you, sir—

BEN You don't have to be. It is a good loan for Hubbard Company, or my father wouldn't be taking it. We'll meet tomorrow, you and I, and work out the details.

BIRDIE Oh, you won't have any trouble with me, Mr. Ben.

BEN You wanted five thousand dollars, Miss Birdie. I have asked my father to lend you ten thousand.

BIRDIE (*puzzled—worried*) Oh. Mr. Ben, I don't need—

BEN (*quickly*) You can take five now, but if you should happen to need more, it will be there for you.

BIRDIE But I won't need ten thousand dollars. No, indeed I won't. It's very kind of you, but—

BEN (*carefully*) You will only get five. I will keep the rest waiting for you. That's the way these things are done—(*smiles*)—sometimes.

BIRDIE But it's bad enough to owe five thousand, not less ten—

BEN *You will only owe five.* Now don't worry about it. Will you take my advice now about something else? Don't speak to my father about the loan. It is all arranged. And he's a man of such culture, as you say, that talk of money would disturb him on his music night.

BIRDIE (*gently*) Oh, of course. After all, it's a party, and as worried and pushing as I am, I wouldn't ever have talked business with him at a party.

BEN (*smiles down at her*) Good breeding is very useful. Thank you, Miss Birdie.

BIRDIE (*gently*) No, sir. It is I who must thank you.

(*He bows, stands aside, indicates porch. She moves to it, sits down.* BEN *stands in the doorway. The music continues. After a minute we see* OSCAR *trying to move into the room. He leans over, bends down, moves rapidly into room, passes* BEN. LAURETTE *turns and* OSCAR *beckons to her to come into room.*)

OSCAR Papa going to play all night? (*Crosses to get a drink*) Laurette's getting restless, sitting there.

BEN She's not accustomed to a sitting position? Have another drink. I got a feeling you're going to need it.

LAURETTE (*enters the room from the porch*) Squee. I don't like this punch. It don't mean anything.

BEN Can I put in a little brandy? I think that would make it mean more.

(MARCUS *appears on the porch, comes up the aisle of chairs. He bows to* BIRDIE *and to* JOHN, *comes into room.* OSCAR *rushes to get him a drink of punch.*)

OSCAR Papa, this is Miss Sincee.

MARCUS (*finishes drink, hands glass to* OSCAR) How do you do?

LAURETTE Finely, thank you. (MARCUS *stares at her. She becomes very nervous.*) I love music, Mr. Hubbard. I had an uncle who played. *He* taught me to love music.

OSCAR (*too brightly*) Did he play the violin, like Papa?

LAURETTE Er. Er. No. He had a little drum.

OSCAR (*very fast*) He liked Mozart. You told me, remember?

LAURETTE Yeah. Sure did.

(REGINA *and* BIRDIE, *followed by* JOHN *and* LAVINIA, *come in from the porch.*)

MARCUS Miss Sincee pleases me. Her uncle played Mozart on a little drum. Have you ever heard of that, Miss Bagtry?

BIRDIE Oh. Well, *I* haven't, but I'm sure there must be such an arrangement.

MARCUS (*looks at her with interest*) That's very kind of you, to be so sure. Do you play any instrument, Miss Bagtry? Not the little drum?

BIRDIE Yes, sir. Not well. The piano.

MARCUS Then you would oblige me—(*she smiles, moves toward the piano, quickly*)—some other night, very soon.

BIRDIE (*very flustered*) Yes. Yes, sir.

OSCAR It's a coincidence, ain't it, that Laurette's Papa liked Mozart?

REGINA (*to* LAURETTE) I thought it was your uncle? Was your Papa the same as your uncle?

LAURETTE What do you mean? Do you mean mon père was on one side of my family, and mon oncle on the other? I can understand *that*.

BEN (*fills her glass from the brandy decanter*) Your family were French?

LAURETTE No. I learned that from a French gentleman who came from France. I don't know where he is now. I liked him.

BEN Perhaps we could locate him for you.

LAURETTE No. He married money.

REGINA Oh, dear. All foreigners do, I guess. Light wines and light money.

LAURETTE I never blamed him. I figured, well— (*Looks at* REGINA) You've had some bad experiences with Frenchmen?

(REGINA, BEN, *and* MARCUS *laugh.*)

BIRDIE (*to* MARCUS—*making conversation*) John's been to Europe, you know.

MARCUS I didn't know.

BIRDIE Yes, he was. Just a few months before the war. Paris, France; London, England; St. Petersburg, Russia; Florence, Italy; Lake Como, Switzerland—

MARCUS Your geography is remarkable.

BIRDIE Oh, I only know because John kept a book. Pictures and notes and menus—if the war hadn't come, and my Papa had lived, I would have gone to Europe. It was planned for me to study water color.

MARCUS Water color?

BIRDIE Small water color. I like small water color.

MARCUS   Is that very different from large water color?

LAURETTE   (*belligerently*) She means she likes small water color. What's the matter with that?

BIRDIE   (*smiles at her*) Yes. (*To* MARCUS) You've been to Europe, Mr. Hubbard?

MARCUS   (*laughs*) No, but I'm going. Might even settle down there. Yes, Regina?

REGINA   (*looks at* JOHN, *nervously*) Maybe some day, Papa. Chicago first.

MARCUS   Of course, we'll take our residence in Greece, but some place gayer, for Regina, at first. Perhaps you'd advise us, Captain Bagtry?

JOHN   I'd like to, sir. But I have no memory of Europe.

MARCUS   (*turns elaborately in his chair*) Something unpleasant took it from your mind?

JOHN   No, sir. I just don't remember. It's as if I had never been there.

LAVINIA   I used to have a good memory. (*Quickly*) I still have. Most of the time.

MARCUS   (*very politely, to* JOHN.) Captain Bagtry, does anything stay in your memory, anything at all?

JOHN   (*looks at* MARCUS, *but the tone has been polite*) The war.

REGINA   (*softly*) Only the war?

LAVINIA   (*to* JOHN, *motherly*) Well, I just bet. That's natural: you rode off so young.

JOHN   (*turns to her*) Yes, ma'am. I can't remember the years before, and the years after have just passed like a wasted day. But the morning I rode off, and for three years, three months, and eight days after, well, I guess I remember every soldier, every gun, every meal, even every dream I had at night—

(BEN *is pouring* LAURETTE *another drink.* OSCAR *is trying to keep her from having it. She pushes* OSCAR's *hand.*)

LAURETTE   I wouldn't ever name a boy Oscar. It's silly.

REGINA   Well?

(MARCUS *and* BEN *laugh. The others look embarrassed.* OSCAR *makes an angry move, decides not to speak.*)

LAVINIA   I can't remember why we chose the name. Can you, Marcus?

MARCUS (*to* LAVINIA) Your father's name was Oscar.

LAVINIA (*worried, crushed*) Oh, goodness, yes.

BIRDIE (*embarrassed, speaks quickly*) John's just wonderful about the war, Mr. Hubbard. Just as good as having a history book. He was everywhere: Vicksburg, Chattanooga, Atlanta.

MARCUS And he remembers it *all?* What now seems to you the most important of your battles, Captain Bagtry?

JOHN (*annoyed*) I don't know. But there's no need for us to talk about the war, sir.

MARCUS Oh, I'm interested. I know more of the Greek wars than I do of our own.

LAURETTE Bet you anything there's a good reason for that. There's a good reason for everything in this vale of tears.

(MARCUS *turns to stare at her.*)

BIRDIE John, Mr. Hubbard says he's interested. Bet he'd like to hear about Vicksburg, just the way you always tell it to Mama and me.

(JAKE *appears at the door.*)

JAKE Supper's laid out, waiting.

MARCUS (*to* JOHN) People remember what made them happy, and you were happy in the war, weren't you?

JOHN Yes, sir. I was happy. I thought we would win.

MARCUS I never did. Never, from the first foolish talk to the last foolish day. (JOHN *sharply turns away*) I have disturbed you. I'm most sorry. I speak the truth—whenever I can.

BIRDIE (*hastily*) Oh, John doesn't mind. He means—well, you see, it's hard for us to understand anybody who thought we'd lose—

JOHN (*sharply*) It's still hard for a soldier to understand.

BIRDIE (*quickly*) John means once a soldier, always a soldier. He wants to go to Brazil right now. Of course you know, Mr. Hubbard, the radical people down there are trying to abolish slavery, and ruin the country. John wants to fight for his ideals.

MARCUS Why don't you choose the other side? Every man needs to win once in his life.

JOHN (*angrily*) I don't like that way of saying it. I don't necessarily fight for slavery, I fight for a way of life.

MARCUS Supper, Captain. (*Turns, calls to the porch*)
  Put away the music, gentlemen, and have a little more
  to eat. (*Turns back to* REGINA) What is disturbing you,
  Regina?

(LAVINIA, BIRDIE, OSCAR, *and* LAURETTE *exit to dining room.*)

REGINA (*sharply*) Nothing.

(BEN *exits.*)

MARCUS (*looks at* JOHN) You disapprove of me, Captain?

JOHN I am in your house, sir, and you forced me into
  this kind of talk.

(PENNIMAN *and* JUGGER *come through the room, go into
  the dining room.*)

MARCUS Well, I disapprove of you. Your people deserved
  to lose their war and their world. It was a backward
  world, getting in the way of history. Appalling that you
  still don't realize it. Really, people should read more
  books.

REGINA (*angrily*) Papa, I didn't ask John here to listen
  to you lecture and be nasty and insulting.

MARCUS *You* asked him here? You asked *John?* (*Sharply*)
  Come in to supper, Regina.

REGINA (*very sharply*) When I'm ready, Papa. (MARCUS
  *looks at her, hesitates for a second, then goes into din-
  ing room. There is a pause. She goes to* JOHN) I am so
  sorry.

JOHN Why should you be sorry? It's the way you feel, too.

REGINA (*impatiently*) All that damn war nonsense—
  Don't worry about Papa. I'll take care of him. You didn't
  give me a chance to tell you about Chicago—

JOHN You didn't give me a chance to tell you about Brazil.

REGINA Will you stop that foolish joke—

JOHN It may not be a joke. Birdie has a plan. She won't
  tell me about it. Anyway, she says there's going to be
  money to run Lionnet and enough for me to borrow a
  little. I'll go on down to Brazil right away. Cod Carter
  says there's no trick in getting a commission with good
  pay. The planters there are looking for Confederate
  officers. I want to be with fighting men again. I'm lonely
  for them.

REGINA Now you stop frightening me. I'm going to Chicago, and a month later you're coming and we'll get married. When Papa finds out he'll have a fit. Then we'll come on home for a while, and I'll talk him out of his fit—

JOHN (*gently, smiles*) Now you're joking. Don't talk silly, honey.

REGINA (*softly*) You don't want to come with me? You don't want to marry me?

JOHN (*after a second*) You don't ask that seriously.

REGINA (*softly*) Answer me, please.

JOHN No. I don't. I never said I did. (*Comes to her*) I don't want to talk this way, but I don't want to lie, either. Honey, I like you so much, but—I shouldn't have let us get like this. You're not in löve with me. I'm no good for you—

REGINA I am in love with you. I've never loved before, and I won't love again.

JOHN My darling child, everybody thinks that, the first time. You're a lonely girl and I'm the first man you've liked. You can have anybody you want—

REGINA John. Come away with me. We'll be alone. And after a while, if you still don't want me, then— (*Softly*) I've never pleaded for anything in my life before. I might hold it against you.

JOHN Oh, Regina, don't speak of pleading. You go away. By the time you come back, you'll be in love with somebody else, and I'll be gone.

REGINA (*stares at him*) Where did you say Miss Birdie was getting this money, this money for you to travel with?

JOHN I don't know where: she won't tell me. But she says we'll have five thousand dollars this week.

REGINA (*after a second*) Five thousand?

JOHN (*nods*) I'd guess she's arranged something about the Gilbert Stuart or the West. We haven't anything but the portraits—

REGINA Is that what you'd guess? Well, I'd guess different. So she's planning to get you away from me?

JOHN Nobody's *planning* anything. Oh, look, honey. This isn't any good. We'll go home now—

REGINA (*quickly, looking toward dining room*) Papa's

coming. Please go in to supper now. It will be bad for
me if you make any fuss or left now— (*Softly*) We'll
talk tomorrow. I love you. Go in to supper.

(MARCUS *appears in the dining-room door.*)

JOHN (*who has his back to the door*) I'm sorry, honey,
if— (*He turns, moves across room, passes* MARCUS *in the
doorway, disappears into the dining room.*)

(MARCUS *stares at* REGINA; *she does not look at him.*)

MARCUS Who is sillier, who is more dead, the captain or
his cousin? (*She doesn't answer him*) You have a reason
for not joining us at supper?

REGINA I wanted to talk to—to Captain Bagtry.

MARCUS Can he talk of anything but war?

REGINA Have you agreed to make Ben's loan on Lionnet?

MARCUS Ben's loan? Of course I'll make it. It is good for
me, and bad for them. Got nothing to do with Ben.

REGINA No? Have you asked yourself why Ben wants it
so much?

MARCUS I am not interested in Ben's motives. As long as
they benefit me, he is welcome to them.

REGINA How much money did he say Miss Birdie had
asked for?

MARCUS Ten thousand. (REGINA *smiles*) Why does this
interest you?

REGINA (*rises*) Don't make the loan, Papa. I don't like
the girl. I think she's come here tonight to make fun of
us. She's snubbing all of us, laughing up her sleeve. Why
should you pay her to do it?

MARCUS (*stares at her*) That's not true and I don't think
you think it is. You're lying to me about something. Stop
it. It hurts me. Tell me why you were talking to that
man, why he called you honey—

REGINA (*carefully*) Ben is sometimes smarter than you
are, and you are so sure he isn't that you get careless
about him. (*Nods toward dining room*) Bagtry doesn't
know about *your* loan on Lionnet, but the girl told him
she was getting five thousand dollars this week. *Five
thousand dollars, not ten.* I'd like to bet the extra five is
meant for Ben to keep. (*Carefully, as he stares at her*)
You're getting older, Papa, and maybe you're getting

tired and don't think as fast. I guess that happens to everybody. You'll have to start watching Ben even more—

MARCUS   (*sharply*)   All right, Regina.

(PENNIMAN *and* JUGGER *come in from the dining room. They stand awkwardly, not knowing what to do.* REGINA *goes into dining room.*)

PENNIMAN   (*hesitates*)   Shall we—would you like us to continue the music?

MARCUS   As soon as you have finished overeating.

(PENNIMAN *coughs, embarrassed.* JUGGER *starts forward angrily, then stops, follows* PENNIMAN *out to the porch.* LAVINIA *comes in from the dining room.*)

LAVINIA   I think that Miss Laurette has a touch of heart trouble. I asked the poor child what she was doing for it. She said she was trying to see if good strong drinks would help. I've never heard that, although Ben says it's a good cure. She's a nice little thing.

MARCUS   You've always been a good judge of people, Lavinia, but that's true of all the pure in heart, isn't it?

(LAURETTE, *followed by* OSCAR, *comes into the room. She is steady, but the liquor has blinded her a little, and she bumps into things.* OSCAR *follows her, very nervous, staring at* MARCUS, *who does not turn around.*)

LAVINIA   (*speaks to* LAURETTE *only because she is nervous*) Hello.

(LAURETTE *now finds herself near the piano. She strikes a note. Pleased, she presses her right hand on the keyboard. Delighted, she presses both hands.* OSCAR *jumps toward her.*)

LAURETTE   Hello . . . I never had opportunities . . . (OSCAR *grabs both her hands, she pulls them away, pounds again, grins, indicates* MARCUS) Your Papa likes music, she says.

MARCUS   (*to* OSCAR)   Is there any effective way of stopping that?

(LAURETTE *throws off* OSCAR, *comes over to* MARCUS.)

LAURETTE   Oskie says he wants to marry little old Laurette.

MARCUS   Does little old Laurette think that fortunate?

LAURETTE   (*laughs—puts her hand through his arm*)

Sometimes yes, sometimes no. We're going on down to New Orleans.

(BEN *and* BIRDIE *come in from the dining room.*)

MARCUS   (*takes* LAURETTE's *hand from his arm*)   This will sound very rude but I have a nervous dislike of being grabbed.

LAURETTE   Oh, sure. Me, too. Can't stand people pressing me unless I know about it, I mean. (*Glares at* OSCAR) Don't you ever press me, Oskie, unless I know about it.

MARCUS   That reminds me. I'm told you work for a living. That is good: Oscar is not a rich man.

LAURETTE   (*laughs*)   Rich? How could he be, on that stinking slave salary you pay him? That's why you're sure to repent and help us, Oskie says. When you die you're going to leave it to him anyway, so why not now, Oskie says?

MARCUS   (*softly*)   Oscar is a liar. Always has been. (BIRDIE *moves toward porch*) And he steals a little. Nothing much, not enough to be respectable. But you know all that, of course.

LAVINIA   Oh, Marcus. (*Turns to* BIRDIE)   My husband makes little jokes. All the time—

OSCAR   (*very loudly, to* MARCUS)   It's not true. It's just not true—

MARCUS   (*to* BIRDIE)   Miss Bagtry, don't you find that people always think you're joking when you speak the truth in a soft voice?

BIRDIE   (*very embarrassed*)   No, sir. I—

MARCUS   (*back to* LAURETTE)   If you want him, Miss Laurette, do have him.

OSCAR   (*with dignity*)   Come on, Laurette. I'll settle this later.

(MARCUS *laughs.*)

LAURETTE   Well, I'll just about say you will. A Papa talking about his son! No animal would talk about their own son that way. I heard tales about you ever since I was born, but—

OSCAR   (*frantic*)   Come on, Laurette.

LAURETTE   You old bastard.

(MARCUS *slowly rises.*)

LAVINIA (*to* LAURETTE) Dear child—

LAURETTE (*to* MARCUS) Everybody in this country knows
how you got rich, bringing in salt and making poor, dying people give up everything for it. Right in the middle of the war, men dying for you, and you making
their kinfolk give you all their goods and money—and
I heard how they suspected you of worse, and you only
just got out of a hanging rope. (*Points to* OSCAR) Why,
the first night he slept with me, I didn't even want to
speak to him because of you and your doings. My uncle
used to tell me about—

BEN Go on, Oscar. Get out.

(JOHN *and* REGINA *come in from dining room.*)

MARCUS (*to* OSCAR) Take that girl out of here. Then
come back. And come back quickly.

(OSCAR *stares at him, starts to speak, changes his mind.
Then he hurries to* LAURETTE, *takes her arm, moves her
out.* JOHN *crosses to* BIRDIE.)

LAVINIA (*in an odd tone*) Why, Marcus. The girl only
told the truth. Salt is just a word, it's in the Bible quite a
lot. And that other matter, why, death, is also just a
word. And—

MARCUS You grow daring, Lavinia. (*Moves toward her*)
Now stop that prattling or go to your room—

BEN (*moves in front of him*) We have guests.

JOHN (*takes* BIRDIE'S *arm, comes forward*) Good night
and thank you, Mrs. Hubbard. (*Coldly, to others*) Good
night.

MARCUS You came to beg a favor, and you stayed to be
amused. Good night.

BIRDIE (*scared*) Mr. Hubbard, please . . .

JOHN Came to ask a favor? From you? Who in this county
would be so dishonored? If you were not an old man,
Mr. Hubbard, I—

MARCUS There is never so great a hero as the man who
fought on a losing side.

BIRDIE (*goes to* JOHN—*desperate*) Stop it, John. Go outside. Wait for me in the carriage.

JOHN I don't want you here. Come on, Birdie—

BIRDIE   (*firmly*)   I want to stay for a few minutes. Please
   go outside. *Please. Please.*

(*He stares at her, then he turns, moves quickly out of the
   room.* MARCUS *is watching* REGINA. REGINA *looks at* MAR-
   CUS, *then turns and moves quickly after* JOHN. MARCUS
   wheels around as if to stop REGINA.)

BIRDIE   Mr. Hubbard, I am sorry. John is upset. You know
   that his twin brother was killed that night in the massacre, and any mention of it—

MARCUS   (*sharply*)   What night do you speak of, Miss
   Birdie, and what massacre?

BIRDIE   (*desperately*)   Oh, I don't know. I—I'm just so
   sorry it has been unpleasant. I was hoping we could all
   be nice friends. Your family and mine—

MARCUS   (*smiles*)   Your mother hasn't bowed to me in the
   forty years I've lived in this town. Does she wish to be
   my nice friend now?

BIRDIE   (*desperate*)   Mama is old-fashioned. I'll speak to
   her and after a bit— (*Pauses, looks down*) Oh. I've said
   the wrong thing again. I don't know how to— (*Turns
   to him, simply*) I guess I just better say it simple, the
   way it comes to me. I didn't only come tonight for the
   loan. I *wanted* to come. I was frightened, of course, but,
   well, it was a big holiday for me, and I tried to get all
   dressed up in Mama's old things, and that was why we
   were late because I haven't had a new dress, and I've
   never had a party dress since I was four years old, and
   I had to get the dress without Mama's knowing why or
   where we were going, and I had to sew—

MARCUS   Then it *is* too bad you troubled yourself, because
   I have bad news for you: I have decided not to make
   the loan.

(BIRDIE *draws back, turns to* BEN, *starts to speak, puts her
   hands to her face.*)

BEN   (*slowly*)   Why? Why? You said yourself—

BIRDIE   (*moves toward him*)   Oh, please, Mr. Hubbard.
   Please. I went around all day telling our people they
   might be paid and— I'll give more, whatever you want—

MARCUS   That is unjust of you. I am not bargaining.

BEN (*angrily, to* MARCUS) I want to know why you have changed your mind. •

MARCUS I will tell you, in time. (*Turns to* BIRDIE) I am sorry to disappoint you. Please come another night, without a motive, just for the music.

BIRDIE Yes, I had a motive. Why shouldn't I have? It was why I was asked here— Oh, I mustn't talk proud. I have no right to. Look, Mr. Hubbard, I'll do anything. I'm sure you like good pictures: we have a Stuart and a West, and a little silver left. Couldn't I give—couldn't I bring them to you—

MARCUS (*gently, hurt*) Miss Birdie, Miss Birdie, please spare us both.

BIRDIE (*softly*) I was going to use the first money to buy molasses and sugar. All that land and cotton and we're starving. It sounds crazy, to need even molasses—

MARCUS Everybody with cotton is starving.

BIRDIE (*angrily*) That's just a way of using a word. That isn't what I mean. I mean starving. (*She looks up at him, her voice changes, sighs*) I should have known I couldn't do anything right. I never have. I'm sorry to have told you such things about us. You lose your manners when you're poor. (*Goes to* LAVINIA) Thank you, ma'am.

LAVINIA (*smiles gently, takes her hand*) Good night, child. You ride over and see me, or come down by the river and we'll read together.

BIRDIE (*smiles, crosses to* BEN) Thank you, Mr. Ben. I know you acted as my good friend.

MARCUS (*laughs*) Good night.

(*She nods, runs out.*)

LAVINIA (*after a second*) Goodness, Marcus. Couldn't you have—it's pig mean, being poor. Takes away your dignity.

MARCUS That's correct, Lavinia. And a good reason for staying rich.

PENNIMAN'S VOICE We're waiting for you, Mr. Hubbard.

MARCUS (*calling out*) That will be all for tonight.

(REGINA *appears from the hall.*)

REGINA (*to* MARCUS) I didn't intend you to insult them and make enemies of them.

MARCUS Why are you so disturbed about the Bagtrys?
(BEN *laughs*) You are amused?

BEN Yes. I am amused.

MARCUS All right. Enjoy yourself—for a few minutes.
(PENNIMAN *and* JUGGER *appear carrying their instru-
ments.* MARCUS *turns to them*) The Mozart was carelessly performed. The carriage is waiting to take you to
the station. Good night.

JUGGER "Carelessly performed." What do you know about
music? Nothing, and we're just here to pretend you do.
Glad to make a little money once a month— (*Angrily*)
I won't do it any more, do you hear me?

MARCUS Very well. Good night.

(JUGGER *moves quickly out.* PENNIMAN *comes forward,*
nervously.)

PENNIMAN He didn't mean— Gil is tired— Why, we're
just as happy to come here— (*No answer. Desperately*)
Well, see you next month, sir. Just as usual. Huh?

(*When* MARCUS *doesn't answer,* PENNIMAN *sighs, exits as*
OSCAR *appears from porch.*)

OSCAR (*rushes toward* BEN) Trying to ruin my life, are
you? Pouring liquor down her. Come on outside and
fight it out like a man. I'll beat you up for it, the way
you deserve—

LAVINIA (*as if she had come out of a doze*) Oh, goodness! The blood of brothers. (*To* BEN) You in trouble,
Ben? (*Sees* OSCAR) Oh, *you're* in trouble, Oscar.

OSCAR Come on—

BEN Oh, shut up.

(MARCUS *laughs.*)

OSCAR (*turns on* MARCUS, *angrily*) You laugh. I told you
he had his eye on Birdie and Lionnet, and me getting it
for him. So I fool him by bringing Laurette here. And
then *he* fools *you*: gets Laurette drunk, and you get mad.
That's just what he wanted you to do. And you did it for
him. I think the joke's kind of on you.

REGINA You must have told the truth once before in your
life, Oscar, but I can't remember it.

MARCUS (*to* BEN) You're full of tricks these days. Did
you get the girl drunk?

BEN Just as good for Oscar to marry a silly girl who owns cotton as a silly girl who doesn't even own the mattress on which she—

(OSCAR *springs toward* BEN, *grabs his shoulder.*)

MARCUS (*to* OSCAR) Will you stop running about and pulling at people? Go outside and shoot a passing nigger if your blood is throwing clots into your head.

OSCAR I'm going to kill Ben if he doesn't stop—

MARCUS Are you denying the girl makes use of a mattress, or do you expect to go through life killing every man who knows she does?

OSCAR (*screaming*) Papa, stop it! I am deeply and sincerely in love.

MARCUS In one minute I shall put you out of the room. (*Looks at* BEN) So that was the way it was supposed to work? Or better than that: the girl was to borrow ten thousand from me and you were to keep five of it, and take your chances on her being a fool, and nobody finding out.

BEN (*slowly*) I understand now. (*Softly to* REGINA) Bagtry told *you.* Yes? (REGINA *nods, and smiles, sits down.*)

MARCUS Your tricks are getting nasty and they bore me. I don't like to be bored: I've told you that before.

BEN (*shrugs*) I want something for myself. I shouldn't think you were the man to blame me for that.

MARCUS I wouldn't have, if you hadn't always been such a failure at getting it. (*Goes to* BEN) I'm tired of your games, do you hear me? You're a clerk in my store and that you'll remain. You won't get the chance to try anything like this again. But in case you anger me once more, there won't be the job in the store, and you won't be here. Is that clear?

BEN (*slowly*) Very clear.

OSCAR (*who has been thinking*) Papa, you couldn't condemn a woman for a past that was filled with loathing for what society forced upon her; a woman of inner purity made to lead a life of outward shame?

MARCUS What are you talking about?

REGINA He's read a book.

MARCUS (*softly*) At nine years old I was carrying water

for two bits a week. I took the first dollar I ever had and
went to the paying library to buy a card. When I was
twelve I was working out in the fields, and that same
year I taught myself Latin and French. At fourteen I
was driving mules all day and most of the night, but
that was the year I learned my Greek, read my classics,
taught myself— Think what I must have wanted for sons.
And then think what I got. One unsuccessful trickster,
one proud illiterate. No, I don't think Oscar's ever read
a book.

LAVINIA   He did, Marcus. I used to read my Bible to him.

MARCUS   (*to* OSCAR) If you want to go away with this
girl, what's detaining you?

OSCAR   (*eagerly*) Your permission, sir.

MARCUS   Talk sense. Do you mean money?

OSCAR   Just a loan. Then we'd ship on down to New Orleans—

MARCUS   How much?

OSCAR   Could invest in a little business Laurette knows
about— (REGINA *laughs loudly*) Ten thousand could
start me off fine, Papa—

MARCUS   There will be a thousand dollars for you, in an
envelope, on that table by six in the morning. Get on
the early train. Send a Christmas card each year to an
aging man who now wishes you to go upstairs.

OSCAR   (*starts to protest, changes his mind*) Well, thank
you. Seems kind of strange to be saying good-bye after
twenty-five years—

REGINA   (*gaily*) Oh, don't think of it that way. We'll be
coming to see you some day. You'll have ten children,
and five of the leaner ones may be yours.

LAVINIA   Good-bye, son. I'm sorry if— I'm sorry.

OSCAR   I'll write you, Mama. (*To* BEN, *sharply*) You've bul-
lied me since the day I was born. But before I leave—
(*Fiercely*)—you're going to do what I tell you. You're
going to be on the station platform tomorrow morning.
You're going to be there to apologize to Laurette.

MARCUS   Goodness, what a thousand dollars won't do!

OSCAR   And if you're not ready on time—(*takes a pistol
from his pocket*)—I'll get you out of bed with this. And

then you won't apologize to her standing up, but on
your knees—

MARCUS (*violently, turning around*) Put that gun away.
How dare you, in this house—

BEN (*smiles*) You've always been frightened of guns,
Papa. Ever since that night, wasn't it?

LAVINIA That's true, ever since that night.

MARCUS (*very angry*) *Put that gun away. And get upstairs. Immediately.*

OSCAR (*to* BEN) See you at the station. (*He crosses room,
exits.*)

BEN (*after a second*) No need to be so nervous. I could
have taken the gun away from him.

LAVINIA And they had hot tar and clubs and ropes that
night—

MARCUS *Stop your crazy talk, Lavinia.*

LAVINIA (*softly*) I don't like that word, Marcus. No, I
don't. I think you use it just to hurt my feelings.

BEN (*smiles*) He's upset, Mama. Old fears come back,
strong.

MARCUS (*slowly, to* BEN) You're wearing me thin.

REGINA (*yawns*) Oh, don't you and Ben start again. (*She
pats* BEN *on the arm*) You know Papa always wins. But
maybe you'll have your time some day. Try to get along,
both of you. After Mama and I leave you'll be here alone
together.

MARCUS I don't know, darling. I'm going to miss you. I
think I may join you.

REGINA (*turns, hesitantly*) Join me? But—

BEN That would spoil the plan.

MARCUS (*to* REGINA) I'll let you and Lavinia go ahead.
Then I'll come and get you and we'll take a turn in New
York. And then Regina and I will go on to Europe and
you'll come back here, Lavinia.

LAVINIA Oh, Marcus, you just can't have been listening to
me. I been telling you since yesterday, and for years before *that*—

MARCUS (*looks at* REGINA) You want me to come, darling?

REGINA   (*nervously*) Of course. When were you thinking
of coming, Papa? Soon or—

BEN   (*to* REGINA—*laughs*) I'm dying to see you get out of
this one, honey.

MARCUS   (*angrily, to* BEN) What are you talking about?

BEN   I'm going to be sorry to miss the sight of your face
when Regina produces the secret bridegroom. (MARCUS
wheels to stare at REGINA) Oh, you know about it. You
guessed tonight. Captain Bagtry. I don't think he wants
to marry her. I don't think he even wants to sleep with
her any more. But he's a weak man and— (MARCUS *is
advancing toward him*) That won't do any good. I'm going to finish. Yesterday, if you remember, Regina wanted
you to make the loan to the girl. Tonight, when she
found out John Bagtry wanted to use a little of the
money to leave here, and her, she talked you out of it.

REGINA   *Ben, be still.* Ben— (*Goes swiftly to* MARCUS)
Don't listen, Papa. I have seen John, I told you that. I
like him, yes. But don't you see what Ben is doing? He
wanted to marry me off to money, he's angry—

BEN   (*to* MARCUS) I'm telling the truth. The whole town's
known it for a year.

LAVINIA   Don't, Benjamin, don't! Marcus, you look so bad—

BEN   You do look bad. Go up to him, Regina, put your arms
around him. Tell him you've never really loved anybody
else, and never will. Lie to him, just for tonight. Tell him
you'll never get in bed with anybody ever again—

(MARCUS *slaps* BEN *sharply across the face.*)

LAVINIA   (*desperately*) God help us! Marcus! Ben!

BEN   (*softly*) I won't forget that. As long as I live.

MARCUS   Lock your door tonight, and be out of here before I am down in the morning. Wherever you decide to
go, be sure it's far away. Get yourself a modest job, because wherever you are, I'll see to it that you never get
any other.

BEN   I spent twenty years lying and cheating to help make
you rich. I was trying to outwit you, Papa, but I guess
I couldn't do it. (*He exits.*)

LAVINIA   Twenty years, he said. Then it would be my
fault, my sin, too— (*She starts for hall door, calling*)

Benjamin! I want to talk to you, son. You're my first-born, going away—

(*She disappears. There is a long pause.* MARCUS *sits down.*)

MARCUS How could you let him touch you? When did it happen? How could you— *Answer me.*

REGINA (*wearily*) Are they questions that can be answered?

MARCUS A dead man, a foolish man, an empty man from an idiot world. A man who wants nothing but war, any war, just a war. A man who believes in nothing, and never will. A man in space—

REGINA (*softly—comes to him*) All right, Papa. That's all true, and I know it. And I'm in love with him, and I want to marry him. (*He puts his hands over his face. She speaks coldly*) Now don't take on so. It just won't do. You let me go away, as we planned. I'll get married. After a while we'll come home and we'll live right here—

MARCUS *Are you crazy?* Do you think I'd stay in this house with you and—

REGINA Otherwise, I'll go away. I say I will, and you know I will. I'm not frightened to go. But if I go that way I won't ever see you again. And you don't want that: I don't think you could stand that. My way, we can be together. You'll get used to it, and John won't worry us. There'll always be you and me— (*Puts her hand on his shoulder*) You must have known I'd marry some day, Papa. Why, I've never seen you cry before. It'll just be like going for a little visit, and before you know it I'll be home again, and it will all be over. You know? Maybe next year, or the year after, you and I'll make that trip to Greece, just the two of us. (*Smiles*) Now it's all settled. Kiss me good night, darling. (*She kisses him, he does not move. Then she moves toward door as* LAVINIA *comes in.*)

LAVINIA Ben won't let me talk to him. He'd feel better if he talked, if he spoke out— I'm his Mama and I got to take my responsibility for what—

REGINA Mama, I think we'll be leaving for Chicago sooner

than we thought. We'll start getting ready tomorrow morning. Good night. (*She exits.*)

LAVINIA (*softly, after a minute*) Did you forget to tell her that I can't go with her? Didn't you tell them all where I'm going? I think you better do that, Marcus—

MARCUS (*softly—very tired*) I don't feel well. Please stop jabbering, Lavinia.

LAVINIA You tell Regina tomorrow. You tell her how you promised me. (*Desperately*) Marcus. It's all I've lived for. And it can't wait now. I'm getting old, and I've got to go and do my work.

MARCUS (*wearily*) It isn't easy to live with you, Lavinia. It really isn't. Leave me alone.

LAVINIA (*gently*) I know. We weren't ever meant to be together. You see, being here gives me—well, I won't use bad words, but it's always made me feel like I sinned. And God wants you to make good your sins before you die. That's why I got to go now.

MARCUS I've stood enough of that. Please don't ever speak of it again.

LAVINIA Ever speak of it? But you swore to me over and over again.

MARCUS Did you ever think I meant that nonsense?

LAVINIA But I'm going!

MARCUS You're never going. Dr. Seckles knows how strange you've been, the whole town knows you're crazy. Now I don't want to listen to any more of that talk ever. I try to leave you alone, try to leave me alone. If you worry me any more with it, I'll have to talk to the doctor and ask him to send you away. (*Softly— crying*) Please go to bed now, and don't walk around all night again.

LAVINIA (*stares at him*) Coralee. . . . Coralee! He never ever meant me to go. He says I can't go. Coralee— (*She starts to move slowly, then she begins to run*) Coralee, are you in bed—

Curtain

Act Three

SCENE: *Same as Act One, early the next morning.*
At rise of curtain, LAVINIA *is moving about in the living room.*

LAVINIA   (*singing*)
> Got one life, got to hold it bold
> Got one life, got to hold it bold
> Lord, my year must come.

(*She comes on the porch. She is carrying a small Bible.*)
> Got one life, got to hold it bold
> Got one life, got to hold it bold
> Lord, my year must come.

(BEN, *carrying a valise, comes from the living room.* LA-VINIA *gets up.*)

LAVINIA   All night I been waiting. You wouldn't let your Mama talk to you.

BEN   I put all my stuff in the ironing room. I'll send for it when I find a place.

LAVINIA   (*softly*) Take me with you, son. As far as Alta-loosa. There I'll get off, and there I'll stay. Benjamin, he couldn't bring me back, or send me, or do, or do. He couldn't, if you'd protect me for a while and—

BEN   I, protect you? (*Smiles*) Didn't you hear him last night? Don't you know about me?

LAVINIA   I don't know. I heard so much. I get mixed. I know you're bad off now. (*She reaches up as if to touch his face*) You're my first-born, so it must be my fault some way.

BEN   Do you like me, Mama?

366

LAVINIA (*after a second*) Well. You've grown away from— I loved you, Benjamin.

BEN (*turns away*) Once upon a time.

LAVINIA Take me with you. Take me where I can do my little good. The colored people are forgiving people. And they'll help me. You know, I should have gone after that night, but I stayed for you children. I didn't know then that none of you would ever need a Mama. Well, I'm going now. *I tell you I'm going.* (*Her voice rises*) I spoke with God this night, in prayer. He said I should go no matter. Strait are the gates, He said. Narrow is the way, Lavinia, He said—

BEN (*sharply*) Mama! You're talking loud. (*Turns to her*) Go to bed now. You've had no sleep. I'm late. (*Starts to move.*)

LAVINIA Take me, Benjamin!

BEN (*sharply*) Now go in to Coralee before you get yourself in bad shape and trouble.

LAVINIA You've got to take me. Last night he said he'd never ever meant me to go. Last night he said if ever, then he'd have Dr. Seckles, have him, have him— (*Turns, her fist clenched*) Take me away from here. For ten years he swore, for ten years he swore a lie to me. I told God about that last night, and God's message said, "Go, Lavinia, even if you have to tell the awful truth. If there is no other way, tell the truth."

BEN (*turns slightly*) The truth about what?

LAVINIA I think, now, I should have told the truth that night. But you don't always know how to do things when they're happening. It's not easy to send your own husband into a hanging rope.

BEN What do you mean?

LAVINIA All night long I been thinking I should go right up those steps and tell him what I know. Then he'd have to let me leave or— (*Puts her hands to her face*) I've always been afraid of him, because once or twice—

BEN Of course. But you're not afraid of me.

LAVINIA Oh, I been afraid of you, too. I spent a life afraid. And you know that's funny, Benjamin, because way down deep I'm a woman wasn't made to be afraid.

What are most people afraid of? Well, like your Papa, they're afraid to die. But I'm not afraid to die because my colored friends going to be right there to pray me in.

BEN (*carefully*) Mama, what were you talking about? Telling the truth, a hanging rope—

LAVINIA And if you're not afraid of dying then you're not afraid of anything. (*Sniffs the air*) The river's rising. I can tell by the azalea smell.

BEN (*tensely, angrily*) For God's sake, Mama, try to remember what you were saying, if you were saying anything.

LAVINIA I was saying a lot. I could walk up those steps and tell him I could still send him into a hanging rope unless he lets me go: I could say I saw him that night, and I'll just go and tell everybody I did see him—

BEN *What night?*

LAVINIA The night of the massacre, of course.

BEN (*tensely, sharply*) Where did you see him, how—

LAVINIA You being sharp with me now. And I never been sharp with you. Never—

BEN (*carefully*) Mama. Now listen to me. It's late and there isn't much time. I'm in trouble, bad trouble, and you're in bad trouble. Tell me fast what you're talking about. Maybe I can get us both out of trouble. Maybe. But only if you tell me now. *Now.* And tell me quick and straight. You can go away and I—

LAVINIA (*rises*) I saw him, like I told you, the night of the massacre, on the well-house roof.

BEN All right. I understand what you mean. All right. But there's a lot I don't know or understand.

LAVINIA (*as if she hadn't heard him*) One time last night, I thought of getting his envelope of money, bringing it out here, tearing it up, and watching his face when he saw it at breakfast time. But it's not nice to see people grovel on the ground for money—

BEN The envelope of money? The little envelope of money or the big envelope?

LAVINIA I could get it, tear it up.

BEN (*carefully*) Why not? Get it now and just tear it up.

LAVINIA   And I thought too about giving it to the poor.
But it's evil money and not worthy of the poor.

BEN   No, the poor don't want evil money. That's not the
way.

LAVINIA   (*turns to him*)   Oh, I am glad to hear you say
that, but you can see how I have been tempted when I
thought what the money could do for my little school.
I want my colored children to have many things.

BEN   (*desperately*)   You can have everything for them if—

LAVINIA   Oh, nobody should have everything. All I want
is a nice school place, warm in winter, and a piano, and
books and a good meal every day, hot and fattening.

BEN   (*comes to her, stands in front of her*)   Get up, Mama.
Come here. He'll be awake soon. (LAVINIA *rises, he takes
her by the arms*)   Papa will be awake soon.

LAVINIA   (*looks at him, nods*)   First part of the war I was
so ill I thought it was brave of your Papa to run the
blockade, even though I knew he was dealing with the
enemy to do it. People were dying for salt and I thought
it was good to bring it to them. I didn't know he was
getting eight dollars a bag for it, Benjamin, a little bag.
Imagine taking money for other people's misery.

BEN   (*softly*)   Yes, I know all that, Mama. Everybody
does now.

LAVINIA   (*puzzled*)   But I can't tell what you know, Benjamin. You were away in New Orleans in school and it's
hard for me to put in place what you know and— (BEN
moves impatiently)   So—well, there was the camp where
our boys were being mobilized. It was up the river,
across the swamp fork, back behind the old delta fields.

BEN   Yes, I know where it was. And I know that Union
troops crossed the river and killed the twenty-seven
boys who were training there. And I know that Papa was
on one of his salt-running trips that day and that every
man in the county figured Union troops couldn't have
found the camp unless they were led through to it, and
I know they figured Papa was the man who did the
leading.

LAVINIA   He didn't lead them to the camp. Not on purpose.
No, Benjamin, I am sure of that.

BEN I agree with you. It wouldn't have paid him enough, and he doesn't like danger. So he didn't do it. And he proved to them he wasn't here so he couldn't have done it (*Turns to her*) So now where are we?

LAVINIA They were murder mad the night they found the poor dead boys. They came with hot tar and guns to find your Papa.

BEN (*softly*) But they didn't find him.

LAVINIA But I found him. (*She opens the Bible, holds it up, peers at it.* BEN *comes toward her*) At four-thirty o'clock Coralee and I saw him and heard him, on the well-house roof. We knew he kept money and papers there, and so we guessed right away where to look, and there he was.

BEN (*looks at her, smiles, softly*) And there he was.

LAVINIA So you see I hadn't told a lie, Benjamin. He wasn't ever in the *house*. But maybe half a lie is worse than a real lie.

BEN (*quickly*) Yes, yes. Now how did he get away, and how did he prove to them—

LAVINIA Coralee and I sat on the wet ground, watching him. Oh, it was a terrible thing for me. It was a wet night and Coralee caught cold. I had to nurse her for days afterward, with—

BEN (*looks up at balcony*) Mama! It's got to be quick now. Shall I tell you why? I've got to go unless— Now tell me how did he get away, and how did he prove to them that all the time he had been down Mobile road?

LAVINIA (*opens her Bible*) Twenty minutes to six he climbed down from the roof, unlocked the well-house door, got some money from the envelope, and went on down through the back pines. Coralee and I ran back to the house, shivering and frightened. I didn't know what was going to happen, so we locked all the doors and all the windows and Coralee coughed, and sneezed, and ran a fever.

BEN (*angrily*) I don't give a damn about Coralee's health.

LAVINIA (*gently*) That's the trouble with you, Benjamin. You don't ever care about other folks.

(*There is the sound of a door closing inside the house.*)

BEN (*quietly*) There is not much time left now. Try, Mama, try hard. Tell me how he managed.

LAVINIA (*looks down at the Bible*) Well, three days later, no, two days later, the morning of April 5, 1864, at exactly ten-five—

BEN (*sharply*) What are you reading?

LAVINIA He rode back into town, coming up Mobile road. They were waiting for him and they roped him and searched him. But he had two passes proving he had ridden through Confederate lines the day before the massacre, and didn't leave till after it. The passes were signed by—(*looks at Bible*)—Captain Virgil E. McMullen of the 5th Tennessee from Memphis. They were stamped passes, they were good passes, and they had to let him go. But he had no money when he came home. So Coralee and I just knew he paid Captain Virgil E. McMullen to write those passes. (*Looks down at book*) Virgil E. McMullen, Captain in the 5th Tennessee—

BEN (*tensely—points to Bible*) It's written down there?

LAVINIA Coralee and I were half wild with what was the right thing to do and the wrong. So we wrote it all down here in my Bible and we each put our hand on the Book and swore to it. That made us feel better—

BEN I'm sure of it. Give me the Bible, Mama—

LAVINIA I think there's one in your room, at least there used to be—

BEN Oh, Mama. For God's sake. I need it. It's the only proof we've got, and even then he'll—

LAVINIA You don't need half this proof. That's the trouble with your kind of thinking, Benjamin. My, I could just walk down the street, tell the story to the first people I met. They'd believe me, and they'd believe Coralee. We're religious women and everybody knows it. (*Smiles*) And then they'd want to believe us, nothing would give them so much pleasure as, as, as, well, calling on your Papa. I think people always believe what they want to believe, don't you? I don't think I'd have any trouble, if you stood behind me, and gave me courage to do the right talking.

BEN (*laughs*) I'll be behind you. But I'd like the Bible behind me. Come, Mama, give it to me now. I need it for us (*Slowly she hands the Bible to him*) All right. Now I'd like to have that envelope.

LAVINIA But what has the money got to do with—I don't understand why the envelope—I'm trying hard to understand everything, but I can't see what it has—

BEN I can't either. So let's put it this way: it would make me feel better to have it. There's nothing makes you feel better at this hour of the morning than an envelope of money.

LAVINIA (*thinks*) Oh. Well. (*Points into living room*) It's in the small upper left-hand drawer of your Papa's desk. But I don't know where he keeps the key.

BEN (*laughs*) That's very negligent of you. We won't need the key. (*Takes her hand, takes her under balcony*) Now call Papa. I'll be back in a minute.

LAVINIA Oh, I couldn't do that. I never have—

BEN (*softly*) You're going to do a lot of things you've never done before. Now I want you to do what I tell you, and trust me from now on, will you?

LAVINIA I'm going to do what you tell me.

BEN (*goes into living room*) All right. Now go ahead.

(JAKE *appears. He is carrying a mop and a pail.*)

JAKE You all up specially early, or me, am I late?

LAVINIA (*calling*) Marcus. Marcus. (*To* JAKE) What do you think of that, Jake?

JAKE (*takes a nervous step toward her—softly*) I don't think well of it. Please, Miss Viney, don't be doing—

LAVINIA Marcus! Marcus! I want—we want to speak to you. (*To* JAKE) Hear what I did? (*Nervously*) Everything's different—Marcus!

(MARCUS *appears on the porch. He has been dressing; he is now in shirtsleeves. He peers down at* LAVINIA.)

MARCUS Are you shouting at me? What's the matter with you now, Lavinia?

LAVINIA Well, I just—

MARCUS You are up early to give your blessings to your departing sons?

LAVINIA I haven't seen Oscar.

MARCUS Benjamin has gone?

LAVINIA (*looks into drawing room*) No, Marcus. He hasn't gone. He's inside knocking off the locks on your desk. My, he's doing it with a pistol. The other end of the pistol, I mean.

(*During her speech, we hear three rapid, powerful blows. MARCUS grips the rail of the porch. BEN comes onto the porch, the pistol in one hand, a large envelope in the other. He looks up at MARCUS. There is a long pause.*)

MARCUS Put the gun on the table. Bring me that envelope.

LAVINIA Same old envelope. Like I said, I used to dream about tearing up that money. You could do it, Benjamin, right now. Make you feel better and cleaner, too.

BEN I feel fine. (*To MARCUS*) I like you better up there. So stay there. *Stay there.* (BEN *turns to* JAKE, *takes another envelope from his pocket, puts in money from first envelope*) Take this over to Lionnet. Ask for Miss Birdie Bagtry and talk to nobody else. Give her this and ask her to forget about last night.

MARCUS Take that envelope from him, Lavinia, and bring it to me quickly.

LAVINIA I can't walk as fast as I used to, Marcus, I'm getting old—

BEN (*to* JAKE) Tell Miss Birdie I'll call on her in the next few days and we'll attend to the details then. Go on, be quick—

MARCUS (*to* JAKE) Come back here! (*To* BEN) How dare you touch—

BEN Well, come and get it from me. (*Turns again to* JAKE) And tell her I wish Captain Bagtry good luck. And stop at the wharf and buy two tickets on the sugar boat.

LAVINIA Thank you, son. (*There is a long pause. She is puzzled by it*) Well. Why doesn't somebody say something?

BEN We're thinking.

MARCUS Yes. Shall I tell you what I'm thinking? That

I'm going to be sorry for the scandal of a son in jail.

BEN   What would you put me in jail for?

MARCUS   For stealing forty thousand dollars.

BEN   (*looking at the envelope, smiles*) That much? I haven't had time to count it. I always said there wasn't a Southerner born before the war who ever had sense enough to trust a bank. Now do you want to know what *I'm* thinking?

MARCUS   Yes, I'm puzzled. This piece of insanity isn't like you. In the years to come, when I do think about you, I would like to know why you walked yourself into a jail cell.

BEN   In the years to come, when you think about me, do it this way. (*Sharply*) You had been buying salt from the Union garrison across the river. On the morning of April 2nd you rode over to get it. Early evening of April 3rd you started back with it—

MARCUS   Are you writing a book about me? I would not have chosen you as my recorder.

BEN   You were followed back—which is exactly what Union officers had been waiting for—at eleven o'clock that night—

LAVINIA   Marcus didn't *mean* to lead them back. I explained that to you, Benjamin—

MARCUS   (*sharply*) *You* explained it to him? What—

BEN   Eleven o'clock that night twenty-seven boys in the swamp camp were killed. The news reached here, and you, about an hour later.

LAVINIA   More than that. About two hours later. Or maybe more, Benjamin.

MARCUS   What the hell is this? Lavinia, I want—

BEN   And the town, guessing right, and hating you anyway, began to look for you. They didn't find you. Because you were on the well-house roof.

LAVINIA   Yes, you were, Marcus, that's just where you were. I saw you.

MARCUS   (*softly*) I don't know why I'm standing here listening to this foolishness, and I won't be for long. Bring me the envelope, and you will still have plenty of time to catch the train. You come up here, Lavinia—

BEN I'll tell you why you're standing there: you are very, very, very—as Mama would say—afraid.

MARCUS (*carefully*) What should I be afraid of, Benjamin? (*Sharply*) A bungler who leaves broken locks on a desk to prove he's stolen, and gives away money to make sure I have further proof? Or a crazy woman, who dreams she saw something sixteen years ago?

LAVINIA Marcus, I must ask you to stop using that awful word and—

MARCUS And I must ask you to get used to it because within an hour you'll be where they use no other word—

BEN (*as* LAVINIA *makes frightened motion*) Mama, stop it. (*To* MARCUS) And you stop interrupting me. Mama saw you on the well-house roof. Coralee saw you. They saw you take money from an envelope—

LAVINIA The same one. My, it wore well, didn't it?

BEN To buy the passes that saved you from a hanging. You bought them from—

MARCUS (*tensely*) Get out of here. I—

BEN From a Captain Virgil E. McMullen. Now I'd figure it this way: by the grace of Captain McMullen you got sixteen free years. So if they swing you tonight, tell yourself sixteen years is a long time, and lynching is as good a way to die as any other.

LAVINIA Benjamin, don't talk like that, don't, son—

MARCUS (*in a different voice*) Walk yourself down to the sheriff's office now. I'll catch up with you. If you're fool enough to believe some invention of your mother's, understand that nobody else will believe it. The whole town knows your mother's been crazy for years, and Dr. Seckles will testify to it—

BEN Let's put it this way: they think Mama is an eccentric, and that you made her that way. And they know Seckles is a drunken crook. They know Mama is a good woman, they respect her. They'll take her word because, as she told me a little while ago, people believe what they want to believe.

MARCUS (*carefully*) Lavinia, you're a religious woman, and religious people don't lie, of course. But I know you are subject to dreams. Now, I wonder why and when you had this one. Remember, will you, that you were ill right after the incident of which you speak so incorrectly, and remember please that we took you— (*sharply, to* BEN)—not to that drunken Seckles, but to Dr. Hammanond in Mobile. He told me then that you were— (LAVINIA *draws back*) And he is still living to remember it, if you can't.

LAVINIA   (*worried, rattled*)   I was ill after that night. Who wouldn't have been? It had nothing to do with, with my nerves. It was taking part in sin, your sin, that upset me, and not knowing the right and wrong of what to do—

MARCUS   She didn't tell you about that illness, did she? You think they'd believe her against Hammanond's word that she was a very sick woman at the time she speaks about? (*Very sharply*) Now stop this damned nonsense and get out of here or—

BEN   Go change your dress, Mama. Get ready for a walk.

LAVINIA   But you told Jake—you said I could go on the sugar boat.

BEN   You can still catch the boat. We won't be walking long. And if you have to stay over a few hours more, I figure you can wear the same costume to a lynching as you can on a boat. We'll walk around to old Isham first, whose youngest son got killed that night. John Bagtry will be mighty happy to remember that his twin brother also died that night. And Mrs. Mercer's oldest son and the two Sylvan boys and— We won't have to go any further because they'll be glad to fetch their kinfolk and, on their way, all the people who got nothing else to do tonight, or all the people who owe you on cotton or cane or land. Be the biggest, happiest lynching in the history of Roseville County. All right. Go change your clothes—

MARCUS   (*softly, carefully*)   Lavinia. I—

LAVINIA   A lynching? *I don't believe in lynching.* If you lynch a white man, it can lead right into lynching a black man. No human being's got a right to take a life in the sight of God.

MARCUS   (*to* BEN)   You're losing your witness. What a

clown you turned out to be. Only you would think your
mother would go through with this, only you would
trust her—

BEN (*sharply*) She won't have to do much. I'm taking
her Bible along. (*Opens the book*) On this page, that
night, she wrote it all down. The names, the dates, the
hours. Then she and Coralee swore to it. Everybody
will like the picture of the two lost innocents and a
Bible, and if they don't, sixteen-year-old ink will be
much nicer proof than your Mobile doctor. (*Softly*)
Anyway, you won't have time to get him here. Want to
finish now?

LAVINIA (*who has been thinking*) I never told you I was
going to have anything to do with a lynching. No, I
didn't.

MARCUS Of course you wouldn't. Of course you wouldn't.
Not of your husband—

LAVINIA Not of my husband, not of anybody.

BEN Mama, go upstairs and let me finish this—

LAVINIA I only said I was going to tell the truth to everybody. And that I'm going to do. (*To* MARCUS) If there's
any nasty talk of lynching, I'm going to plead for your
life hard as I can, yes I am.

BEN (*laughs*) Now, that's merciful of you. I'm going to
do the same thing. I'm going to plead with them for
Papa's life.

LAVINIA That's the least a son can do for his father.

BEN (*to* MARCUS) Better than that. I'll come tomorrow
morning and cut you down from the tree, and bury you
with respect. How did the Greeks bury fathers who were
murdered? Tell me, and I'll see to it. You'd like that,
wouldn't you?

LAVINIA Benjamin, don't talk that way—

MARCUS You gave him the right to talk that way. You
did, Lavinia, and I don't understand anything that's
been happening. Do you mean that you actually wrote
a lie in your Bible, you who—

LAVINIA (*very angry*) Don't you talk like that. Nobody
can say there's a lie in my Bible— You take that back.
You take it back right away. I don't tell lies, and then

I don't swear to them, and I don't swear on my Bible
to a false thing and neither does Coralee. You just
apologize to me and then you apologize to Coralee,
that's what you do—

MARCUS (*quickly*) No, no. I don't mean you knew it was
a lie. Of course not, Lavinia. But let me see it, and then
tell me—

LAVINIA (*puts out her hand*) Let him see it. Of course.

BEN Tell him to come down and look at it. I'll put it here,
under the gun.

LAVINIA Bibles are there for all people. For grown people. I'm not going to have any Bibles in my school.
That surprise you all? It's the only book in the world
but it's just for grown people, after you know it don't
mean what it says. You take Abraham: he sends in his
wife, Sarah, to Pharaoh, and he lets Pharaoh think
Sarah is his sister. And then Pharaoh, he, he, he. Well,
he does, with Sarah. And afterward Abraham gets mad
at Pharaoh because of Sarah, even though he's played
that trick on Pharaoh. Now if you didn't understand, a
little child could get mighty mixed up—

MARCUS (*gently*) You want to go to your school, don't
you, Lavinia?

LAVINIA Or about Jesus. The poor are always with you.
Why, I wouldn't have colored people believe a thing
like that: that's what's the matter now. You have to be
full grown before you know what Jesus meant. Otherwise you could make it seem like people ought to be
poor.

BEN All right. Go upstairs now and start packing. You're
going to be on the sugar boat.

LAVINIA Am I? Isn't that wonderful—

MARCUS Lavinia. (*She turns toward him*) It would be
wrong of me to say ours had been a good marriage. But
a marriage it was. And you took vows in church, sacred
vows. If you sent me to trouble, you would be breaking
your sacred vows—

BEN Oh, shut up, Papa.

LAVINIA I don't want trouble, for anybody. I've only
wanted to go away—

MARCUS   (*slowly, as he comes down from balcony*)   I was wrong in keeping you.

BEN   (*laughs*)   Yes. That's true.

MARCUS   It was wrong, I can see it now, to have denied you your great mission. I should have let you go, helped you build a little schoolhouse in Altaloosa.

BEN   I built it about ten minutes ago.

LAVINIA   What? Oh, about the marriage vows, Marcus. I had a message last night, and it said it was right for me to go now and do my work. Once I get a message, you know.

MARCUS   Yes. Yes, you'll want a lot of things for your colored pupils. A schoolhouse isn't enough—you'll need books and—

LAVINIA   That's absolutely true. And I want to send for a teacher— I'm getting old and I'm ignorant— I want to make a higher learning.

MARCUS   Lavinia. I'll get them for you.

LAVINIA   Thank you. But of course, it isn't just getting them, I've got to keep up the schoolhouse every year—

MARCUS   Certainly. Did your, did your messages suggest any definite figure?

LAVINIA   Why, yes, they did.

MARCUS   How much was suggested?

LAVINIA   To tell you the truth, my message said a thousand dollars a year would make my colored children happy. But I think ten thousand a year would make them happier. Altaloosa's a mighty poor little village and everybody needs help there—

MARCUS   Ten thousand wouldn't be enough. I think—

LAVINIA   (*firmly*)   It would be enough. I'd make it enough. Then, of course, I been forgetting about Coralee coming with me. And Coralee supports a mighty lot of kinfolk right here in town. She got a crippled little cousin, her old Mama can't take washing any more—

MARCUS   Oh, that's too bad. What could I do for them?

LAVINIA   Maybe two hundred dollars a month would take Coralee's mind from worrying.

MARCUS   I should think so. They'll be the richest family in the South. But, of course, your friends should have the best.

LAVINIA   You're being mighty nice to me, Marcus. I wish it had always been that way.

MARCUS   (*quickly*) It started out that way, remember? I suppose little things happened, as they do with so many people—

LAVINIA   No, I don't really think it started out well. No, I can't say I do.

MARCUS   Oh, come now. You're forgetting. All kinds of pleasant things. Remember in the little house? The piano? I saved and bought it for you and—

LAVINIA   Bought it for me? No, I don't remember it that way. I always thought you bought it for yourself.

MARCUS   But perhaps you never understood why I did anything, perhaps you were a little unforgiving with me.

BEN   (*to* MARCUS) Aren't you getting ashamed of yourself?

MARCUS   For what? For trying to recall to Lavinia's mind that we were married with sacred vows, that together we had children, that she swore in a church to love, to honor—

BEN   If I wasn't in a hurry, I'd be very amused.

LAVINIA   (*thoughtfully*) I did swear. That's true, I—

BEN   (*quickly*) Mama, please go upstairs. Please let me finish here. You won't get on the boat any other way—

MARCUS   Indeed you will, Lavinia. And there's no need to take the boat. I'll drive you up. We can stay overnight in Mobile, look at the churches, have a nice dinner, continue on in the morning—

LAVINIA   How did you guess? I always dreamed of returning that way. Driving in, nice and slow, seeing everybody on the road, saying hello to people I knew as a little girl, stopping at the river church—church . . . (*To herself*) Every Sunday here I always saved and put a dollar in the collection box. They're going to miss the dollar. You all know, in my vanity, what I'd like to have when I'm gone to Altaloosa?

MARCUS   What, Lavinia? I am most anxious to know.

LAVINIA   A mahogany pew, with my name on it, in brass.

MARCUS Brass! It shall be writ in gold—

LAVINIA I don't like gold. Brass. Now, what else did I think about last night?

MARCUS We'll be in constant communication. And if you have more practical messages from God we can take care of them later. Now bring me the envelope and the Bible, and we'll start immediately—

(*She puts her hand on the Bible, as if to pick it up.*)

BEN (*quickly takes her hand*) Do I really have to explain it to you? Do I really have to tell you that unless you go through with it, he's got to take you to the hospital? You don't really think that he's going to leave you free in Altaloosa with what you know, to tell anybody— Why do you think he took you to Dr. Hammonond in the first place? Because he thought you might have seen him, and because it wouldn't hurt to have a doctor say that you were—

MARCUS (*very sharply*) That's a lie.

BEN Maybe it is. But then you're only sorry you didn't think of it that way.

MARCUS Lavinia—

LAVINIA (*softly*) I don't ever want to hear such things again, or one person do or say, to another.

MARCUS Lavinia, you'll get what you want. You know I am not a stingy man or one who—

BEN You'll get nothing. For the very simple reason that he isn't going to have a nickel to buy it with.

LAVINIA (*wearily*) Oh. That isn't what worries me— It's that Marcus may have been saying things he didn't mean. (*Softly*) Would you really have told me you would drive me to Mobile and then you would have taken me—

MARCUS *Of course not.* If you listen to that scoundrel— You're my wife, aren't you? I also took vows. I also stood up and swore. Would I break a solemn vow—

LAVINIA (*appalled*) Oh, now, I don't believe what you're saying. One lie, two lies, that's for all of us: but to pile lie upon lie and sin upon sin, and in the sight of God—

BEN (*sharply*) Write it to him, Mama. Or you'll miss your boat.

LAVINIA   Oh, yes. Oh, I wouldn't want to do that. (*She picks up the Bible, exits.*)

MARCUS   You're a very ugly man.

BEN   Are you ready now?

MARCUS   For what?

BEN   To write a piece of paper, saying you sell me the store for a dollar.

MARCUS   (*pauses*)   All right. Bring me that envelope. I'll sell you the store for a dollar. Now I have had enough and that will be all.

BEN   You'll write another little slip of paper telling Shannon in Mobile to turn over to me immediately all stocks and bonds, your safe-deposit box, all liens, all mortgages, *all* assets of Marcus Hubbard, Incorporated.

MARCUS   I will certainly do no such thing. I will leave you your proper share of things in my will, or perhaps increase it, if you behave—

BEN   (*angrily*)   You're making fun of me again. A will? That you could change tomorrow? You've made fun of me for enough years. It's dangerous now. One more joke. So stop it now. Stop it.

MARCUS   All right. But I would like to give you a little advice—you're so new at this kind of thing. If you get greedy and take everything there's bound to be a lot of suspicion. And you shouldn't want that. Take the store, take half of everything else, half of what's in the envelope. Give me the rest. I'll go on living as I always have, and tell everybody that because you're my oldest son, I wanted you to have—

BEN   You'll tell nobody anything, because you can't, and you'll stop bargaining. You're giving me everything you've got. Is that clear? If I don't have to waste any more time with you, I'll give you enough to live on, here or wherever you want to go. But if I have to talk to you any longer, you won't get that. I mean what I'm saying, and you know I do. And it's the last time I'll say it. (*There is no answer. He smiles*) All right. Now start writing things down. When you finish, bring them to me. You're waiting for something?

MARCUS   (*softly, as he goes up the porch steps*)   To tell you the truth, I am trying to think of some way out.

BEN   If I told you that it's been a large temptation to see you—to do it the other way, you will believe me, I know; remember the past and don't waste your time, or put yourself in further danger, or tempt me longer. Ever since you started your peculiar way of treating me, many years ago, I have had many ugly dreams. But this is better than I ever dreamed— Go in and start writing now. I consider you a lucky man: you'll die in bed.

MARCUS   You will give me enough for a clean bed?

BEN   Yes, of course.

MARCUS   Well, I daresay one could make some small bargains with you still. But I don't like small bargains. You win or you lose—

BEN   And I don't like small talk. (MARCUS *turns, goes into his room.* BEN *waits for a second, then crosses to kitchen door, calls in*) Breakfast here, please. (*As* JAKE *comes from street side of porch*) Yes? Did you find Miss Birdie?

JAKE   Yes, sir. She was mighty happy and said to thank you.

BEN   All right. Did you get the tickets?

JAKE   Sure. Boat's loading now.

BEN   (*sits down at* MARCUS's *table*) Take them up to Miss Lavinia, get the carriage ready. Get me coffee first.

JAKE   (*as he goes off*) Lot of running around this morning.

(*The sound of knocking is heard from the hall of the second floor.*)

OSCAR's VOICE   (*with the knocking*) Papa! Papa! It's me. Hey, Papa. Please. Open your door. (*After a second* OSCAR *runs in from the living room, runs up the porch steps, calls into* MARCUS's *room*) Papa. I'm all ready. (*Pounds on* MARCUS's *door.*)

BEN   (*looking up at* OSCAR) Traveling clothes? You look nice.

OSCAR   What you doing there? I told you to get on down to the station to make your apologies. I ain't changed my mind.

BEN   Oh, I never thought you meant that silly talk.

OSCAR You didn't, huh? (*Looks down, sees the gun on the table*) What's my pistol doing out?

BEN Waiting for you.

OSCAR You just put it back where you found it— (*Then as if he remebered*) Papa. Please. Let me in. *Please.* Papa, I .can't find it. Papa— (REGINA *appears on the balcony. She is arranging her hair. She has on a riding skirt and shirt*) Regina, go in and tell him, will you? *Please, Regina.* Laurette's waiting for me to fetch her up—

REGINA (*looks down at* BEN *on the porch. Looks at* OSCAR) Oh, God. I slept late, hoping you'd both be gone. What's the matter with you, Oscar, what are you carrying on about?

(JAKE *appears with coffee tray, brings cup to* BEN, *puts tray down, and exits.*)

OSCAR (*desperately*) The thousand dollars on the table. But it's *not* on the table. You heard him promise last night—

REGINA Go look again. Papa certainly wouldn't stop your going.

OSCAR I tell you it's not there. I been over the whole house. I crawled around under the table—

BEN Come on down and crawl some more.

REGINA (*softly*) You're in Papa's chair, Ben, eating breakfast at Papa's table, on Papa's porch.

OSCAR (*softly, very puzzled*) I'm telling you that Ben is a crazy Mama's crazy son.

BEN (looks up at REGINA) Come on down and have breakfast with me, darling. I'm lonely for you.

REGINA Papa told you to be out of here.

BEN (*smiles*) Come on down, honey.

REGINA No, I'm going out before the horse-whipping starts.

BEN Going to look for a man who needs a little persuading?

REGINA That's right.

OSCAR Regina. Help me. It's *not* there. (*Screaming*) Papa! *Papa!*

REGINA (*disappears into her room*) Oh, stop that screaming.

OSCAR Papa, I got to go. The money's not there. Papa, answer me—

MARCUS (*comes out from his room*) You looking for me, son? Speak up.

OSCAR (*softly*) It's getting late. The money. You forgot to leave it. (*When he gets no answer, his voice changes to a sudden shriek*) It just ain't there.

MARCUS A voice injured at your age is possibly never recovered. The money isn't there, Oscar, because I didn't put it there. (*To* BEN) Would you like to give him a little—some—explanation, or will I, or—

BEN (*shakes his head*) I'm eating.

(OSCAR *stares down at* BEN, *stares at* MARCUS.)

MARCUS (*to* OSCAR) An unhappy event interfered. I am thus unable to finance your first happy months in the rose-covered brothel about which you have always dreamed. I assure you I am most sorry, for many reasons, none of them having anything to do with you.

OSCAR What the hell does all that mean? That you're *not* giving me the money to leave here—

BEN (*nods*) It means that. And it means that Papa has found a new way of postponing for a few minutes an unpleasant writing job. Go back in, Papa.

(OSCAR *stares at* MARCUS, *stares down at* BEN. *Then he suddenly runs down the steps, off the porch, going toward the street.* BEN *smiles,* MARCUS *smiles.*)

MARCUS Where would you prefer me to have breakfast? A tray in my room, this side of the porch, or the dining room or—

BEN Any place you like. My house is your house.

MARCUS I eat a large breakfast, as you know. Should that continue?

BEN Certainly. But before you eat this large breakfast on this large morning, I want you to finish the papers I'm waiting for.

MARCUS Naturally, I've been inside thinking. Is there any chance I could get out of here and on the train without your interfering with me?

BEN No, I don't think so. I've thought of that. And if you did, I feel confident I could bring you back.

MARCUS (*pleasantly*) Yes. Thank you, Benjamin.

(*He re-enters his room as* REGINA *comes on the porch. She hears his last sentence, stares at* MARCUS. *She comes down the steps, goes to the table, pours herself coffee, takes a biscuit, looks curiously at* BEN *and sits down.*)

REGINA (*after a minute*) What's the matter with Papa?

BEN He's changed. You think it's age?

REGINA (*annoyed*) Why aren't you getting on the train?

BEN I'm going to build a new house. I never liked this house; it wasn't meant for people like us. Too delicate, too fancy. Papa's idea of postwar swell.

REGINA (*stares at him*) I want to know why you aren't leaving this morning?

BEN I can't tell you why. (*Laughs*) My lips are sealed in honor.

REGINA Before there's any more trouble you better go quiet down Mama. She's *packing*. She says she's going to her destiny. You know what that always means. And I'm sick of fights—

BEN But that's where she is going.

REGINA (*bewildered*) Papa said she could go?

BEN No . . . I said so.

REGINA And who have you become?

BEN A man who thinks you have handled yourself very badly. It's a shame about you, Regina: beautiful, warm outside, and smart. That should have made a brilliant life. Instead, at twenty, you have to start picking up the pieces, and start mighty fast now.

REGINA (*gets up, laughs*) I like the pieces, and I'm off to pick them up.

BEN To try to persuade the Captain by the deed of darkness to a future legal bed? So early in the morning?

REGINA (*pleasantly, as she passes him*) I'm sure something very interesting has happened here. (*Sharply. Turns to him*) But whatever it is, don't talk that way to me.

BEN Can I talk this way? You're not going to Chicago. And for a very simple reason. Papa has no money at all

—now. No money for you to travel with, or to marry
with, or even to go on here with.

REGINA (*stands staring at him. Then, quietly*) *What are
you talking about? What's happened?* What's he done
with his money—

BEN Given it to me.

REGINA Do you take that new drug I've been reading
about? What would make you think he had given it to
you?

BEN You mean what were his reasons? Oh, I don't know.
I'm the eldest son: isn't that the way with royalty?
Maybe he could find me a Greek title— Go up and talk
to him. I think he's been waiting.

(*Slowly she starts for the staircase. Then the speed of her
movements increases, and by the time she is near the
door of* MARCUS'S *room she is running. She goes into the
room.* BEN *picks up his newspaper. There is low talking from* MARCUS'S *room.* BEN *looks up, smiles. After a
moment,* REGINA *comes slowly out of* MARCUS'S *room.
She crosses porch, starts downstairs.*)

REGINA (*slowly*) He says there is nothing he will tell me.
He says there's nothing he can tell me. He's crying.
What does all that mean?

BEN It means there is nothing he can tell you, and that
he's crying. Don't you feel sorry for him?

REGINA Why can't he tell me? I'll make him—

BEN He can't tell you, and I won't tell you. Just take my
word: you're, er, you're not well off, shall we say?

REGINA (*tensely*) What have you been doing to Papa or—

BEN A great deal. Whatever you think of me, honey,
you know I'm not given to this kind of joke. So take it
this way: what is in your room is yours. Nothing else.
And save your time on the talk. No Chicago, honey. No
nothing.

REGINA You can't stop my going, and you're not going to
stop it—

BEN Certainly not. What people want to do, they do.
You go ahead, your own way. Ride over to your soldier.
Stand close and talk soft: he'll marry you. But do it
quickly: he was angry last night and I think he wants

to get away from you as fast as he can. Catch him quick. Marry him this morning. Then come back here to pack your nice Chicago clothes, and sell your pearls.

REGINA Do you think I'm going to take your word for what's happening, or believe I can't talk Papa out of whatever you've done to him—

BEN Believe me, you can't. Not because your charms have failed, but because there's nothing to talk him out of. I have it now, and your charms won't work on me. Money from the pearls will be plenty to take you to Brazil, and love and war will feed you. People in love should be poor.

REGINA Ben, tell me, what storm happened here this morning. Tell me so that I can—can find out what I think or—

BEN Or if you don't want to go to the war in Brazil, stay here and starve with them at Lionnet. I'd love to see you in the house with those three ninnies, dying on the vine. Either way, he'd leave you soon enough and you'd find out there's never anybody nastier than a weak man. Hurry— or have a cup of coffee.

REGINA (*softly, tensely*) I'll find out what's happened, and—

BEN No you won't.

REGINA And the day I do, I'll pay you back with carnival trimmings.

BEN Good girl. I won't blame you. But in the meantime, learn to win, and learn to lose. And don't stand here all day losing, because it's my house now, and I don't like loser's talk.

REGINA You've ruined everything I wanted, you've—

BEN Now, look here. Write *him* a poem, will you? I've ruined nothing. You're not marrying a man who didn't love you. You can't go away, or at least not on my money, and therefore a willful girl can't have a willful way. You're not in love; I don't think anybody in this family can love. You're not a fool; stop talking like one. The sooner you do, the sooner I'll help you.

REGINA You heard me say I'd pay you back for this?

BEN All right. Be a fool.

(MARCUS *opens his door, comes out on the porch, comes down the steps.* REGINA *turns to look at him.* MARCUS *comes to* BEN, *hands him two pieces of paper.* BEN *takes them, reads them.* MARCUS *puts his hand out to take the newspaper.* BEN *smiles, shakes his head,* MARCUS *quickly takes his hand away.*)

REGINA (*desperately, to* MARCUS) You still won't tell me? You're willing to see—

MARCUS (*softly*) Regina, honey, I can't, I—

(OSCAR, *dejected and rumpled, appears.*)

REGINA (*to* OSCAR) Do you know what's happened here? Did you have anything to do with it?

OSCAR What?

(REGINA *turns away from him.* OSCAR *sits down, puts his head in his hands.*)

REGINA (*after a minute*) Well, what's the matter with you then? Ben Hubbard trouble?

OSCAR She wouldn't wait. She wouldn't even wait for a few days until Papa could give me the money again.

BEN Again?

OSCAR That's how much she cared for me. Wouldn't even wait. Said she was going on to New Orleans, anyway. That she'd had enough— My God, I talked and begged. I even tried to carry her off the train.

MARCUS Oh, how unfortunate.

BEN I think it's charming. How did you do it, Oscar?

OSCAR (*to nobody*) You know what she did? She spat in my face and screamed in front of everybody that she was glad I wasn't coming, that she had never cared for me, and had only been doing the best she could. If I didn't have the money, what the hell did she need me for?

REGINA (*sympathetic*) Spat in your face! How could she do a thing like that?

MARCUS How does one spit in your face?

BEN Why, I imagine the way one spits in anybody's face.

REGINA But it's special in a railroad station. How did she do it, Oscar? You can't just up and spit—

OSCAR (*in his sorrow, spits out on the porch*) Just like that. The way you wouldn't do with a dog. And all the while yelling I was to let her alone, with everybody staring and laughing—(MARCUS, REGINA, *and* BEN *laugh.* OSCAR *rises*) So. So, making fun of me, huh?

REGINA Now really, Oskie, can you blame us? You on a railroad station trying to carry off a spitting—girl? You'd laugh youself, if you didn't always have indigestion.

OSCAR (*carefully*) Your love didn't laugh. Your love, looking like a statue of Robert E. Lee. Dressed up and with his old medals all over him. (REGINA *rises.* MARCUS *rises*) So you didn't know he was going on the train, huh? I thought not. So you're no better off than me, are you, with all your laughing. Sneaked out on you, did he?

REGINA So you arranged that, too, so that I couldn't—

BEN All right. That's enough. I'm sick of love. Both of you follow the trash you've set your hearts on, or be still about it from now on. I don't want any more of this.

OSCAR *You* don't want any more. What the—

BEN (*to* REGINA) You, early-maturing flower, can go any place you want and find what it's like to be without Papa's money. (*To* OSCAR) And you, lover, can follow your spitting heart and get yourself a wharf job loading bananas. Or you can stay, keep your job, settle down. I got a girl picked out for you—make yourself useful.

OSCAR (*completely bewildered, turns to* MARCUS) What's he talking about, Papa? Since when—

BEN It's not necessary to explain it to you. (*To* REGINA) Now, honey, about you, if you're staying. You're a scandal in this town. Papa's the only person didn't know you've been sleeping with the warrior.

MARCUS Benjamin—

BEN (*laughs*) Papa, and Horace Giddens in Mobile. How soon he'll find out about it, I don't know. Before he does, we're taking you up to see him. You'll get engaged to him by next week, or sooner, and you'll get married in the first church we bump into. Giddens isn't bad off, and if you're lucky it'll be years before he hears about you and the Brazilian general. I don't say it's a brilliant future, but I don't say it's bad. You could have done a lot better, but girls who have been despoiled in this part of the country—

MARCUS   (*softly*) You don't have to marry a man, Regina, just because— We can go away, you and I—

OSCAR   (*goes toward kitchen door*) I certainly don't know what's happened here. I certainly don't. I'm hungry. (*Calls in*) Where's breakfast, you all?

REGINA   (*sharply*) Order breakfast for me, too, selfish.

BEN   (*laughs*) That's my good girl. (*Picks up the newspaper*) Nothing for anybody to be so unhappy about. You both going to do all right. I'm going to help you. I got ideas. You'll go to Chicago some day, get everything you want— Then—

REGINA   (*softly*) When I'm too old to want it.

MARCUS   Regina, you didn't hear me. We could go away, you and I— I could start over again just as I started once before.

REGINA   When you did—whatever Ben made you do, did you realize what you were doing to me? Did you care?

MARCUS   (*slowly*) I cared very much.

REGINA   And what good did that do?

OSCAR   Sure must have been an earthquake here since last night. You go to bed and Papa's one kind of man, and you wake up—

BEN   (*reading newspaper*) They got that ad in again, Oscar. Dr. Melgoyd's "All Cure." Two bits, now, on special sale, for gentlemen only. Sluggish blood, cure for a wild manhood, nothing to be ashamed of, it says—

REGINA   He's still got the last bottle.

(JAKE *appears with a large tray. He has on his hat and coat.*)

OSCAR   (*annoyed*) I never bought that rot. Don't believe in it. Somebody gave it to me.

REGINA   (*laughing*) That was tactless, wasn't it?

BEN   Big goings on all over the country. Railroads going across, oil, coal. I been telling you, Papa, for ten years. Things are opening up.

OSCAR   (*who has started to eat*) That don't mean they're opening up in the South.

BEN   But they are. That's what nobody down here sees

or understands. Now you take you, Papa. You were smart in your day and figured out what fools you lived among. But ever since the war you been too busy getting cultured, or getting Southern. A few more years and you'd have been just like the rest of them.

MARCUS (*to* JAKE) Bring my breakfast, Jake.

JAKE Belle will have to do it, Mr. Marcus. Last breakfast I can bring. I got the carriage waiting to take Miss Viney. (*He exits.*)

BEN But now we'll do a little investing, nothing big, because unlike Papa I don't believe in going outside your class about anything—

OSCAR (*his mouth full*) Think we've got a chance to be big rich, Ben?

BEN I think so. All of us. I'm going to make some for you and Regina and—

(LAVINIA *appears in the living-room door. She is carrying a purse and the Bible. Coralee is standing behind her.*)

LAVINIA Well, I'm off on my appointed path. I brought you each a little something. (*Goes to* REGINA) This is my pin. (REGINA *gets up,* LAVINIA *kisses her*) Smile, honey, you're such a pretty girl. (*Goes to* OSCAR) Here's my prayer book, Oscar. I had it since I was five years old. (OSCAR *kisses her. She goes to* BEN) I want you to have my Papa's watch, Benjamin.

BEN Thank you, Mama. (*He kisses her, she pats his arm.*)

LAVINIA (*goes to* MARCUS) I didn't have anything left, Marcus, except my wedding ring.

MARCUS (*gets up, smiles*) That's kind, Lavinia.

LAVINIA Well, I guess that's all.

BEN Mama, could I have your Bible instead of Grandpa's watch? (MARCUS *laughs*) It would make me happier, and I think—

MARCUS Or perhaps you'd give it to me. I can't tell you how happy it would make me, Lavinia.

LAVINIA Oh, I wouldn't like to give it up. This Bible's been in my Papa's family for a long time. I always keep it next to me, you all know that. But when I die, I'll leave it to you all. Coralee, you hear that? If I die before you, you bring it right back here.

CORALEE Come on, Miss Viney.

LAVINIA I'll be hearing from you, Benjamin?

BEN You will, Mama. Every month. On time.

LAVINIA Thank you, son. Thank you in the name of my colored children.

CORALEE Miss Viney, it's late.

LAVINIA Well. (*Wistfully*) Don't be seeing me off, any of you. Coralee and I'll be just fine. I'll be thinking of you, and I'll be praying for you, all of you. Everybody needs somebody to pray for them, and I'm going to pray for you all. (*Turns to* MARCUS) I hope you feel better, Marcus. We got old, you and me, and— Well, I guess I just mean it's been a long time. Good-bye.

MARCUS Good-bye, Lavinia.

(LAVINIA *and* CORALEE *exit.* MARCUS *goes to sit by* REGINA.)

MARCUS (*softly*) Pour me a cup of coffee, darling.

(REGINA *looks at him, gets up, crosses to table, pours coffee, brings it to him.* MARCUS *pulls forward the chair next to him.* REGINA *ignores the movement, crosses to chair near* BEN, *sits down.* BEN *smiles.*)

Curtain

The
Autumn
Garden

FOR DASH

Characters

(In the order of their speaking)

ROSE GRIGGS	FLORENCE ELDRIDGE
MRS. MARY ELLIS	ETHEL GRIFFIES
GENERAL BENJAMIN GRIGGS	COLIN KEITH-JOHNSTON
EDWARD CROSSMAN	KENT SMITH
FREDERICK ELLIS	JAMES LIPTON
CARRIE ELLIS	MARGARET BARKER
SOPHIE TUCKERMAN	JOAN LORRING
LEON	MAXWELL GLANVILLE
CONSTANCE TUCKERMAN	CAROL GOODNER
NICHOLAS DENERY	FREDRIC MARCH
NINA DENERY	JANE WYATT
HILDA	LOIS HOLMES

The play was presented by KERMIT BLOOMGARDEN
on the night of March 7, 1951,
at the Coronet Theater, New York.

The play was directed by HAROLD CLURMAN
and the settings were designed by
HOWARD BAY.

Scene

The time is September 1949.
The place is the Tuckerman house in
a summer resort on the Gulf of Mexico,
about one hundred miles
from New Orleans.

ACT ONE
Monday night after dinner.

ACT TWO
Scene I. The following Sunday morning.
Scene II. That night.

ACT THREE
Early the next morning.

Act One

SCENE: *The living room of the Tuckerman house in a town on the Gulf of Mexico, a hundred miles from New Orleans. A September evening, 1949, after dinner. To the right of the living room is a side porch, separated from the room by a glass door. Upstage left is a door leading into the entrance hall of the house: through this door we can see the hall and staircase. On the porch are chairs and tables. The furniture of the living room is handsome but a little shabby. It is all inherited from another day. (Right and left are the audience's right and left.)*

ON STAGE AT RISE OF CURTAIN: GENERAL GRIGGS, *a good-looking man of fifty-three, is seated at one side of the room reading a newspaper. His wife—*

ROSE GRIGGS, *ex-pretty, soft-looking and about forty-three, is seated at a table wearing an evening dress that is much too young for her. She is chatting across the room with—*

CARRIE ELLIS, *a distinguished-looking woman of about forty-five, who is sitting on a side chair, near her son, Frederick, and her mother-in-law—*

MRS. MARY ELLIS, *in her seventies, sprightly in manner and movement when she wishes to be, broken and senile when she wishes to be broken and senile. She has piled cushions on her chair so she can read a manuscript over the shoulder of her grandson—*

FREDERICK ELLIS, *a pleasant-looking young man of around twenty-five. Occasionally he makes a correction in the manuscript, looks up amused and annoyed at his grand-mother. On the right porch—*

EDWARD CROSSMAN, *about forty-six, tired and worn-looking as if he is not in good health, is sitting alone, his back to those in the room. There is a second of silence after the curtain goes up.*

ROSE   (*Gets up from her chair. She finds silence uncomfortable and breaks into song: "We stroll the lane together"*). Now where is it? Everything's been so topsy-turvy all evening. If I can't have it immediately after dinner then I just about don't want it. At home you can bet it's right waiting for us when we leave the dining room, isn't it, Ben? Too bad it's Thursday. I'd almost rather go and see him than go to the party. (*To* MRS. ELLIS) I think it's what keeps you awake, Mrs. Ellis. I mean a little is good for your heart, the doctor told me always to have a little, but my goodness the amount you have every night.

MRS. ELLIS   (*Pleasantly*) Would you mind telling me what you're talking about, Mrs. Griggs? You said if it wasn't for the party you'd go and see *him*, but you thought *I* drank too much on a Thursday?

ROSE   (*Giggles*) Coffee. I mean you drink too much coffee.

MRS. ELLIS   Then it is coffee you wish to go and see?

ROSE   Now, now. You're teasing. You know very well I mean Robert Taylor in that thing.

MRS. ELLIS   Believe me, I did *not* know you meant Robert Taylor in that thing. You know, General Griggs, after seven summers I have come to the conclusion that your wife considers it vulgar to mention anything by name. There's nothing particularly genteel about pronouns, my dear. Coffee is coffee and not it, Robert Taylor is Robert Taylor and not him, I suppose, and a fool is a fool and not her.

ROSE   (*Pleasantly*) I know. It's a naughty habit. Ben has been telling me for years. (*She is close to* BEN.) Do you like my dress, Ben?

GRIGGS It's nice.

ROSE Have I too much rouge? (*To others*) Know what she used to say? (*Quickly*) Ben's mother, I mean. She used to say it before she died. (*To* CROSSMAN) Come and join us. (*To others*) She used to say that Southern women painted a triangle of rouge on their faces as if they were going out to square the hypotenuse. Ben came from Boston, and his mother was sometimes a little sharp about Southerners.

MRS. ELLIS Who could have blamed her?

ROSE (*Calling out to* CROSSMAN) Know what she told me last winter when I met her at the Club?

CROSSMAN (*Turns, smiles*) Ben's mother?

ROSE No. Your sister, of course. She said we see more of you here on your summer vacation than she sees all year round in New Orleans. She says you're getting to be a regular old hermit. You have to watch that as you get older. You might get to like being alone—and that's dangerous.

MRS. ELLIS I used to like being alone. When you get old, of course, then you don't any more. But somewhere in the middle years, it's fine to be alone. A room of one's own isn't nearly enough. A house, or, best, an island of one's own. Don't you agree, General Griggs? (*Very quickly*) Happiest year of my life was when my husband died. Every month was springtime and every day I seemed to be tipsy, as if my blood had turned a lovely *vin rosé*.

CARRIE You're lyrical, Mother.

MRS. ELLIS (*To* FREDERICK) Do you know I almost divorced your grandfather, Frederick? During the racing season in 1901.

FREDERICK (*Looks up, laughs*) You don't feel it's a little late to talk about it?

(*The phone rings.*)

MRS. ELLIS Thought you might like to write my biography —when you're finished with regional poetry.

(*As the phone rings again,* SOPHIE *comes into the hall to answer it.*)

SOPHIE (*Into the phone*) No, sir. We do not take transient guests. No, never, sir. Only permanent guests. You might telephone to Mrs. Prescott in the village. Thank you, sir.

ROSE *(Calls into hall)* Dear Sophie, where *is* coffee?

*(*SOPHIE *comes to the hall door. She is a plain-looking, shy girl of about seventeen. She has a hesitant, overpolite manner and speaks with a slight accent. She has on a party dress, covered by a kitchen apron.)*

SOPHIE Aunt Constance is most sorry for the delay. We bring it immediately.

(She disappears.)

ROSE Frederick, do you know I've been giving Sophie dancing lessons, or trying to? She's a charming child, your intended, but she's never going to be a dancer.

FREDERICK *(Pleasantly)* Terrible expression, Mrs. Griggs: my intended. Sounds like my indentured. Did you tell Mrs. Griggs, Mother? I thought we agreed that since there were no definite plans as yet—

CARRIE *(A little uncomfortable)* It's natural that I should speak about my son's marriage, isn't it?

ROSE Why, goodness, yes indeed it is. I'd have felt hurt—

GRIGGS Don't you know that women have no honor, Frederick, when it comes to keeping secrets about marriage or cancer?

FREDERICK *(Looks at his mother)* No, sir. I didn't know. I'm too young for my age.

MRS. ELLIS *(Who has been busy reading the manuscript)* I know I'm too young to be reading Payson's book. Full of the most confused sex. I can't tell who is what. And all out of doors. Is that new, so much sex out of doors? Is it, General?

GRIGGS I don't think it's a question of "new." I think it's a question of climate.

MRS. ELLIS *(Points to book)* But aren't sexual relations the way they used to be: between *men and women?* It's so twitched about in Mr. Payson's book. You know, I think the whole country is changing.

GRIGGS *(As if he wished to help* FREDERICK*)* Has Payson written a good book, Fred?

FREDERICK It's a wonderful book. I think he's going to be the most important young writer—

CARRIE You said the first two books were wonderful, Frederick. And they didn't sell very well.

MRS. ELLIS I don't know why they didn't— I always thought houses of prostitution had a big lending-library trade.

(FREDERICK *gets up, as if he were angry.*)

CARRIE Will this new book sell, Frederick?

FREDERICK I don't know, Mother.

CARRIE I hope it sells. Any man is better off supporting himself.

FREDERICK (*Smiles*) Mother, sometimes I think no people are quite so moral about money as those who clip coupons for a living.

MRS. ELLIS And why not? Particularly your mother, who is given the coupons already clipped by me who has the hardship of clipping them. That leaves her more time to grow moral. And then, of course, you who don't even have that much trouble are left at leisure to be moral about those who have to go to the trouble of living on unearned money.

CARRIE (*To* GENERAL GRIGGS) You mustn't look uncomfortable, General. You should know by this time that my mother-in-law enjoys discussing family matters in public. And the more uncomfortable you look, the longer she will continue.

GRIGGS Do I look uncomfortable? I was thinking how hard it is to be young.

ROSE (*To* BEN) Won't you come to the party? (*To others*) Ben has never gone to the Carter party. I am sure they're just as insulted every year—

GRIGGS I don't think so.

ROSE But what will you do with yourself? Why don't you go to see Robert Taylor? It's that war picture where he does so well and you'll want to see if it's accurate.

GRIGGS No. I don't want to see if it's accurate.

ROSE Do you like my dress?

GRIGGS It's nice.

MRS. ELLIS You are a patient man. (*To* ROSE) Do you

know you've asked him that five times since rising from dinner?

ROSE Well, I feel young and gay, and I'm going to a party. I wish the Denerys would come before we leave. I like meeting new people and they sound so interesting. I thought they were supposed to arrive in time for dinner. (*To* CARRIE) Is he absolutely fascinating?

CARRIE I don't know, Mrs. Griggs. I haven't seen him in twenty years or more.

ROSE (*Calling to* CROSSMAN) Is he fascinating, Mr. Crossman?

CROSSMAN (*Pleasantly*) You're making it a little harder than usual. Is who fascinating?

ROSE Nicholas Denery, of course.

CROSSMAN Of course. I don't know.

ROSE But, goodness. Didn't you all grow up together? I mean you and Constance and Mrs. Ellis and—

CROSSMAN I don't remember any of us as fascinating. Do you, Carrie?

(CARRIE *shakes her head, laughs.* SOPHIE, *carrying a tray with brandy and brandy glasses, comes into the room. She is followed by* LEON, *a young, colored butler, carrying coffee and coffee cups.* FREDERICK *rises and takes the tray from* SOPHIE. *She looks at him and smiles.*)

ROSE Let's see your dress, Sophie. (SOPHIE *smiles shyly, begins to take off her apron as* LEON *pours coffee*) Oh. It's right nice. But you should wear tighter things, dear. (*Comes in back of her, begins to fool with her hair*) I'd like to try your hair again. (SOPHIE *moves to help* LEON *but is cornered by* ROSE) Now you just sit down. How's this?

(CROSSMAN *comes into the room.*)

CROSSMAN Makes her look like everybody else. That's desirable, isn't it?

ROSE What does Frederick think? We're out to please Frederick, after all, aren't we, dear?

FREDERICK (*Turns to look*) I like Sophie her own way.

SOPHIE (*Smiles*) I have no "way."

ROSE But most European girls have such chic— (GENERAL GRIGGS *gets up, as if he were annoyed*) They have, Ben.

You said it yourself when you came back from the Pacific, and I was jealous.

MRS. ELLIS   Pacific? I thought you fought in Europe.

GRIGGS   I did. Robert Taylor fought in the Pacific.

(*He rises, wanders off to the porch.*)

ROSE   (*Holding* SOPHIE's *hair another way*)   Or is *this* better?

FREDERICK   (*Smiles to* SOPHIE)   Don't you mind being pulled about?

SOPHIE   No. Well. (*Gently pulls away*) I am grateful for the trouble that Mrs. Griggs— Thank you.

CROSSMAN   Sophie doesn't mind anything. All she has said all summer is thank you.

(*Through his speech the phone rings.* FREDERICK *starts for the phone. At the same time,* CONSTANCE TUCKERMAN *comes through the hall. She is a handsome woman of forty-three or forty-four. She is carrying two flower vases. She puts down one of the vases in order to answer the phone.*)

CONSTANCE   Yes. Just a minute. Frederick. Mr. Payson would like to speak to you. (*She picks up the other vase, comes into the door, as if she were in a hurry.* FREDERICK *immediately moves to the phone*) Sorry coffee was late. You all want more just ring. And do, Carrie, explain to the Carters why I can't come to their party this year—

ROSE   Any news from them, Constance?

CONSTANCE   (*Carefully*)   News from whom?

ROSE   (*Laughs*)   Oh, come now. Stop pretending. When do the Denerys arrive?

CONSTANCE   Don't wait up for them, Rose. You'll see them at breakfast.

(*She turns, goes out and goes up the stairs.*)

ROSE   My, Constance is nervous. Well, I suppose I should be if I were seeing an old beau for the first time in— But I don't believe in old beaux. Beaux should be brand-new, or just friends, don't you think? (CROSSMAN *starts out to porch, carrying his coffee and the brandy bottle.* ROSE *points outside, meaning* GENERAL GRIGGS *and* CROSSMAN) Now are you boys just going to sit here and share the bottle—

CROSSMAN   General Griggs is only being kind when he says he shares the bottle with me.

(*He goes off.* FREDERICK *comes in, starts to speak, changes his mind.*)

CARRIE   (*Carefully*)   Was that Mr. Payson on the phone? Is he coming to the party?

FREDERICK   How many generations do you have to summer in this joint before you're invited to the Carters'?

MRS. ELLIS   Oh, that's not true. They're very liberal lately. (*Points to* ROSE) After all, the last few years they've always included Mrs. Griggs. (*To* ROSE) And nobody can be more *nouveau riche* than your family, can they? I mean your brother during the war and all that.

ROSE   (*Giggles*)   My. Everybody is so jealous of Henry.

MRS. ELLIS   Well, of course we are. I wish we were *nouveau riche* again.

FREDERICK   (*Sharply*)   All right, Grandma.

ROSE   Oh, I don't mind. I enjoy your grandmother.

FREDERICK   (*To his mother*)   I'm sorry I'm not going to be able to take you to the party. I hope you'll excuse me, Sophie. Mother. Grandma.

CARRIE   (*Carefully*)   What has happened, Frederick?

FREDERICK   Payson has a wire from his publishers. They want the manuscript in the mail tomorrow morning. (*He goes to take the manuscript from the table*) So I'll have to proofread it with him tonight. It's a nasty job alone, almost impossible—

CARRIE   (*Slowly*)   I don't understand.

ROSE   (*Hurriedly*)   I must fix my face. As you get older your face needs arranging more often.

(*She goes off.*)

CARRIE   We're ready to leave, Frederick.

FREDERICK   Mother, I'm not going to the party, I wasn't making a joke—

CARRIE   Oh. I hoped you were. You have no obligation to us, or Sophie? An appointment broken, because Payson summons you?

FREDERICK   I am sorry, Sophie. Maybe I can pick you up later. (*Haltingly*) I am sorry.

SOPHIE   I do not mind, really. It is better this way.

CARRIE   Don't you? Why not? (*No answer*) Why don't you mind, Sophie?

SOPHIE   (*Smiles*) I do not like parties. I did not want to go. Now Frederick has some important business and must leave quickly—

CARRIE   Perhaps you are going to make *too* good a wife.

FREDERICK   Suppose you let me decide that, Mother. Good night. Have a good time. See you in the morning—

CARRIE   I want to talk to you, Frederick.

FREDERICK   (*Stops, smiles*) When you use that tone of voice you need two hours. Let's make it in the morning, Mother.

(SOPHIE *has turned away, gone upstage, as if she wanted to be as far away as possible.*)

CARRIE   I ask you to break your appointment with Payson. As a favor to me.

FREDERICK   There's nothing important about my being at the party and it is important to him. He wants to consult me—

CARRIE   (*Sharply*) He is always consulting you. You talk like a public accountant or a landscape gardener. Why should he want to consult *you* about his work?

FREDERICK   (*Hurt*) Maybe because I try to write and maybe because he thinks I know a little. I realize that's hard for you to believe—

CARRIE   I didn't mean that.

FREDERICK   I think you did. Good night.

CARRIE   You have no sense of obligation to me. (*Looks around for* SOPHIE, *who is trying at this minute to leave the room*) And none to Sophie. Who evidently won't speak for herself. Do stay here, Sophie, it's your business as well as mine— (SOPHIE *stands still*) I am getting tired of Mr. Payson, Frederick, and with good reason. When he came to stay with us in town last winter, I fully understood that he was a brilliant and gifted man and I was glad for you to have such a friend. But when he followed you down here this summer—

FREDERICK   (*Slowly, angrily*) He did not follow me down here and I wouldn't like you to put it that way again.

He came here for the summer and is that your business, Mother?

CARRIE There is just too much of Mr. Payson. Every day or every evening— How often do you take Sophie with you? (*Sharply*) How often have you seen Mr. Payson this summer, Sophie? (*There is no answer*) Please answer me.

FREDERICK And please stop using that tone to Sophie. Say what you have to say to me.

CARRIE (*Turning to* MRS. ELLIS, *who has been watching them*) Mother—

MRS. ELLIS I've been dozing. How many hours have passed?

CARRIE (*Slowly*) You are always dozing when there is something unpleasant to face out with Frederick.

MRS. ELLIS What better time? You all want to know something's been worrying me all day? Nobody in the South has tapeworm any more. In my day that was all you ever heard. Tapeworm, tapeworm, tapeworm. (*Gets up*) Now kiss your mother good night, boy. Otherwise she'll be most unhappy. And say you forgive her.

FREDERICK I have nothing to forgive her for, Grandma.

MRS. ELLIS Of course not. But even when your mother starts out being right she talks and talks until she gets around to being wrong.

(*She exits. There is silence.*)

CARRIE (*Softly*) I'm sorry if I spoke unfairly, or at the wrong time—

FREDERICK (*Comes to her, smiling*) You didn't, you didn't. Now don't feel bad. Nothing's happened. And don't let Grandma tease you.

CARRIE I know. (*She turns to go*) You go ahead, dear. Try to join us later.

(*He kisses her. She smiles, pleased, and goes out.* FREDERICK *turns to* SOPHIE.)

FREDERICK Sophie, Mother didn't mean to be sharp with you. But when she is, you mustn't let her. She's a little bossy from time to time, but no harm in it. You look so worried.

SOPHIE (*Very puzzled*) Your mother is not angry now?

FREDERICK Of course not. You mustn't take these things too seriously. Mother is like that.

SOPHIE (*Smiles*) You know it is most difficult in another language. Everything in English sounds so important. I get a headache from the strain of listening.

FREDERICK (*Laughs*) Don't. It's not worth it. (*Looks at her, then slowly*) Mother is right: I have been rude and neglectful. But I haven't meant to be, Sophie.

SOPHIE No, no. You have not been.

FREDERICK And in two weeks Mother and I will be going off to Europe. I hope you don't mind about the European trip. It was all arranged long before you and I— (*Stares at her, smiles*) engaged. (SOPHIE *smiles at him as if she were embarrassed, then she coughs and clears her throat*) We're an awkward pair. I like you, Sophie.

SOPHIE (*Warmly*) I like you, Frederick.

FREDERICK Sophie, I think we'll have to sit down soon and talk about ourselves. I don't think we even know how we got engaged. We haven't said much of anything—

SOPHIE Sometimes it is better not to say things. There is time and things will come as they come.

FREDERICK The day we got engaged, we tried to speak as honestly as we both knew how but we didn't say very much—

SOPHIE And I think we should not try so hard to talk. Sometimes it is wise to let things grow more roots before one blows them away with many words— (*Shyly touches his hand*) It will come better if we give it time.

FREDERICK We will give it time. And you'll make no decisions and set no dates until you are sure about what you think and feel.

SOPHIE Oh, I have made the decision for myself. And I am pleased.

FREDERICK (*Pleased*) And you are quite sure of your decision?

SOPHIE You know, sometimes I have thought that with rich people— (*Very quickly*) with educated people, I mean, decisions are made only in order to speak about changing them. It happens often with Aunt Constance and with your mother, also, I think. And the others.

FREDERICK   Yes. (*Takes her hand*) We'll get along fine. I want you to know that I feel very lucky—

SOPHIE   Lucky? You will have to be patient with me. I am not a good success here.

FREDERICK   Now, you stop that. I don't want you a good success. And you're to stop thinking it. You're to stop a lot of things: letting Mother boss you about, letting Mrs. Griggs tell you what to wear, or pull your hair—

SOPHIE   Oh, I do not mind. Because I look so bad makes Mrs. Griggs think she looks so good.

FREDERICK   (*Smiles*)   Good night, my dear.

SOPHIE   (*Smiles*)   Good night.

(*He exits.* SOPHIE *begins to pick up the coffee cups, brandy glasses, etc. After a minute* ROSE GRIGGS *comes down the steps carrying a light summer wrap. She comes into the room.*)

ROSE   Where are the Ellises?

SOPHIE   They went to the party, Mrs. Griggs.

ROSE   No! Without me? I *must* say that's very rude. They can't have done that, Sophie— (*She hurries to the hall, looks out. Then she comes back in, goes to the porch*) Ben. (*He looks up*) The Ellises left without me, Ben!

GRIGGS   Yes?

ROSE   You'll have to walk me over. I just won't go in, alone.

GRIGGS   It's across the street, Rose. Not a very dangerous journey.

ROSE   (*Gently*)   Ben. (*He rises, comes in*) You know, I think it's shocking. In front of other people. God knows what they know or guess this summer. (*Suddenly notices* SOPHIE *who is collecting cups*) Sophie. Don't wait here listening.

(SOPHIE *turns, surprised, but before she can speak . . .*)

GRIGGS   (*Sharply*)   Rose!

ROSE   (*Who is always charming at this point. To* SOPHIE) I am sorry, my dear. Please most earnestly I ask your pardon—

SOPHIE   Yes, ma'am.

ROSE   (*Tries to catch her at door*) I'm just a nervous old
silly these days. Now say you forgive me—

(SOPHIE *disappears.*)

GRIGGS   (*Smiles, as if he has seen this before*) All right,
Rose. You're charming.

ROSE   You won't even walk over with me, just to the door?

GRIGGS   Certainly I will.

ROSE   (*Smiles*) No, you don't have to. I just wanted to see
if you would. Will you call for me, at twelve, say?

GRIGGS   No.

ROSE   Then will you meet me at twelve, at the tavern?

GRIGGS   No. What mischief is this, Rose?

ROSE   Is it mischief to want to talk with you?

GRIGGS   Again? Tonight? And every night and every day?
The same things over and over? We're worn out, Rose,
both of us. (*Kindly*) There is no more to say.

ROSE   (*Softly*) No more to say. Do people get divorces,
after twenty-five years, by just saying they want them
and that's all and walking off?

GRIGGS   I suppose some men do. But I haven't walked off
and I have said all I know how to say.

ROSE   But you haven't really explained anything to me.
You tell me that you want a divorce— And I ask why,
why, why. We've been happy together.

GRIGGS   (*Looks at her*) You don't believe that.

ROSE   When people get our age, well, the worst is over—
and what else can one do? (*Exasperated*) I never really
heard of such a thing. I'm just not taking you seriously
and I do wish you'd stop talking about it. (*After a
pause*) You've never given me a good reason. I ask you
ten times a day if there's another woman. I could understand that. Of course you say no, naturally—

GRIGGS   There is no other woman.

ROSE   (*Giggles*) You know what I think? I think it's that
little blonde at the drugstore, and the minute my back
is turned—

GRIGGS   Please, Rose. Please stop that.

ROSE   Never at any time, during this divorce talk, have you
mentioned them. You'd think we didn't have sons, and
the awful effect on them. Did you write them today?

GRIGGS I did not write them because you begged me not to.

ROSE Oh, yes, I forgot. It will break their hearts.

GRIGGS Their hearts won't be broken. They won't even bother to finish the letter.

ROSE (*Softly, shocked*) You can't love them, to speak that way.

GRIGGS I don't love them. I did love them but I don't now. They're hard men to love.

ROSE Oh, I don't believe a word you say. You've always enjoyed shocking me. You've been a wonderful father and you're just as devoted to them as they are to you.

GRIGGS They aren't the least devoted to me—when they think about me it is to find my name useful and when it isn't useful they disapprove of me.

ROSE (*Moving to door*) Look, Ben. I just can't stay and talk all night. I'm late now. There's no use our saying the same things over and over again— (*He laughs*) If you won't come to the party what are you going to do?

GRIGGS I am going down by the water, sit on a bench and study from a Chinese grammar.

ROSE You'll be lonely.

GRIGGS Yes, but not for parties.

ROSE It's very hard to take seriously a man who spends the evening with a Chinese grammar. I'll never forget that winter with the Hebrew phonograph records. (*Pats his arm*) Now, good night, darling. And don't worry about me: I am going to try to have a good time. We'll talk about all this another day.

(*She starts out.*)

GRIGGS (*Sharply*) No. No, we're not going to do that. You're turning it into a pleasure, Rose, something to chatter about on a dull winter night in the years to come. I've told you it isn't going to be that way. (*She is in the hall*) It isn't going to be that way. When you go back to town next week I'm not going with you.

(*He turns to see that she has gone.*)

ROSE'S VOICE (*From the hall*) Good night, darling.

GRIGGS (*He stands still for a minute. Then he turns, sees his book on the porch table. Goes out to the porch, re-*

alizes the doors have been open. To CROSSMAN). I guess
we thought the doors were closed. I am sorry.

CROSSMAN Don't be.

GRIGGS There are so many things I want to do that I don't
know which to do first. Have you ever thought about
starting a new life?

CROSSMAN (*Smiles*) I've often thought that if I started
all over again, I'd go right back to where I started and
start from there. Otherwise, it wouldn't prove anything.

GRIGGS (*Laughs*) Where'd you start from?

CROSSMAN (*Laughs*) Nowhere. That's the trouble.

GRIGGS I started with mathematics. Seems strange now,
but that's why I went to West Point—wonderful mathematics department. So I got myself two wars instead. I
want to go somewhere now and study for a few years,
or— (*Smiles*) Anyway, sit down by myself and think.

CROSSMAN Europe?

GRIGGS I don't think so. Europe seemed like a tourist joint
the last time. With all the aimless, dead bitterness of—
tourist joints. I don't want sentimental journeys to old
battlefields. I'll start tame enough: I've written my sister
that I'd like to stay with her for a month or two.

CROSSMAN Isn't that a sentimental journey?

GRIGGS I suppose it is. I really want to see her because she
looks like my mother. The last six months I've thought
a lot about my mother. If I could just go back to her for
a day. Crazy at my age—

CROSSMAN I know. We all do at times. Age has nothing to
do with it. It's when we're in trouble.

GRIGGS I don't know why I want to say this but, well, don't
think too badly of my wife.

CROSSMAN Why should I think badly of anybody?

GRIGGS (*As he turns to go*) All professional soldiers marry
Rose. It's in the Army Manual. She is as she always was.
It is my fault, not hers.

CROSSMAN Haven't you lived in the South long enough to
know that nothing is ever anybody's fault?

(GENERAL GRIGGS *laughs, starts out as* CONSTANCE *comes
downstairs.* CONSTANCE *has on a different dress and is
buttoning the belt as she comes into the room.* GENERAL

GRIGGS *crosses the room and exits by the stage left windows.* CONSTANCE *looks around, finds the room is neat, goes out to the porch, talking as she goes.*)

CONSTANCE I *think* everything is ready. I've put Nick in Sophie's room— Sophie says she doesn't mind sleeping down here. Anyway it happens every summer. And I've given Mrs. Denery the yellow room. They wanted *two* rooms, Nick said on the phone.

CROSSMAN Fashionable people don't sleep together, don't you know that? It's not sanitary.

CONSTANCE (*Sits down*) I'm tired, Ned.

CROSSMAN Have a brandy.

CONSTANCE No. It would make me nervous.

CROSSMAN Remarkable the things that make people nervous: coffee, brandy, relatives, running water, too much sun, too little sun. Never anything in themselves, eh, Constance?

CONSTANCE They have a maid and a chauffeur. I'll have to put them in the boathouse. It's all so much work at the end of the season. Sophie's been cleaning all day, and I've been cooking— Why did I say they could come?

CROSSMAN (*Smiles*) I wonder why.

CONSTANCE Well, of course, I want to see Nick again. But I am nervous about meeting her. (*Points to his glass*) Do you think perhaps a sip?

CROSSMAN Only drunkards borrow other people's drinks. Have one of your own.

(*Through her next speech he pours her a drink and hands it to her. When she finishes it, he will take back the glass and pour himself a drink.*)

CONSTANCE I got out Mama's good, old linen sheets. I don't care how rich the Denerys are, or where they've been, they never could have had finer linen. And I've stuffed some crabs and there's white wine— Remember how Nick loved stuffed crabs?

CROSSMAN (*Smiles*) No. I don't remember.

CONSTANCE It was twenty-three years ago, the eighteenth of next month. I mean the night he decided to go to Paris to study. Not so many young men from New Orleans went to Paris in those days.

CROSSMAN   Just as many young men met rich young ladies on boats.

CONSTANCE   (*Sharply*) *He fell in love.* People can't be blamed for changing their hearts—it just happens. They've had a fine marriage, and *that's* given me happiness all these years.

CROSSMAN   How do you know they've had a "fine" marriage?

CONSTANCE   (*Smiles*) I know.

CROSSMAN   The rest of us don't know anything about any marriage—but you know all about one you've never seen. You're very wise, Constance. It must come from not thinking.

CONSTANCE   Is this dress all right?

CROSSMAN   You've changed your dress three times since dinner.

CONSTANCE   My dresses are all sort of— She'll think they're cheap. (*Smiles*) Well, and so they are. (*There is silence. Then*) Have we changed much, Ned?

CROSSMAN   Yes, my dear. You've changed, I've changed. But you're still handsome, if that's what you mean.

CONSTANCE   Ned, you don't look so well this summer. (*He is pouring himself another brandy. She points to bottle*) I wanted to tell you— Don't you think—

CROSSMAN   (*Very pleasantly*) Don't I think you should mind your business? Yes, I do.

(SOPHIE *comes into living room carrying sheets, a quilt, a pillow, puts them down and moves to porch.*)

CONSTANCE   Isn't what happens to you my business?

SOPHIE   You look pretty, Aunt Constance.

CONSTANCE   (*To* CROSSMAN) Sophie made this dress for me.. Last winter. What could the girls at school have thought? Sophie sitting sewing for an old country aunt when she could have been out dancing—

SOPHIE   I sew better than I dance.

CONSTANCE   (*To* CROSSMAN) Sophie's mother taught her to sew. You know that Ann-Marie is a modiste?

SOPHIE   (*Laughs*) Oh, she is not. She is what you call here a home-seamstress, or sometimes a factory worker.

CONSTANCE But she *designs*. She wrote me and you told me—

SOPHIE (*Laughs*) Oh no. You did not understand. She does—

(*Outside the house there is the noise of a car coming to a stop.* CONSTANCE *turns towards the room, then steps back, moves around the table and suddenly runs into the house.* CROSSMAN *turns to stare at her.*)

SOPHIE (*Timidly, pointing out towards living room*) Should I— Should I stay, Mr. Ned?

CROSSMAN I don't know the etiquette of such meetings.

SOPHIE Why is Aunt Constance so nervous about the visit of this lady and gentleman?

CROSSMAN Because she was once in love with Nicholas Denery, this gentleman.

SOPHIE Oh. Such a long, long time to stay nervous. (*Sententious*) Great love in tender natures. And things of such kind. (*As he turns to stare at her*) It always happens that way with ladies. For them it is once and not again: it is their good breeding that makes it so.

CROSSMAN What is the matter with you?

SOPHIE (*Laughs*) I try very hard to sound nice. I try too hard, perhaps?

(*She begins to move out into the room; then, as she hears voices, she runs out of the room, exits off porch.*)

NICK'S VOICE (*Offstage*) Constance?

(NICK *appears in the hall and comes into the room. He is about forty-five, handsome, a little soft-looking and in a few years will be too heavy. He is followed by* NINA DENERY, *who is a woman of about forty, good-looking, chic, tired and delicate. She stops and stands in the doorway.*)

NICK (*Calling*) Constance!

(NICK *and* NINA *are followed by a maid,* HILDA, *who stands waiting in the hall. She is carrying a jewelry case, an overnight bag, two coats.* CROSSMAN *starts to come forward, changes his mind, draws back.*)

HILDA (*In German*) Shall I take the bags upstairs, madame?

NINA (*In German*) We don't know where upstairs is.

NICK   Oh, I know where upstairs is. I know every foot of this house. (*Examining the room*) It was *the* great summer mansion and as kids we were here more than we were at home— (*Softly*) The great summer mansion! Did the house change, or me? (*Sees* NINA *in doorway*) Come on in.

NINA   Perhaps it would be pleasanter for you to see old friends without me. In any case. I am very tired—

NICK   Oh, now don't get tired. We've just come. What have you got to be tired about? Do you realize how often these days you're tired?

NINA   I realize it very well. And I know it bores you.

NICK   It *worries* me. (*By this time,* NICK, *wandering around the room, has reached the porch.* CROSSMAN *turns and, realizing that he has been seen, now comes forward*) Could you tell me where we could find Miss Tuckerman?

CROSSMAN   Hello, Nick. Good to see you.

NICK   (*After a second*) My God, Willy. How many years, how many years? (*He puts his arm around* CROSSMAN, *embraces him*) Nina, this may be my oldest and best friend in the world. Nina, tell Willy how often I've talked about him and what I said.

CROSSMAN   (*Who is shaking hands with* NINA, *amused*) Then I hope he told you that my name is Edward, not Willy.

NINA   (*Amused*) I hope so—but I am not sure.

NICK   Your mother always called you Willy. Don't you remember?

CROSSMAN   (*Goes out into the hall*) No. I thought it was my brother's name. (*Calls out, loudly*) Constance, Nick is here.

NICK   (*Coming to* CROSSMAN) Tell me before I see her. What has happened here? I don't know anything.

CROSSMAN   There's very little to know. Old man Tuckerman surprised everybody by dying broke. Constance sold the New Orleans house and managed to hang on to this by turning it into what is called a summer guest house. That's about all, Nick.

NICK   Where is Mrs. Tuckerman? I was crazy about her, Nina: she had style.

CROSSMAN I don't know where she is, although I've asked myself often enough. She died shortly after Mr. Tucker-man—just to show him anybody could do it.

NICK (*Laughs, pats* CROSSMAN) Good to see you, boy. You know, if anybody had asked me, I would have said this room was as large as an eighteenth-century ballroom and as elegant. I think it shrank. All the fine things were sold?

CROSSMAN The size hasn't changed. And nothing was sold.

NICK Could I have been so wrong all these years? Seems so shabby now and—

NINA (*Quickly*) I think it is a pleasant room.

NICK Does Sam live here?

CROSSMAN Sam died during the war. He went to Europe, oh, in the thirties, married there and never came back. You'll meet his daughter. Constance imported her five years ago.

NICK Well, Sam was always the devoted brother until it came to being devoted. And Constance sacrificed her life for him.

CROSSMAN (*To* NINA) Nick is still a Southerner. With us every well-born lady sacrifices her life for something: a man, a house, sometimes a gardenia bush. Is it the same where you come from?

NINA (*Smiles*) New York is too cold for gardenias.

(*Through* CROSSMAN'S *speech,* CONSTANCE *appears in the hall. As she moves into the room, she trips, recovers herself, smiles nervously and waits for* NICK *to come to her. He takes her face in his hands and kisses her. Then he stands back to look at her.*)

NICK This is a good hour of my life, Constance.

CONSTANCE (*Softly*) And of mine.

NICK (*Holds her face*) You've changed and you've changed well. Do you still have the portrait, Constance?

CONSTANCE (*Smiles*) *Still* have the portrait! It's the only important thing I have got— (*Then she remembers* NINA, *becomes confused, moves away from him and comes to* NINA) Forgive me, Mrs. Denery.

NINA (*Puts out her hand, warmly*) Hello. .

CONSTANCE (*Flossy*) I should have been here to make

you as welcome as you truly are. I was reading when you arrived, reading a book, and I didn't hear the car.

(*She sees* CROSSMAN *is staring at her and she looks nervously away from him.*)

NICK   I had expected you standing in the driveway with the sun in your face, in the kind of lovely pink thing you used to wear—

NINA   The sun is not usually out at night—even for you.

NICK   (*To* CONSTANCE) Instead, you are reading. As if you were waiting for the groceries to come.

CONSTANCE   (*Quickly*) I wasn't reading. It was a silly lie. I was just pretending— (*Embarrassed*) Well, I'm even forgetting my manners. You must be hungry, Mrs. Denery, and I've got—

NICK   (*Laughs, takes her hands, pulls her to the couch*) No, no. Stop your manners, girl. There's a great deal I want to know. (*They sit down*) Now. Is the portrait as good as I remember it? I want Nina to see it. Nina knows a great deal about painting. Sometimes I think she knows more than I.

CONSTANCE   (*Smiles to* NINA, *nods. Then to* NICK) You know, Nick, I subscribe to the New York Sunday *Times*. Because of the art section. I wanted to follow your career.

NICK   (*Carefully*) You haven't often found me in the *Times*. I've only exhibited in Europe.

CONSTANCE   (*Relieved*) Oh. That explains it.

(*There is a slight, awkward pause.*)

I like painting. I like Renoir best. The summer ladies in the gardens, so very, very pretty.

NICK   (*Bored*) Yes, very pretty. This is the same wonderful place— My God, we had happy summers here, all of us. We loved each other so very much. Remember, Ned?

CROSSMAN   I don't remember that much love.

NINA   (*Laughs*) I like you, Mr. Crossman.

NICK   Of course you like him. These are my oldest friends. I think as one grows older it is more and more necessary to reach out your hand for the sturdy old vines you knew when you were young and let them lead you back

to the roots of things that matter. (NINA *coughs.* CROSS-
MAN *moves away, smiling. Even* CONSTANCE *is a little
overwhelmed*) Isn't that true, Ned? Now what have you
been up to all these years?

CROSSMAN   I still work in the bank and come here for my
vacation. That's about all.

NICK   I bumped into Louis Prescott in Paris a couple of
years ago and he told me you and Constance had never
married—

(*Pats* CONSTANCE's *hand;* CONSTANCE *looks embarrassed.*)
Couldn't understand it. No wonder you drink too much,
Ned.

CROSSMAN   Louis Prescott go all the way to Paris to tell you
that?

NICK   (*Anxious, gets up*) Oh, look old boy. I didn't mean
anything— I drink too much myself. I only want to
know about you and have you know about me. I hope
you didn't mind, Ned.

CROSSMAN   Not a bit. I want to know about you, too. Ever
had syphilis, Nick? Kind of thing one has to know right
off, if you understand me.

CONSTANCE   (*Gets up, very disturbed*) Ned, how can you
speak that way?

NICK   (*Smiles*) You've grown edgy. I didn't remember
you that way.

CROSSMAN   (*Pleasantly*) Oh, I don't think I've changed.
See you in the morning.

NICK   Hope you'll take me around, show me all the old
places—

CROSSMAN   Of course I will. Good night, Mrs. Denery.

(*He exits up staircase.*)

NICK   (*To* CONSTANCE, *meaning* CROSSMAN) I'm sorry if I
said anything—

CONSTANCE   You know, for years I've been meeting you
and Mrs. Denery—in my mind, I mean—and I've played
all kinds of roles. Sometimes I was the dignified old
friend, and sometimes I was a very, very old lady wel-
coming you to a gracious table. It was so important to
me—our first meeting— (*Sadly*) And now when it happens—

NICK (*Heartily*) Nonsense. My homecoming is just as it should be. It's as if I had gone away yesterday. We took up right where we left off: even Ned and I. Let us be as we were, my dear, with no years between us, and no pretending.

CONSTANCE (*Delighted with him, warmly*) Thank you. (*Goes to* NINA) All these years I wanted to write you. I did write but I never sent the letters. It seemed so intrusive of me. I could see you getting the letter and just not knowing who I was.

NICK I told Nina about you the first night I met her and through the years she has done quite a little teasing— You are too modest, Constance. (*Suddenly*) Now are you going to let me do another portrait of you?

CONSTANCE (*Laughs*) Another portrait? No, no, indeed. I want to remember myself as I was in the picture upstairs.

NICK Go and get it for me. I want to look at it with you. (*She smiles, exits. There is silence*) You haven't been too warm or gracious, Nina.

NINA What can I do when I don't even know the plot?

NICK What are you talking about?

NINA You told me about Constance Tuckerman the first night we met? And about dear Willy or Ned, and I've done quite a little teasing about her all these years?

NICK I did tell you about her immediately—

NINA You mentioned her very casually, last week, years after the night you met me and you said that you could hardly remember anything more about her than a rather silly—

NICK (*Quickly*) Are you going to be bad-tempered for our whole visit here? For years I've looked forward to coming back—

(NINA *laughs.*)

NINA So you came to do her portrait?

NICK No, I didn't "come to do her portrait." I thought about it driving down here. If the one I did is as good as I remember, it would be wonderful for the show. The young girl, the woman at forty-five. She's aged. Have we changed that much? I don't think you've changed, darling.

NINA I've changed a great deal. And I wouldn't want it pointed out to me in a portrait to be hung side by side with a picture of what I used to be. (*He doesn't answer her*) That isn't a nice reason for being here and if I had known it—

NICK We have no "reason" for being here. I just wanted to come back. Nothing mysterious about it—

NINA You're simply looking for a new area in which to exercise yourself. It has happened many, many times before. But it *always* happens when we return from Europe and spend a month in New York. It's been too important to you, for many years, that you cannot manage to charm my family. And so, when our visit is finished there, you inevitably look around for— Well, you know. You know what's been and the trouble.

NICK (*Cheerfully*) I don't know what the hell you're talking about.

NINA I'm tired of such troubles, Nick—

NICK Do you know that these sharp moods of yours grow more sharp with time? Now I would like to have a happy visit here. But if something is disturbing you and you'd prefer not to stay, I'll arrange immediately—

NINA (*As if she were a little frightened*) I'd only prefer to go to bed. Sorry if I've been churly about your— homecoming. (*She starts out, meets* CONSTANCE *who comes in carrying portrait*) Will you excuse me, Constance? The long drive gave me a headache.

CONSTANCE I am sorry. Will I bring you a tray upstairs?

NINA No, thank you.

(CONSTANCE *moves as if to show her the way.*)

NICK Come, I want to see the picture. Nina will find her way.

(*He takes the picture from* CONSTANCE.)

CONSTANCE The yellow room on the left. Your maid is unpacking. I peeked in. What lovely clothes. Can I come and see them tomorrow?

NINA (*Going up the stairs*) Yes, of course. Thank you and good night.

(CONSTANCE *watches her and then comes into room.*)

NICK   (*Who is looking at the picture*) I was nervous about seeing it. Damn good work for a boy of eighteen.

CONSTANCE   You were twenty-two, Nick.

NICK   No, I wasn't. I—

CONSTANCE   You finished it the morning of your birthday. (*She points to windows*) And when you put down your brushes you said damn good work for a boy of twenty-two, and then you asked me to marry you. Don't you remember— (*She stops, embarrassed*) Why should you remember? And I don't want to talk that way.

NICK   (*Who is preoccupied with the picture*) Oh, non-sense. Talk any way you like. We were in love, very much in love, and why shouldn't we speak of it?

CONSTANCE   (*Hastily, very embarrassed*) After I die, the picture will go to the Delgado Museum.

NICK   (*Laughs*) I want to borrow it first. I'm having a retrospective show this winter, in London. I've done a lot of fancy people in Europe, you know that, but I'll be more proud of this— And I want to do another por-trait of you as you are now. (*Moves toward window, excited*) You standing here. As before. Wonderful idea; young girl, woman at— Be a sensation. Constance, it's fascinating how faces change, mold firm or loose, have lines that start in youth and—

CONSTANCE   (*Amazed*) Oh, Nick. I don't want to see myself now. I don't want to see all the changes. And I don't want other people to stand and talk about them. I don't want people to laugh at me or pity me. (*Hurt*) Oh, Nick.

NICK   I see. (*Turns*) Well, it would have meant a lot to me. But that's that. I'll be off to bed now—

CONSTANCE   (*Coming after him*) But we haven't had a minute. And I have supper all ready for you—

NICK   Good night, my dear.

CONSTANCE   (*Slowly*) You think I'm being selfish and vain? I mean, am I the only woman who wouldn't like—

NICK   No, I think most women would feel the same way. (*He starts out.*)

CONSTANCE Do you prefer breakfast in bed? And what shall I make for your dinner? Pompano—

(*He is at the door as* CARRIE *and* ROSE *come into the hall.* CARRIE *is holding* ROSE's *arm.*)

CARRIE Hello, Nick.

NICK (*Takes her hands*) My God, Carrie. I didn't know you were here. How come? It's wonderful—

CARRIE We come every summer.

NICK You're handsome, Carrie. But you always were.

CARRIE (*Smiles*) And you always remembered to say so. (ROSE *coughs delicately*) This is Mrs. Griggs. (*To* CONSTANCE) Mrs. Griggs didn't feel well, so I brought her home. She became a little dizzy, dancing.

ROSE (*To* NICK, *who is shaking hands with her*) You're a famous gentleman in this town, sir, and I've been looking forward so to seeing you. We lead dull lives here, you know—

NICK (*Laughs*) *You* don't look as if you do.

ROSE Oh, thank you. But I don't look well tonight. I became suddenly a little ill—

CARRIE (*Tartly*) Yes. Well, come along. If you still feel ill.

NICK Can I help you, Mrs. Griggs?

ROSE (*Delighted*) Oh, thank you. That would be nice. I haven't been well this summer—

(NICK *starts into hall.*)

CONSTANCE Nick—

(*He pays no attention.* CARRIE *moves quickly ahead of him, takes* ROSE's *arm.*)

CARRIE Come. Good night, Nick. I look forward to seeing you in the morning. Hope you're staying for a while.

NICK I think we'll have to leave tomorrow.

ROSE Oh, don't do that. (*Then*) Constance, if Ben comes in would you tell him I was taken ill?

(CARRIE *impatiently pushes her ahead and up the steps.*)

NICK (*Meaning* ROSE) Pretty woman, or was. (*Looks at* CONSTANCE) What is it, Con?

CONSTANCE How can you talk of leaving tomorrow? (*He doesn't answer*) Don't be mad with me, Nick.

NICK I don't get mad, darling.

CONSTANCE (*Catches him as he is almost out the door*)
Please, Nick, please let me change my mind. You are
welcome to take this picture and I am flattered you wish
to do another. But I'll have to pose early, before they're
all down for breakfast—

NICK (*turns casually*) Good. We'll start in the morning.
Do you make a living out of this place, darling?

CONSTANCE (*Gaily*) Not much of one. The last few years
have been a little hard. I brought Sam's daughter from
Europe—she and her mother went through the occupation and were very poor—and I've tried to send her to
the best school and then she was to make her debut, only
now she wants to get married, I think, and—

NICK The girl expected all that from you?

CONSTANCE Oh, no. Her mother didn't want to come and
Sophie didn't want to leave her mother. I finally had
really to *demand* that Sam's daughter was not to grow
up— Well, I just can't describe it. At thirteen she was
working in a fish store or whatever you call it over there.
I just *made* her come over—

NICK Why didn't you ever marry Ned?

CONSTANCE I can't answer such questions, Nick. Even for
you.

NICK Why not? I'd tell you about myself or Nina.

CONSTANCE Oh, it's one thing to talk about lives that have
been good and full and happy and quite another— Well,
I don't know. We just never did marry.

NICK (*Bored*) Well, then, tomorrow morning. I'll do a
good portrait of you because it's the face of a good
woman—

(*He stops as* SOPHIE *comes in. She sees* NICK *and* CON-
STANCE *and draws back a little.*)

CONSTANCE Sophie. (SOPHIE *comes into the room*) This
is Sam's daughter.

NICK (*Very warmly to* SOPHIE) I've been looking forward
to meeting you for many years.

(CONSTANCE *turns, puzzled.*)

SOPHIE How do you do, sir?

NICK You follow in the great tradition of Tuckerman
good looks.

SOPHIE   Er. Er.

CONSTANCE   (*Smiles*) Don't er, dear. Say thank you.
(GRIGGS *enters from left porch*) Do come in. (GRIGGS
comes in) This is General Griggs. My very old friend,
Nicholas Denery.

NICK   Are you General Benjamin Griggs? I've read about
you in Raymond's book and Powell's.

GRIGGS   (*As they shake hands*) I hear they disagree about
me.

NICK   We almost met before this. When your boys marched
into Paris. I was in France during the German occupation.

(SOPHIE *turns sharply.*)

GRIGGS   That must have been unpleasant for you.

NICK   Yes, it was. But in the end, one has to be just; the
Germans were damn smart about the French. They
acted like gentlemen.

GRIGGS   (*Pleasantly*) That's a side of them I didn't see.
(*Looks over at* SOPHIE) You didn't either, Sophie?

(*During his speech* HILDA, *the maid, appears in the doorway.*)

HILDA   (*In German*) Excuse me, Mr. Denery. Mrs. Denery would like you to come for a minute before you
retire. She has a little surprise gift she bought for you in
New Orleans.

NICK   (*In German*) No. Tell Mrs. Denery I will see her
in the morning. Tell her to take a sleeping pill.

HILDA   (*In German*) Thank you, sir.

CONSTANCE   (*Who hasn't understood the German but who
is puzzled because* SOPHIE *is frowning and* GRIGGS *has
turned away*) Can I— Does Nina want something?

NICK   No, no, she's fine. (SOPHIE *begins to make up the
couch.* NICK *turns to her*) That means one of us must
have put you out of your room. I'm sorry and I thank
you.

SOPHIE   Not at all, sir. It is nothing.

NICK   (*Comes to her*) You're a sweet child and I look
forward to knowing you. Good night. (*To* GRIGGS) Good
night, sir. A great pleasure. (GRIGGS *bows.* NICK *kisses*
CONSTANCE) Wonderful to be here, darling.

(*He goes out.* CONSTANCE *moves to help* SOPHIE *make up the couch. There is silence for a minute while they arrange the bedclothes.* GRIGGS *watches them.*)

CONSTANCE I suppose I shouldn't ask but what did the German maid want? Something from the kitchen or— (*No answer*) Sophie. (*No answer*) Sophie.

SOPHIE (*Slowly*) Mrs. Denery wanted to say good night to Mr. Denery.

GRIGGS Mrs. Denery had bought a little gift for him in New Orleans and wanted to give it to him.

CONSTANCE After all these years. To have a little gift for him. Isn't that nice? (*She looks at* GRIGGS *and* SOPHIE. *Neither answers her. She becomes conscious of something strained*) What did Nick say?

SOPHIE He said she should take a sleeping pill and go to sleep.

CONSTANCE Just like that?

SOPHIE Down at the beach there is the frankfurter concession. I think I will get the sleeping-pill concession and grow very rich.

CONSTANCE Why, Sophie. Are you disturbed about something, dear? (*Looks at her dress*) You didn't go to the party! I've been so busy, I didn't realize— Why, where's Fred and—

SOPHIE I did not wish to go to the party, Aunt Constance. And Frederick had a most important appointment.

CONSTANCE More important than being with you? Young people get engaged and act toward each other with such— I don't know. (*To* GRIGGS) In our day we made marriage more romantic and I must say I think we had more fun. If you can't have fine dreams now, then when can you have them? (*Pats* SOPHIE) Never mind. I guess the new way is more sensible. But I like our way better. (*To* GRIGGS) Didn't you? Oh, what's the matter with me? I forgot. Rose came back from the party. She said she was ill. I mean, I think she just didn't feel well— Carrie is upstairs with her. (*He doesn't move*) I think Carrie probably wants to go back to the party and is waiting for you to come.

GRIGGS Yes. Of course. Thank you. Good night.

(*He exits.*)

CONSTANCE   (*She kisses* SOPHIE)   You'll be comfortable? See you in the morning, dear.

(*She exits through the hall.* SOPHIE *finishes with the couch, goes out. After a second,* CROSSMAN *comes down the stairs. He sticks his head in the door, sees nobody, crosses the room, goes out to the porch, takes the bottle of brandy and a glass, moves back into the room and crosses it as* SOPHIE *returns carrying pajamas and a robe.*)

CROSSMAN   (*His voice and his manner are slightly different now*)   I needed another book and another bottle. Royalty gone to bed? Does anybody improve with age? Just tell me that, Sophie, and I'll have something to lie awake and think about.

SOPHIE   I do not know, Mr. Ned.

CROSSMAN   For God's sake, Sophie, have an opinion about *something*. Try it, and see what comes out.

SOPHIE   (*Laughs*)   Some people improve with age, some do not.

CROSSMAN   (*Nods, amused*)   Wonderful, Sophie, wonderful. Some improve with age, some do not. Medical statistics show that 61 per cent of those who improve have bought our book on Dianetics and smoke Iglewitz cigarettes. You're beginning to talk like an advertisement, which is the very highest form of American talk. (*Sharply*)   It's not *your* language, nor your native land. You don't have to care about it. You shouldn't even understand it.

SOPHIE   Sometimes I understand.

CROSSMAN   That's dangerous to admit, Sophie. You've been so busy cultivating a pseudo-stupidity. Not that you'd ever be a brilliant girl, but at least you used to be normal. Another five years and you won't be *pseudo*-stupid.

SOPHIE   (*Smiles*)   I will not mind. It will be easier. (*Carefully*)   You notice me too much, Mr. Ned. Please do not feel sorry or notice me so much.

CROSSMAN   You came here a nice little girl who had seen a lot of war and trouble. You had spirit, in a quiet way, and you were gay, in a quiet way, which is the only way women should be gay since they are never really gay at all. Only serious people are ever gay and women are very seldom serious people. They are earnest instead. But earnestness has nothing to do with seriousness. So. (*Suddenly*) What the hell is this marriage business between you and Fred Ellis?

SOPHIE (*Softly*) It is the marriage business between me and Fred Ellis.

GROSSMAN But what's the matter with you? Haven't you got sense enough to know—

SOPHIE (*Quickly*) I do the best I can. I do the best I can. And I thank you for worrying about me, but you are an educated man with ideas in English that I am not qualified to understand.

CROSSMAN Listen to me, Sophie. Sometimes when I've had enough to drink—just exactly enough—I feel as if I were given to understand that which I may not understand again. And sometimes then—but rarely—I have an urge to speak out. Fewer drinks, more drinks, and I'm less certain that I see the truth, or I get bored, and none of my opinions and none of the people and issues involved seem worth the trouble. Right now, I've had just enough: so listen to me, Sophie. I say turn yourself around, girl, and go home. Beat it quick.

SOPHIE You take many words to say simple things. All of you. And you make the simple things—like going to sleep—so hard, and the hard things—like staying awake —so easy. Go home, shall I? Just like that, you say it. Aunt Constance has used up all her money on me, wasted it, and for why and what? How can I go home?

CROSSMAN If that's all it is I'll find you the money to go home.

SOPHIE (*Wearily*) Oh, Mr. Ned. We owe money in our village, my mother and I. In my kind of Europe you can't live where you owe money. Go home. Did I ever want to come? I have no place here and I am lost and homesick. I like my mother, I— Every night I plan to go. But it is five years now and there is no plan and no chance to find one. Therefore I will do the best I can. (*Very sharply*) And I will not cry about it and I will not speak of it again.

CROSSMAN   (*Softly, as if he were moved*)   The best you can?

SOPHIE   I think so. (*Sweetly*) Maybe you've never tried to do that, Mr. Ned. Maybe none of you have tried.

CROSSMAN   Sophie, lonely people talking to each other can make each other lonelier. They should be careful because maybe lonely people are the only people who can't afford to cry. I'm sorry.

(*He exits through the hall, goes up the stairs as the curtain falls.*)

Act Two

SCENE I

SCENE: The same as ACT ONE. *A week later, eight-thirty Sunday morning.*

AT RISE: CONSTANCE *is standing against the outside edge of the porch, leaning on the railing.* NICK *is standing in front of an easel.* CONSTANCE *has on a most unbecoming house dress and her hair is drawn back tight. She looks ten years older. In the living room,* SOPHIE *has finished folding her bedclothes and is hurrying around the room with a carpet sweeper. After a second,* LEON *appears from the direction of the dining room with a tray and dishes and moves out to the porch. He puts down the tray, moves the table, begins to place the dishes.* CONSTANCE *tries desperately to ask him if everything is all right in the kitchen. She does this by moving her lips and trying not to move her head.* LEON *sees her motions but doesn't understand what she is trying to say. The noise of the rattling dishes, and the carpet sweeper, becomes sharp.*

NICK Constance, please ask them to stop that noise. (*Waves his hand to* LEON *and* SOPHIE) Go away, both of you.

CONSTANCE They can't, Nick. I explain it to you every morning! We simply have to get ready for breakfast. (*Quietly*) Sophie, is everything all right in the kitchen?

SOPHIE Yes, ma'am. Everything is fine.

431

NICK   (*To* CONSTANCE, *sharply*)   Please keep the pose. Just a few minutes more.

CONSTANCE   (*To* LEON)   Tell Sadie not to cook the liver until everybody is downstairs, like she always does. Did she remember about the grits this Sunday? (*To* NICK, *sees his face*) All right. I'm sorry. But really, I can't run a boardinghouse and pose for—

(*She sighs, settles back.* SOPHIE *picks up her bedclothes and exits through the hall.* LEON *finishes with the porch table and comes back into the living room as* MRS. ELLIS *comes down the steps.*)

MRS. ELLIS   (*To* LEON)   My breakfast ready?

LEON   No, ma'am. We'll ring the bell.

MRS. ELLIS   What's the matter with my breakfast?

LEON   Nothing the matter with it. It will be like always.

MRS. ELLIS   It gets later and later every day.

LEON   No, ma'am. That's just you. Want it in the dining room or on the porch?

MRS. ELLIS   Too damp on the porch. Whole house is damp. I haven't slept all summer, Leon.

LEON   Just as well not to sleep in summer.

MRS. ELLIS   (*As* LEON *exits*)   You're going to have to explain that to me sometime. (*She turns, goes toward porch, comes around in front of* CONSTANCE) Constance, he's made you look right mean and ten years older. Why have you done that, Nicholas?

(SOPHIE *comes back into living room with a large urn of coffee and small cups. She puts the tray on a table.*)

NICK   (*To* MRS. ELLIS)   Shoo, shoo. This is forbidden ground.

MRS. ELLIS   (*Calls*)   Sophie, give me a cup. I have to stay awake for church. (*To* CONSTANCE) Ten years older. When you pay an artist to paint your portrait he makes you ten years younger. I had my portrait done when I was twenty-one, holding my first baby. And the baby looked older than I did. Was rather a scandal or like those people in Tennessee.

NICK   You know if you wouldn't interrupt me every morning, I think I'd fall in love with you.

MRS. ELLIS   (*She goes toward* SOPHIE *to get her coffee. Dur-*

ing her speech, SOPHIE *puts three spoons of sugar in the small cup*) I wouldn't like that. Even if I was the right age I wouldn't like it. Although I realize it would make me dangerously different from every older woman in the world. You would never have been my dish of tea, and isn't that a silly way of saying it? (*To* SOPHIE: *she is now in the living room*) You're the only one who ever remembers about my sugar. Sophie, will you come up to town (CROSSMAN *comes down the steps and into the room*) and stay with me for a few weeks while Carrie and Frederick are in Europe?

SOPHIE   I would like that.

MRS. ELLIS   Ned, what shall I give Sophie for her wedding present? My pearls or my mother's diamonds?

CROSSMAN   (*To* SOPHIE) The rich always give something old and precious to their new brides. Something that doesn't cost them new money. Same thing true in your country?

SOPHIE   (*Smiles*) I do not know the rich in my country.

MRS. ELLIS   He's quite right, Sophie. Not only something old but something so old that we're sick of it.

CROSSMAN   Why don't you give her a nice new check?

MRS. ELLIS   Only if I have to.

CONSTANCE   (*On porch*) Nick, my neck is breaking—

NICK   All right. All finished for this morning.

(*Turns the picture around so that* CONSTANCE *cannot see it.* SOPHIE *brings two cups of coffee to the porch.*)

CONSTANCE   (*Collapsing in a chair*) Whew.

(*Takes the coffee from* SOPHIE, *pats her arm.* SOPHIE *takes the other cup to* NICK.)

NICK   You're the girl I want to paint. Change your mind and we'll start today. Why not, Sophie?

(*He is holding her hand.*)

SOPHIE   I am not pretty, Mr. Nicholas.

NICK   You are better than pretty.

(CROSSMAN *comes out to the porch.* SOPHIE *disengages her hand, moves off.*)

CROSSMAN   (*staring at* CONSTANCE) My God, you look awful, Constance. What did you get done up like that for? You're poor enough not to have to pretend you are poor.

NICK (*Laughing*) Go away, Ned. You've got a hangover. I know I have.

(NINA *comes down the steps, comes into the room, says good morning to* MRS. ELLIS *who says good morning to her. She pours herself a cup of coffee. She is close enough to the porch to hear what is said.*)

CONSTANCE You know, I waited up until twelve o'clock for you both—

NICK We were late. We had a good get-together last night. Like old times, wasn't it, Ned? (*To* CONSTANCE) If you have the normal vanity you'd be pleased at the amount of time we spent on you. Ned loosened up and talked—

CROSSMAN I did? I thought that was you.

NICK (*Laughs*) I knew you wouldn't remember what you'd said— Don't regret it: did you good to speak your heart out—for once.

CROSSMAN My heart, eh?

NICK In a juke-box song called Constance.

CONSTANCE What? I don't understand.

CROSSMAN (*Who has turned sharply, then decided to laugh*) Neither do I. The stage of not remembering, or speaking out my heart, will come in time, I am sorry to say. But I hope it hasn't come yet.

(*As he turns to go out,* LEON *appears in the hall with a bell and begins to ring the bell.*)

NINA (*A little timidly*) Good morning, Mr. Crossman.

CROSSMAN Good morning, Mrs. Denery. I'm sorry you didn't join us last night—to hear me pour my heart out.

NINA I'm never invited to the pouring of a heart.

CROSSMAN I looked for you, but Nick said you had a headache.

NINA Nick always says I have a headache when he doesn't want me to come along, or sees to it that I do have one.

MRS. ELLIS (*Gets up quickly*) All right, Leon. I'm ready. I haven't eaten since four this morning. (*Goes out. As she passes stairs, she shouts up*) Carrie! Frederick! I simply won't wait breakfast any longer.

(CROSSMAN *follows her out.*)

CONSTANCE (*Gets up*) Well, they seemed to have managed in the kitchen without me. I reckon I better change now. Where'd you get this dress, Nick?

NICK Place on Dreyenen Street.

CONSTANCE In a Negro store! You bought this dress in a Negro store! (*He looks at her and laughs*) I don't mean that. I mean Ned's right. You must have wanted to make me look just about as awful as— For some reason I don't understand. Nick, what *are* you doing? And why won't you let me see the portrait?

NICK Haven't you yet figured out that Ned is jealous?

CONSTANCE Jealous of what?

NICK He's in love with you, girl. As much as he was when we were kids. You're all he talked about last night. How lonely he's been, how much he's wanted you, how often he asked you to marry him—

CONSTANCE I just don't believe you. Ned never talks about himself. I just don't believe he said such things—

NICK You know damn well he loves you and you know he's rotting away for you. He said last night—

CONSTANCE (*Prissy*) Nick, if he did talk, and it's most out of character, I don't think I should hear what he said in confidence just to you.

NICK Oh, run along, honey. You're pleased as punch. When you're not pretending to be genteel.

CONSTANCE (*Laughs*) Genteel? How awful of me. Mama used to say gentility was the opposite of breeding and— (*She has started to move out of the room*) Did Ned say—er—

(NICK *laughs, she laughs, and exits.* NICK *begins to put away portrait and to fold easel as* NINA *puts down her coffee and comes out to the porch.*)

NICK (*Kisses her*) Morning, darling. (NINA *sits down, watches him*) What's the matter?

(LEON *appears with breakfast dishes. He serves* NICK *and* NINA *during the next few speeches.*)

NINA Why have you done that? To Constance?

NICK Done what? Tell her the truth?

NINA How could you know it to be the truth? I don't believe Crossman talked to you—

NICK Look, it makes her happy—and if I can get a little sense into her head it will make him happy. I don't have to have an affidavit to know what's going on in the human heart.

(*He leans over, kisses her, sits down to eat his breakfast.*)

NINA (*Laughs*) Oh, you are enjoying yourself so much here. I've seldom seen it this hog-wild. (LEON *exits*) You're on a rampage of good will. Makes me nervous for even the trees outside. But there's something impertinent about warning an oak tree. How should I do it?

NICK (*Laughs*) First tell me how to understand what you're talking about.

(*They eat in silence for a minute.*)

NINA Are we staying much longer, Nick?

NICK A few more days. The house officially closes this week, Constance says. The Ellises go tomorrow and the Griggs on Tuesday, I think. Just till I finish.

NINA Finish what?

NICK (*Carefully*) The portrait, Nina.

(ROSE GRIGGS *comes down the stairs, carrying a small overnight case. She is done up in a pretty, too fussy, hat and a pretty, too fussy, dress. She looks in the room, puts the case down, comes hurrying out to the porch.*)

ROSE Oh, good morning. Sorry to interrupt. You look so handsome together. (*Makes a gesture to* NICK *meaning "Could you come here?"*) Nick—

NICK (*Hospitable*) Come on out.

ROSE I'd rather. Could you—

NICK Come and join us.

ROSE (*Hesitantly*) Well, I wanted to tell *you* but I don't want to worry Nina. You see—

NINA I'd go away, Mrs. Griggs, but I've been dismissed from so many meals lately that I'm getting hungry.

ROSE (*Smiles to* NINA. *Speaks to* NICK) I called him last night. Just like you advised. And I'm driving right over now. He's the executor of my trust fund, you know. He's very wise: I've got gilt-edged securities.

NICK Who is this?

ROSE My brother, of course. Henry, like I told you. (*To*

NINA) It sounds so mysterious, but it isn't. He's much older. You know he builds ships, I mean during our wars. I'll tell him the whole story, Nick, and he'll know what to do.

NICK (*Amused*) Of course he will.

ROSE I'm going to drive over to my doctor's. He's going to wait for me on a hot Sunday. It'll be expensive— (*To* NINA) I had a heart murmur. They had to take me out of school for a year.

NINA Recently?

(NICK *chokes back a laugh.*)

ROSE (*Giggles*) That's charming—"recently." (*To* NICK) There's so much I wanted to consult you about. I waited up for you last night, but—well. Should I do *just* as you told me yesterday?

NICK (*Who doesn't remember what he told her*) Sure.

ROSE Everything?

NICK Well—

NINA I think, Mrs. Griggs, you'll have to remind Nick what he told you. Yesterday is a long time ago when you have so many ladies to attend to—

ROSE (*As* NICK *laughs*) I shouldn't have brought it up like this. Oh, Mrs. Denery, you might as well know: it's about a divorce, and Nick has been most kind.

NINA I am sure of it.

ROSE Just one more thing. What should I do about our boys? Should I telephone them or let Henry? One of our sons works on the atom bomb, you know. He's the religious one and it will be traumatic for him. What do you think, Nick?

NINA (*Gets up quickly, trying not to laugh, moves away*) Goodness.

NICK I think you should go and have your breakfast. It's my firm belief that women only look well in hats after they've eaten.

ROSE (*To* NICK, *softly, secretly*) And I'm going to just *make* Henry commission the portrait—and for the very good price that he can afford to pay. You remember though that I told you she can't take the braces off her teeth for another six months.

NICK   (*Laughs*) Go along now, my dear.

ROSE   (*Pleased*) Thank you for all you've done. And forgive me, Nina. I'll be back tonight, Nick, before you go to bed because you'll want to know how everything turns out.

(*She exits through room.* NINA *stands without speaking.*)

NICK   (*Looks up at her*) There was a day when we would have laughed together about this. Don't you have fun any more?

NINA   I don't think so.

NICK   She's quite nice, really. And very funny.

NINA   I suppose it's all right to flirt with, or to charm, women and men and children and animals but nowadays it seems to me you include books-in-vellum and sirloin steaks, red squirrels and lamp shades.

NICK   (*Smiles*) Are you crazy? Flirt with that silly woman? Come and eat your breakfast, Nina. I've had enough seriousness where none is due.

(*Through this speech,* CARRIE *has come down the steps. She meets* SOPHIE *who is going through the hall to the dining room.* SOPHIE *is carrying a tray.*)

CARRIE   Good morning, dear. Is Frederick in the dining room?

SOPHIE   No. He has not come down as yet.

(*She goes on past.* CARRIE *comes into the room, continues on to the porch.*)

CARRIE   (*To* NICK *and* NINA) Good morning. Your maid said you wanted to see me, Nick.

NICK   (*Hesitantly*) Carrie, I hesitated all day yesterday. I told myself perhaps you knew, but maybe, just maybe, you didn't.

NINA   (*Laughs*) Oh, it sounds so serious.

CARRIE   (*Smiles*) It does indeed.

NICK   (*Carefully*) Don't you know that man's reputation, Carrie? You can't travel around Europe with him.

CARRIE   Travel around Europe with *him?* I'm going to Europe with Frederick. (*Then sharply, as she sees his face*) What do you mean, Nick?

NICK   I—

(SOPHIE *comes into room, goes out to porch. During next speeches, she pours coffee.*)

CARRIE Please tell me.

NICK I saw Frederick in the travel agency yesterday with a man I once met in Europe. Not the sort of man you'd expect to see Frederick with.

CARRIE Are you talking about Mr. Payson?

NICK Yes, I am. Well, I waited until they left the travel place and then I went in.

NINA Why did you go in?

NICK Luther hadn't seen me since we were kids and we got to talking. He said he had booked your passage on the *Elizabeth* and now he had another for Mr. Payson and Fred had just paid for it— (CARRIE *gets up, turns sharply, does not speak*) I didn't know whether you knew, Carrie, or if I should tell you—

CARRIE I didn't know. I thank you for telling me. (*After a second, she turns*) What did you mean, Nick, when you asked me if I knew Payson's reputation? I don't like to press you for gossip, but—

NINA He didn't mean anything, Mrs. Ellis—

NICK Oh, look here, Nina, you know he's part of Count Denna's set, and on the nasty fringe of that.

(SOPHIE, *very quietly, leaves the porch.*)

CARRIE What does that mean: Count Denna's set and the nasty fringe of· that?

NINA (*Quickly*) It means very little. The Count is a foolish old man who gives large parties—

NICK (*To* NINA) Would you want your young son with such people at such parties?

NINA (*Angrily*) I have no son. And I don't know: perhaps I would have wanted only to leave him alone—

CARRIE (*Gently*) All people who have no children think that, Mrs. Denery. But it just isn't true. (*To* NICK) I don't know much about Mr. Payson but I've been worried for a long time that he's taken Frederick in. Frederick admires his writing, and— Yet I know so little about him. He stayed with us a few weeks in town last winter. He'd just come back from Europe then—

NICK   He'd just come back from a filthy little scandal in Rome. It was all over the papers.

NINA   You don't know it was true.

CARRIE   What kind of scandal? (*No answer. Softly*) Please help me. I don't understand.

NICK   (*Gets up*) Look, Carrie, there's nothing to understand. The guy is just no good. That's all you need to know. He's nobody to travel around Europe with.

CARRIE   How could Fred have— (*She hesitates for a minute*) It was kind and friendly of you to tell me. I am grateful to you both.

(*She goes slowly across the room and into the hall toward the dining room. There is a long pause:* NICK *takes a sip of coffee, looks around at* NINA.)

NICK   What would you have done?

NINA   (*Idly*) I don't know. Have you ever tried leaving things alone?

NICK   I like Carrie. She doesn't know what the hell it's all about—and the chances are the boy doesn't either. I'm sorry for them. Aren't you? (*When she doesn't answer*) What's the matter, Nina?

NINA   I can smell it: it's all around us. The flower-like odor right before it becomes troublesome and heavy. It travels ahead of you, Nick, whenever you get most helpful, most loving and most lovable. Down through the years it runs ahead of us—I smell it—and I want to leave.

NICK   (*Pleasantly*) I think maybe you're one of the few neurotics in the world who didn't marry a neurotic. I wonder how that happened?

NINA   *I want to leave.*

NICK   (*Sharply*) Then leave.

NINA   (*After a second*) You won't come?

NICK   I told you: we'll go Friday. If you want to go before, then go. But stop talking about it, Nina. Or we'll be in for one of your long farewells—and long returns. I don't think I can stand another. Spare yourself, darling. You pay so heavy, inside. (*Comes to her, puts his arms around her*) Friday, then. And in the meantime, gentle down to the pretty lady you truly are.

(*He kisses her. Exits.* NINA *stands quietly for a minute.* SOPHIE *comes onto the porch, begins to gather the dishes.*)

SOPHIE   (*Gently*)   Would you like something, Mrs. Denery?

NINA   (*Softly*)   No, thank you.

(*She moves off, through the room and toward the staircase. As she starts up the stairs,* FREDERICK *comes down.*)

FREDERICK   Good morning.

NINA   Good morning, Mr. Ellis. (*Stops as if she wanted to tell him something*) I—er. Good morning.

(*She goes up as* SOPHIE, *who has heard their voices, leaves the dishes and comes quickly into the room.*)

SOPHIE   (*Calling into the hall*)   Fred. Fred. (*He comes in. Shyly*) Would you like to have your breakfast on the kitchen porch?

FREDERICK   Sure. Why?

SOPHIE   Your mother is—er— (*Points toward dining room*) She has found out that— Come.

FREDERICK   Denery told her he saw me in the travel agency. I was sure he would. There's nothing to worry about. I intended to tell her this morning.

SOPHIE   But perhaps it would be more wise—

FREDERICK   (*Smiles to her*)   We'll be leaving here tomorrow and for Europe on the sixteenth. You and I won't see each other for six months. Sophie, you're sure you feel all right about my going?

SOPHIE   (*Quickly*)   Oh, I do.

FREDERICK   We will visit your mother. And—

SOPHIE   (*Very quickly*)   No, no, please do not do that. I have not written to her about us—

FREDERICK   Oh.

SOPHIE   You see, we have as yet no date of time, or—

FREDERICK   (*Smiles*)   I don't think you want a date of time, Sophie. And you don't have to be ashamed of wishing you could find another way. But if there isn't any other way for you, then I'll be just as good to you as I know how. And I know you will be to me.

SOPHIE   You are a kind man. And I will also be kind, I hope.

FREDERICK   It isn't any deal for you. You are a girl who should love, and will one day, of course.

SOPHIE   (*Puts her hand up to her mouth*)   Shssh. Such things should not be said. (*Cheerfully*) It will be nice in your house with you, and I will be grateful for it.

FREDERICK   I have no house, Sophie. People like me never have their own house, so-to-speak.

SOPHIE   Never mind. Whatever house. It will be nice. We will make it so.

(*He smiles, pats her arm.*)

FREDERICK   Everybody in the dining room? (*She nods. He starts for hall*) Might as well face it out.

SOPHIE   I would not. No, I would not. All of you face out too much. Every act of life should not be of such importance—

FREDERICK   (*calling into dining room*) Mother. (SOPHIE *shrugs, smiles, shakes her head, and exits.* FREDERICK *comes back into room, pours himself a cup of coffee. After a minute,* CARRIE *appears. She comes into the room obviously very disturbed. But she does not speak*) There's nothing to be so upset about.

CARRIE   (*After a pause*)   You think that, really?

(MRS. ELLIS *appears in the hall.*)

FREDERICK   We're going to have a companion. That's all. We know nothing of traveling and Payson knows all of Europe.

MRS. ELLIS   Of course. You're lucky to get Mr. Payson to come along.

(*Both of them turn to look at her.*)

FREDERICK   (*After a second, to* CARRIE)   What is it, Mother?

CARRIE   I can't say it. It's shocking of you to take along a guest without consulting me. You and I have planned this trip for three years and—

FREDERICK   I didn't consult you because the idea came up quickly and Payson had to get his ticket before the travel office closed for the week end—

CARRIE   *Payson* had to get *his* ticket?

FREDERICK   I thought you'd given up going through my checkbooks.

CARRIE   *Please don't speak that way to me.* (*Pause, quietly, delicately*) We are not going to Europe.

FREDERICK   (*After a second, quietly*) I am.

CARRIE   We are not going, Fred. We are not going.

MRS. ELLIS   Your mother's feelings are hurt. She had looked forward to being alone with you. Of course.

FREDERICK   (*Uncomfortably*) We'll still be together.

CARRIE   (*To* MRS. ELLIS) I don't wish to be interpreted, Mother. (*To* FREDERICK) There's no sense talking about it: we'll go another time.

FREDERICK   (*Laughs, unpleasantly*) Will you stop acting as if you're taking me back to school? I will be disappointed if you don't wish to come with me but I am sailing on the sixteenth. (*Then, quietly*) I've never had much fun. Never seen the things I wished to see, never met the people I wanted to meet or been the places where I could. There are wonderful things to see and to learn about and to try to understand. We're lucky to have somebody who knows about them and who is willing to have *us* tag along. *I'm* not much to drag around— (*Softly*) I'll come back, and you can take up my life again. Six months isn't much to ask.

MRS. ELLIS   Six months? Sad to ask so little.

CARRIE   (*As if she recognized a tone of voice*) Mother, please. I—

MRS. ELLIS   Perhaps you won't want to come back at all? I wouldn't blame you.

CARRIE   (*Nervously*) Fred, don't make a decision now. Promise me you'll think about it until tomorrow and then we'll talk quietly and—

MRS. ELLIS   (*To* FREDERICK) Don't make bargains with your mother. Everything always ends that way between you. I advise you to go now, or stay.

FREDERICK   I am going. There is nothing to think about. I'm going.

(*He turns and exits, goes up staircase. There is a pause.*)

CARRIE   (*Angry*) You always do that, Mother. You always arrange to come out his friend and make me his enemy. You've been amusing yourself that way all his life.

MRS. ELLIS   There's no time for all that, Carrie. I warned you to say and do nothing. I told you to make the best of it and go along with them.

CARRIE (*Softly*) How could I do that? That man is a scoundrel and Fred doesn't know it, and won't believe it. What am I to do now?

MRS. ELLIS You're to go upstairs and say that you are reconciled to his leaving without you but that Frederick is to make clear to his guest that his ten thousand a year ends today and will not begin again. Tell him you've decided young people have a happier time in Europe without American money—

CARRIE (*Sharply*) I couldn't do that. He'd hate me for it. Maybe we'd better let him go, and perhaps I can join him later, Time will— (*Sees* MRS. ELLIS's *face*) I will not cut off his allowance.

MRS. ELLIS I didn't know it was you who wrote the check.

CARRIE (*With dignity*) Are you quite sure you wish to speak this way?

MRS. ELLIS Relatively sure.

CARRIE Then I will say as sharply that the money is his father's money, and not yours to threaten him, or deprive him, in any proper sense.

MRS. ELLIS In any *proper* sense. There is no morality to money, Carrie, and very immoral of you to think so.

CARRIE If you stop his allowance, Mother, I will simply send him mine.

MRS. ELLIS Then I won't give you yours. (CARRIE *turns sharply, as if she were deeply shocked.* MRS. ELLIS *now speaks, gently*) Yes, old people are often harsh, Carrie, when they control the purse. You'll see, when your day comes. And then, too, one comes to be bored with those who fool themselves. I say to myself—one should have power, or give it over. But if one keeps it, it might as well be used, with as little mealymouthness as possible. Go up now, and press him hard, and do it straight. (CARRIE *turns slowly to exit*) Tell yourself you're doing it for his own good.

CARRIE (*Softly*) I wouldn't be doing it otherwise.

MRS. ELLIS Perhaps. Perhaps not. Doesn't really matter.

(*Laughs, amused*) I'm off to church now. You can skip church today, Carrie.

CARRIE Thank you for the dispensation.

(*She begins to move off toward hall and toward stairs as* ROSE *comes from the direction of the dining room and into the room.*)

MRS. ELLIS   (*To* CARRIE, *as* CARRIE *moves off*)   Quite all right. You have God's work to do. (*She turns to watch* ROSE, *who is elaborately settling herself in a chair as if she were arranging for a scene—which is what she is doing*) What are you doing, Mrs. Griggs? (ROSE *nervously points to left window.* MRS. ELLIS *looks toward it, watches* ROSE *fix her face*) Is it Robert Taylor you're expecting or Vice-President Barkley? (GRIGGS *comes in from the left windows. He has on riding pants and an old shirt*) Oh.

GRIGGS (*To them both*) Good morning.

MRS. ELLIS Your wife's getting ready to flirt. You'd be safer in church with me.

(*She exits as* GRIGGS *laughs. He goes to coffee urn.*)

ROSE (*Meaning* MRS. ELLIS) Nasty old thing. (*Then*) I'm driving over to see him. I'm sorry I had to make such a decision, but I felt it was necessary now.

GRIGGS Are you talking about your brother?

ROSE Yes, of course. Now, I know it will be bad for you, Ben, but since *you're* being so stubborn, I didn't know what else to do.

GRIGGS I think you should see Henry.

ROSE But he's going to be very, very angry, Ben. And you know how much influence he has in Washington.

GRIGGS (*Turns, carefully*) Tell him to use his influence. And tell him to go to hell.

ROSE (*Giggles*) On a Sunday?

GRIGGS (*Gently*) Rose, no years will make you serious.

ROSE You used to like me that way.

GRIGGS So you always wanted to believe.

ROSE How can I just walk into Henry's happy house and say Ben wants a divorce, and I don't even know the reason. I *ask* him and I *ask* him but he says there is no reason—

GRIGGS I never said there was no reason. But it isn't the reason that you like, or will accept. If I were in love with another woman you'd rather enjoy that. And certainly Henry would.

ROSE It would at least be human. And I am not convinced it isn't so. I've done a good deal of thinking about it, and I've just about decided it's why you stayed in Europe so long.

GRIGGS I didn't arrange World War II and don't listen to the rumors that I did.

ROSE He said it at the time. He said he had known a good many professional soldiers but nobody had managed to make so much fuss about the war as you did, or to stay away so long. Henry said that.

GRIGGS I guessed it was Henry who said that.

ROSE (*Laughs*) But you didn't guess that it was Henry who got you the last promotion.

GRIGGS Rose, stop that. You're lying. You always do it about now. (*Turns to her*) Give Henry this reason: tell him my wife's too young for me. For Henry's simple mind, a simple reason.

ROSE I've wanted to stay young, I've—

GRIGGS You've done more than stay young: you've stayed a child.

ROSE What about your mother, Ben, have you thought of her? It would kill her—

GRIGGS She's been dead sixteen years. Do you think this will kill her?

ROSE You know what I mean. She loved me and she was happy for our marriage.

GRIGGS No, she didn't. She warned me not to marry— (*With feeling*) I began my life with a serious woman. I doubt if any man gets over that, or ever really wants any other kind of woman.

ROSE *Your mother loved me.* You have no right to malign the dead. I say she loved me, I know she did.

GRIGGS (*Wearily*) What difference does it make?

ROSE You never think anybody loves me. Quite a few men have found me attractive—

GRIGGS (*Quickly*) And many more will, my dear.

ROSE I always knew in the end I would have to tell you although I haven't seen him since you came home. That I promise you. I told him you were a war hero with a glorious record and he said he wouldn't either any longer—

GRIGGS (*Who is at the left window*) Henry's chauffeur is outside, Rose.

ROSE He was very, very, very, very much in love with me while he was at the Pentagon.

GRIGGS Good place to be in love. The car is outside, Rose.

ROSE Even after we both knew it, he kept on saying that you didn't make love to a friend, more than a friend's, wife.

GRIGGS (*Gently*) Rose, don't let's talk this way.

ROSE Does it hurt you? Well, you've hurt me enough. The third time you went to Europe was when it really began, maybe the second. Because I, too, wanted affection.

GRIGGS (*Gently*) I can understand that.

ROSE Ask me who it was. Ask me, Ben, and I will tell you. (*No answer*) Just ask me.

GRIGGS No, I won't do that, Rose.

ROSE Remember when the roses came from Teheran, I mean wired from Teheran, last birthday? That's who sent them. You didn't even like Teheran. You said it was filthy and the people downtrodden. But he sent roses.

GRIGGS He sounds like the right man. Go to him, Rose, the flying time is nothing now.

ROSE (*Angrily*) You just stop being nasty. (*Then*) And now I am going to tell you who it is.

GRIGGS (*Begins to move toward door, as if he were backing away from her*) Please, Rose. We have had so many years of this— Please. (*As she is closer to him*) Do I have to tell you that I don't care who it is?

ROSE (*She begins to move on him*) I'd like to whisper it. I knew if I ever told you I'd have to whisper it. (*He begins now really to back away*) Ben, you come right here. Ben, stand still. (*He starts to laugh*) Stop that laughing. (*Very loudly, very close to him*) It was your cousin, Ralph Sommers. There. (*She turns away*) There. You won't ever speak with him about it?

GRIGGS You can be sure of that.

ROSE (*Outside an automobile horn is sounded*)   Oh, I'm late. I can't talk any more now, Ben. (*She starts for door, stops*) What am I going to tell Henry? Anyway, you know Henry isn't going to allow me to give you a divorce. You know that, Ben. (*Carefully*) And therefore I won't be able to do what you want, and the whole day is just wasted. Please tell me not to go, Ben.

GRIGGS (*As if he has held on to himself long enough*) Tell Henry that I want a divorce. But in any case I am going away. I am leaving. That is all that matters to me or need matter to you or him. I would prefer a divorce. But I am going, whatever you and Henry decide. Understand that, Rose, the time has come to understand it.

ROSE (*Gently, smiling*) I am going to try, dear. Really I am. It's evidently important to you.

(*She exits through hall. GRIGGS sits down as if he were very tired. A minute later, CROSSMAN comes from the direction of the dining room, carrying the Sunday papers. He looks at BEN, goes to him, hands him the front page. BEN takes it, nods, sits holding it. CROSSMAN crosses to a chair, sits down, begins to read the comic section. A second later, NINA comes down the stairs, comes into the room, starts to speak to BEN and CROSSMAN, changes her mind and sits down. Then CONSTANCE, in an old-fashioned flowered hat and carrying a large palmetto fan, comes through the hall and into the room.*)

CONSTANCE I'm off to church. Anybody want anything just ring for Leon or Sophia. (*Bravely*) Want to come to church with me, Ned? (*He peers over his paper, amazed*) All right. I just thought— Well, Nick told us that you told him last night—

CROSSMAN (*Laughs*) I think perhaps I shall never again go out at night.

CONSTANCE Oh, it's good for all of us to confide in somebody— (*She becomes conscious of NINA and GRIGGS, smiles awkwardly and then with great determination leans over and kisses CROSSMAN*) Good-by, darling.

(*Surprised, he gets up, stands watching her leave the room. Then he sits down, staring ahead.*)

NINA (*after a minute, hesitantly*) I've got a car and a full picnic basket and a cold bottle of wine. Would you— (*Turning to* CROSSMAN *and then to* GRIGGS) like to come along? I don't know where to go, but—

CROSSMAN Got enough in your picnic basket for lunch *and* dinner?

NINA (*Smiles*) I think so.

CROSSMAN Got a mandolin?

NINA (*Smiles*) No. Does that rule me out?

CROSSMAN Almost. But we'll make do. The General whistles very well.

GRIGGS (*Smiles, gets up*) Is one bottle of wine enough on a Sunday?

NINA (*Laughs as she goes toward hall*) Not for the pure in heart. I'll get five or six more.

(GRIGGS *follows her out through hall.* CROSSMAN *gets up, folds the comic section, puts it under his arm, exits through hall. As he exits,* SOPHIE *comes onto the porch. She begins to pile the breakfast dishes on a tray. She sees a half-used roll and a piece of bacon, fixes it for herself, goes out carrying the tray and chewing on the roll as the curtain falls.*)

Act Two

SCENE II

SCENE: The same. Nine-thirty that evening.

AT RISE: NICK *is lying on the couch. Next to him, on the floor, is an empty champagne glass. On the table, in a silver cooler, is a bottle of champagne.* CONSTANCE *is sitting at the table playing solitaire and humming to the record on the phonograph. On the porch,* SOPHIE *is reading to* MRS. MARY ELLIS.

NICK (*Looks up from couch to* CONSTANCE, *irritably*) Please don't hum.

CONSTANCE Sorry. I always like that so much, I—

NICK And please don't talk. Mozart doesn't need it.

CONSTANCE Haydn.

NICK Mozart.

CONSTANCE (*Tartly*) I'm sorry but it's Haydn.

NICK You know damn well I know what I'm talking about.

CONSTANCE You don't know what you're talking about. Go look.

NICK (*Gets up, picks up his glass, goes to phonograph, shuts it off, looks down, turns away annoyed, picks up the champagne bottle, pours himself a drink, then brings the bottle to* CONSTANCE) Ready for another?

CONSTANCE I haven't finished this.

(NICK *carries the bottle out to the porch.*)

MRS. ELLIS (*Looks up at him*) For the fourth time, we don't want any. Please go away. We're having a nice time. We're in the part I like best.

NICK A nice time? Will I think such a time is a nice time when I am your age? I suppose so.

MRS. ELLIS No, Mr. Denery. If you haven't learned to read at your age, you won't learn at mine.

NICK (*Laughs, pats her shoulder*) Never mind, I like you.

MRS. ELLIS You must be damn hard up. People seldom like those who don't like them.

NICK (*Pleased*) You haven't forgotten how to flirt. Come on inside and talk to me. My wife disappears, everybody disappears— (*Stretches*) I'm bored, I'm bored.

MRS. ELLIS And that's a state of sin, isn't it?

NICK Unfortunately, it isn't. I've always said I can stand any pain, any trouble—but not boredom.

MRS. ELLIS My advice is to try something intellectual for a change. Sit down with your champagne—on which you've been chewing since early afternoon—and try to make a paper hat our of the newspaper or get yourself a nice long piece of string.

NICK (*Goes to* SOPHIE) Sophie, come in and dance with me.

MRS. ELLIS (*Calls in*) Constance, whistle for Mr. Denery, please.

NICK (*To* SOPHIE) You don't want to sit here and read to Mrs. Ellis.

SOPHIE Yes, sir, I do. I enjoy the adventures of Odysseus. And the dollar an hour Mrs. Ellis pays me for reading to her.

NICK (*Laughs, as* MRS. ELLIS *laughs*) Give you two dollars an hour to dance with me.

MRS. ELLIS It's not nearly enough, Sophie.

NICK (*Pats* MRS. ELLIS) You're a corrupter of youth— you steal the best hours.

MRS. ELLIS (*Shakes his hand off her shoulder*) And you're a toucher: you constantly touch people or lean on them. Little moments of sensuality. One should have sensuality whole or not at all. Don't you find pecking at it ungratifying? There are many of you: the touchers and the leaners. All since the depression, is my theory.

NICK   (*Laughs, pats her again*)   You must have been quite a girl in your day.

MRS. ELLIS   I wasn't. I wasn't at all. (NICK *wanders into the room.* MRS. ELLIS *speaks to* SOPHIE) I was too good for those who wanted me and not good enough for those I wanted. Like Frederick, Sophie. Life can be hard for such people and they seldom understand why and end bitter and confused.

SOPHIE   I know.

MRS. ELLIS   Do you? Frederick is a nice boy, Sophie—and that is all. But that's more than most, and precious in a small way.

SOPHIE   Yes, I think so.

(MRS. ELLIS *smiles, pats her hand;* SOPHIE *begins again to read.*)

NICK   (*near the phonograph, to* CONSTANCE)   Dance with me?

CONSTANCE   I don't know how any more.

NICK   (*Turns away from the phonograph*)   Has it been wise, Constance, to lose all the graces in the service of this house?

CONSTANCE   Do you think I wanted it that way?

NICK   I'm not sure you didn't. You could have married Ned, instead of dangling him around, the way you've done.

CONSTANCE   Ned has come here each summer because, well, because I guess this is about the only home he has. I loved Ned and honored him, but—I just wasn't in love with him when we were young. You know that, and you'd have been the first to tell me that you can't marry unless you're in love— (*He begins to laugh*) What are you laughing at?

NICK   "Can't marry unless you're in love." What do you think the rest of us did? I was in love with you. I've never been in love again.

CONSTANCE   (*Very sharply*)   *I don't want you to talk to me that way.* And I don't believe you. You fell in love with Nina and that's why you didn't come back— (*Desperately*) You're *very* much in love with Nina. Then and now. Then—

NICK   Have it your way. What are you so angry about?

Want to know something: I've never been angry in my life. (*Turns to her, smiles*) In the end, we wouldn't have worked out. You're a good woman and I am not a good man.

CONSTANCE Well, whatever the reason, things turned out for the best. (*Carefully*) About Ned. What did he say last night? I mean did he really talk about me?

NICK (*Expansively*) He said he loved you and wanted you and had wasted his life loving you and wanting you. And that he wasn't coming here any more. This is his last summer in this house.

CONSTANCE (*She turns, pained, startled*) His last summer? He said that? He really said it was his last summer—

(CARRIE *comes quickly into the room.*)

CARRIE Has Fred come back?

NICK (*To her*) Well, where have *you* been? Come and have a drink and talk to me.

(*He moves to pour her a drink as she crosses to the porch.*)

CARRIE (*Softly, to* MRS. ELLIS) I've been everywhere. Everywhere possible. I even forced myself to call on Mr. Payson.

MRS. ELLIS And what did he say?

CARRIE That Fred came in to see him after he left here this morning, stayed a few minutes, no more, and he hasn't seen him since.

MRS. ELLIS Ah, that's good.

CARRIE What's good about it? It means we don't know where he's been since ten this morning. (*Softly, as she sits down*) I don't know what else to do or where else to look. What should I do? Shall I call the police, what else is there to do?

MRS. ELLIS Nothing.

CARRIE How can I do nothing? You shouldn't have made me threaten him. We were wrong. It wasn't important that he wanted to go to Europe with a man his own age. What harm was there in it?

MRS. ELLIS All his life you've been plucking him this way and plucking him that. Do what you like. Call the police.

NICK   (*Who has come to the door carrying a glass for* CAR-RIE. *He hears the last few speeches; gently*). Can I do anything, Carrie?

CARRIE   I don't know, Nick. I only found one person who had seen him, down by the water—

NICK   Is he—would he have—is that what you're thinking, Carrie?

CARRIE   I'm afraid, I'm afraid.

NICK   (*Quickly, the kind of efficiency that comes with liquor and boredom*)   Then come on, Carrie. You must go to the police right away. I'll get a boat. Tell the police to follow along. Right away.

(CARRIE *gets up. Starts toward* NICK. SOPHIE *gets up.*)

SOPHIE   (*Angrily, in French, to* NICK)   Do not enjoy the excitement so much. Stop being a fool.

NICK   (*Amazed*)   What?

SOPHIE   (*In German*)   I said don't enjoy yourself so much. Mind your business.

CARRIE   What? What is it, Sophie?

SOPHIE   (*To* CARRIE)   Frederick is in the cove down by the dock. He has been there all day.

NICK   (*To* SOPHIE)   You said I was a fool. I don't like such words, Sophie. I don't.

CARRIE   (*Carefully, to* SOPHIE)   You've let me go running about all day, frantic with terror—

SOPHIE   He wanted to be alone, Mrs. Ellis. That is not so terrible a thing to want.

CARRIE   How dare you take this on yourself? How dare you—

MRS. ELLIS   I hope this is not a sample of you as a mother-in-law.

SOPHIE   (*Gently, to* CARRIE)   He will return, Mrs. Ellis. Leave him alone.

NICK   (*Softly*)   Sophie, I think you owe me an apology. You are by way of being a rather sharp little girl underneath all that shyness, aren't you? I'm waiting. (*No answer*) I'm waiting.

MRS. ELLIS   Well, wait outside, will you?

(*He stares at her, turns, goes in the room.*)

NICK (*Very hurt, to* CONSTANCE) I don't think I like it around here, Constance. No, I don't like it.

(*He goes out left windows as* CONSTANCE *stares at him.*)

CARRIE Since Frederick has confided in you, Sophie, perhaps you should go to him.

SOPHIE He has not confided in me. Sometimes his troubles are his own.

(*She gets up, walks through room, sits down near* CONSTANCE, *who looks at her curiously. On the porch,* MRS. ELLIS *leans over and whispers to* CARRIE.)

CARRIE Not tonight.

MRS. ELLIS Why not tonight? We'll be leaving in the morning.

CARRIE Because I've changed my mind. I think it best now that we let him go to Europe.

MRS. ELLIS (*Gets up*) He will not want to go to Europe. Haven't you understood that much?

CARRIE (*Hesitantly*) How do you know what he wants or feels—

MRS. ELLIS I know. (*She comes into room, sits near* CONSTANCE *and* SOPHIE. *After a second* CARRIE *follows her in, stands near them*) Sophie, I think a decision had best be made now. There should be no further postponement.

CARRIE (*Very nervous*) This isn't the time. Fred will be angry—

MRS. ELLIS (*To* SOPHIE) I don't want to push you, child, but nothing will change, nothing. I know you've wanted to wait, and so did Frederick, both of you hoping that maybe— But it will all be the same a year from now. Miracles don't happen. I'm telling you the truth, Sophie.

SOPHIE Yes, Mrs. Ellis, and I agree with you. Nothing will change. If Frederick is willing for an early marriage then I am also willing.

CONSTANCE Is this the way it's been? *Willing* to marry, *willing* to *marry*—

SOPHIE (*Looks at her*) I do not use the correct word?

CONSTANCE (*To* MRS. ELLIS *and* CARRIE) If that's the way it is, then I am not willing. I thought it was two young people who—who—who loved each other. I didn't ever understand it, and I didn't ask questions, but— Willing to get married. What have you been thinking of, why— (*Sharply, hurt*) What kind of unpleasant thing has this been?

CARRIE   I—I know. I can't—

MRS. ELLIS   (*To* CONSTANCE *and* CARRIE) Why don't you take each other by the hand and go outside and gather in the dew?

SOPHIE   I think Aunt Constance is sad that we do not speak of it in the romantic words of love.

CONSTANCE   Yes. I am. And shocked. When Carrie first talked to me about the marriage, I asked you immediately and you told me you were in love—

SOPHIE   I never told you that, Aunt Constance.

CONSTANCE   I don't remember your exact words but of course I understood— You mean you and Frederick have never been in love? Why? Then why have you—

SOPHIE   Aunt Constance, I do not wish to go on with my life as it has been. I have not been happy, and I cannot continue here. I cannot be what you have wished me to be, and I do not want the world you want for me. It is too late—

CONSTANCE   (*Softly*) Too late? You were thirteen years old when you came here. I've tried to give you everything—

SOPHIE   I came from another world and in that world thirteen is not young. I know what you have tried to give me, and I am grateful. But it has been a foolish waste for us both.

CONSTANCE   (*Softly*) Were you happy at home, Sophie?

SOPHIE   I did not think in such words.

CONSTANCE   Please tell me.

SOPHIE   I was comfortable with myself, if that is what you mean, and I am no longer.

CONSTANCE   (*Gently, takes her hand*) I have been so wrong. And so careless in not seeing it. Do you want to go home now?

SOPHIE   No. My mother cannot— Well, it is not that easy. I do not— (*As if it were painful*) I do not wish to go home now.

CONSTANCE   (*Puzzled*)   It's perfectly simple for you to go home. Why, isn't it?

SOPHIE   I do not want to say, Aunt Constance. I do not want to. (*With feeling*) Please do not talk of it any more. Please allow me to do what I wish to do, and know is best for me. (*Smiles*) and don't look such a way. Frederick and I will have a nice life, we will make it so.

(*Goes out.*)

CARRIE   (*Sharply*)   Don't be too disturbed, Constance. I have decided that Frederick should go to Europe and this time I am not going to allow any interference of any kind.

(FREDERICK *appears in the hall, comes into the room.*)

FREDERICK   I'm not going to Europe, Mother.

CARRIE   (*Turns to him*)   I have had a bad day. And I have thought of many things. I was mistaken and you were right. You must go wherever you want—however you want to go.

FREDERICK   I am not going, Mother. Payson made that very clear to me this morning.

MRS. ELLIS   Don't, Frederick. It's not necessary. I know.

FREDERICK   But evidently Mother doesn't. . . . Payson made it clear to me that I was not wanted and never had been unless I supplied the money

(CONSTANCE *gets up, moves off to the porch.*)

CARRIE   (*After a second*)   I— Er— I don't believe he meant that. You just tell him that it's all been a mistake and there will certainly be money for the trip. Just go right back and say that, Frederick—

FREDERICK   (*Very sharply*)   Mother! I don't want to see him again! Ever.

CARRIE   You often imagine people don't like you for yourself. *I'll* go and tell Mr. Payson that it's all fixed now—

MRS. ELLIS   Carrie, you're an ass. (*To* FREDERICK) But I hope you haven't wasted today feeling bitter about Mr. Payson. You have no right to bitterness. No right at all. Why shouldn't Mr. Payson have wanted your money, though I must say he seems to have been rather boorish about not getting it. People like us should pay for the interest of people like him. Why should they want us otherwise? I don't believe he ever pretended to feel anything else about you.

FREDERICK (*softly*) No, he never pretended.

MRS. ELLIS Then understand that you've been the fool, and not he the villain. Take next week to be sad: a week's long enough to be sad in, if it's true sadness. Plenty long enough.

FREDERICK (*Smiles*) All right, Grandma. I'll take a week.

(SOPHIE *appears at the hall door.*)

SOPHIE (*To* FREDERICK) You have had no dinner? (*Puts out her hand*) Then come. I have made a tray for you.

(*He turns, goes to her, takes her hand, goes out.*)

MRS. ELLIS (*Gets up, looks at* CARRIE) Are you going to interfere this time, Carrie? (*No answer. Gently*) I hope ·not.

(*She goes out.* CARRIE *stands for a minute near the porch. Then she goes out to* CONSTANCE.)

CARRIE I don't like it either.

CONSTANCE (*Wearily*) Whole thing sounds like the sale of a shore-front property. I don't know. Seems to me I've been so mixed up about so much. Well, maybe you all know what you're doing.

CARRIE I don't know what I'm doing.

CONSTANCE Why did you want the marriage, Carrie? I mean a month ago when you spoke to me—

CARRIE I don't even know that.

CONSTANCE You always seem so clear about everything. And so strong. Even when we were girls. I envied you that, Carrie, and wanted to be like you.

CARRIE (*Laughs*) Clear and strong? I wish I could tell you what I've missed and what I've wanted. Don't envy me, Con.

(*She exits toward hall and staircase. As she does,* NICK *comes in. He is now a little more drunk than when he went out.*)

NICK Come on out, Carrie. It's wonderful night. Take you for a sail.

CARRIE (*Laughs*) Good night, Nick.

NICK (*As she goes up steps*) I'm lonely, Carrie. I

wouldn't leave you if you were lonely. (*When she doesn't answer, he goes into room, looks around, sees* CONSTANCE *sitting on the porch, goes over, stands in the door looking out. After a second*) I wish I wanted to go to bed with you, Con. I just can't want to. I don't know why. I just don't want it.

CONSTANCE   (*Very sharply*)   Stop talking that way. You've had too much to drink.

(*She gets up, comes into room. He grabs her arm.*)

NICK   Now you're angry again. (*Puts his arms around her*) I'll sing you a lullaby. Will you like that?

CONSTANCE   Look, Nick, you've been rather a trial tonight. Do go to bed.

NICK   I'm not going to bed. I'm lonely. I'm—

(*The phone rings,* CONSTANCE *goes to it.* NICK *pours himself a glass of champagne*).

CONSTANCE   Yes? General Griggs isn't in, Rose. Oh. Yes. Just a minute. (*To* NICK) Rose Griggs wants to talk to *you.*

NICK   What's the matter, she got some new trouble?

CONSTANCE   (*Annoyed*)   Do you want the call or don't you?

NICK   Tell her I'm busy.

CONSTANCE   (*In phone*)   He's busy drinking, Rose. Shall I leave a message for General Griggs— Oh. (*She puts the phone down, annoyed*) She says it's absolutely and positively urgent that she speak with *you.* Not her husband. Absolutely and positively.

(*She exits through hall.* NICK *rises and goes to phone.*)

NICK   Look here, my dear, don't be telling people you want to speak to me and not to your husband. Sounds awful. (*Laughs*) Oh. A most agreeable doctor. Must get to know him. Look, you don't have to convince me. Save it for your husband. Oh, come on. You're getting like those people who believe their own press agents. Anyway, I once knew a woman with heart trouble and it gave her a nice color. You didn't go to the doctor to believe him— (*Sighs, listens*) All right, of course I'm sorry. It sounds jolly nice and serious and I apologize. (*Listens*) Oh. Well, that is kind of you. Yes, tell your brother I'd like to stay with him. Oh, by Friday, certainly. How old is your niece? Is she the one with the braces on her teeth? (NINA *appears from the hall entrance. She is followed by* GRIGGS, *who is carrying the picnic basket*) No, I won't paint anything out. That big a hack I'm not. Yes, we'll have plenty of time together. You're a good friend. (*To* NINA *and* GRIGGS) Had a nice day? (*Into phone*) No, I'm talking to your husband. Oh. Good-by. Take care of yourself. (*He hangs up. To* GRIGGS) That was Rose. (*Gaily, to* NINA) I've had a dull day, darling. (CROSSMAN *comes in*) Where'd you skip to?

NINA   We drove over to Pass Christian.

NICK   Did you put the car in the garage?

CROSSMAN   (*Gives* NINA *the keys*) Yes, all safe.

NICK   Did you drive, Ned? That heavy Isotta? (*To* NINA) Nobody who drinks as much as Ned should be driving that car. Or any car belonging to me.

NINA   And nobody as tight as you are should talk that way.

NICK   (*Laughs*) Have a drink, Ned.

(*He brings* CROSSMAN *a glass.*)

CROSSMAN   Thank you, no.

(NICK *turns, hands glass to* GRIGGS.)

GRIGGS   No, thank you.

NICK   What the hell is this? Refusing to have a drink with me— (*To* CROSSMAN) I'm trying to apologize to you. Now take the drink—

NINA   Nick, please—

NICK   Stay out of it, Nina. Women don't know anything about the etiquette of drinking.

CROSSMAN   (*Laughs*) Has it got etiquette now? (*As* NICK *again hands him glass. Shakes his head*) Thank you.

NICK   (*Drunk, hurt*) Look here, old boy, I say in the light of what's happened, you've just got to take this. It's my way of apologizing and I shouldn't have to explain that to a gentleman.

(*He grabs* CROSSMAN'S *arm, playfully presses the glass to* CROSSMAN'S *lips.*)

CROSSMAN   (*Quietly*) Don't do that.

NICK   Come on, old boy. If I have to pour it down you—

CROSSMAN   Don't do that.

(NICK, *laughing, presses the glass hard against* CROSSMAN'S *mouth,* CROSSMAN *pushes the glass and it falls to the floor.*)

NINA   (*Sits down*)   Well, we got rid of that glass. But there are plenty more, Nick.

NICK   (*Sad, but firm to* CROSSMAN)   Now *you've* put *yourself* on the defensive, my friend. That's always tactically unwise, isn't it, General Griggs?

GRIGGS   I know nothing of tactics, Mr. Denery. Certainly not of yours.

NICK   Then what the hell are you doing as a general?

GRIGG   Masquerading. They had a costume left over and they lent it to me.

NICK   (*To* CROSSMAN)   I'm waiting, Ned. Pour yourself a drink, and make *your* apologies.

CROSSMAN   You are just exactly the way I remember you. And that I wouldn't have believed of any man.

(*He turns, goes out.*)

NICK   (*Like a hurt child*)   What the hell does that mean? (*Calling*) Hey, Ned. Come on back and have it your way. (*Gets no answer, turns, hearty again*) Come on, General. Have a bottle with me.

NINA   Are we going to start again?

NICK   General, got something to tell you: your wife telephoned but she didn't want to speak to you.

GRIGGS   That's most understandable. Good night, Mrs. Denery, and thank you for a pleasant day.

NICK   But she'll want to speak to you in the morning. Better stick around in the morning.

GRIGGS   (*Stares at him*)   Thank you. Good night.

NICK   (*Following him*)   I think you're doing the wrong thing, wanting to leave Rose. You're going to be lonely at your age without—

GRIGGS   If my wife wishes to consult you, Mr. Denery, that's her business. But I don't wish to consult you.

(*He exits.*)

NICK   Sorry. Forget it.

(NICK *turns, takes his drink to the couch, lies down.*)

NINA   (*After a pause*) You know, it's a nasty business hating yourself.

NICK   Who's silly enough to do that?

NINA   Me.

NICK   (*Warmly*) Come on over here, darling, and tell me about yourself. I've missed you.

NINA   To hate yourself, all the time.

NICK   I love you, Nina.

NINA   (*Gets up*) Here we go with that routine. Now you'll bait me until I tell you that you've never loved any woman, or any man, nor ever will. (*Wearily*) I'll be glad to get out of this house before Constance finds you out. She can go back to sleeping with her dreams. (*After a second*) You still think you can wind up everybody's affairs by Friday?

NICK   Oh, sure. Friday. Then we're going up to spend a month with Rose's brother, Henry something or other. In New Orleans.

NINA   (*Carefully*) What are you talking about?

NICK   Rose fixed it for me. I'm going to do a portrait of her niece, the heiress to the fortune. The girl is balding and has braces. (*Looks at her*) Five thousand dollars.

NINA   Are you crazy?

NICK   Not a bit.

NINA   It's all right to kid around here—

NICK   (*Gets up*) I *don't* know what you mean.

NINA   (*Violently*) Please don't let's talk this way. Just tell Mrs. Griggs that you've changed your mind—

NICK   I demand that you tell me what you mean.

NINA   (*Angrily*) How many years have we avoided saying it? Why must you walk into it now? (*Pauses, looks at him*) All right. Maybe it's time: you haven't finished a portrait in twelve years. And money isn't your reason for wanting to do this portrait. You're setting up a silly flirtation with Mrs. Griggs. I'm not going to New Orleans, Nick. I am not going to watch it all again. I can't go on this way with myself— (*Then softly*) Don't go. Call it off. You know how it will end. Please let's don't this time— We're not young any more, Nick. Somewhere we must have learned something.

NICK   (*Softly, carefully*) If I haven't finished every picture I started it's because I'm good enough to know they weren't good enough. All these years you never understood that? I think I will never forgive you for talking that way.

NINA   Your trouble is that you're an amateur, a gifted amateur. And like all amateurs you have very handsome reasons for what you do not finish—between trains and boats.

NICK   You have thought that about me, all these years?

NINA   Yes.

NICK   Then it was good of you and loyal to pretend you believed in me.

NINA   Good? Loyal? What do they mean? I loved you.

NICK   Yes, good and loyal. But I, too, have a little vanity— (*She laughs; he comes to her*) And no man can bear to live with a woman who feels that way about his work. I think you ought to leave tomorrow, Nina. For good and forever.

NINA   (*Softly*) Yes. (*She turns*) Yes, of course.

(*She starts to exit. He follows behind her, talking.*)

NICK   But it must be different this time. Remember I said years ago— "Ten times of threatening is out, Nina," I said—the tenth time you stay gone.

NINA   All right. Ten times is out. (*Quietly, desperately*) I promise for good and forever.

NICK   (*She is climbing the staircase*) This time, spare yourself the return. And the begging and the self-humiliation and the self-hate. And the disgusting self-contempt. This time they won't do any good. (*He is following her but we cannot see him*) Let's write it down, darling. And have a drink to seal it.

(*On the words "disgusting self-contempt,"* CONSTANCE *comes into the hall. She hears the words, recognizes* NICK's *voice and stands, frowning, and thoughtful. Then she turns out the lights on the porch, puts out all lights except one lamp, comes back into the living room and begins to empty the ashtrays, etc.* SOPHIE *comes into the room carrying pillow, sheets, quilts, a glass of milk, and crosses to couch. Without speaking,* CONSTANCE *moves to help her and together they begin to make the couch for the night.*)

SOPHIE   (*After a minute, smiles*) Do not worry for me, Aunt Constance.

CONSTANCE   I can't help it.

SOPHIE   I think perhaps you worry sometimes in order that you should not think.

CONSTANCE   (*Smiles*) Yes, maybe. I won't say any more. I'll be lonely without you, Sophie. I don't like being alone, any more. It's not a good way to live. And with you married, I'll be alone forever, unless— Well, Ned's loved me and it's been such a waste, such a waste. I know it now but—well— I don't know. (*Shyly, as a young girl would say it*) You understand, Sophie? (SOPHIE *stares at her, frowning. Then* CONSTANCE *speaks happily*) Sleep well, dear.

(*She comes to* SOPHIE, *kisses her, exits, closing door.* SOPHIE *finishes with the bed, brings her milk to the bed table, takes off her robe, puts it around her shoulders, gets into bed, and lies quietly, thinking. Then she turns as she hears footsteps in the hall and she is staring at the door as* NICK *opens it. He trips over a chair, recovers himself, turns on a lamp.*)

NICK   (*Sharply*) Constance! What is this—a boys' school with lights out at eleven! (*He sees* SOPHIE) Where's your aunt? I want to talk to her. What are you doing?

SOPHIE   I think I am asleep, Mr. Denery.

NICK   You're cute. Maybe too cute. (*He pours himself a drink*) I'm going down to the tavern and see if I can get up a beach party. Tell your aunt. Just tell her that. (*Going toward door*) Want to come? You couldn't be more welcome. (*She shakes her head*) Oh, come on. Throw on a coat. I'm not mad at you any more. (*He comes back toward her, looks down at her*) I couldn't paint you, Sophie. You're too thin. Damn shame you're so thin. (*Suddenly sits down on bed*) I'm sick of trouble. Aren't you? Like to drive away with me for a few days? (*Smiles at her*) Nobody would care. And we could be happy. I hate people not being happy. (*He lies down. His head*

is now on her knees) Move your knees, baby, they're
bony. And get me a drink.

SOPHIE   Take the bottle upstairs, Mr. Denery.

NICK   Get me a drink. And make it poison. (*Slowly, wearily, she gets up, takes his glass, goes to bottle, pours
drink. He begins to sing. She brings glass back to him.
He reaches up to take the glass, decides to pull her
toward him, and spills the liquid on the bed*) Clumsy,
honey, clumsy. But I'll forgive you.

(*He is holding her, and laughing.*)

SOPHIE   (*Calmly*) Please go somewhere else, Mr. Denery.

NICK   (*Springs up, drunk-angry*) People aren't usually
rude to me, Sophie. Poor little girls always turn rude
when they're about to marry rich little boys. What a
life you're going to have. That boy doesn't even know
what's the matter with him—

SOPHIE   (*Very sharply*) Please, Mr. Denery, go away.

NICK   (*Laughs*) Oh, you know what's the matter with
him? No European would be as innocent of the world as
you pretend. (*Delighted*) I tricked you into telling me.
Know that?

SOPHIE   You are drunk and I am tired. Please go away.

NICK   (*Sits down across the room*) Go to sleep, child. I'm
not disturbing you. (*She stares at him, decides she can't
move him, gets into bed, picks up a book, begins to
read*) I won't say a word. Ssh. Sophie's reading. Do you
like to read? Know the best way to read? With someone
you love. Out loud. Ever try it that way, honey? (*He
gets up, comes to bed, stands near her, speaking over
her shoulder*) I used to know a lot of poetry. Brought up
on Millay. My candle and all that. "I had to be a liar.
My mother was a leprechaun, my father was a friar."
Crazy for the girl. (*Leans over and kisses her hair. She
pulls her head away*) Ever wash your hair in champagne, darling? I knew a woman once. (*Tips the glass
over her head*) Let's try it.

SOPHIE   (*Sharply*) Let us not try it again.

NICK   (*Sits down beside her*) Now for God's sake don't
get angry. (*Takes her shoulders and shakes her*) I'm sick
of angry women. All men are sick of angry women, if

angry women knew the truth. Sophie, we can always go away and starve. I'll manage to fall in love with you.

SOPHIE   (*He is holding her*) Mr. Denery, I am sick of you.

NICK   (*Softly*) Tell me you don't like me and I will go away and not come back.

SOPHIE   No, sir. I do not like you.

NICK   People have hated me. But nobody's ever not liked me. If I thought you weren't flirting, I'd be hurt. Is there any aspirin downstairs? If you kiss me, Sophie, be kind to me for just a minute, I'll go away. I may come back another day, but I'll go all by myself— (*Desperately*) Please, Sophie, please.

SOPHIE   (*Sighs, holds up her face to him*) All right. Then you will go, remember. (*He takes her in his arms, pulls her down on the bed. She struggles to get away from him. She speaks angrily*) Do not make yourself such a clown. (*When she cannot get away from him*) I will call your wife, Mr. Denery.

NICK   (*Delighted*) That would be fun, go ahead. We're getting a divorce. Sophie, let's make this night our night. God, Julie, if you only knew what I've been through—

SOPHIE   (*Violently*) Oh, shut up.

(*She pulls away from him with great effort. He catches her robe and rolls over on it.*)

NICK   (*Giggles as he settles down comfortably*) Come on back. It's nice and warm here and I love you very much. But we've got to get some sleep, darling. Really we have to.

(*Then he turns over and lies still. She stands looking at him.*)

SOPHIE   (*After a minute*) Get up, Mr. Denery. I will help you upstairs. (*No answer*) Please, please get up.

NICK   (*Gently, half passed-out*) It's raining out. Just tell the concierge I'm your brother. She'll understa— (*The words fade off.* SOPHIE *waits a second and then leans over and with great strength begins to shake him*) Stop that. (*He passes out, begins to breathe heavily. She turns, goes to hall, stands at the foot of the steps. Then she changes her mind and comes back into the room.*

She goes to the couch, stands, looking at him, decides to pull him by the legs. Softly) I'll go away in a few minutes. Don't be so young. Have a little pity. I am old and sick.

(SOPHIE *draws back, moves slowly to the other side of the room as the curtain falls.*)

Act Three

SCENE: *Seven o'clock the next morning.* NICK *is asleep on the couch.* SOPHIE *is sitting in a chair, drinking a cup of coffee. A minute after the rise of the curtain,* MRS. ELLIS *comes down the steps, comes into the room.*

MRS. ELLIS I heard you bumping around in the kitchen, Sophie. The older you get the less you sleep, and the more you look forward to meals. Particularly breakfast, because you've been alone all night, and the nights are the hardest— (*She sees* NICK, *stares, moves over to look at him.*) What is this?

SOPHIE It is Mr. Denery.

MRS. ELLIS (*Turns to stare at her*) What's he doing down here?

SOPHIE He became drunk and went to sleep.

MRS. ELLIS He has been here all night? (SOPHIE *nods*) What's the matter with you? Get him out of here immediately.

SOPHIE I cannot move him. I tried. Shall I get you some coffee?

MRS. ELLIS (*staring at her*) Are you being silly, Sophie? Sometimes it is very hard to tell with you. Why didn't you call Constance or Mrs. Denery?

SOPHIE I did not know what to do. Mr. and Mrs. Denery had some trouble between them, or so he said, and I thought it might be worse for her if— (*Smiles*) Is it so much? He was just a little foolish and sleepy. (*Goes toward door*) I will get Leon and Sadie and we will take him upstairs.

468

MRS. ELLIS   (*Crosses to door*) You will not get Leon and
Sadie. Rose Griggs may be President of the gossip club
for summer Anglo-Saxons, but Leon is certainly President of the Negro chapter. You will get this, er, out of
here before anybody else sees him. (*She crosses back to
bed, pulls blanket off* NICK) At least he's dressed. Bring
me that cup of coffee. (SOPHIE *brings cup*) Mr. Denery!
Sit up! (NICK *moves his head slightly. To* SOPHIE) Hold
his head up.

(SOPHIE *holds* NICK's *head;* MRS. ELLIS *tries to make him
drink.*)

NICK   (*Very softly*) Please leave me alone.

MRS. ELLIS   (*Shouting in his ear*) Mr. Denery, listen to
me. *You are to get up and get out of here immediately.*

NICK   (*Giving a bewildered look around the room; then he
closes his eyes*). Julie.

SOPHIE   He has been speaking of Julie most of the night.

MRS. ELLIS   (*Very sharply*) Shall I wake your wife and
see if she can locate Julie for you, or would you rather be
cremated here? Get up. Mr. Denery.

(*He opens his eyes, shuts them again.*)

SOPHIE   You see how it is? (*She tries to pull her robe from
under him*) Would you get off my robe, Mr. Denery?

MRS. ELLIS   (*Stares at her*) Sophie, you're a damned little
ninny. (*Very loudly, to* NICK) Now get up. You have no
right to be here. You must get up immediately. I say
you, you get up. (*Shouting*) Get to your room. Get out
of here.

NICK   (*Turns, opens his eyes, half sits up, speaks gently*)
Don't scream at me, Mrs. Ellis (*Sees* SOPHIE, *begins to
realize where he is, groans deeply*) I passed out?

SOPHIE   Yes, sir. Most deeply.

MRS. ELLIS   I'm sure after this he won't mind if you don't
call him "sir."

NICK   Champagne's always been a lousy drink for me. How
did I get down here? (*He turns over*) I'm sorry, child.
What happened?

SOPHIE   You fell asleep.

NICK   (*Hesitantly*) Did I— God, I'm a fool. What did I—
Did I do anything or say anything? Tell me, Sophie.

MRS. ELLIS   Please get up and get out of here.

NICK   I'm thirsty. I want a quart of water. Or a bottle of beer. Get me a bottle of cold beer, Sophie, will you? (*Looks around the bed*) Where'd you sleep? Get me the beer, will you?

MRS. ELLIS   (*Carefully*)   Mr. Denery, you are in Sophie's bed, in the living room of a house in a small Southern town where for a hundred and fifty years it has been impossible to take a daily bath without everybody in town advising you not to dry out your skin. You know that as well as I do. Now get up and go out by the side lawn to the boathouse. Put your head under water, or however you usually treat these matters, and come back through the front door for breakfast.

NICK   (*Laughs*)   I couldn't eat breakfast.

MRS. ELLIS   I don't find you cute. I find only that you can harm a young girl. Do please understand that.

NICK   Yes, I do. And I'm sorry. (*He sits up, untangling himself from the robe*) What's this? Oh, Sophie, child, I must have been a nuisance. I am *so* sorry.

MRS. ELLIS   (*Very loudly*)   Get up and get the hell out of here.

(*The door opens and* ROSE, *carrying her overnight handbag, sticks her head in.*)

ROSE   (*To* MRS. ELLIS, *who is directly on a line with the door*)   You frightened me. I could hear you outside on the lawn, so early. Oh, Nick. How nice you're downstairs. I never expected it—(*Her voice trails off as she sees* SOPHIE *and realizes* NICK *is on the bed*) Oh. (*Giggles, hesitantly*) You look like you just woke up, Nick. I mean, just woke up where you are.

MRS. ELLIS   (*To* NICK)   Well, that's that. Perhaps you wanted it this way, Mr. Denery.

(*She starts out as* LEON *appears carrying the coffee urn.* ROSE *stands staring at* NICK.)

LEON   (*Very curious, but very hesitant in doorway*)   Should I put it here this morning, like every day, or—

MRS. ELLIS   Who told you, Leon?

LEON   Told me what, Mrs. Ellis? Sadie says take on in the urn—

MRS. ELLIS I'm not talking about the urn. Who told you about Mr. Denery being here?

LEON Told me? Why Miss Sophie came in for coffee for them.

MRS. ELLIS (*After a second, shrugs, points to coffee urn*) Take it into the dining room.

LEON You want me come back and straighten up, Miss Sophie?

MRS. ELLIS (*Waves him out*) Mrs. Griggs will be glad to straighten up.

(*She exits.*)

ROSE (*Softly to* NICK) You were here all night? I come back needing your help and advice as I've never before needed anything. And I find you—

NICK Rose, please stop moving about. You're making me seasick. And would you go outside? I'd like to speak to Sophie.

ROSE I am waiting for you to explain, Nick. I don't understand.

NICK There is no need for you to understand.

ROSE I'm not judging you. I know that there's probably a good explanation— But please tell me, Nick, what happened and then I won't be angry.

NICK What the hell are you talking about? What's it your business? Now go upstairs, Rose.

ROSE (*Softly, indignant*) "Go upstairs, Rose," "What's it your business?" After I work my head off getting the commission of the portrait for you and after I go to the doctor's on your advice, although I never would have gone if I had known, and I come back here and find you this way. (*Sits down*) You've hurt me and you picked a mighty bad day to do it.

(*The door opens and* CONSTANCE *comes in. She goes to* NICK, *stands looking at him.*)

CONSTANCE Nick, I want you to go to the window and look across the street. (*He stares at her. Then he gets up slowly and slowly moves to the window*) The Carters have three extra guests on their breakfast porch, the Gable sisters are unexpectedly entertaining— (*With feeling*) This house was not built to be stared at.

NICK   (*Gently*)   It can't be that bad, Constance.

CONSTANCE   It is just that bad.

NICK   I'm sorry. I was silly and drunk but there's no sense making more out of it than that.

CONSTANCE   I am not making anything out of it. But I know what is being made out of it. In your elegant way of life, I daresay this is an ordinary occurrence. But not in our village. (*The telephone rings.* CONSTANCE *picks up phone, says "Hello," pauses, "Hello, Mrs. Sims." Then her face becomes angry and she hangs up. She stands looking at the phone, and then takes it off the hook. Turns to* NICK) Please explain to me what happened. (*Points to telephone and then across the street*) I only know what they know.

SOPHIE   Mr. Denery came down looking for someone to talk to. He saw me, recited a little poetry, spoke to me of his troubles, tried to embrace me in a most mild fashion. He was uncertain of my name and continued throughout the night to call me Julie although twice he called for Cecile. And fell into so deep a sleep that I could not move him. Alcohol. It is the same in my country, every country.

CONSTANCE   (*Softly, as if it pained her*)   You are taking a very light tone about it, Sophie.

SOPHIE   (*Turns away, goes toward couch, and through the next speeches will strip the bed and pile the clothes*) I will speak whichever way you think most fits the drama, Aunt Constance.

CONSTANCE   Will you tell me why you stayed in the room? Why didn't you come and call me, or—

NICK   Oh, look here. It's obvious. The kid didn't want to make any fuss and thought I'd wake up and go any minute. Damn nice of you, Sophie, and I'm grateful.

CONSTANCE   It was the most dangerous "niceness" I've ever heard of.

(SOPHIE *looks up, stares at* CONSTANCE.)

NICK   I know it's hard for you, Constance, but it's not all that much.

CONSTANCE   Isn't it? You've looked out of the window.

Now go down to the drugstore and listen to them and
I think you'll change your mind.

NICK Look. A foolish guy drinks, passes out—

ROSE (*Amazed as she turns to look at* SOPHIE) Why, look
at Sophie. Just as calm as can be. Making the bed. Like
it happened to her every night.

CONSTANCE (*Turns, realizes* ROSE *is in the room*) What
are you doing here, Rose?

ROSE Sitting here thinking that no man sleeps in a girl's
bed unless she gives him to understand— (CONSTANCE
stares at her) You can blame Nick all you like. But you
know very well that a nice girl would have screamed.

CONSTANCE How dare you talk this way? Whatever gave
you the right— I hope it will be convenient for you to
leave today. I will apologize to the General.

ROSE (*Softly*) That's all right, Constance. I must leave
today, in any case. You see, I have to— (*Sighs, sincerely*) You won't be mad at me for long when you
know the story. Oh, I'm very tired now. Could I have
my breakfast in bed? Doctor's orders. (*She goes out,
passes* CROSSMAN *who is coming in. In sepulchral tones*)
Good morning, dear Ned. (*Then in a sudden burst*)
Have you heard—?

CROSSMAN (*cheerful*) Good morning. Yes, I've heard. I'm
not the one deaf man in town.

(*Passes her. She stares at his back, reluctantly exits.*)

CONSTANCE (*Turns*) Ned, what should we do?

CROSSMAN Is there always something that can be done,
remedied, patched, pulled apart and put together again?
There is nothing to "do," Con. (*Smiles to* SOPHIE,
amused) How are you, Sophie?

SOPHIE I am all right, Mr. Ned.

NICK Ned, is it as bad as (*Gestures toward window and*
CONSTANCE) Constance thinks?

CONSTANCE What's the difference to you? You're just sitting there telling yourself what provincial people we
are and how you wish you were in the Ritz bar with
people who would find it amusing with their lunch.
(*Very angrily*) You came here as my friend and in our
small life—in our terms—you have dishonored my

house. It has taken me too many years to find out that you—

CROSSMAN   All right, Con, maybe that's the truth; but what's the good of discussing Nick's character and habits now?

NICK   (*Sincerely, to* CONSTANCE)   Whatever you think of me, I didn't want this. I know what it will mean to Sophie and I'll stay here and face anything that will help you. Anything I can say or do—

SOPHIE   (*She finishes folding the clothes*)   What will it "mean" to me, Mr. Ned?

CONSTANCE   (*Softly*)   You're old enough to know. And I believe you do know.

SOPHIE   I want to know from Mr. Ned what he thinks.

CROSSMAN   (*To* SOPHIE)   I know what you want to know: the Ellis name is a powerful name. They won't be gossiped about out loud. They won't gossip about you and they won't listen to gossip about you. In their own way they'll take care of things. (*Carefully*)   You can be quite sure of that. Quite sure.

SOPHIE   (*After a second*)   And that is all?

CROSSMAN   That is all.

SOPHIE   (*Softly, carefully*)   Thank you, Mr. Ned.

CONSTANCE   Take care of things? She hasn't done anything. Except be stupid. The Tuckerman name is as good as the Ellis name—

CROSSMAN   Yes, yes. Sure enough.

(SOPHIE *looks at* CROSSMAN, *exits. She passes* LEON *in the hall. He is carrying his hat.*)

LEON   Mrs. Ellis is cutting up about her breakfast. And Sadie's waiting for orders. We're messed this morning, for good.

CONSTANCE   Not at all. Tell Sadie I'm coming. (*She goes toward door*)   What's your hat for, Leon?

LEON   Well, kind of a hot sun today.

CONSTANCE   Not in here. Rest your hat: you'll have plenty of time to gossip when the sun goes down.

(*She goes out.*)

NICK   (*Miserably*)   Ned. Ned, you understand I never thought it would make all this— Is Constance being—

I mean, is she being old-maid fussy or is it really unpleasant—

CROSSMAN   It is unpleasant. She loves the girl, and she's worried for her.

NICK   (*Groans*) If I could do something—

CROSSMAN   You did; but don't make too much of it.

NICK   (*The first kind word he's heard*) Thank you, boy.

CROSSMAN   Or too little. (NICK *groans*) Nobody will blame you too much. The girl's a foreigner and they don't understand her and therefore don't like her. You're a home-town boy and as such you didn't do anything they wouldn't do. Boys will be boys and in the South there's no age limit on boyishness. Therefore, she led you on, or whatever is this morning's phrase. You'll come off all right. But then I imagine you always do.

NICK   You think this is coming off all right?

CROSSMAN   No, I don't.

NICK   I didn't even want her. Never thought of her that way.

CROSSMAN   (*Too sympathetic*) That *is* too bad. Better luck next time. You're young—in spirit.

(*He exits into hall toward dining room as* HILDA, *carrying a jewel case, and hat box, comes down the steps. She has on her hat and gloves.*)

NICK   (*Who is sitting on a line with the door and sees her, speaks in German*) Where you going?

HILDA   (*In German*) Good morning, sir. I am taking madame's luggage to the nine-thirty train.

(*She moves off as* NINA *appears.* NINA *has on a hat and gloves. On her heels is* ROSE *in a fluffy negligee.* ROSE *is talking as she follows* NINA *down the steps.*)

ROSE   I'm not trying to excuse him. Of course it was indiscreet but you're a woman of the world, Nina, and you know what young girls are with a tipsy man. Nina, do believe that I saw them this morning and he didn't have the slightest interest in her. Nina—

NINA   (*Turns to her, very pleasantly*) I know it's eccentric of me, Mrs. Griggs, but I dislike being called by my first name before midnight.

ROSE   (*Hurt, softly*) You shouldn't allow yourself such a

nasty snub. I'm only trying to help Nick. I know him
well enough to know that he didn't do a thing— (NINA
laughs) He's been my good friend. I'm trying to be a
friend to him.

NINA You will have every opportunity.

NICK (*very angry*) Will you please not stand there in
the hall discussing me?

ROSE Oh! (*Looks at* NICK, *then at* NINA, *steps back into
hall, calls toward kitchen*) Leon! Could I have my tray
upstairs? (*As she goes past room and upstairs*) Anybody seen my husband this morning?
(*Exits.*)

NICK Nina. (*She comes in*) I just want to say before you
go that they're making an awful row about nothing—

NINA You don't owe me an explanation, Nick.

NICK Nothing happened, Nina, I swear. Nothing happened.

NINA Try out phrases like "nothing happened" on women
like Mrs. Griggs.

NICK (*Smiles*) I'm sorry as all hell but they sure are cutting up—

NINA Well, it is a tasty little story. Particularly for a girl
who is going to be married.

NICK My God, I'd forgotten about the boy. I must say he's
an easy boy to forget about. Now I'll have to take *him*
out and explain—

NINA Don't do that, Nick. He isn't a fool.

NICK (*Looks around, thinking of anything to keep her in
the room*) Shall I get you a cup of coffee, darling?

NINA No. Darling will have it on the train.
(*She turns.*)

NICK Nina, I swear I didn't sleep with her.

NINA I believe you. The girl doesn't like you.

NICK Doesn't she? She's been very kind to me. She could
have raised hell. That doesn't sound as if she doesn't
like me. (NINA *laughs*) Don't laugh at me this morning.
(*After a second*) What can I do for her, Nina?

NINA You used to send wicker hampers of white roses.
With a card saying "White for purity and sad parting."

NICK   Stop being nasty to me. (*Then he smiles and comes toward her*) Or maybe it's a good sign.

NINA   It isn't. I just say these things by rote. (*Turns*) I don't know how long I'll be in New York, but you can call Horace and he'll take care of the legal stuff for us.

NICK   (*Close to her*) I told you last night that I would agree to the separation because I knew with what justice you wanted to leave me.

NINA   (*Coldly*) That's not at all what you said.

NICK   I was tight. It was what I meant to say—

NINA   (*Very angry*) You're lying. You said just what you meant to say: I was to leave. And not make you sick with my usual begging to come back—

NICK   Stop, Nina. Take any kind of revenge you want, but—please—some other day. (*Leans down, puts his face against her face*) Don't leave me. Don't ever leave me. We've had good times, wild times. They made up for what was bad and they always will. Most people don't get that much. We've only had one trouble; you hate yourself for loving me. Because you have contempt for me.

NINA   For myself. I have no right—

NICK   No, nobody has. No right at all.

NINA   I wouldn't have married you, Nick, if I had known—

NICK   You would have married me. Or somebody like me. You've needed to look down on me, darling. You've needed to make fun of me. And to be ashamed of yourself for doing it.

NINA   (*Softly*) Am I that sick?

NICK   I don't know about such words. You found the man you deserved. That's all. I am no better and no worse than what you really wanted. You like to—to demean yourself. And so you chose me. You must say I haven't minded much. Because I've always loved you and known we'd last it out. Come back to me, Nina, without shame in wanting to. (*He leans down, kisses her neck*) Put up with me a little longer, kid. I'm getting older and I'll soon wear down.

NINA   (*She smiles, touched*) I've never heard you speak of getting old.

NICK (*Quickly*) Yes. (*Then*) The *Ile* sails next week.
Let's get on. We'll have fun. Tell me we're together
again and you're happy. Say it, Nina, quick.

NINA I'm happy.

(*He takes her in his arms, kisses her. Then he stands away,
looks at her, and smiles shyly.*)

NICK There'll be no more of what you call my "home-
comings." Old friends and all that. They are damn
bores, with empty lives.

NINA Is that so different from us?

NICK If we could only do something for the kid. Take her
with us, get her out of here until they get tired of the
gossip—

NINA (*Laughs*) I don't think we will take her with us.

NICK (*Laughs*) Now, now. You know what I mean.

NINA I know what you mean—and we're not taking her
with us.

NICK I suppose there isn't anything to do. (*Softly, his
hand to his head*) I feel sick, Nina.

NINA You've got a hangover.

NICK It's more than that. I've got a sore throat and my
back aches. Come on, darling, let's get on that train.

NINA You go. I'll stay and see if there's anything I can do.
That's what you really want. Go on, Nicky. Maybe it's
best.

NICK I couldn't do that.

NINA Don't waste time, darling. You'll miss the train. I'll
bring your clothes with me.

NICK (*Laughs, ruefully*) If you didn't see through me so
fast, you wouldn't dislike yourself so much. (*Comes to
her*) You're a wonderful girl. It's wonderful of you to
take all this on—

NINA I've had practice.

NICK (*Hurt*) That's not true. You know this never happened before.

NINA (*Smiles*) Nicky, it always confuses you that the
fifth time something happens it varies slightly from
the second and fourth. No, it never happened in this
house before. Cora had a husband and Sylvia wanted
one. And this isn't a hotel in Antibes, and Sophie is not

a rich Egyptian. And this time you didn't break your arm on a boat deck and it isn't 1928—

NICK   This is your day, Nina. But pass up the chance to play it too hard, will you? Take me or leave me now but don't—

NINA   You're right. Please go, darling. Your staying won't do any good. Neither will mine, but maybe—

NICK   When will you come? I tell you what: you take the car and drive to Mobile. I'll get off there and wait at the Battle House. Then we can drive the rest of the way together. Must be somewhere in Mobile I can waste time for a few hours—

NINA   (*Gaily*)   I'm sure. But let's have a week's rest. Now go on.

NICK   (*Takes her in his arms*)   I love you, Nina. And we'll have the best time of our lives. Good luck, darling. And thank you. (*He kisses her*) They won't rag you, Nobody ever does. We'll get the bridal suite on the *Ile* and have all our meals in bed. (*He moves away*) If you possibly can, bring the new portrait with you. I can finish it now. And try to get me the old portrait, darling. Maybe Constance will sell it to you—(NINA *laughs*) All right. Think what you want and I'll be what I am. I love you and you love me and that's that and always will be.

(*He exits. She stands quietly.*)

NINA   You love me and I love you and that's that and always will be. (*Then she turns, goes to the bell cord, pulls it. After a second,* CONSTANCE *appears in the hall.* NINA *does not turn*) Leon, could I have breakfast on the porch?

CONSTANCE   (*In the doorway. She is carrying a tray*)   Yes, of course. I'll tell Leon to bring it.

(NINA *turns, stares at her.*)

NINA   I am very sorry, Constance.

CONSTANCE   I am sorry, too, my dear.

NINA   I don't know what else to say. I wish—

CONSTANCE   There's nothing for us to say. (*There is an awkward pause.*) Well. I'll tell Leon. Old lady Ellis is having her second breakfast. She always does on her last day. I don't know why. (*She starts out as* CARRIE, *followed by* FREDERICK, *comes down the steps.* CARRIE *has on her hat, etc., as if she were ready for traveling.* FREDERICK *is carrying two valises*) Shall I send breakfast up to Nick?

NINA   (*Very quickly*)   No, no. I'll just have mine and—

FREDERICK   (*Calling to* CONSTANCE)   Where's Sophie?

CONSTANCE   I'll send her in.

FREDERICK   (*Smiles*)   Don't sound so solemn, Miss Constance.

CONSTANCE   (*Sharply*)   I didn't mean to.

(*She disappears in the direction of the dining room.* FREDERICK *and* CARRIE *come into the room.*)

NINA   Mr. Ellis, I should be carrying a sign that says my husband is deeply sorry and so am I.

(*He smiles at her. She turns, goes out on the porch, closes the door behind her.*)

CARRIE   (*Hesitantly*)   She's a nice woman, I think. Must be a hard life for her.

FREDERICK   (*Laughs*)   I don't think so. (*Turns as he hears* SOPHIE *in the hall*) Now remember, Mother. (SOPHIE *appears in the door.* FREDERICK *goes to her, takes her chin in his hand, kisses her*) I want to tell you something fast. I don't know how to explain it but I'm kind of glad this foolishness happened. It makes you seem closer to me, some silly way. You must believe that, although I can't make it clear. Now there are two things to do right away. Your choice.

SOPHIE   I have made bad gossip for you, Frederick. We must speak about that. Right away.

FREDERICK   There's no need to speak about it again. It's a comic story and that's all. And you must begin to laugh about it.

SOPHIE   (*Smiles*)   I did laugh but nobody would laugh with me. And nobody will laugh in New Orleans, either. Is that not so, Mrs. Ellis?

CARRIE   I think you should travel with us, Sophie. Right now. Whatever is to be faced, we will do much better if we face it all together and do it quickly.

FREDERICK   (*Looks at her, as if they had had previous talk*)

You're putting it much too importantly. There's nothing to be faced.

CARRIE   I didn't mean to make it too important. Of course, it isn't—

SOPHIE   (*Puts her hand on his arm*)   It is important to you. And you must not be kind and pretend that—

FREDERICK   (*Firmly*)   I'm not being kind. I told you the truth. I've been in trouble, now you've been in a little. That's all, now or ever. (*Shyly*) As far as I'm concerned, it makes us seem less like strangers. I'd hope you'd feel the same way—

CARRIE   (*Quickly*)   Run and pack a bag, Sophie. It's a lovely day for driving and we'll be in town for lunch. I think you and I will have it at the club— Now let's not talk about it any more—

SOPHIE   No. It would be most mistaken of me to come now. My leaving here would seem as if I must be ashamed and you shamed for me. I must not come with you today. I must stay here. (*Smiles*) It must be faced.

FREDERICK   All right. That makes sense. Mother and Grandma will drive up and I'll stay here—

SOPHIE   (*Very quickly*)   No, no. You must not stay here. (*Points to window, meaning town*) They knew you had made plans to leave today as usual. And so you must leave. We must act as if nothing had happened, and if we do that, and are not worried, it will all end more quickly. (*Goes to* FREDERICK) Believe me, Frederick. You know what I say is true. All must seem to be as it has been. (*To* CARRIE) You tell him that, please, Mrs. Ellis.

CARRIE   I don't know. You belong with us now, Sophie. We don't want to leave you, or Constance. I think she should come along and—

SOPHIE   Oh, she would not do that. You know she would not. (*Smiles, very cheerfully*) Now. You are both very kind. But you know what I say is best for us all, and of no importance whether I come one week or the next. (*Takes* FREDERICK's *arm*) You have said I must laugh about it. I do laugh, and so it will be nothing for me to stay.

(MRS. ELLIS *comes to the door from the direction of the dining room.*)

CARRIE Good-by, Sophie. We will be waiting for you.

(*She exits, passing* MRS. ELLIS *without speaking.*)

FREDERICK (*Unhappily*) You all seem to know what's right, what's best, so much faster than I do. I—

SOPHIE (*Smiles, puts her hand over his mouth*) This is best. Please.

FREDERICK Then let us come back this weekend. Can I do that?

SOPHIE (*She touches his face*) I think so. You are a nice man, Frederick.

FREDERICK (*Kisses her*) And you're a nice girl to think so. See you in a few days. (*Turns to go out, passes* MRS. ELLIS) I feel happy, Grandma.

(MRS. ELLIS *nods, waits for him to exit.* SOPHIE *sits down.*)

MRS. ELLIS (*After a second*) Sophie.

SOPHIE (*Smiles as if she knew what was coming*) Yes.

MRS. ELLIS Did *Carrie* ask you to leave with us? (SOPHIE *nods*) Ah. That's not good. When Carrie gets smart she gets very smart. Sophie, Frederick meant what he said to you. But I know them both and I would guess that in a week, or two or three, he will agree to go to Europe with his mother and he will tell you that it is only a postponement. And he will believe what he says. Time and decisions melt and merge for him and ten years from now he will be convinced that you refused to marry him. And he will always be a little sad about what could have been.

SOPHIE Yes. Of course.

MRS. ELLIS Carrie never will want him to marry. And she will never know it. Well, she, too, got cheated a long time ago. There is very little I can do—perhaps very little I want to do any more. Don't judge him too harshly, child.

SOPHIE (*Smiles*) No, I will not judge. I will write a letter to him.

MRS. ELLIS That's my girl. Don't take from us what you don't have to take, or waste yourself on defeat. (*She gets up*) Oh, Sophie, feel sorry for Frederick. He is nice and he is nothing. And his father before him and my other sons. And myself. Another way. Well. If there is ever a chance, come and see me.

(*She moves out.* SOPHIE *remains seated. After a second* CONSTANCE *comes in from the hall. She looks at* SOPHIE.)

CONSTANCE (*Hesitantly*) Carrie tells me you'll be going up to town in a few weeks to stay with them. I'm glad. (*No answer*) Er. Why don't you go up to my room, dear, and lie down for a while? (*Points to porch*) She's on the porch. I'm going to ask the Denerys to leave today. I am sure they will want to, anyway. And the Griggses will be going and then just you and I—

SOPHIE I will not be going to New Orleans, Aunt Constance, and there will be no marriage between Frederick and me.

CONSTANCE (*Stares at her*) But Carrie told me—

SOPHIE Now she believes that she wants me. But it will not be so.

CONSTANCE (*After a second*) I wish I could say I was surprised or angry. But I'm not sorry. No marriage without love—

SOPHIE (*Pleasantly*) Yes. Yes.

CONSTANCE (*Gently*) You're not to feel bad or hurt.

SOPHIE I do not.

CONSTANCE I'm— I'm glad. Mighty glad. Everything will work out for the best. You'll see. After everybody goes, we'll get the house and the accounts cleaned up and straightened out as usual. (*Gaily*) And then I think you and I will take a little trip. I haven't seen Memphis in years and maybe in a few months— (*Gently*) You know what? We can even sell, rent, the place, if we want to. We can pick up and go anywhere we want. You'll see, dear. We'll have a nice time.

SOPHIE (*Almost as if she were speaking to a child*) Yes, Aunt Constance. (CONSTANCE *goes out.* SOPHIE *turns to watch* LEON *who, during* CONSTANCE's *speech, has come out on the porch and is serving breakfast to* NINA. SOPHIE *rises and goes out to the porch. She takes the coffee pot from* LEON—*he has finished placing the other dishes—nods to him, and pours* NINA's *coffee.* LEON *exits.*

NINA *turns, sees* SOPHIE, *turns back*) You are a pretty woman, Mrs. Denery, when your face is happy.

NINA   And you think my face is happy *this* morning?

SOPHIE   Oh, yes. You and Mr. Denery have had a nice reconciliation.

NINA   (*Stares at her*) Er. Yes, I suppose so.

SOPHIE   I am glad for you. That is as it has been and will always be. (*She sits down*) Now could I speak with you and Mr. Denery?

NINA   (*Uncomfortably*) Sophie, if there is anything I can do— Er. Nick isn't here. I thought it best for us all—

SOPHIE   (*Softly*) Ah. Ah, my aunt will be most sad.

NINA   Sophie, there's no good my telling you how sorry, how— What can I do?

SOPHIE   You can give me five thousand dollars, Mrs. Denery. American dollars, of course. (*Demurely; her accent from now on grows more pronounced*) I have been subjected to the most degrading experience from which no young girl easily recovers. (*In French*) A most degrading experience from which no young girl easily recovers—

NINA   (*Stares at her*) It sounds exactly the same in French.

SOPHIE   Somehow sex and money are simpler in French. Well. In English, then, I have lost or will lose my most beloved fiancé; I cannot return to school and the comrades with whom my life has been so happy; my aunt is uncomfortable and unhappy in the only life she knows and is now burdened with me for many years to come. I am utterly, utterly miserable, Mrs. Denery. I am ruined. (NINA *bursts out laughing.* SOPHIE *smiles*) Please do not laugh at me.

NINA   I suppose I should be grateful to you for making a joke of it.

SOPHIE   You make a mistake. I am most serious.

NINA   (*Stops laughing*) Are you? Sophie, it is an unpleasant and foolish incident and I don't wish to minimize it. But don't you feel you're adding considerable drama to it?

SOPHIE   No, ma'am. I did not say that is the way I thought of it. But that is the way it will be considered in this place, in this life. Little is made into very much here.

NINA   It's just the same in your country.

SOPHIE   No, Mrs. Denery. You mean it is the same in Brussels or Strasbourg or Paris, with those whom you would meet. In my class, in my town, it is not so. In a poor house if a man falls asleep drunk—and certainly it happens with us each Saturday night—he is not alone with an innocent young girl because the young girl, at my age, is not so innocent and because her family is in the same room, not having any other place to go. It arranges itself differently; you have more rooms and therefore more troubles.

NINA   Yes. I understand the lecture. (*Pauses*) Why do you want five thousand dollars, Sophie?

SOPHIE   I wish to go home.

NINA   (*Gently*) Then I will be happy to give it to you. Happier than you know to think we can do something.

SOPHIE   Yes. I am sure. But I will not accept it as largesse —to make you happy. We will call it a loan, come by through blackmail. One does not have to be grateful for blackmail money, nor think of oneself as a charity girl.

NINA   (*After a second*) Blackmail money?

SOPHIE   Yes ma'am. You will give me five thousand dollars because if you do not I will say that Mr. Denery seduced me last night. (NINA *stares at her, laughs*) You are gay this morning, madame.

NINA   (*Shocked*) Sophie, Sophie. What a child you are. It's not necessary to talk this way.

SOPHIE   I wish to prevent you from giving favors to me.

NINA   I intended no favors. And I don't like this kind of talk. Nick did not seduce you and I want no more jokes about it. (*Pleasantly*) Suppose we try to be friends—

SOPHIE   I am not joking, Mrs. Denery. And I do not wish us to be friends.

NINA   (*Gets up*) I would like to give you the money. And I will give it to you for that reason and no other.

SOPHIE   It does not matter to me what you would like. You will give it to me for my reason—or I will not take it.

(*Angrily,* NINA *goes toward door, goes into the room, then turns and smiles at* SOPHIE.)

NINA   You are serious? Just for a word, a way of calling something, you would hurt my husband and me?

SOPHIE   For me it is more than a way of calling something.

NINA   You're a tough little girl.

SOPHIE   Don't you think people often say other people are tough when they do not know how to cheat them?

NINA   (*Angrily*) I was not trying to cheat you of anything—

SOPHIE   Yes, you were. You wish to be the kind lady who most honorably stays to discharge—within reason—her obligations. And who goes off, as she has gone off many other times, to make the reconciliation with her husband. How would you and Mr. Denery go on living without such incidents as me? I have been able to give you a second, or a twentieth, honeymoon.

NINA   (*Angrily*) Is that speech made before you raise your price?

SOPHIE   (*Smiles*) No. A blackmail bargain is still a bargain.

(CROSSMAN *appears in the hall,* SOPHIE *sees him.*)

NINA   How would— How shall we make the arrangements?

SOPHIE   (*Calling*) Mr. Ned. (*Pleasantly, to* NINA) Mr. Ned will know what to do.

NINA   (*After a second to* CROSSMAN) I'd like to get a check cashed. It's rather a large check. Could you vouch for me at the bank?

CROSSMAN   Sure. That's easy enough. The bank's just around the corner.

SOPHIE   Would you like me to come with you, Mrs. Denery?

NINA   (*Smiles*) You know, I think perhaps it's wisest for you to stay right here. You and I in a bank, cashing a check, this morning, could well be interpreted as a pay-off, or blackmail.

(*She goes out.*)

SOPHIE   I will be going home, Mr. Ned.

CROSSMAN   (*Smiles*) Good. (*Looks at her, turns to stare at* NINA, *as she passes him and goes into hall*) At least I hope it's good.

SOPHIE   I think it is more good than it is not good.

(*He goes out.* ROSE *comes down the steps. Her manner is hurried, nervous. She goes immediately to windows. She looks out as if she saw somebody coming. Then she turns and sees* SOPHIE.)

ROSE   (*Very nervous*)   Oh. Good morning, Sophie.

SOPHIE   We have seen each other earlier this morning, Mrs. Griggs.

ROSE   Oh. It's like a nightmare to me, as if a year had gone by. I've asked for my breakfast tray twice and nobody pays any attention. And the doctor says that's the way it *must* be.

SOPHIE   (*Exiting*)   I will get it for you.

ROSE   (*Back at the window, speaks to* SOPHIE *who has left the room*)   Not you, Sophie. You have your own troubles, God knows. I don't know how any of us can eat anything today. (GRIGGS, *in riding pants and old shirt, comes in through the windows. Because she is upstage of the windows, he does not see her until she speaks*)   I've been looking everywhere for you, Ben.

GRIGGS   (*Turns*)   Rose. You knew where I was.

ROSE   That was all we needed here today: a telephone call to the stables. Oh, Ben, it was I who found them. But you don't know about it—

GRIGGS   I've heard all about it.

ROSE   Terrible, isn't it?

GRIGGS   Not very.

ROSE   He's been a disappointment to me. I've been lying on the bed thinking about it. Nick Denery, I mean.

GRIGGS   I'm sorry.

ROSE   You know, Ben, I've just about come to the conclusion that I'm often wrong about people, mostly men.

GRIGGS   And what did you and Henry—ah—put together, Rose?

ROSE   It was so hot in town. Henry's got that wonderful air conditioning, of course, but it's never like your own air. I think Sunday's the hottest day of the year, anyway. Athalia's braces cost twenty-five hundred dollars at that Greek dentist's and believe me they don't make anybody look prettier—

GRIGGS What point did you come to about my decision?

ROSE Decision? Your decision—

GRIGGS (*Tensely*) Please stop playing the fool. I'm afraid of you when you start playing that game.

ROSE *You* afraid of *me?*

GRIGGS Yes, me afraid of you. This very minute. Be kind, Rose, and tell me what has been decided for me.

ROSE (*Softly, very nervous*) It wasn't like that. Before I saw Henry I went to see Dr. Wills. You know he won't ever see patients on Sunday.

GRIGGS Not unless the fee is over a hundred.

ROSE I've always been sorry you didn't like Howard Wills. He's known as the best man in the South, Ben. He gave up a beach picnic with that woman, you know. Only that famous a man could buck having an open mistress—

GRIGGS I don't want to hear about Wills. Come to the point. What did you and Henry—

ROSE (*Grows sober, recognizing the tone*) I've been uneasy. I've sometimes been in pain, all summer. But I guess I knew because I guess I've known since that army doctor in 1934—I didn't want to talk about it—(*Moves toward him, frightened*) I have bad heart trouble, Ben.

GRIGGS (*After a second, as if he were sick*) Don't play that trick, Rose. It's just too ugly.

ROSE I am not playing a trick. Wills wrote you a letter about it.

(*She reaches in the pocket of her robe, hands him a folded paper. He takes it from her, reads it.*)

GRIGGS (*Violently*) How much did Henry pay Wills for this?

ROSE (*Gently, seriously*) It wasn't bought. Even Henry couldn't buy it.

(*She turns, goes toward door, as if she were a dignified woman.*)

GRIGGS (*Softly*) Tell me about it.

ROSE There isn't much to tell. I've known some of it for

years, and so have you. I just didn't know it was this
bad, or didn't want to. Wills says I must lead a—well,
a very different life. I'll have to go to the country somewhere and rest most of the day—not climb steps or go
to parties or even see people much. I like people, I—
Well, I just don't understand what I can do, except sit
in the sun, and I hate sun— Oh, I don't know. He said
worse than I am saying— I can't say it—

GRIGGS Yes. (*After a second*) I'm sorry.

ROSE I know you are. You've been my good friend. I'm
frightened, Ben. I play the fool, but I'm not so big a fool
that I don't know I haven't got anybody to help me.
I pretend about the boys and what they're like but I
know just as well as you do that they're not very kind
men and won't want me and won't come to help me.
(*With feeling*) And of course I know about Henry—
I always have. I've got nobody and I'm not young and
I'm scared. Awful scared.

GRIGGS You don't have to be.

ROSE (*Who is crying, very quietly*) Wills says that if I
take good care I might be, probably will be, in fine
shape at the end of the year. Please stay with me this
year, just this year. I will swear a solemn oath—believe
me I'm telling the truth now—I will give you a divorce
at the end of the year without another word. I'll go and
do it without any fuss, any talk. But please help me
now. I'm so scared. Help me, please. One year's a lot
to ask, I know, but—

(GRIGGS *comes to her, presses her arm.*)

GRIGGS Of course. Of course. Now don't let's speak of it
again and we'll do what has to be done.

(*She turns, goes out. He stands where he is. A minute
later,* CROSSMAN *comes in, stares at* GRIGGS *as if he knew
something was wrong. Then he speaks casually.*)

CROSSMAN Seen Sophie?

GRIGGS (*As if it were an effort, idly*) In the kitchen, I
guess. Tough break for the kid, isn't it?

CROSSMAN Perhaps it isn't. I don't know.

(*He watches as* GRIGGS *takes out a cigarette and lights it.*

GRIGGS's *hands are shaking and as he puts out the match, he stares at them.*)

GRIGGS (*Smiles*) My hands are shaking.

CROSSMAN What's the matter?

GRIGGS Worst disease of all. I'm all gone. I've just looked and there's no Benjamin Griggs.

CROSSMAN (*After a second*) Oh, that. And you've just found that out?

GRIGGS Just today. Just now.

CROSSMAN My God, you're young.

GRIGGS (*Laughs*) I guess I was. (*Slowly, carefully*) So at any given moment you're only the sum of your life up to then. There are no big moments you can reach unless you've a pile of smaller moments to stand on. That big hour of decision, the turning point in your life, the someday you've counted on when you'd suddenly wipe out your past mistakes, do the work you'd never done, think the way you'd never thought, have what you'd never had—it just doesn't come suddenly. You've trained yourself for it while you waited—or you've let it all run past you and frittered yourself away. (*Shakes his head*) I've frittered myself away, Crossman.

CROSSMAN Most people like us.

GRIGGS That's no good to me. Most people like us haven't done anything to themselves; they've let it be done to them. I had no right to let it be done to me, but I let it be done. What consolation can I find in not having made myself any more useless than an Ellis, a Denery, a Tuckerman, a—

CROSSMAN Say it. I won't mind. Or a Crossman.

GRIGGS The difference is you've meant to fritter yourself away.

CROSSMAN And does that make it better?

GRIGGS Better? Worse? All I know is it makes it different. Rose is a sick woman. But you know I'm not talking only about Rose and me, don't you?

CROSSMAN I know.

GRIGGS (*Very slowly*) I am not any too sure I didn't partly welcome the medical opinion that made it easier for me to give up. (*Then in a low voice as if to himself*)

And I don't like Rose. And I'll live to like her less.

(*He starts toward door.* CONSTANCE *appears in the hall carrying a tray. She is followed by* SOPHIE, *who is carrying a carpet sweeper and a basket filled with cleaning rags, etc.* CONSTANCE *comes to the door. She speaks wearily.*)

CONSTANCE   (*To* GRIGGS)   Sorry about Rose's breakfast. I forgot it. Sophie is going to help Rose to get packed. I don't mean to sound inhospitable but since you were going tomorrow, anyway–(*Gently*) I'm just tired and it would be easier for us. Please forgive me but you're an old friend and you will understand.

GRIGGS   (*Smiles, pats her arm*)   I'll take the tray.

(*He takes it from her, goes up the steps.* CONSTANCE *comes in the room, sighs, sits down.*)

CROSSMAN   Sophie. (SOPHIE *comes to him*) I was asked to give you this.

(*He hands her an envelope.*)

SOPHIE   Thank you, Mr. Ned.

CONSTANCE   (*Idly, without much interest*)   Secrets?

CROSSMAN   That's right. Secrets. Old love letters or something.

(SOPHIE *laughs, goes out.*)

CONSTANCE   (*After a silence*)   I hate this house today.

CROSSMAN   Well, they'll all be gone soon.

CONSTANCE   You won't go? Please.

CROSSMAN   I'll stay for a few days if you'd like me to.

CONSTANCE   Oh, yes. I need you to stay.

CROSSMAN   (*Points out of window*)   Don't worry about what the town thinks. Just act as if nothing had happened and they'll soon stop talking.

CONSTANCE   Oh, I'm not worrying about that. (*Pauses*) I feel so lost, Ned. As if I distrusted myself, didn't have anything to stand on. I mean, right now, if you asked me, I just wouldn't know what I thought or believed, or ever had, or– (*Shyly*) Well, what *have* I built my life on? Do you know what I mean?

CROSSMAN   Sure. I know.

CONSTANCE   (*As if she had trouble with the words*)   It's– it's so painful. (*Then as if she wished to change the sub-*

ject quickly) Sophie will be going back to Europe. She just told me. She *wants* to go. Did you know that?

CROSSMAN Is that so?

CONSTANCE I was so sure I was doing the right thing, bringing her here. You see? That's part of what I mean by not knowing the things I thought I knew. Well. She wants me to come with her and live with them, but I told her I'd be no happier in a new life than she was. (*Pauses as if she were coming to something that frightens her*) Nick said you wouldn't be coming here next summer. Did you say anything like that, or was it one of Nick's lies? (*He does not answer her. She stares at him*) Why, Ned?

CROSSMAN Hasn't anything to do with you, Con. Just think I'd be better off. You know, it's kind of foolish—two weeks a year—coming back here and living a life that isn't me anymore. (*Laughs*) It's too respectable for me, Con. I ain't up to it anymore.

CONSTANCE Oh. It's what I look forward to every summer. What will I— (*Very quickly*) Where is Nick? I haven't seen him. I wish they'd leave—

CROSSMAN They've gone.

CONSTANCE (*Stares at him*) Without a word to me? Exactly the way he left years ago. I didn't ever tell you that, did I? We had a date for dinner. He didn't come. He just got on the boat. I didn't ever tell anybody before. (*Violently*) What a fool. All these years of making a shabby man into the kind of hero who would come back some day all happy and shining—

CROSSMAN Oh, don't do that. He never asked you to make him what he wasn't. Or to wait twenty years to find him out.

CONSTANCE No, he didn't. That's true. (*She rises, goes to the portrait and stands staring at it*) Do I look like this?

CROSSMAN You look nice.

CONSTANCE Come and look at it.

CROSSMAN No, I don't want to.

CONSTANCE Much older than I thought or— And I don't look very bright. (*Puts the picture away from her*) Well, I haven't been very bright. I want to say something to you. I can't wait any longer. Would you forgive me?

CROSSMAN Forgive you? For what?

CONSTANCE For wasting all these years. For not knowing what I felt about you, or not wanting to. Ned, would you have me now?

CROSSMAN (*After a second*) What did you say?

CONSTANCE Would you marry me? (*There is a pause. Then* SOPHIE *comes from the direction of the dining room carrying a carpet sweeper and a cleaning basket. As she goes up the steps she is singing a cheerful French song.* CONSTANCE *smiles*) She's happy. That's good. I think she'll come out all right, always.

CROSSMAN (*Stares at* CONSTANCE, *then slowly, carefully*) I live in a room and I go to work and I play a game called getting through the day while you wait for night. The night's for me—just me—and I can do anything with it I want. There used to be a lot of things to do with it, good things, but now there's a bar and another bar and the same people in each bar. When I've had enough I go back to my room—or somebody else's room—and that never means much one way or the other. A few years ago I'd have weeks of reading— night after night—just me. But I don't do that much anymore. Just read, all night long. You can feel good that way.

CONSTANCE I never did that. I'm not a reader.

CROSSMAN (*As if he hadn't heard her*) And a few years ago I'd go on the wagon twice a year. Now I don't do that anymore. And I don't care. (*Smiles*) And all these years I told myself that if you'd loved me everything would have been different. I'd have had a good life, been worth something to myself. I wanted to tell myself that. I wanted to believe it. Griggs was right. I not only wasted myself, but I wanted it that way. All my life, I guess, I wanted it that way.

CONSTANCE And you're not in love with me, Ned?

CROSSMAN No, Con. Not now.

CONSTANCE (*Gets up, goes to him*) Let's have a nice din-

ner together, just you and me, and go to the movies.
Could we do that?

CROSSMAN I've kept myself busy looking into other people's hearts so I wouldn't have to look into my own.
(*Softly*) If I made you think I was still in love, I'm
sorry. Sorry I fooled you and sorry I fooled myself. And
I've never liked liars—least of all those who lie to themselves.

CONSTANCE Never mind. Most of us lie to ourselves,
darling, most of us.

Curtain

About the Author

LILLIAN HELLMAN was born in New Orleans and educated at New York University and Columbia University. In addition to the plays included in this volume, she wrote *The Searching Wind* and *Toys in the Attic* and collaborated with Richard Wilbur on the libretto for a musical version of Voltaire's *Candide*. In recent years she has written three books of autobiography: *An Unfinished Woman*, *Pentimento*, and *Scoundrel Time*, which have been published in one volume under the title *Three*.

THE CRYPTOGRAM
by David Mamet

"First-rate . . . spooky, elliptical, full of wit. . . . Not in any stage literature that I know has childhood been as movingly evoked as it is in *The Cryptogram*." —Vincent Canby, *The New York Times*

In this gripping short play, David Mamet combines mercurial intelligence with genuinely Hitchcockian menace. *The Cryptogram* is a journey back into childhood and the moment of its vanishing—the moment when the sheltering world is suddenly revealed as a place full of dangers.

Drama/0-679-74653-6

OLEANNA
by David Mamet

"David Mamet has raised outrage to an art form. . . . *Oleanna* is . . . a scorcher. The woods are burning, and all of us are being seared in the fire." —*Boston Globe*

A male college instructor and his female student sit down to discuss her grades and in a terrifyingly short time become the participants in a modern reprise of the Inquisition.

Drama/0-679-74536-X

SIMPATICO
A Play in Three Acts
by Sam Shepard

"Breathtaking . . . *Simpatico* is Mr. Shepard writing at his distinctive, savage best." —*The New York Times*

Set within the netherworld of thoroughbred racing, this hair-raising, funny new play launches the reader into regions where high society meets the low life and, along the way, explores classical themes of memory, loyalty, and restitution.

Drama/0-679-76317-1